and Ad

J. Ranade Workstation Series

BAMBARA/ALLEN • *PowerBuilder: A Guide for Developing Client/Server Applications*, 0-07-005413-4

CERVONE • *AIX/6000 System Guide*, 0-07-024129-5

CHAKRAVARTY, CANNON • *PowerPC: Concepts, Architecture, and Design*, 0-07-011192-8

CHAKRAVARTY • *Power RISC System/6000: Concepts, Facilities, and Architecture*, 0-07-011047-6

CHAPMAN • *OS/2 Power User's Reference: From OS/2.2 Through Warp*, 0-07-912218-3

DEROEST • *AIX for RS/6000: System and Administration Guide*, 0-07-036439-7

GOPAUL • *OS/2 Programmer's Desk Reference*, 0-07-023748-4

GRAHAM • *Solaris 2.x: Internals & Architecture*, 0-07-911876-3

HENRY, GRAHAM • *Solaris 2.X System Administrator's Guide*, 0-07-029368-6

JOHNSTON • *OS/2 Connectivity & Networking: A Guide to Communication Manager/2*, 0-07-032696-7

JOHNSTON • *OS/2 Productivity Tool Kit*, 0-07-912029-6

KELLY • *AIX/6000 Internals and Architecture*, 0-07-034061-7

LAMB • *MicroFocus Workbench and Toolset Developer's Guide*, 0-07-036123-3

LEININGER • *AIX/6000 Developer's Tool Kit*, 0-07-911992-1

LEININGER • *HP-UX Developer's Tool Kit*, 0-07-912174-8

LEININGER • *Solaris Developer's Tool Kit*, 0-07-911851-8

LEININGER • *UNIX Developer's Tool Kit*, 0-07-911646-9

LOCKHART • *OSF DCE: Guide to Developing Distributed Applications*, 0-07-911481-4

PETERSON • *DCE: A Guide to Developing Portable Applications*, 0-07-911801-1

RANADE, ZAMIR • *C++ Primer for C Programmers*, 2/e, 0-07-051487-9

RIORDAN • *Windows NT Power User's Tool Kit*, 0-07-912301-5

ROBERTSON, KOOP • *Integrating Windows and Netware*, 0-07-912126-8

ROBERTSON, KOOP • *Windows 95 and Windows NT Networking*, 0-07-912983-8

SANCHEZ, CANTON • *Graphics Programming Solutions*, 0-07-911464-4

SANCHEZ, CANTON • *High Resolution Video Graphics*, 0-07-911646-9

SANCHEZ, CANTON • *PC Programmer's Handbook*, 2/e, 0-07-054948-6

SANCHEZ, CANTON • *Solutions Handbook for PC Programmers*, 2/e, 0-07-912249-3

WALKER, SCHWALLER • *CPI-C Programming in C: An Application Developer's Guide to APPC*, 0-07-911733-3

WIGGINS • *The Internet for Everyone: A Guide for Users and Providers*, 0-07-067019-8

To order or receive additional information on these or any other McGraw-Hill titles, please call 1-800-822-8158 in the United States. In other countries, contact your local McGraw-Hill representative.

KEY = WM16XXA

HP-UX System and Administration Guide

Jay Shah

McGraw-Hill

New York   San Francisco   Washington, D.C.   Auckland   Bogotá
Caracas   Lisbon   London   Madrid   Mexico City   Milan
Montreal   New Delhi   San Juan   Singapore
Sydney   Tokyo   Toronto

Library of Congress Cataloging-in-Publication Data

Shah, Jay.
    HP-UX system and administration guide / Jay Shah.
        p.   cm. — (J. Ranade workstation series)
    Includes index.
    ISBN 0-07-057277-1 (pb)
    1. Operating systems (Computers) 2. HP-UX. I. Title.
II. Series.
QA76.76.O63S498 1996
005.4'3—dc20   96-30856
                                        CIP

McGraw-Hill

*A Division of The **McGraw·Hill** Companies*

1 2 3 4 5 6 7 8 9 0 DOC/DOC 9 0 1 0 9 8 7 6

ISBN 0-07-057277-1

The sponsoring editor for this book was Judy Brief, the editing supervisor was Paul R. Sobel, and the production supervisor was Pamela A. Pelton. It was set in Century Schoolbook by Ron Painter of McGraw-Hill's Professional Book Group composition unit.

Printed and bound by R. R. Donnelley & Sons Company.

To my children: Anand and Tulsi
who entertained me through the months I spent writing the
book. No Tulsi, I cannot read this book for you—not yet. No
Anand, you cannot compare this book with Thomas
Edison's works.

Contents

Preface

This book describes HP-UX computers, system management activities and the programming environment. HP-UX is Hewlett-Packard's implementation of the Unix operating system. Starting from HP-UX Version 10, released in 1995, the operating system conforms well with industry standards like POSIX and AT&T System V Interface Definition. When comparing sales, HP-UX systems generate more revenue than any other Unix implementation in the world. This book provides:

- an overview of HP-UX hardware systems.
- an implementation overview of the HP-UX operating system.
- a description of common software layered products.
- techniques and commands for using HP-UX effectively.
- a guide for system administration tasks.

While there is no prerequisite to understanding the material in the book, some knowledge of generic Unix systems will be helpful. Common Unix terminology and commands are not described; the book concentrates on HP's flavor of Unix. The book is intended for:

- fresh and novice HP-UX system administrators.
- experienced Unix system administrators, who have not worked on HP-UX.
- HP-UX software developers; programmers, systems analysts, and software project leaders.
- data center managers, operators, and other computing professionals who are familiar with non-HP computing environments and now are acquiring HP-UX products in their shop.

As this is a *getting-started* book, many topics are introduced in broad terms; HP manuals and other books should be consulted for complete details. Foreign languages and locales are supported on HP-UX, however, this book does not explain how. I believe this does not undermine the utility of this book to non-U.S. readers.

Acknowledgments

I wish to thank my manuscript reviewers, Sanjay Chikarmane, Harish Dindigal and Henryk Mozman. They did a great job polishing up the material. I would also like to thank my colleagues and managers who have provided me a congenial work environment, Tony Buccheri, David Chien, John Giuliano, Vince Harding, David Kuttler, Rohit Mehra, Tom Nicastri and Alex Valentin. Jay Ranade, the book series editor, is always a pleasure to work with.

Jay Shah

Trademarks

Alpha, AlphaServer, Digital, OpenVMS are trademarks of Digital Equipment Corporations.

UNIX is a registered trademark, licensed exclusively through X/Open Company Ltd.

X Window System is a trademark of the Massachussetts Institute of Technology.

MS-DOS, Microsoft and Windows are U.S. registered trademarks of Microsoft Corporation.

MOTIF is a registered trademark of the Open Software Foundation, Inc.

SUN, NFS, SPARC and SPARCstation are trademarks and registered trademarks of Sun Microsystems, Inc.

PostScript is a trademark of Adobe Systems Inc.

Ethernet is a trademark of Xerox Corp.

HP, HP-UX, HP VUE and HP Openview are trademarks and registered trademarks of Hewlett-Packard Company.

Other brands, product names and company names mentioned in this book are trademarks and registered trademarks of their respective holders.

HP-UX System
and Administration Guide

1

Introduction to HP-UX Computer Systems

1.1 HP as a Company

Hewlett-Packard, based in Palo Alto, California, was founded in 1939 by William Hewlett and David Packard. In the beginning the company engineered and sold instrumentation and measurement products. In 1966, HP introduced process control computers. Business and commercial systems came in 1972. In 1986, HP-UX was released on servers based on HP-PA (HP Precision Architecture). HP did not have a significant presence in the workstation marketplace; hence, it acquired one of the leading workstation vendors, Apollo Computers, in 1989. The HP 9000 Series 300 and Series 400 workstations, now obsolete, were based on Apollo design. Apollo's PRISM RISC architecture was eventually abandoned and HP-PA evolved into the current PA-RISC architecture. (RISC stands for Reduced Instruction Set Computer.)

HP has another line of commercial computer systems, the HP 3000 series, which run the MPE/iX operating system. MPE preceded HP-UX and was HP's main computer business until the industry decided to move to Unix systems. MPE/iX is a proprietary operating system, somewhat like Digital's OpenVMS. The HP 3000 systems have a higher profit margin than HP-UX–based systems. Current implementations of the HP 3000 hardware are based on the PA-RISC architecture.

HP's current lines of business (and shares of revenue) are computers and peripherals (78 percent), test and measurement equipment (11 percent), medical instrumentation (5 percent), analytical devices (3 percent), and components (3 percent).

Why is a latecomer to the Unix world, HP, doing so well with HP-UX? In my opinion, the main reason is that HP has the best engineering resources in the industry. It has designed top-quality products in all the fields it operates in. To underscore this fact, witness the number of products for which HP ranks number one in the world:

- LED lamps and displays
- Each category of laser, inkjet, and color printers
- Digital audiotape (DAT) products
- Hospital patient monitoring systems
- Cardiac ultrasound imaging systems
- DOS-based palmtops
- Network analyzers
- Spectrum analyzers
- Logic analyzers
- Cesium (atomic) clocks
- Unix-based systems

A company culture focused on high-quality design and human factor engineering has led HP to the number one position in the Unix marketplace.

1.2 Unix History

As can be seen in Table 1.1, HP-UX is a comparatively new Unix implementation.

1.3 HP 9000 Hardware

All HP-UX systems now run on systems with CPUs based on the PA-RISC architecture. The architecture was first introduced in 1986 with the PA-7100 CPU chip. This was followed by the PA-7100LC (LC for low cost), the PA-7150, the PA-7200, and now the 64-bit PA-8000 RISC chip. The newer chips have graphics and multimedia functionality built-in. The PA-RISC architecture is available to other vendors; however, few non-HP products using the architecture are commercially available.

HP-UX runs on these HP 9000 series systems, all based on the PA-RISC architecture:

- *The T500 and T520 series server:* These are high-end systems supporting up to 14 CPUs in an SMP configuration. They are supposed to displace mainframes, though I do not believe they have the expansion capabilities mainframes have. The T series is comparable to Digital's AlphaServers 8000 series, though the Alpha CPU is a 64-bit processor and has a higher clock speed, hence the AlphaServers have an edge.

TABLE 1.1   Unix Milestones

1969	Unix developed on a Digital Equipment Corporation PDP-7 system.
1975	AT&T licenses Unix to universities.
1977	Berkeley Software Distribution V1.0.
	SCO Unix.
1979	Berkeley gets ARPAnet contract. TCP/IP is widely adopted.
1981	SUN Unix is born.
1983	AT&T System V.
	HP-UX announced.
1984	DEC Ultrix is born.
	X/Open formed.
1985	Sun's NFS released.
	POSIX founded.
1986	HP-UX released on the HP-PA RISC architecture.
	BSD V4.3.
1989	AT&T SYSV Release 4.
	OSF founded, Motif announced.
	HP acquires Apollo Computers mainly for its workstations.
1990	IBM AIX released.
	OSF/1 operating system announced.
1992	Digital Alpha systems implement fastest Unix, OSF/1.
1995	Digital Unix is only OSF/1 implementation.
	HP-UX Version 10 released.
	"Single Unix" being worked on by X/Open.
	Common Desktop Environment (CDE) implemented.
1996	PA-8000 64-bit RISC architecture announced.

- *The K series server:* Current versions are based on PA-7200 32-bit and PA-8000 64-bit RISC CPUs. A K system has up to four CPUs. CPU clock speeds start at 100 MHz. These are typical minicomputers with adequate expansion capabilities. The systems can be upgraded from PA-7200 to use the 64-bit PA-8000 CPUs. They are comparable to Sun Microsystems' Sparc2000 systems, which run the Solaris operating system; or to IBM's RISC/6000 J30 or R30 series, which are based on the PowerPC architecture and run the AIX operating system.

- *The D series server:* These are low-cost computers that support up to two CPUs. The systems can be upgraded to PA-8000 CPUs. The system has extensive expansion capabilities for its price.

- *The E series server:* These are small minicomputers, older than the D series, with limited expansion capabilities; they do not support fiber optic (FDDI) interfaces. They can run the complete gamut of HP-UX software. Comparable to IBM's RISC/6000 Model 590.

- *The HP 700 series workstations:* PA-RISC systems for low-end graphics or other desktop use. An example is the 715 workstation.

- *The C series and the J series workstations:* These are high-performance workstations using the PA-7200 RISC CPUs supporting SMP. CPU clock speeds start at 100 MHz. The workstations can be upgraded to use the 64-

bit PA-8000 CPUs. The C series is newer than the J series. The workstations are comparable to the Digital AlphaStation 250.

- *The HP 9000 Model EPS20 Enterprise parallel servers:* These are glorified K series systems joined with an FDDI link. Limited software is available to use all the systems as a single parallel processing system. Clustering and high availability are supported with the MC/ServiceGuard software.

- *The SPP1200 series scalable parallel processors:* These systems support over a hundred PA-RISC chips in a parallel processing configuration. The design was by Convex Computer Corporation, which had a license to use the PA-7200 chips in its products. Convex was bought by HP, which is now marketing one of the Convex systems as the number cruncher SPP1200.

The G, H, and I series servers are older systems. They fall between the E and K series in performance and expandability. They cannot be upgraded to PA-8000 RISC. The 700 series workstations are also older; they cannot be expanded to PA-8000 RISC. These systems are still shipping, though. Figures 1.1, 1.2, and 1.3 show HP servers, and Fig. 1.4 shows an HP 9000 J series workstation. Figure 1.5 shows a two-node EPS20 server.

Table 1.2 is a performance comparison of the models. Table 1.3 compares HP with other vendors using the SPEC95 test suites.

Figure 1.6 is a block diagram of a two-CPU K200 system. HP's line of X-stations are called Envizex (for high-end, CAD/CAM use) and Entria (for low-end terminal use). Figure 1.7 shows an HP X-terminal. DAT tape-drive tech-

Can be configured with up to 12 CPUs.
A T520 can have up to 14 CPUs.

Figure 1.1 A T500 system. (*Copyright 1995, Hewlett-Packard Company. Reprinted with permission.*)

Can be configured with up to 4 CPUs.
Can be updated to PA-8000 64-bit CPUs.

Figure 1.2 A K series system. (*Copyright 1995, Hewlett-Packard Company. Reprinted with permission.*)

Can be configured with up to 2 CPUs.
Can be upgraded to PA-8000 64-bit CPUs.

Figure 1.3 A D series system. (*Copyright 1995, Hewlett-Packard Company. Reprinted with permission.*)

nology (DDS format) is popular on HP systems. SCSI-2 devices are commonly used. RAID disk arrays, optical storage, and tape jukeboxes are well supported in software. For example, the HP A3232A disk array consists of 20 disks of 2 Gbytes supporting RAID in firmware. SCSI-2 technology is used. The array can be configured in standalone and RAID 0, 1, or 5 formats. Popular CRT

J210 single CPU
performance 57MFLOPS.

Can be configured with
2 CPUs.

Can be configured to
PA-8000 64-bit CPUs.

Figure 1.4 J series workstation. (*Copyright 1995, Hewlett-Packard Company. Reprinted with permission.*)

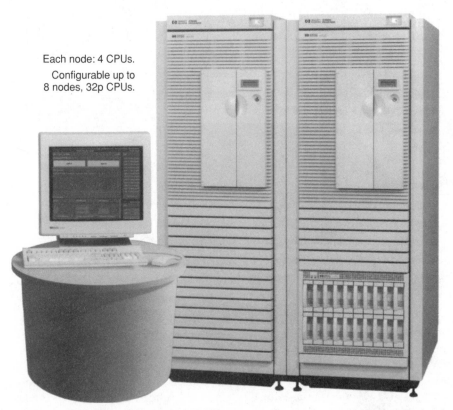

Each node: 4 CPUs.

Configurable up to
8 nodes, 32p CPUs.

Figure 1.5 EPS20 parallel server HP-UX system. (*Copyright 1995, Hewlett-Packard Company. Reprinted with permission.*)

TABLE 1.2   Model Comparisons

Model	SPECrate_int92	Maximum CPUs	Maximum memory	Other information
T500-12	~23,000	12	2 Gbyte	256 Mbyte/s I/O bus
K400	~12,000	4	2 Gbyte	Per CPU 256K/256K cache for Instr/Data
E55	~2,500	1	512 Mbyte	4 HP-PB I/O slots
D350-1	~3,341	2	768 Mbyte	8 I/O slots
J200	~3,000	2	1 Gbyte	Optional graphics accelerator hardware

TABLE 1.3   Multivendor Model Comparisons

Model	CPU	SPECint_base95	SPECfp_base95
HP C110	120 MHz PA-7200	4.41	7.45
HP K400	100 MHz PA-7200	3.58	6.21
Digital AlphaStation 600 5/300	300 MHz 21164	7.33	11.59
IBM POWERServer 591	77 MHz POWER2	3.67	11.20

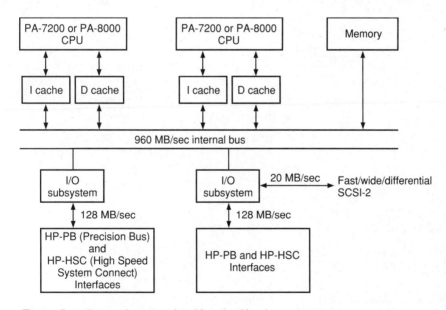

The configuration can be extrapolated for other K series systems.

Figure 1.6   Block diagram of an HP 9000 two-CPU K200 system.

Can be configured with up to 2 CPUs.
Can be upgraded to PA-8000 64-bit CPUs.

Figure 1.7   An HP X-terminal. (*Copyright 1995, Hewlett-Packard Company. Reprinted with permission.*)

• Multisessions
• Windowing
• 8 programmable softkeys with
  corresponding help on bottom of screen

Figure 1.8   An HP CRT terminal, model 700/600. (*Copyright 1995, Hewlett-Packard Company. Reprinted with permission.*)

terminals are HP 700/60 and 700/70. The terminals have programmable soft-keys and can display menus at the bottom of the screen. This functionality is exploited by some HP software. However, VT100-compatible terminals are also fairly well supported. Figure 1.8 shows an HP CRT terminal.

1.4   Major Software Components

Basic HP-UX is a typical commercial Unix operating system implementation. Commonly used enhancements include:

- *SAM: System Administration Manager:*   This menu-oriented and (Graphics user interface) GUI-based bundled software simplifies most system administration tasks.

- *fbackup and frestore:*   These are upgraded versions of the Unix *dump* and *restore* commands. These commands are adequate for most routine back-ups. In fact, *sam* has a backup and recovery menu that is essentially a GUI front end to fbackup and frestore.

- *LaserROM:* This is on-line documentation that is distributed on a CD-ROM. The software allows browsing, searching, and creation of custom bookshelves. The software is bundled with the system. LaserROM is very useful for all types of users.

- *Software Distributor:* This is the standard software distribution and installation tool. Software can be stored at a common network site, called a *depot,* and can be installed on multiple systems with ease.

- *Logical Volume Manager:* LVM is now available on most Unix implementations. Disks can now be partitioned into flexible logical volumes instead of the rigid slices that were used before.

- *OpenView:* This was originally a network management tool. However, it is now a framework of products that support, among other functionality, SNMP-based and OSI-based network management (comparable to IBM NETVIEW), performance management of multiple systems on a network, and operations management of systems on the network. A separately licensed product.

- *OmniBack II:* This is a GUI-based backup and restore tool that allows backups over the network. It has especially convenient features like checking how many times tapes are written to and warning when there have been too many writes on a tape. A separately licensed product.

- *Softbench:* A visual development environment supporting program editing, compiling, debugging, and the like in an integrated manner. A separately licensed product.

- *GlancePlus and other performance products:* GlancePlus is a real-time performance monitoring and troubleshooting tool. It has a GUI interface and shows information in graphical or tabular form. Its Advisor component can be programmed to display alarms when there are abnormal conditions. Performance data can be collected with the Measurement Interface (midaemon). The data can be graphed and studied with PerfRX and PerfView. These products are separately licensed.

2

Using HP-UX:
A Beginner's Guide

2.1 Introduction

This chapter is intended for users starting off on HP-UX, though seasoned users may get some nuggets out of some sections. The chapter is by no means comprehensive; it provides a flavor of what is available on HP-UX. Information on Unix concepts, processes, utilities, interprocess communications, networking, and other topics is available in the plethora of Unix books available.

2.2 Logging In

Typically, there are two login interfaces to HP-UX: X-stations, and "dumb" terminals. X-stations include terminals, PCs with X software, other Unix systems with graphics terminals, or any other system supporting the X protocol. Dumb terminals are character display–oriented, like HP's 700/96 or the industry standard VT100 terminals.

2.2.1 X-station login

To log into HP-UX from an X-station, the X server should be brought up and a connection to the HP-UX system established by the XDMCP protocol. Most PC X software packages usually have a configuration option to do this. On AIX Unix systems, the following command can be issued after logging into the graphics terminal from a command line:

```
# X -query hpsystem
```

HP's Entria and Envizex X-terminals are slightly more convenient to set up and use compared with other X-stations, because the keyboard has the F1 to F8 softkeys and HP's fonts are loaded by default.

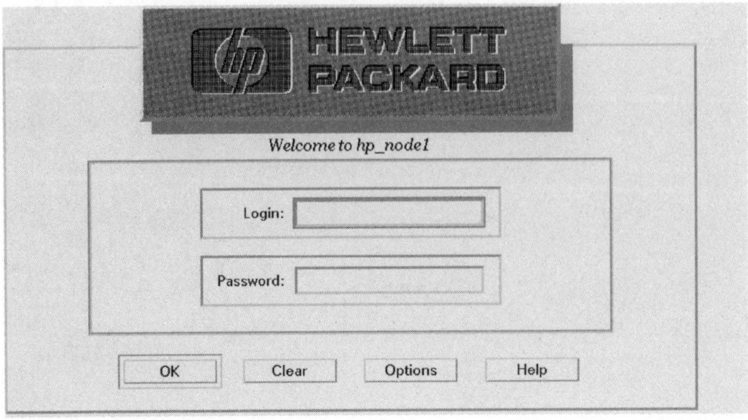

Figure 2.1 HP VUE login screen.

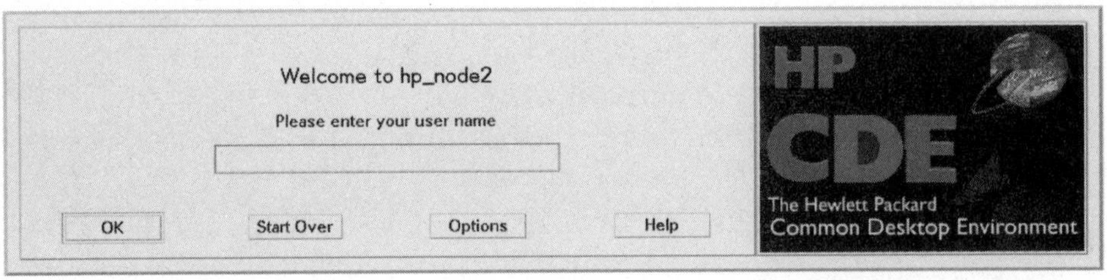

Figure 2.2 HP CDE login screen.

You should see a login screen, either from VUE (Fig. 2.1) or from CDE (Fig. 2.2), depending on which of the two GUI window manager interfaces is configured on your system. Note that CDE replaces the older VUE. VUE is short for Visual User Environment, and CDE is short for Common Desktop Environment. VUE and CDE are X protocol–based window managers. Both are covered in Chapter 12.

Once you are logged in, a desktop of commonly used products is displayed. Example applications are File Manager, Terminal Emulator, and Mail. Shell commands can be entered by bringing up a terminal emulator window.

2.2.2 Dumb terminal login

Character display terminals may be connected directly to the HP system via serial cables or across the network. Some HP-UX software takes advantage of hpterm features like softkeys; hence, HP's terminals are slightly more convenient to use. However, VT100 and other terminals are also well supported. In a multiple-Unix shop, VT100-compatible terminals may be more suitable.

The login prompts are:

```
login:
password:
```

2.2.3   TSM: Terminal Session Manager

When working from an X-terminal, you can pop up many windows of hpterm, xterm, VT100, and other dumb terminals. However, on a real dumb terminal, you can normally have only one session. TSM is a utility that allows you to use multiple sessions from a dumb terminal. To run TSM, log into the system from a terminal and enter *tsm*. A copyright and help screen will be displayed. Entering *return* then displays a message that indicates that TSM is running and shows which of nine possible sessions you are using, depending on TSM setup:

```
$ tsm
( copyright and help screen)
>>>Session 1 is active<<<
$
```

The session is now a normal Unix session. ctrl-T is used to communicate with TSM. When ctrl-T is pressed, a menu, shown in Fig. 2.3, will be displayed. The *select* submenu displays a list of sessions; selecting one will allow you to work with that session. TSM will restore the screen contents of that session so you will see exactly what you had on the screen when you left that session for another session. On hpterms, softkeys can be used to select sessions, as displayed at the bottom of the screen. The *quit* menu item will cause TSM to terminate, following which the normal Unix single session will be in effect. TSM supports many dumb terminals like dumb hpterms, VT100, and VT220.

2.2.4   Logging out

On X-stations, pressing the appropriate button of the mouse causes a popup menu to be displayed. One of the options on this menu is for terminating the

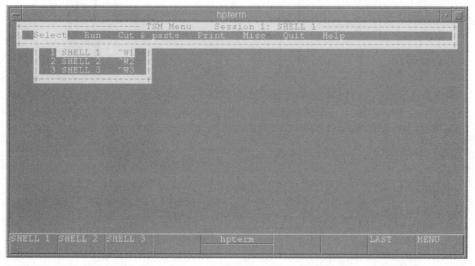

Figure 2.3 Terminal Session Manager supporting three Unix sessions from a terminal.

VUE session. Terminating the session will cause the VUE login screen to be displayed. If logged in via the XDMCP protocol, the X-station vendor's documentation should be consulted to terminate the XDMCP session.

To log out from a character display terminal, enter *logout* at the command line.

2.3   Shells: Bourne, C, Korn, POSIX, dtksh, and keysh

After logging in, a shell displays the command line prompt, for example,

```
#
```

The shell is your interface to the operating system. Your login shell is specified in the /etc/passwd file. Shells interpret and execute some commands like *echo*; however, most other command names, like *tar,* are interpreted as names of files to be run with the specified command line. The files are searched for in the directories specified by the PATH environment variable, which is described later. Although a number of shells are available, POSIX is the standard shell on HP-UX.

2.3.1   The command line

The precise syntax of the command line will depend on the shell being used. Moreover, utilities and other programs may not follow conventions. In most cases, shells support the following syntax:

```
# commandname   -qualifier -qualifier ...  parameter parameter ...
```

An example command is

```
# ls -a -R  file1 file2
```

Many times a qualifier is a single letter. Such qualifiers can be combined, as in

```
# ls -aR  file1 file2
```

Qualifiers may have optional parameters as in

```
# tar -b 5000 -xvf  /dev/cd0
```

Here, the tar command has no parameters, the b qualifier has the parameter 5000, and the f qualifier has the parameter /dev/cd0. This relationship is more clear in the equivalent command

```
# tar -b 5000 -f /dev/cd0 -x -v
```

At times, qualifiers are not single letters, as in

```
# tail -35  file1
```

2.3.2 Comparing the shells

Bourne shell, or B-shell, is one of the oldest shells. Korn shell, or K-shell, was developed later, in 1986. It is (very nearly) a superset of the B-shell. Both B- and K-shells are products of AT&T Bell Laboratories. C-shell leans toward a C language–style syntax. It was developed at the University of California at Berkeley. All these three shells should be available on all Unix implementations.

POSIX shell is based on the standard defined by IEEE P1003.2. The POSIX shell is Korn shell with minor differences.

Key shell, or Keysh, is Korn shell with extensions by HP. The extensions relate to HP terminals that support user-programmable softkeys. Obviously, shell scripts using softkey extensions will not be portable to other Unix platforms.

Desktop Korn shell (*dtksh*) is the standard shell under the Common Desktop Environment (CDE), which is being adopted by the major Unix vendors. dtksh is Korn shell–93 with extensions to support X-windowing features. GUI scripts can be written without resorting to standard programming languages.

Which shell should you use? My recommendation would be *dtksh* if you have access to it on all your Unix platforms. POSIX (or Korn) shell should be the next choice.

Differences between POSIX and Korn shells.   Functions can be defined in POSIX or Korn shell scripts. These functions act as commands. The shells also have built-in commands like echo. In Korn shell, the built-in commands are searched before functions; in POSIX shell, the functions are searched before built-in commands. Hence, in POSIX you can replace built-in commands with your functions.

- As a result of the above POSIX shell feature, a new built-in command called *command* can be used to execute a command without looking up functions.

- The time keyword is removed; the POSIX-compliant /bin/time should be used instead.

- In the POSIX shell, read-only and export commands print variables in a format suitable for reinput to the shell as commands. For example:

```
# /usr/bin/ksh        # Korn shell
# readonly a345       # Define a variable read-only
# readonly           # Does nothing
```

```
# /usr/bin/sh          # POSIX shell
# readonly a345
# readonly             # Print read-only variables
a345
```

Similarly, *export* will list variables with no values, as, for example,

```
# export | grep a345
a345          # Korn shell output
a345 = ''     # POSIX shell output
```

- *unalias* removes an alias in both Korn and POSIX shells. *unalias -a* removes all aliases in POSIX shell. The *-a* qualifier is not present in Korn shell; hence, there is no simple way to remove all aliases.

2.3.3 Changing your shell and shell paths

To run a different shell, enter the name of the shell executable file, as in

```
# /usr/dt/bin/dtksh    # Desktop Korn shell
# /usr/bin/sh          # POSIX shell
# /usr/bin/ksh         # Korn shell
# /usr/bin/csh         # C-shell
# /usr/bin/keysh       # Key shell
# /usr/old/bin/sh      # Bourne shell
```

To change the shell permanently for all logins, the *chsh* command can be used with your username and the shell path as parameters, as in

```
chsh  jayshah /usr/dt/bin/dtksh
```

2.3.4 Customizing logins

Most users want a small set of commands automatically executed when they log in. For users having ksh, POSIX shell, or dtksh, /etc/profile and .profile in the user's home directory are executed every time the user logs in. /etc/profile is normally used by the system administrator to execute commands for all users logging into the system. Users normally cannot edit this file. Each user can enter his or her own login commands in .profile in the home directory. Note that these commands are run only when the user logs in, not when the user invokes the shells again during the session.

To automatically execute a set of commands every time one of the above three shells is invoked, the ENV (environment) variable should be set to point to the file containing the commands to be run on shell invocation. Normally, ENV is set in your .profile. Typically, it points to .kshrc, as in

```
export ENV=~/.kshrc
```

The symbol ~ is shorthand for the home directory.
Note that the ENV file is executed at login also.

2.4 Pipe

Pipes allow the output of one program to be sent as input to another program. A pipe is represented by the vertical bar (|) character. For example, the *who* command output can be sent to the word count (also line count) program (wc) as in:

```
# who | wc
```

This construct is useful to determine how many users are logged onto the system. The who program generates no terminal output, since its standard output is the pipe. The wc program does not accept input from the terminal; it accepts input from the pipe. Output of the wc program is displayed on the terminal.
Pipes can be cascaded as in

```
# cat file1 | sort | uniq
```

2.5 I/O Redirection

Programs get their input from a virtual device called *standard input* and send their output to a virtual device called *standard output*. Normally, the terminal is the input and output device. The input can be specified to be from a file by the symbol <, and output can be sent to a file by the symbol >. For example,

```
# wc < inputfile
```

will provide count information of data in the file *inputfile*. In

```
# wc < inputfile > cntfile
```

the count is performed on the data in inputfile and output is sent to cntfile instead of the terminal. Incidentally, the last command is equivalent to

```
# cat inputfile | wc | cat > cntfile
```

The symbol > is used to create a new file with the output; >> can be used to append output to an existing file. For example,

```
who >> tmpfile
```

will append *who* output to tmpfile. The file will be created if it does not exist.

2.6   File Operations

A new file can be created by the cat command, which accepts data from its standard input and sends it to its standard output. By redirecting standard output, a file can be created, as

```
cat > testfile
```

Text can be entered from the terminal and terminated by control-d, the end-of-file character. All entered text is directed to testfile. The ls command lists the files in the current directory. Files with names beginning with a period are considered hidden files which can also be displayed with the ls -a command:

```
# ls -a
.          .Xauthority   .dtprofile   .profile   .sh_history
..         .dt           .login       .rhosts    testfile
```

Other common file manipulation commands are

```
more testfile                # Display file one screen at a time.
mv testfile newfile          # Rename file from testfile to newfile.
cp testfile newfile          # Make a copy of testfile in newfile.
rm testfile                  # Delete a file.
lp testfile                  # Print file on default printer.
lp -d psprint testfile       # Print file on printer psprint.
diff testfile testfile2      # Compare contents of two files.
```

2.7   Directories

Directories on Unix systems are hierarchical; hence

```
/usr/bin/pgm
```

represents the file named pgm under the bin directory, which in turn is under the usr directory, which is under the root directory. The root directory is represented by the slash /. It is the topmost directory of the system. This is in contrast to MS-Windows and some other operating systems, which have a top-level directory for each disk device, as in c:\user\win\file. When a new disk is added, a file system is created on it and attached to a mount point in the existing directory structure. For example, the file system on a disk could be attached to the mount point directory /home/products. Then /home/products/Cobol/pgm represents the file pgm on the new disk.

Each user on the system has a default directory when he or she logs in. This directory is called the user's home directory. A file can be specified using an absolute path as in /disk1/home/jayshah/pgm/p1 or using a relative path as in pgm/pl. The relative path is relative to the current directory. Hence, the absolute and relative paths to the file will be identical if the user's current directory is /disk1/home/jayshah. Some common directory manipulation commands are:

```
pwd                        # Print working directory. Displays current directory.
cd /home/peter             # Change current directory to the one specified.
mkdir /home/jay/filedir    # Create specified directory.
mkdir filedir              # Make specified directory under the current directory.
rmdir filedir              # Delete directory.
rmdir -R filedir           # Remove specified directory/files/subdirectories.
cp -r /home/peter jayshah  # Copy a directory tree to another directory.
```

2.8   Wildcards

There are two wildcards for manipulating files and directories: * and ?. The * matches any number of characters, while ? matches any one character. Example uses are:

```
ls f*t      # Display all file names beginning with t and ending with t.
ls f?t      # File names beginning with f, ending with t, and 3 characters long.
ls f*t?t*f  # (Exercise for you.)
```

2.9   The *find* Command: Searching for Files

find is useful for searching all file names under a directory tree meeting specified conditions. An example command is:

```
find / -print
```

Here the first argument is the directory under which to look for files. All subdirectories are also scanned. The print option specifies that the file names be sent to standard output, the terminal. In this example, names of all files on the system are printed.

The first argument of find is always a directory. Other arguments may have parameters. These arguments and parameters are treated as boolean expressions when deciding whether the current file name should be processed by further arguments. For example,

```
find /home -user jay -size +50 -print
```

scans all files under the /home tree. For each file, if the owner is not Jay, the file name is not processed further. If the owner is Jay, then if the file size is not greater than 50 blocks, the file name is not processed further. If the size is greater than 50 blocks, the file name is printed. Effectively, this statement prints all names of all files under the tree /home which are owned by Jay and which have a size of more than 50 blocks. The ! operator negates the boolean condition.

Example uses of find are:

```
find / -name "*sh*" -print       # Files with "sh" in the file name.
find /home -size -50 -print      # Files less than 50 blocks in size.
find /home -size -1024c -print   # Files less than 2 blocks in size.
find / -mtime +20 -print         # Files modified more than 20 days ago.
find / ! -mtime +20 -print       # Files not modified more than 20 days ago.
find / -local -print             # Local files as opposed to network, NFS files
find / -mount -print             # Files in the file system where the current directory is.
find / -print | ls -l            # Long file listing of all files on the system.
find / -print > allfiles         # Create a file containing listing of all files on the system.
```

2.10 The grep Command: Searching within Files

grep is used to search for strings and regular expressions (explained later) within files. For example,

```
# grep jay file1
```

searches for the string jay within file1. Lines containing the string are printed. To search all files within the current directory, the command is

```
# grep jay *
```

The search is not case-sensitive. To search for jay, Jay, or even JaY, the command is

```
grep -i jay file1
```

Major options to grep are:

-c	Print the number of lines containing the search string.
-i	Ignore upper- and lowercase distinction when comparing.
-l	Print the file name only of each file containing the search string.
-n	Precede each matching line with its line number in the file.
-v	Print all lines which do *not* have the search string.

2.10.1 Regular expressions

grep stands for global/regular expression/print. A regular expression is a sequence of characters and operators. For example, "d.g" is a regular expression that means the character d followed by any one character, followed in turn by the character g. Regular expressions can be used for searching with grep. For example,

```
grep 'd.g' file1
```

will search for all lines containing dog, dug, dag, dzg, and so on. The single quotes are used so that the shell passes the complete string as-is to grep; otherwise, the shell may interpret some characters before passing them on to grep. Common regular expression operators are:

- The period (.), which matches one character, as described above.

- The asterisk (*), which matches zero or more of the previous regular expression. Example: *ab*cd* matches *a* followed by zero or more *b*'s followed by *c* and *d*. Hence, *acd, abcd, abbbcd* are matches. Another example is *foo.*test*. Here, *foo* followed any number of characters followed by *test* is matched. Note how *foo.*test* and *foo*test* are different.

- A set of characters between square brackets, which match any one of the set of characters. For example, *[abc]* matches any of *a, b,* or *c.* A range of matching characters can be specified within brackets separated with a dash, as in *[a-z]*. Here, all lowercase alphabetic characters will be matched. *[a-zA-Z0-9]* matches lowercase and uppercase alphabets along with any digits. As an example, *grep 'x[0-9]*y' file1* matches any string starting with *x,* followed by zero or more digits, followed by *y.* Valid matches are *x1y, xy, x324y,* and *x01y.*

- Caret (^) and $, which are called anchor characters. They represent the beginning and end of a line. Examples: *grep '^test$' file1* will match any line with the word *test* and nothing else in it. *grep '^$'* will match all lines containing no characters.

2.10.2   egrep and fgrep

egrep handles more regular expressions than grep:

- Plus (+) matches one or more occurrences of the preceding regular expression. For example, *egrep 'b+' file1* matches all lines containing at least one *b.*

- Question mark (?) matches exactly zero or one occurrence of the preceding regular expression.

- Parentheses that group multiple regular expressions as one. For example, *egrep '(ab)+' file1* matches *ab, abab, ababab,* and so on.

- Vertical bar (|), which is an OR operator. For example, *egrep 'book|tome' file1* matches all lines containing book or tome. *egrep 'c(a|u)t' file1* matches cat or cut.

fgrep does not support regular expressions; only strings can be searched by it. It is faster than grep.

2.11   The sort and uniq Commands

The command

```
cat file1 | sort
```

sorts the file *file1* and writes the sorted output to the standard output, normally the terminal. Because the sort has no options, the sort field is the first field of each line. Fields are separated with a space or tab character or end of line. If a field has multiple tabs or spaces in a sequence, the first is considered a separator; the others are part of the next field. The command

```
cat file1 | sort -f > file2
```

sorts the file ignoring upper- and lowercase distinction when comparing alphabets. Common sort options are

-f	Treats upper- and lowercase characters as matches.
-n	Numeric sort. Digits, decimal point, and + and − signs are significant.
-r	Reverse sort.
-tc	Considers the character *c* as the separator instead of the default space or tab.
+p1 −p2	Specifies the sort field instead of the default first field. +p1 specifies the starting field and −p2 specifies the ending field. Multiple such specifications can be given.

Here are some examples:

```
cat file1 | sort -t, +2 -2        Sort on second field; comma is the field separator.
cat file1 | sort +2 -2 +5 -5      Sort on the second field, then on the fifth field.
```

The uniq command is used to remove duplicate lines from a file. An example is

```
cat file1 | sort | uniq
```

The file should be sorted, as uniq compares only adjacent lines. uniq -c file1 displays all lines along with a repeat count of each line. uniq -d file1 displays only lines that have a repeat count greater than 1.

2.12   The Editors

ed, ex, vi, and *EMACS* are popular editors on Unix systems. The latest editor, which is also easy to use, is the one bundled with the Common Desktop Environment (CDE). vi and EMACS are screen-oriented; hence they are more popular than the others. EMACS is not bundled with most Unix systems; hence, the most common editor on unix is vi. A file is edited with a command like

```
# vi file1
```

The TERM environment variable must be set to a valid terminal type using commands like

```
# export TERM=VT100
# export TERM=HPTERM
```

Text can be inserted following the i command, for inserting. To stop insert-

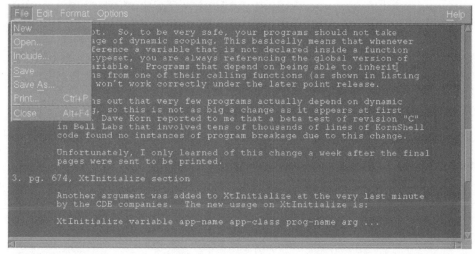

Figure 2.4 The CDE text editor.

ing, press the escape key. There are many single-character commands. Colon (:) and slash (/) are used to enter commands requiring more than one character input. For example, the :w command writes the file to disk, and the :q command causes an exit from the editor back to the command line. vi is a "Unixy" editor; commands are cryptic and nonintuitive. If you have access to CDE and you do not have complex editing requirements, consider using the editor that can be run from the Frontpanel. The CDE editor is like MS-Windows notepad editor.

Figure 2.4 is a screen shot of the CDE editor.

2.13 Mail

Two mail packages are commonly used on HP systems, *elm* and *mailx*. elm is screen-oriented and simple to use; hence, it is the default mail package. mailx is line-oriented; hence, experienced systems administrators like to use it, especially in scripts. elm is invoked by the command

```
# elm
```

Figure 2.5 shows the initial screen. elm is fairly simple to use, as it has extensive menus and prompts.

2.14 man Pages

LaserROM is the best way to search for HP-UX information. Traditionally, however, Unix documentation has been supplied as man pages. To get details on a command—for example, sort—the command is

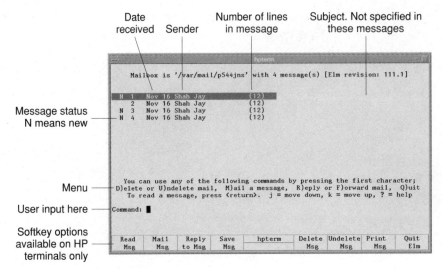

Figure 2.5   elm: screen-oriented mail package, initial screen.

```
# man sort
```

The information is displayed in sections like name, synopsis, and description. Here is a sample output. The indication (1) represents the manual section number.

```
sort(1)                                                              sort(1)

NAME
     sort - sort or merge files

SYNOPSIS
     sort [-m] [-o output] [-bdfinruM] [-t char] [-k keydef] [-y [kmem]] [-z
     recsz] [-T dir] [file ...]
     sort [-c] [-AbdfinruM] [-t char] [-k keydef] [-y [kmem]] [-z recsz] [-T
     dir] [file ...]

DESCRIPTION
     sort performs one of the following functions:

          1. Sorts lines of all the named files together and writes the result
          to the specified output.

          2. Merges lines of all the named (presorted) files together and
          writes the result to the specified output.
          3. Checks that a single input file is correctly presorted.

     The standard input is read if - is used as a file name or no input files
     are specified.

     Comparisons are based on one or more sort keys extracted from each line
     of input. By default, there is one sort key, the entire input line.
     Ordering is lexicographic by characters using the collating sequence of
     the current locale. If the locale is not specified or is set to the
     POSIX locale, then ordering is lexicographic by bytes in machine-collat-
```

ing sequence. If the locale includes multi-byte characters, single-byte
characters are machine-collated before multi-byte characters.
Behavior Modification Options
  The following options alter the default behavior:

  -A   Sorts on a byte-by-byte basis using each character's encoded
              value. On some systems, extended characters will be consid-
              ered negative values, and so sort before ASCII characters. If
              you are sorting ASCII characters in a non-C/POSIX locale,
              this flag performs much faster.
  -c   Check that the single input file is sorted according to the
              ordering rules. No output is produced; the exit code is set
              to indicate the result.
  -m   Merge only; the input files are assumed to be already sorted.

Hewlett-Packard Company   - 1 -   HP-UX Release 10.10:Jan 1996

sort(1)   sort(1)

  -o output   The argument given is the name of an output file to use
              instead of the standard output. This file can be

(Some lines deleted here)

  Ordering Rule Options
    When ordering options appear before restricted sort key specifications,
    the ordering rules are applied globally to all sort keys. When attached
    to a specific sort key (described below), the ordering options override
    all global ordering options for that key.

The following options override the default ordering rules:

  -d   Quasi-dictionary order: only alphanumeric characters and
              blanks (spaces and tabs), as defined by LC_CTYPE are signifi-
              cant in comparisons (see environ(5)).

Hewlett-Packard Company   - 2 -   HP-UX Release 10.10:Jan 1996

sort(1)   sort(1)

  -f   Fold letters. Prior to being compared, all lowercase

(Some lines deleted here)

  Field Separator Options
    The treatment of field separators can be altered using the options:

  -t char   Use char as the field separator character; char is not con-
              sidered to be part of a field (although it can

(Some lines deleted here)

Hewlett-Packard Company   - 3 -   HP-UX Release 10.10:Jan 1996

sort(1)   sort(1)

              below). Note that the -b option is only effective when
              restricted sort key specifications are given.

  Restricted Sort Key

```
        -k keydef  The keydef argument defines a restricted sort key.
                   The format of this definition is
                   field_start[type][,field_end[type]]
```

(Some lines deleted here)

```
Hewlett-Packard Company        - 4 -      HP-UX Release 10.10:Jan 1996

sort(1)                                                           sort(1)
```

```
              Multiple -k options are permitted and are significant in com-
              mand line order. A maximum of 9 -k options can be given. If
              no -k option is specified, a default
```

(Some lines deleted here)

EXTERNAL INFLUENCES

```
Hewlett-Packard Company        - 5 -      HP-UX Release 10.10:Jan 1996

sort(1)                                                           sort(1)
```

```
  Environment Variables
     LC_COLLATE determines the default ordering rules applied to the sort.
```

(Some lines deleted here)

```
International Code Set Support
     Single- and multi-byte character code sets are supported.
```

EXAMPLES
```
     Sort the contents of infile with the second field as the sort key:

         sort -k 2,2 infile

     Sort, in reverse order, the contents of infile1 and infile2, placing the
     output in outfile and using the first two characters of the second field
     as the sort key:

         sort -r -o outfile -k 2.1,2.2 infile1 infile2
```

(Some lines deleted here)

```
Hewlett-Packard Company        - 6 -      HP-UX Release 10.10:Jan 1996

sort(1)                                                           sort(1)
```

```
sort -mu -k 3,3 infile
```

DIAGNOSTICS
```
     sort exits with one of the following values:

         0    All input files were output successfully, or -c was specified
              and the input file was correctly presorted.

         1    Under the -c option, the file was not ordered as specified, or
              if the -c and -u options were both specified, two input
```

(Some lines deleted here)

WARNINGS
>
>   Numbering of fields and characters within fields (-k option) has changed
>   to conform to the POSIX standard. Beginning at HP-UX Release 9.0, the -k
>   option numbers fields and characters within fields, starting with 1.
>   Prior to HP-UX Release 9.0, numbering started at 0.
>
>   A field separator specified by the -t option is recognized only if it is
>   a single-byte character.
>
>   The character type classification categories alpha, digit, space, and
>   print are not defined for multi-byte characters. For languages with
>   multi-byte characters, all characters are significant in comparisons.

FILES
>
>   /var/tmp/stm???
>   /tmp/stm???

AUTHOR
>
>   sort was developed by OSF and HP.

SEE ALSO
>
>   comm(1), join(1), uniq(1), collate8(4), environ(5), hpnls(5), lang(5).

STANDARDS CONFORMANCE
>
>   sort: SVID2, SVID3, XPG2, XPG3, POSIX.2

```
Hewlett-Packard Company        - 7 -     HP-UX Release 10.10:Jan 1996
```

2.14.1   The whatis database: Keyword searching for man pages

The command

```
# catman -w
```

creates a database containing lines each containing a command name and the command synopsis. This database, called the *whatis* database, is in the file /usr/share/lib/whatis. The database can be searched with the man -k command by specifying a string of characters to be searched; for example,

```
# man -k sort
```

bsearch( )(3C)	Binary search of a sorted table.
comm(1)	Select or reject lines common to two sorted files.
qsort( )(3C)	Quicker sort.
scandir( ), alphasort( )(3C)	Scan a directory.
sort(1)	Sort or merge files.
tsort(1)	Topological sort.
uusnaps(1M)	Sort and embellish uusnap output.

The command displays other sorting commands that have man pages. The numbers in parentheses represent the manual section numbers. Manual pages in (1) and (1M) describe commands, and pages in (3C) describe C library functions.

2.15   sed: Stream Editor

sed is a utility that accepts input, performs operations on it a line at a time, and writes the result to standard output. Typically, it is used to perform string replacements with the substitute (s) command:

```
$ sed s/temp1/test2/g infile > outfile
```

Here, all occurrences of *temp1* in the file *infile* are replaced with *test2*. The output is sent to outfile. The slashes are string delimiters for the substitute command; the *g* is for global substitution, which means all search strings (not just the first) in a line are to be processed. Regular expressions like those used in grep are supported. sed has other features for which Unix manuals should be consulted.

2.16   awk: A Scripting Language

awk is more powerful than the shells, though awk is used in conjunction with shell features in most applications. awk processes input a line at a time. In an awk program, $0 represents the line, and $1 through $9 represent the parameters. Here is a sample awk script:

```
$ awk '{
print $2, $3
}' tmpfile
```

The script will print the second and third parameters of all lines in tmpfile. For example, if a line contains

```
a1 a2 a3 a4
```

the output will be

```
a2 a3
```

Parameter delimiters are white spaces; however, the delimiter can be specified to be, for example, a colon with the -F qualifier, as in:

```
$ awk -F: '{
...
```

The awk script can be specified between quotes as shown above or can be put into a file which can be used as:

```
$ awk -f awkscript tmpfile
```

awk has extensive functionality beyond the scope of this book; if you are serious about Unix, learn awk from one of the many books out there.

2.17 Working across the Network

The rlogin and telnet commands are used to log into another system on the network. Example commands are:

```
# rlogin hpsys2
# telnet hpsys2
```

Files can be copied from one system to another using the rcp and ftp commands. An example rcp command is

```
rcp hpsys2:file1 localfile
```

Here, the file *file1* from hpsys2 is copied to the local system as file *localfile*. The rcp command requires your local system name to be entered in the .rhosts file in your home directory on hpsys2. This process is described in Chapter 9, on networking.

ftp is another popular file transfer utility. ftp does not use the .rhosts mechanism; a user name and password are required for the other system on the network. ftp is also described in Chapter 9.

2.18 ps: Displaying Processes on the System

The *ps* command has many options for displaying information on processes running on the system. For example, the -e qualifier displays all processes on the system, and the -f qualifier prints "full" information. Here is an example of use of the *ps* command:

```
# ps -ef
```

UID	PID	PPID	C	STIME	TTY	TIME	COMMAND
root	0	0	0	05:02:26	?	0:00	swapper
root	1	0	0	05:02:35	?	0:00	init
root	2	0	0	05:02:26	?	0:00	vhand
root	3	0	0	05:02:26	?	4:01	statdaemon
root	4	0	0	05:02:26	?	0:02	unhashdaemon
root	7	0	0	05:02:26	?	1:16	ttisr
root	38	0	0	05:02:35	?	0:00	lvmkd
root	39	0	0	05:02:35	?	0:00	lvmkd
root	40	0	0	05:02:35	?	0:00	lvmkd
root	12	0	0	05:02:34	?	0:04	vx_sched_thread
root	13	0	0	05:02:34	?	0:00	vx_iflush_thread
root	14	0	0	05:02:34	?	0:01	vx_inactive_cache_thread
root	15	0	0	05:02:34	?	0:00	vx_delxwri_thread
root	16	0	0	05:02:34	?	0:00	vx_logflush_thread
root	17	0	0	05:02:34	?	0:00	vx_attrsync_thread
root	18	0	0	05:02:34	?	0:00	vx_inactive_thread
root	19	0	0	05:02:34	?	0:00	vx_inactive_thread
root	20	0	0	05:02:34	?	0:00	vx_inactive_thread
root	21	0	0	05:02:34	?	0:00	vx_inactive_thread

```
root       41       0    0    05:02:35  ?              0:00  lvmkd
root       42       0    0    05:02:35  ?              0:00  nvsisr
root       43       0    0    05:02:35  ?              0:00  supsched
root       44       0    0    05:02:35  ?              0:00  strmem
root       45       0    0    05:02:35  ?              0:00  strweld
root     2372       1    0    07:32:04  console        0:00  /usr/sbin/getty console
                                                             console
root      577       1    0    05:03:47  ?              0:00  /usr/sbin/automount -f
                                                             /etc/auto_master
root      685       1    0    05:04:53  ?              0:00  /usr/sbin/inetd
root      403       1    0    05:03:30  ?              0:10  /usr/sbin/syslogd -D
root      912       1    0    05:05:24  ?              0:05  /usr/sbin/xntpd
root      323       1    0    05:03:11  ?              0:01  /usr/sbin/swagentd
daemon    726       1    0    05:04:56  ?              0:00  sendmail -bd -q30m -
                                                             accepting connections
root      269       1    0    05:02:58  ?              0:24  /usr/sbin/syncer
root      522       1    0    05:03:40  ?              0:00  /usr/sbin/portmap
root     1109       1    0    05:05:31  ?              0:00  /usr/dt/bin/dtlogin
root      427       1    0    05:03:31  ?              0:00  /usr/sbin/ptydaemon
root      553       1    0    05:03:40  ?              0:00  /usr/sbin/biod 4
root      562       1    0    05:03:41  ?              0:00  /usr/sbin/rpc.statd
root      554       1    0    05:03:40  ?              0:00  /usr/sbin/biod 4
root      555       1    0    05:03:40  ?              0:00  /usr/sbin/biod 4
root      556       1    0    05:03:40  ?              0:00  /usr/sbin/biod 4
root      568       1    0    05:03:42  ?              0:00  /usr/sbin/rpc.lockd
root     3150     685    0    16:31:22  ?              0:00  ftpd nodep.acme.com:
                                                             usera12: LIST -aFl
root      864       1    0    05:05:17  ?              0:01  /opt/dce/sbin/rpcd
root      866       1    0    05:05:19  ?              0:28  /usr/sbin/ncs/glbd
usera12  3152    3090    4    16:31:45  ttyp1          0:00  ps -ef
root      965       1    0    05:05:26  ?              0:00  /usr/sbin/cron
root     3089     685    0    16:19:42  ttyp1          0:00  rlogind
root      981       1    0    05:05:26  ?              0:00  /usr/sbin/envd
usera12  3090    3089    0    16:19:42  ttyp1          0:00  -sh
root     1082    1081    0    05:05:29  ?              0:00  /usr/sbin/nfsd 4
root     1075       1    0    05:05:29  ?              0:00  /usr/sbin/rpc.mountd
root     1081       1    0    05:05:29  ?              0:00  /usr/sbin/nfsd 4
root     1087    1081    0    05:05:29  ?              0:00  /usr/sbin/nfsd 4
root     1086    1081    0    05:05:29  ?              0:00  /usr/sbin/nfsd 4
```

The fields displayed are UID, PID, PPID (parent process ID), C (CPU scheduling priority), STIME (start time or date), TTY (? means the process is started during the boot init time), TIME (CPU use), and COMMAND. The major processes are

- *swapper:* Process 0 is always this one. It works with vhand and unhash-daemon to handle swapping and paging.

- *init:* Process 1 is always this one. It performs system initializations and processes /etc/inittab.

- *vhand:* Handles virtual memory paging.

- *statdaemon and unhashdaemon:* These work with swapper and vhand to check free memory and to handle paging.

- *ttisr:* Kernel process handling terminal I/O.

- *lvmkd:* Logical Volume Manager kernel daemon. Handles raw I/O for logical volumes.

- *vx_sched_thread and other vx_*_thread processes:* These are part of the Journaled File System (JFS), also known as VxFS. The processes are present even when JFS is not in use.

- *netisr:* Picks up network data and calls appropriate protocol process—one process per processor in an SMP system.

- *nvsisr:* Picks up terminal network data and sends to appropriate pseudo-terminal.

- *supsched:* UP STREAMS scheduler. Part of the STREAMS subsystem.

- *smpsched:* STREAMS multiprocessor scheduler.

- *sblksched:* STREAMS blockable scheduler.

- *strmem, strsched, strmem, strweld:* STREAMS subsystem processes.

- *dtlogin:* The Common Desktop Environment (CDE) login process.

- *automount, biod, and nfsd:* Network File System processes.

- *portmap, rpc.statd, rpc.lockd, rpcd, glbd, rpc.mountd:* Remote Procedure Call–related processes. rpc.statd, rpc.lockd, and rpc.mountd are NFS-related.

- *swagentd:* Software Distributor (SD) agent process.

- syslogd: System message logging daemon.

- *inetd:* Internet superserver daemon; starts other processes based on incoming network information and contents of the file /etc/inetd.conf.

- *sendmail:* Unix mail.

2.19 lp: Printing

A file can be printed by the lp command; for example,

```
$ lp -d pname   /home/user12/file3
```

where pname is the printer queue name. The list of queues can be found by

```
$ lpstat -a
```

and the status of a printing job can be displayed by

```
$ lpstat
```

and a job can be canceled by

```
$ cancel job-name
```

2.20 syslog: Logging System Messages

The *syslog* facility, found on all Unix implementations, standardizes handling of error and other messages. Unfortunately, utilities on HP-UX, as on all

Unix systems, do not always use syslog, and hence there are log files scattered throughout the file system. Nevertheless, syslog is the most important logging mechanism, and it should be used if you need to send messages to the console and log them. syslog log files are under /var/adm/syslog. The log files have one line per entry. Sample contents of the most common log file, /var/adm/syslog/syslog.log, are

```
Mar 20 10:35:04 nodetst3 syslogd: restart
Mar 20 10:35:04 nodetst3 vmunix: inet_clts:ok inet_cots:ok 8 ccio
Mar 20 10:35:04 nodetst3 vmunix: 10 ccio
Mar 20 10:35:04 nodetst3 vmunix: 10/0 c720
Mar 20 10:35:04 nodetst3 vmunix: 10/0.3 tgt
Mar 20 10:35:04 nodetst3 vmunix: Logical volume 64, 0x1 configured as ROOT
Mar 20 10:35:04 nodetst3 vmunix: Logical volume 64, 0x2 configured as SWAP
Mar 20 10:35:04 nodetst3 vmunix: Memory Information:
Mar 20 10:35:04 nodetst3 vmunix: physical page size = 4096 bytes, logical
                                 page size = 4096 bytes
Mar 20 10:35:04 nodetst3 vmunix: Physical: 262144 Kbytes, lockable: 200980
                                 Kbytes,
                                 available: 233320 Kbytes
Mar 20 10:35:04 nodetst3 vmunix:
Mar 20 10:35:05 nodetst3 nettl[424]: nettl starting up.
Mar 20 10:35:15 nodetst3 automount[588]: load yp map auto.master error -1
Mar 20 10:35:16 nodetst3 inetd[601]: Reading configuration
Mar 20 10:35:16 nodetst3 inetd[601]: ftp/tcp: Added service, server
                                 /usr/lbin/ftpd
Mar 20 10:35:45 nodetst3 LVM[904]: lvlnboot -v
Mar 20 10:35:45 nodetst3 /usr/sbin/envd[936]: restart, and read the configu-
                                 ration file
Mar 20 10:35:47 nodetst3 bootpd[687]: hardware address not found:
                                 52515520A0AB
Mar 20 10:36:12 nodetst3 xntpd[818]: peer 43.26.1.46 event 84: Peer reach-
                                 able.
Mar 20 15:45:00 nodetst3 ftpd[2375]: connection from mgmstud31.largo.com
                                 at Wed Mar 20 15:45:00 1995
Mar 20 15:45:03 nodetst3 ftpd[2375]: FTP LOGIN FROM mgmstud31.largo.com,
                                 userwk1
Mar 20 15:46:20 nodetst3 ftpd[2375]: User userwk1 logged out
Mar 21 15:32:10 nodetst3 syslog: su : + ttyp5 userjqp-root
Mar 21 15:32:10 nodetst3 syslog: su : + ttyp5 userjqp-root
```

2.20.1 syslog configuration

Logging is started at system boot with a command like

```
# /usr/sbin/syslogd
```

The syslogd daemon (process) reads the configuration file /etc/syslog.conf, which specifies what kind of messages are to be processed and what action should be taken for each type of message. syslogd gets messages from

/dev/log   Named pipe

/dev/log.un   Unix domain socket

/dev/klog   Kernel log device

By default, programs send messages to /dev/log.un. Here is a typical configuration file, /etc/syslog.conf:

```
# @(#) $Revision: 74.1 $
#
# syslogd configuration file.
#
# See syslogd(1M) for information about the format of this file.
#
mail.debug              /var/adm/syslog/mail.log
*.info;mail.none        /var/adm/syslog/syslog.log
*.alert                 /dev/console
*.alert                 root
*.emerg                 *
```

The lines starting with # are comments. Each entry in the other lines has the format

facility.level info   action

Important note: Tabs and not spaces are used between the two fields. Possible actions are

- Send to console, as /dev/console
- Send to a log file, specified as, for example, /var/adm/syslog/syslog.log
- Send to specified users, specified as, for example, root, users34, userw32
- Send to all logged-in terminals, specified as *
- Send to syslogd on another system, specified as, for example, @lognode

Note how system messages from a networked set of nodes can be sent to a single system by the last method.

Possible values for facility are

kern	Messages generated by kernel
user	Messages generated by typical users
mail	Mail subsystem messages
daemon	Messages from system daemons such as ftpd and inetd
auth	Messages from login, su, getty, and such
lpr	Spooler messages
local0–local7	Reserved for local use

Possible values for level are

emerg	Panic messages, normally sent to all users
alert	Message requiring immediate action
crit	Critical condition such as device hard errors
err	Error messages
warning	Warning messages
notice	Message between info and warning in importance
info	Informational message
debug	Messages sent by debug programs
none	Don't log the message

Messages having a higher level than the one specified in the configuration file are logged. A wildcard in the facility or level field implies all possible values. Multiple facility.level fields can be specified separated by semicolons. Multiple facility values can be specified for the same level; the facility values are separated by commas. For example, in

```
*.info;mail.none
```

all messages at all levels (except debug) are logged except for mail messages; none of the mail messages will be logged when processing that entry. Mail messages, however, are logged by another entry in a different file, as shown in the configuration file above.

Programs can send messages to the syslog facility using the syslog(), openlog(), closelog(), and setlogmask() system calls. The next section shows how to send messages from the command line or scripts.

2.20.2   logger: Sending messages to syslog

The logger command can be used to send a message to the syslog facility. For example,

```
$ logger test logging
```

will generate an entry in the log file as:

```
Mar 20 11:35:04 nodetst3 usertqw test logging
```

Here usertqw is your user name. Actually, the message is sent to syslogd with a facility.level of user.notice. This can be changed with the -p qualifier as in

```
$ logger -p local2.warning system will reboot tonight
```

The action for the local2 facility can be defined in the file /etc/syslog.conf. This way, you can customize logging to suit your site requirements.

2.21   File System Layout

Unix is notorious for having files scattered throughout the file system without much rationale. Effective with V10.0, HP-UX follows the SRV4 file system layout, which is quite logical, though still complicated. Figure 2.6 shows the layout of major directories. Files are broadly classified as dynamic or static. Note that most user application files should be residing under /home. See Chapter 6, on system startup and shutdown, for information on system boot files, including software startup rc files.

```
Dynamic files (Configuration, temporary, and user files)


/dev       Device files.
/etc       System configurations, no programs. For example, the directory
           /etc/rc.config.d contains files with startup configuration informa-
           tion for utilities and other software products.
/home      User directories.
/mnt       Local mounts—for example, for CDROM.
/stand     Kernel files (stand comes from standard kernel).
/tmp       O/S temporary files.
/var       Logs, spooler, and similar files.
           /var/adm        Common system administration files
           /var/adm/cron   Cron queue files
           /var/spool      Spool files
           /var/tmp        Application temporary files


Static files (Executables, libraries, system startup files)


/opt       Layered applications—for example, iFOR/LS, LaserROM, Sybase, and
           Softbench.
/sbin      Minimum commands and programs to boot the system. For example, the
           directory /sbin/init.d contains startup and shutdown scripts for
           utilities and other software products.
           /usr            O/S and system commands.
           /usr/ccs        C compilation system files
           /usr/lib        Object and dynamic link libraries
           /usr/include    C and C++ header files
           /usr/local      Programs and other files developed at the site
           /usr/contrib    Programs and other files from other sites—however,
                           not supported by HP
           /usr/share/man  Manual pages, accessed by the man command
```

Figure 2.6 File system layout.

3

LaserROM:
On-Line Hypertext
Documentation

3.1 Introduction

LaserROM is a full-text search and retrieval system. It is one of the first HP-UX products a system administrator or software developer should learn. The product's browsing and search facilities provide quick and convenient access to HP-UX information. HP-UX LaserROM documentation is available on a single CD-ROM. The documentation is accessed by the LaserROM software, which can be installed from the same CD-ROM. There are two versions of LaserROM: LaserROM/UX for HP-UX, and LaserROM/PC for Microsoft Windows, both on the same CD-ROM. While the versions have a lot of similarity, we will concentrate on the HP-UX version in this chapter.

LaserROM has two user interfaces: a graphics interface for an X-windows system, and a character-based terminal interface for a VT100 or hpterm terminal. The graphic mode interface is typically started from a VUE, CDE, or Motif session. In graphics mode, figures can be displayed and zoomed into. Needless to mention, the graphics interface is more fun to use.

3.2 Invoking LaserROM

When the environment and your PATH variable are properly set up, you need to enter *lrom* from a graphics terminal or *lrom -c* from a character-based terminal. The library screen should show up. Here is a brief troubleshooting/setup checklist:

- Your PATH variable must contain the path /opt/lrom/bin. If it does not, use

```
$ PATH = $PATH:/opt/lrom/bin
```

- The LaserROM documentation CD-ROM must be at the mount point /cdrom. An example mount command is

```
$ /usr/sbin/mount /dev/dsk/c2d0s2 /cdrom
```

- Actually, the CD-ROM mount point can be specified in .lromrc in the current directory, in .lromrc in your home directory, or in /opt/lrom/config/.lromrc. The default mount point is /cdrom. The relevant line in the .lromrc file is

```
cdpath = /cdrom
```

Check that the documentation CD-ROM is mounted at the specified mount point.

3.3 Startup: The Library Window

When the LaserROM software is run, a welcome "splash" window is displayed for a short duration, until various internal initializations are performed. This window displays a copyright notice and the current LaserROM version. The library window is the key initial display of LaserROM. Figure 3.1 shows the library window and explains its components. Typically, you click on a Bookshelf and then click Browse or Search to look at the contents.

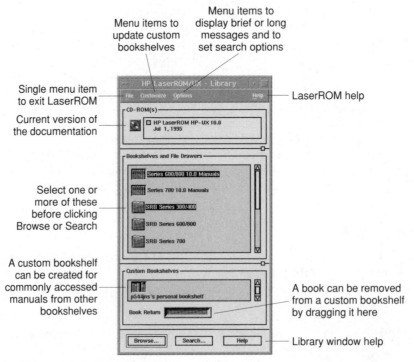

Figure 3.1 LaserROM library window.

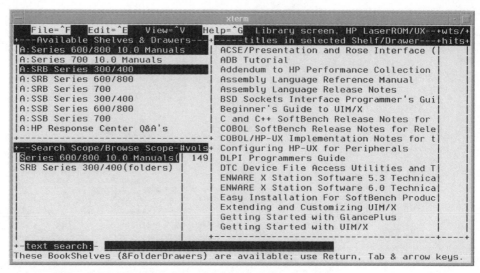

Figure 3.2 LaserROM library window on a "dumb" terminal.

If an X-windowing terminal is not used, the hpterm or VT100 version of LaserROM is invoked. Figure 3.2 shows the dumb-terminal library window. We will not be discussing this interface in this section, though most of the features are available in both interfaces.

3.3.1 Bookshelf

A bookshelf contains a set of related manuals. For example, the Series 700 10.0 manuals include system and software manuals pertaining to the HP 9000 Series 700 workstations.

3.3.2 File drawers

A file drawer consists of information documents like problem resolutions and application notes, information that is not normally supplied in book form. A file drawer may contain *file folders,* which in turn contain information documents.

3.4 Browse: Scanning Manuals and Documents

Browsing is a good way to become familiar with what is on the documentation CD-ROM. From the library window select one or more entries in the book-shelves and file drawers or custom bookshelves subwindows and then click on the Browse button at the bottom. Contents of the selected entries are displayed in the Browse window as shown in Fig. 3.3. Note that one item each can be selected from the left and right subwindows. Contents of a specific document can be browsed by clicking on it in the right subwindow and then clicking the Open button at the bottom. The document will be displayed in a

These three bookshelves
and file drawer were
selected in the library
window before Browse
was clicked

These are the manuals
and folders in the one
selected entry from the
three entries shown
in the left subwindow

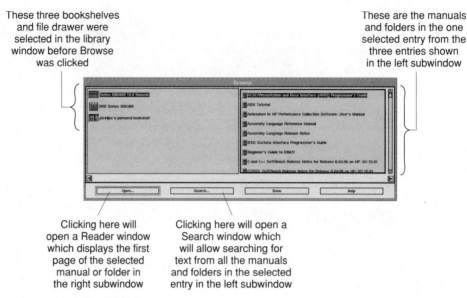

Clicking here will
open a Reader window
which displays the first
page of the selected
manual or folder in
the right subwindow

Clicking here will open a
Search window which
will allow searching for
text from all the manuals
and folders in the selected
entry in the left subwindow

Figure 3.3 Browse window.

Reader window. A text search can be performed on all the manuals or folders by selecting an entry in the left subwindow and clicking on the Search button at the bottom, which will open a Search window.

3.5   Looking at Complete Documents: The Reader Window

The reader window displays pages from a selected document. The document can be selected from the browse window or a *search results* window. The browse window, in turn, is displayed by clicking on Browse in the main library window. Search windows are explained in Section 3.6.

Figure 3.4 shows a reader window. Simple searches can be performed right within the reader window by entering search text in the Pattern Match field and using the adjacent arrow buttons to navigate to the desired search-string location. The string is searched as specified, though the search is case-insensitive. Some of the other items will be explained in a later section.

3.5.1   Snapshots

At times it is helpful to be able to see multiple sections of the same document simultaneously. The reader window has a Snapshot button, which "snaps" the current window and creates a second reader window. The two reader windows can then be independently used to display different parts of the document. Here is an exercise. The new reader window does not have a Snapshot button, yet it is possible to bring up three reader windows with three views of the document. How?

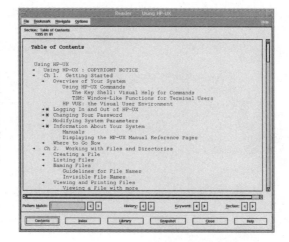

Sections with asterisks contain search hits. Clicking on these asterisks displays the section at the point where the keyword is

Click here to sequentially display search hit locations

Figure 3.4 Reader window.

3.5.2 Printing document sections and saving them as files

The File menu option on the reader window contains two options,

Print ...

Copy to File ...

that can be used to print documents in postscript or PCL format and to save the current section to a disk file. Figure 3.5 shows the print window. Note that the current section is highlighted and will be printed by default; however, multiple sections can be selected by dragging the mouse over the sections, pressing the Shift key, and clicking on a section to select the range of sections between previous selections and the current selection, or by pressing the Ctrl key and clicking on isolated sections, which will be printed individually.

3.6 Searching: The Essence of LaserROM

The search window opens when the Search button is clicked in the browse or library window. Figure 3.6 shows a search window after a search has been performed. There are two kinds of searches: intuitive and boolean. When one or more words are highlighted with the mouse in a reader window and the Start Intuitive Search button on the search window is clicked, documents containing the highlighted words are displayed. (Do not take the description "intuitive" too literally.)

Boolean searching is the most powerful feature of LaserROM. AND, OR, and NOT, along with parentheses, can be used in search terms. Hence, the following are valid search terms:

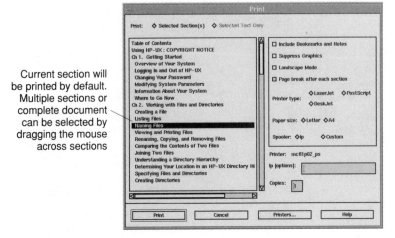

Current section will be printed by default. Multiple sections or complete document can be selected by dragging the mouse across sections

Figure 3.5 Printing from the reader window.

Search term: Find documents containing any of the three words

Search based on term specified at left

Search words highlighted in any reader window

Where to search

Bookshelves and file drawers searched along with the numbers of documents containing the search items

Documents containing the search items along with the number of units in each document

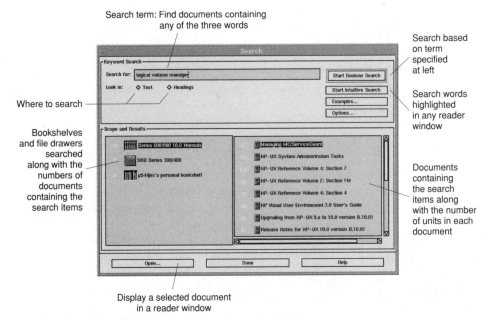

Display a selected document in a reader window

Figure 3.6 Search window.

> Booting and startup
>
> (On-line or hot) and backup
>
> "Logical volume manager"
>
> Logical volume manager

The last term is equivalent to *logical AND volume AND manager*. The term *logical volume manager* means the three words must be consecutively next to each other. Searches are case-insensitive. Wildcards are allowed at the ends of words, as in:

boot*

logi* volume* mana*

"logi* volume* mana*"

Normally, multiple words are searched for in the complete document. Proximity search allows you to specify that two words occur within a specified number of characters in the document. By default, the proximity distance is 100 characters. The proximity search term is specified by using brackets:

[booting startup]

[kernel configuration parameters]

Figure 3.7 shows the search options popup window, which is displayed when the Options button on the search window is clicked. The Proximity Distance scroll bar can be used to specify a value between 0 and 1000 characters.

Searches can be restricted to documents created within a specified range of dates. The start and end dates can be entered if the Show Date Search option is selected in Fig. 3.7.

Search hit documents are displayed on the right subwindow in the search window ranked by the number of hits. The documents will be displayed in alphabetic order if the *Rank Results By # of Hits* button in Fig. 3.7 is deselected.

3.6.1 Stopwords

All documents in LaserROM have an index that is used by the search engine. Common words like *a, the, there, which,* and *with* are not indexed, for better performance and to avoid a large number of hits. These words are called *stopwords.* They are ignored except when they occur in strings where the word is

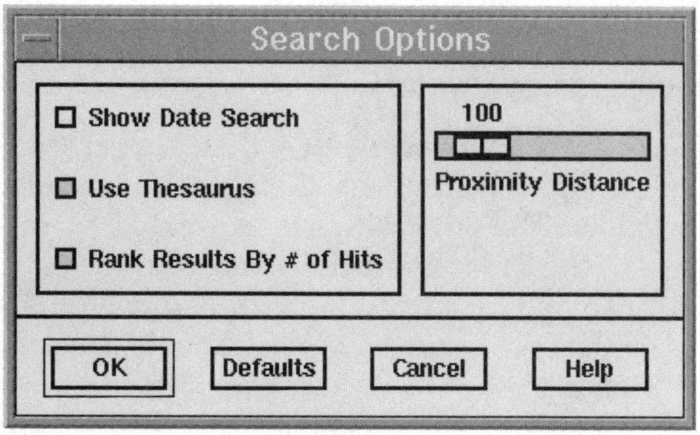

Figure 3.7 Options popup window.

matched with any word containing the same number of characters. Hence "programming with objects" is treated as "programming ???? objects," where ???? is any four-letter word.

3.6.2   The thesaurus: Synonyms, abbreviations, suffix rules

The thesaurus is enabled by default. Figure 3.7 shows the button to use to disable the thesaurus. The thesaurus

1. Has a set of synonyms which allows the search engine to treat some words similarly. Examples are

   control, ctrl

   config, kernel

   internet, ip

   xmit, transmit

   pound, lbs

2. Has suffix rules so that words like *fly* and *flies* are treated similarly.

3. Includes common abbreviations like

   Friday, Fri

   California, CA

   January, Jan

   twelve, 12

   twelfth, 12th

3.6.3   The reader window revisited

After a search is performed, a document containing search hits can be opened by selecting it in the search window and clicking on the Open button. The document will be displayed in the reader window. As shown in Fig. 3.8, there are some search-related options.

3.7   Working with Figures: Zooming and Viewports

Figures in documents are displayed in line with text in reader windows. Figure 3.9 shows an example. Portions of the figure can be enlarged and displayed in a zoom window. The zoom window is created by pressing the left mouse button, dragging the mouse, and releasing the button. The rectangle area selected will be displayed enlarged in a zoom window. The original rectangle area is called a *viewport*. Figure 3.10 illustrates these concepts. The mouse can be used to change the size of the viewport, and the zoom window will be automatically updated. Also, the scroll bars on the zoom window can be used to move the viewport around the figure.

First section
of the book
*HP-UX System
Administrator
Tasks*
The complete
book can
be read or
printed

Clicking on
these arrows
displays the
corresponding
sections

A simple literal
string can be
searched for in
the current
document. A
convenience
feature

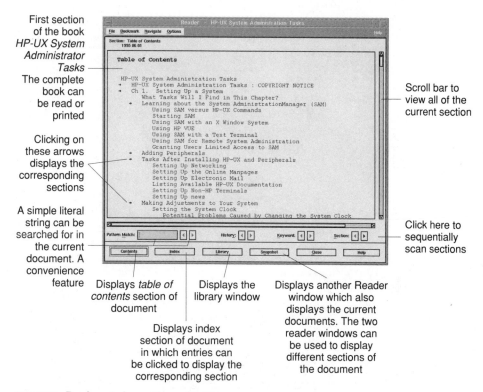

Scroll bar to
view all of the
current section

Click here to
sequentially
scan sections

Displays *table of
contents* section of
document

Displays the
library window

Displays another Reader
window which also
displays the current
documents. The two
reader windows can
be used to display
different sections of
the document

Displays index
section of document
in which entries can
be clicked to display the
corresponding section

Figure 3.8 Reader window with search hits.

3.8 Bookmarks

Bookmarks are useful for noting down various places in a book. To create a bookmark:

- Bring up the reader window with the book in it.
- Select the Bookmark menu option on the window.
- Select the Create suboption.
- A bookmark window, as shown in Fig. 3.11, will pop up. Enter the title and note.
- Click OK. The cursor will become a small bookmark icon.
- Place the bookmark icon at the bookmark location in the book.

The Bookmark menu displays all the bookmarks for the current book, and clicking on any one of them takes you to the bookmark location. When the bookmark icon in the book is clicked, a small popup window displays the bookmark title and three options: *open, move,* and *delete.* open displays more details on the bookmark, move allows you to change the location of the bookmark by dragging the icon, and delete removes the bookmark.

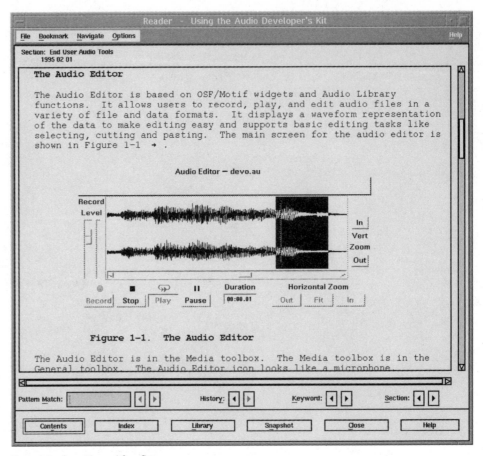

Figure 3.9 A section with a figure.

Information on all bookmarks is stored under .lrom in the home directory so system reboots do not cause the bookmarks to be "lost."

3.9 Custom Bookshelves

A custom bookshelf can be used to keep commonly used books from various other bookshelves and folders.

The Customize menu of the library window has a Create New Bookshelf option. A name has to be entered when the option is selected. Once created, the bookshelf will show up in the Custom Bookshelves subwindow of the library window. Books can be placed in the bookshelf by dragging book names in other windows to the bookshelf name. Books can be removed from the bookshelf by dragging the book name to the Book Return location in the library window.

Viewport mouse can be used to move viewport around over the figure. Zoom window will be updated accordingly

Zoom window scroll bar can be used to move viewport

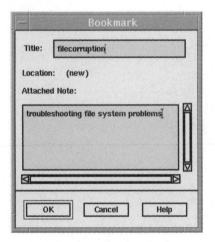

Figure 3.10 Zoom window and viewport.

Figure 3.11 The bookmark Create window.

3.10 Customizations

When you enter the lrom command, the script /opt/lrom/bin/lrom is executed. Though this is a "system" script, it can be customized for special startup requirements.

The CD ROM mount point is determined by the *cdpath* entry, for example,

```
cdpath = /cdrom
```

in the .lromrc file. The .lromrc file is searched for in the following order:

- In the directory pointed to by the variable LROMRC

- In the current directory
- In the user's home directory
- /opt/lrom/config/.lromrc

When using the X-windows version of LaserROM, the X resources like window sizes, colors, keyboard accelerators, and fonts can be customized. The resource values are determined in the following order of precedence:

- Entries in LRom file in the user's home directory.
- Entries in /opt/lrom/lib/X11/app-defaults/C/LRom.
- .X11defaults file. This is used when the window manager—such as Motif or VUE—is started.

Example resource definitions are:

LRom*Foreground: Black

LRom*Background: White

LRom*browseWidth: 70

LRom*ReaderForeground: Black

LRom*ReaderBackground: White

These resource settings will display a much-needed bigger browser window, and the color settings will produce good-quality screen dumps, like those in the illustrations for this chapter.

4

SAM: System Administration Manager

4.1 Introduction

SAM is a menu-driven utility for HP-UX system administration tasks. *smit,* which is available on IBM AIX Unix systems, is a close equivalent of SAM. SAM is a very powerful and useful tool. It "idiot-proofs" many tasks that would otherwise require a string of commands with complex parameters. However, SAM has a few limitations:

- It does not automate all tasks. Hence, system administrators have to be familiar and comfortable with line-mode commands.

- SAM is not scriptable; a common sequence of operations cannot be automated.

- It is slow.

4.2 Starting SAM

SAM can be started with a command like

```
/usr/sbin/sam
```

There are two user interfaces: for X/MOTIF terminals, and for character terminals (HP or VT100/VT320 type terminals). All functionality is available from both interfaces; however, the X/MOTIF interface is more convenient to use. Figure 4.1 shows the initial SAM window for an X-station; Fig. 4.2 shows the initial SAM screen for an HP terminal emulation window. In the following discussion, the X/MOTIF interface is used to illustrate SAM features. The

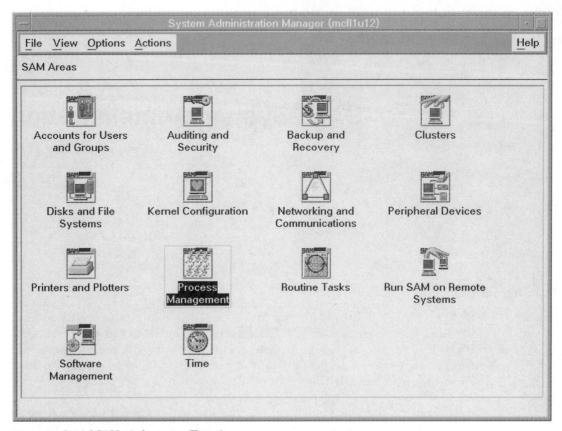

Figure 4.1   Initial SAM window on an X-station.

items in the main window are called SAM function areas. The menu displays options depending on what is being displayed on the screen. Typically the menus are

- *File:*   Exit from SAM and print options.
- *List:*   Not found on initial screen. In listing windows, can be used to display related lists.
- *View:*   Allows filtering and sorting of displayed items. Useful for large lists.
- *Options:*   Display SAM log file, described below, or refresh currently displayed list of items (in case the list changes while SAM is in use).
- *Actions:*   The list of items displayed by this menu depends on the area currently selected. For example, if the Printer and Plotters area is selected,

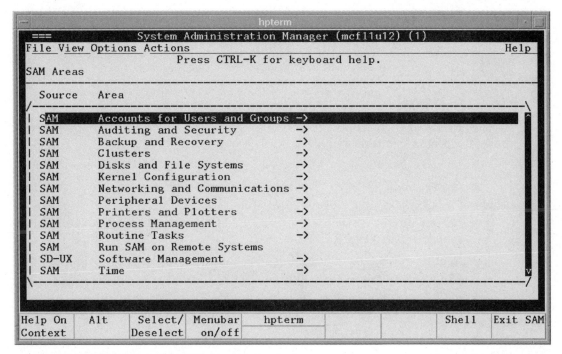

Figure 4.2   Initial SAM screen on an HP character terminal.

the list of printers is displayed in a window and the action menu has options to add printers, stop spooler, and so on.

■ *Help:*   Invokes HP's help system with information relevant to SAM.

4.3   SAM Areas

Each icon on the initial SAM screen represents an area, which displays further icons when double-clicked. Here is a brief description of what is handled in each area:

■ *Accounts for users and groups:*   Add and delete users.

■ *Auditing and security:*   Security issues: events, system calls, users and groups, and global security policies.

■ *Backup and recovery:*   Uses fbackup and frestore internally. Not for OmniBack backups and restores.

■ *Cluster configuration:*   Manages NFS clusters.

- *Disks and file systems:*   Include Logical Volume Manager (LVM) and Networked File System (NFS); configure LVM and NFS.

- *Kernel configuration:*   Change kernel parameters, add/delete drivers, set up swap, configure kernel subsystems.

- *Networking/configuration:*   Manage Internet services, Ethernet/Token Ring/FDDI cards, remote access, UUCP, and NFS.

- *Peripheral devices:*   Configures interface cards, disks, tape drives, modems, printers, and other hardware devices.

- *Printers and plotters:*   Manage spooler subsystem.

- *Process management:*   Configures cron jobs; monitors system performance by sar, vmstat, top, and similar commands.

- *Remote administration:*   Performs SAM operations on other HP systems connected via TCP/IP.

- *Routine tasks:*   Look at common log files, remove large and old files, shut down the system, remove unused product files.

- *Software management:*   Install, list, remove software products. This area is created and handled by Software Distributor (SD).

- *Time:*   Sets lock clock and manages Network Time Protocol (NTP).

Figure 4.3 shows the top-level menu for each area. Each icon may represent a group, in which case additional windows will be displayed when the icon is double-clicked. Other areas not mentioned here may be displayed depending on the version of SAM and customizations.

4.4   A Sample SAM Session: Adding a Remote Printer

We will walk through the steps involved in defining a printer queue on the local system for a printer connected to another system on the network. Double-click on the Printers and Plotters icon to enter that subarea. A list of printing-related icons is displayed. Double-click on Printers and Plotters, which is not the same as the main-window Printers and Plotters. A separate window, shown in Fig. 4.4, opens. This window lists the printers on the local system. Select the Add Remote Printer/Plotter item from the Actions menu. Another window pops up where the printer information has to be entered. Figure 4.5 shows this window. Once the relevant information is filled out and the OK button is pressed, the parent window will list all printers including the newly defined printer. The printer is then available for use.

4.5   SAM for Users: Restricted SAM

On many occasions system administrators were called on to perform tasks they would rather have relegated to the user. Unfortunately these tasks

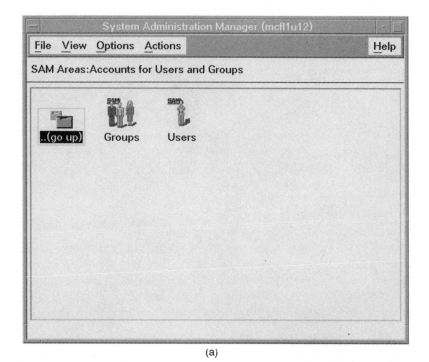

(a)

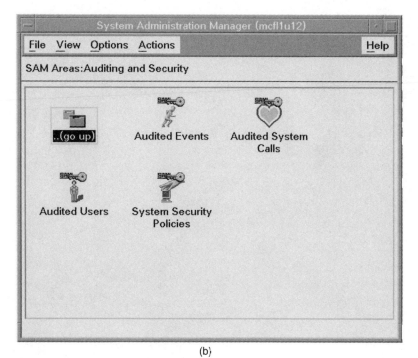

(b)

Figure 4.3 Options within SAM areas.

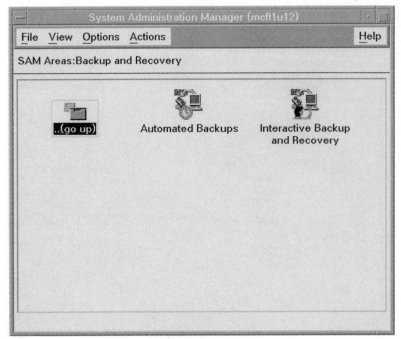

(c)

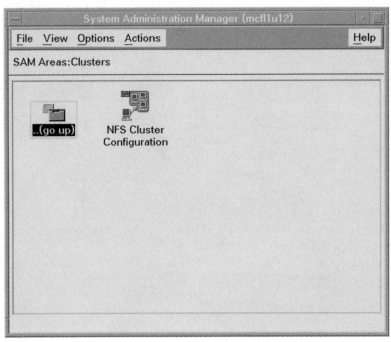

(d)

Figure 4.3 *(Continued)*

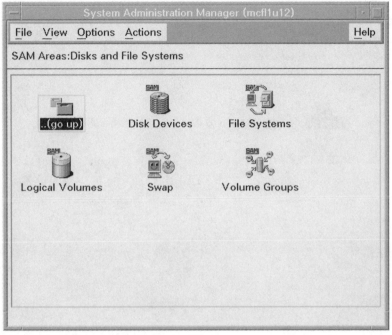

(e)

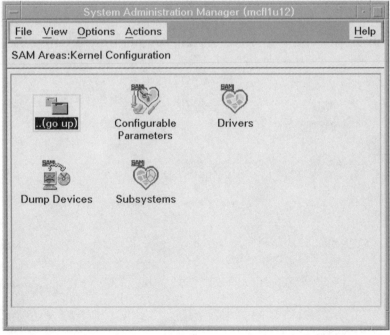

(f)

Figure 4.3 (*Continued*)

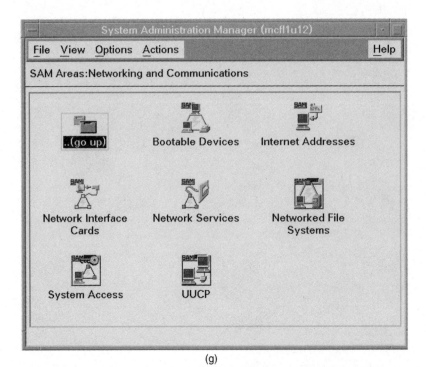

(g)

(h)

Figure 4.3 *(Continued)*

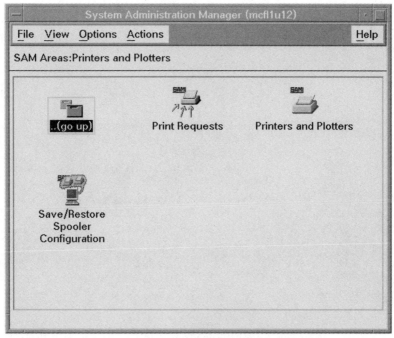

(i)

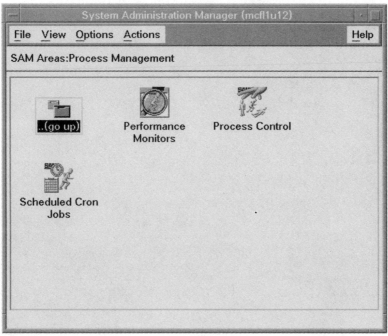

(j)

Figure 4.3 *(Continued)*

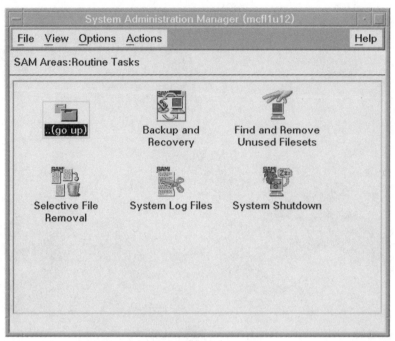

(k)

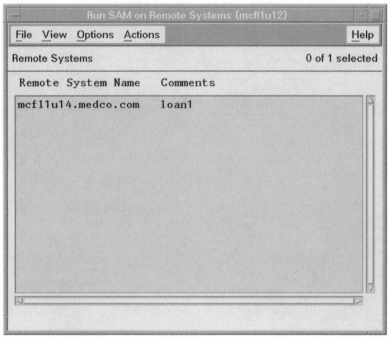

(l)

Figure 4.3   (*Continued*)

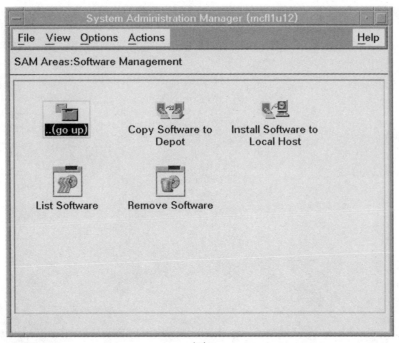

(m)

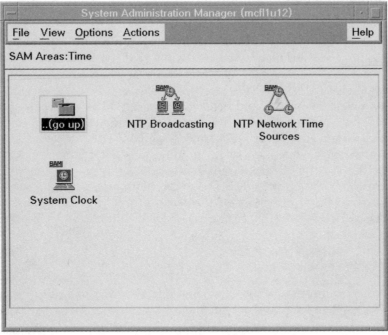

(n)

Figure 4.3 (*Continued*)

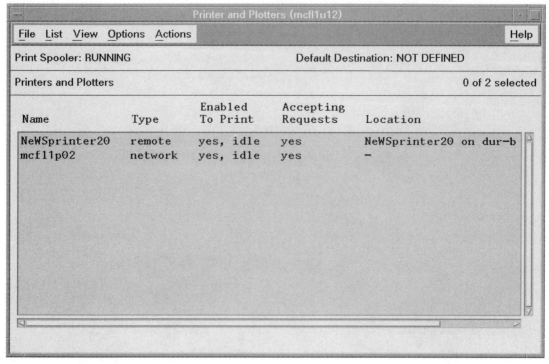

Figure 4.4   Printer list.

required root privileges, which cannot be given to the user. Hence, the most pestered and brave system administrators wrote SETUID scripts that users could execute as *root*. However, these scripts have to be carefully maintained, because if the user found holes in the script, he or she could gain root access to the system. SAM has a better way of giving functionality to users that normally could have been available only to the privileged root user.

On a new system, all tasks mentioned in SAM windows can be performed by the root user only. Nonroot users attempting to run SAM will get an error message. However, SAM can be configured so that a specified user can have access to a subset of the icons and can perform the corresponding tasks. To achieve this, the restricted SAM builder must be started with the command

```
# SAM -r
```

A list of all users on the system is displayed and one user has to be selected. The SAM initial window will then be displayed. The icons will be in one of three background colors:

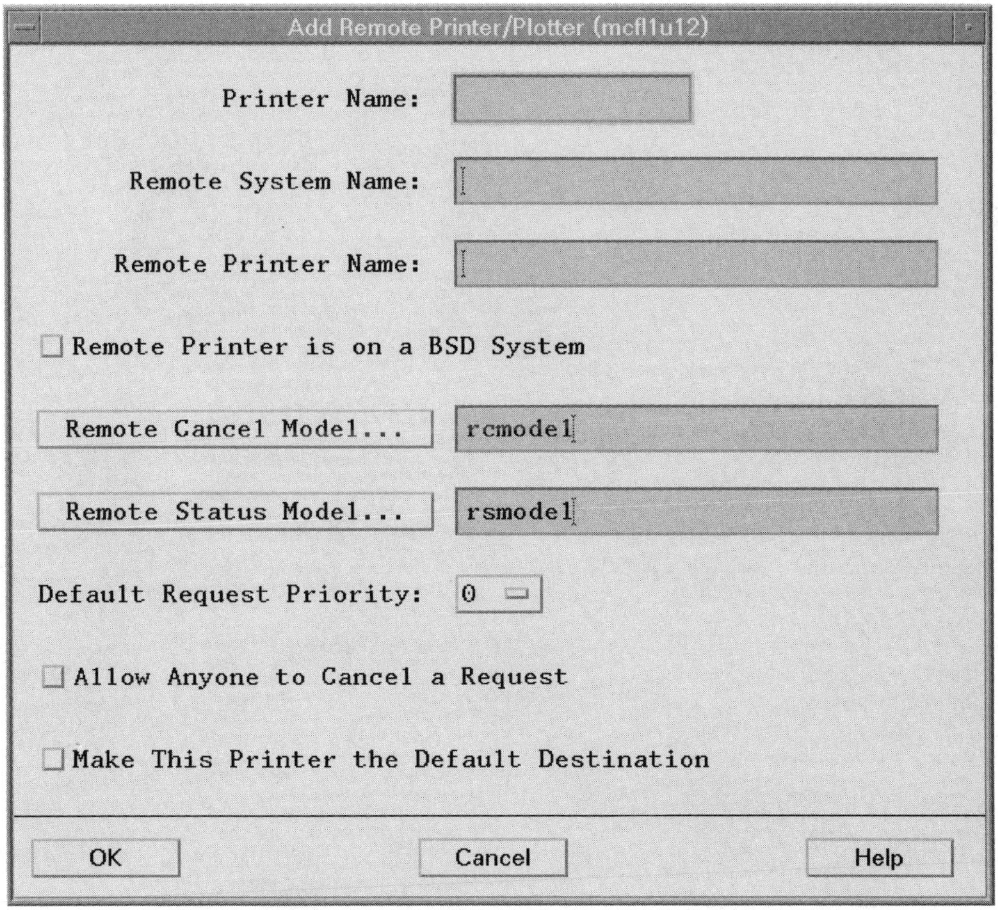

Figure 4.5   Remote printer configuration parameters.

- Red if the area and all submenus are not to be offered to the user
- Yellow if some submenus are not to be offered to the user
- Green if all submenus of the area will be offered to the user

The initial colorings are SAM defaults. To change the default, an icon can be selected and the Enable or Disable menu item can be selected from the Action menu. If only some items are offered within areas, the top-level area icon background will be yellow. After appropriate selections have been made for the user, the Save User Privileges item on the Action menu can be used to save the user's SAM privileges. The user will then be able to run SAM; only the areas and submenu icons which were selected—that is, which were

```
┌─────────────────────────────────────────────────────────────────────┐
│ ─                    SAM Log Viewer (mcfl1u12)                     ↑  │
│ ┌───────────────────────────────────────────────────────────────┐   │
│ │ Current Filters:                                              │   │
│ │                                                               │   │
│ │   Message Level:  ┌Detail          ⊐┐     ┌ User(s)... ┐ All  │   │
│ │                   └─────────────────┘     └────────────┘      │   │
│ │                                                               │   │
│ │  ┌ Time Range... ┐  START: Beginning of Log (Wed 10/25/95 15:21:14) │
│ │  └───────────────┘  STOP: None                               │   │
│ └───────────────────────────────────────────────────────────────┘   │
│                                                                       │
│          ┌ Save... ┐      ┌ Search... ┐      ☐ Include Timestamps    │
│          └─────────┘      └───────────┘                              │
│                                                                       │
│  Filtered SAM Log                          ■ Automatic Scrolling      │
│ ┌───────────────────────────────────────────────────────────────┐   │
│ │        lpmgr -l -xcols=1                                    ↑  │   │
│ │   * lpmgr done, exit value is 0.                              │   │
│ │ ===== Wed Oct 25 19:20:44 1995 Exiting SAM area "Printer and Plotters │
│ │   (mcf11u12)".                                                │   │
│ │ ===== Wed Oct 25 19:20:56 1995 Entering SAM area "Kernel     │   │
│ │   Configuration (mcf11u12)".                                  │   │
│ │   * Performing task "Check if Kernel Regen is Required".      │   │
│ │ ===== Wed Oct 25 19:21:01 1995 Exiting SAM area "Kernel Configuration │
│ │   (mcf11u12)".                                                │   │
│ │ ===== Wed Oct 25 19:21:18 1995 Entering SAM area "Printer and │   │
│ │   Plotters (mcf11u12)".                                       │   │
│ │   * Starting:                                                 │   │
│ │        lpmgr -l -xcols=1                                      │   │
│ │   * lpmgr done, exit value is 0.                          ↓  │   │
│ │ ◁──────────────────────────────────────────────────────▷     │   │
│ └───────────────────────────────────────────────────────────────┘   │
│                                                                       │
│  ┌──────────┐                                      ┌──────────┐       │
│  │    OK    │                                      │   Help   │       │
│  └──────────┘                                      └──────────┘       │
└─────────────────────────────────────────────────────────────────────┘
```

Figure 4.6 SAM log viewer.

green—are displayed on the user's SAM window. The root user can test any user's SAM menu by entering the command

```
# SAM -f username     # Run restricted SAM for user username.
```

Note a limitation of restricted SAM: users are given access to a complete set of operations. Hence, for example, a user cannot be allowed to manage a single printer; the user either manages no printers or manages all printers.

Each user's SAM privileges are stored in /etc/SAM/custom/*username*.cf.

4.6   Log File Viewer

SAM is basically a GUI front end to Unix commands. As SAM performs various operations, it maintains a time-stamped log of commands in the file

/var/sam/log/samlog. This file can be viewed while running SAM by selecting the View SAM Log menu item from the Options menu. Figure 4.6 shows the log file viewer window, which displays the end of the log file. The viewer window was opened just after selecting the Printers and Plotters listing from the Printers and Plotters area. The printer list was shown in Fig. 4.4. Note the log file: it shows that the command lpmgr was used to get the raw data, which SAM then formatted for display. Here is a session where the command is executed from the shell command line:

```
# /usr/SAM/lbin/lpmgr -l -xcols = 1
RUNNING
off

NeWSprinter20
remote
yes, idle
yes
NeWSprinter20 on dur-b.medco.com
0

mcf11p02
network
yes, idle
yes
-
0
```

The log file can be large; hence, the viewer can display selected items from the file. The viewer allows items to be filtered based on level of detail, SAM operations by a specified user (who may be running restricted SAM), and time range. The viewer search option can be used to go to specific entries. The filtered log file output can be saved as an ASCII file using the save button on the viewer window.

The command SAMlog_viewer allows entries to be extracted from the SAM log file without using the graphics interface. SAMlog_viewer has the same filtering options as the SAM viewer window, and its output can be sent to a file.

4.7 Adding Custom Applications

Note how SAM areas are structured. The initial window contains icons representing areas. Double-clicking icons displays subarea icons or applications. Subareas may in turn have other subareas and applications. Hence, SAM selections are a tree of areas with applications at the end of the leaf levels. The application is actually a single shell command.

New areas can be added on the currently displayed window by selecting Add Custom Application Group from the Action menu. A window, shown in Fig. 4.7, is displayed. The entries are

- Label. This will be displayed under the icon.

- Help file. This contains the context-sensitive help, which is displayed when

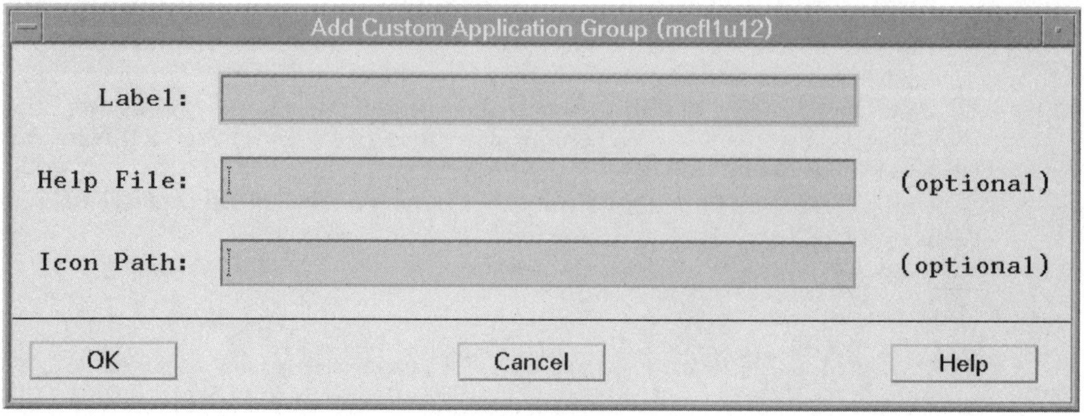

Figure 4.7   Input required to create a new area or subarea.

the icon is selected and the F1 key is pressed. If no file is specified, a help error message will be displayed if the F1 key is used on the icon.

■ Icon path. This must be an XPM (X pixmap) file. It can be created by the icon editor, /usr/vue/bin/vueicon. If no file is specified, a default icon will be displayed.

Once created, the area icon can be double-clicked to display the area window, which initially is empty. Here more subareas can be created if required, or an application can be added by selecting Add Custom Application from the Action menu. Figure 4.8 shows the window that pops up. Here, the entries described above are present, and there are a few more:

■ *Command:* The command to be executed when the icon will be clicked. Full path name must be specified. An example is

```
/usr/bin/tail /usr/vue/Xerrors
```

■ *Execute Using:* Specifies user ID under which the command will be executed.

■ *User Interface Supports:* Specifies whether a character terminal or the Motif interface will be used to execute the command under.

Once created, the application icon can be double-clicked to display a new window with the output from the execution of the specified command.

Customized areas, subareas, and applications can be offered to other users by the restricted SAM builder and, in general, blend in with SAM areas and applications. Customizations can be removed with the Remove from SAM selection under the Action menu.

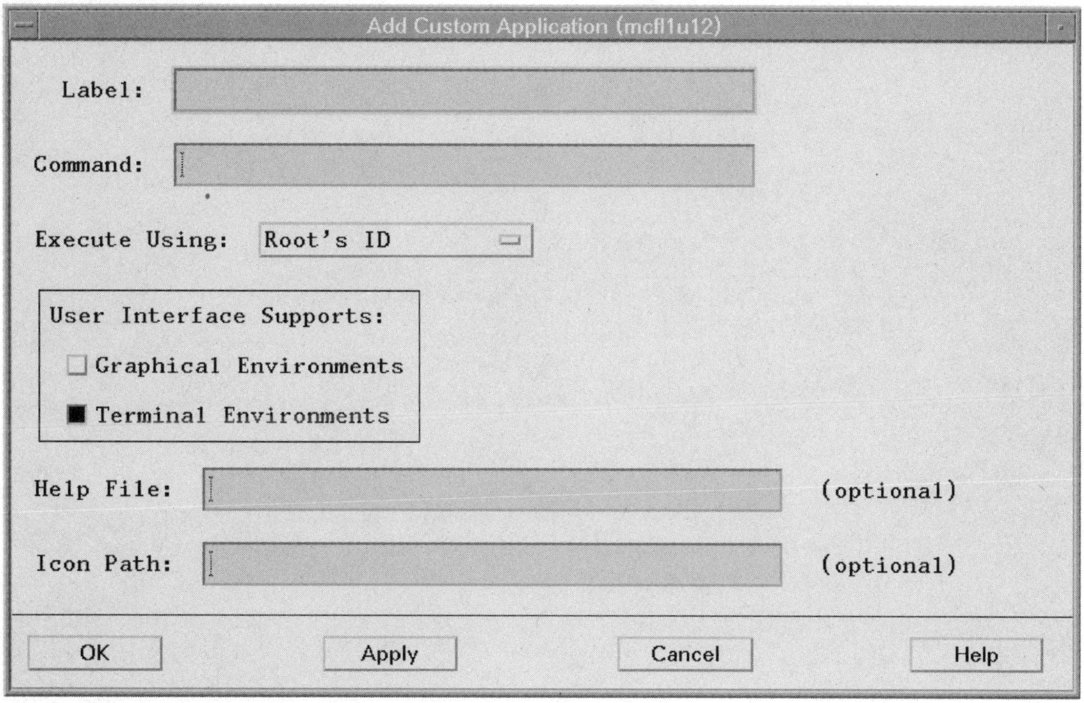

Add Custom Application (mcfl1u12)	

Label: [   ]

Command: [   ]

Execute Using: [Root's ID   ▭]

```
User Interface Supports:
   ☐ Graphical Environments
   ■ Terminal Environments
```

Help File: [   ] (optional)

Icon Path: [   ] (optional)

OK	Apply	Cancel	Help

Figure 4.8 Adding an application icon to SAM.

Chapter

5

HP-UX
Operating System
Installation

5.1 Introduction

When a new system is ordered, HP will preinstall the operating system and purchased layered products for a modest fee. Such a system is called an *Instant Ignition* system. The system can be up and running within minutes of hardware installation. If required, the operating system can be installed from scratch from the installation media, typically CD-ROMs. Such an install is called a *cold install*. On a K series system, cold install from a CD takes about an hour, assuming all required input information is on hand. Layered products are installed with the *swinstall* utility.

The chapters on layered product installation and system startup and shutdown also provide related information.

5.2 Instant Ignition

A new system with Instant Ignition will have the operating system preloaded. Separately purchased products may also be preloaded. When the system is booted the first time, the following information will be prompted for:

- Host name.
- Time zone.
- Date and time.
- IP address.
- IP subnet mask.

- Default gateway (default IP route).
- Root password.
- Whether DNS (BIND) is to be used for, for example, IP address resolution. If yes, enter DNS server address.
- Whether the system should be configured as a font server.
- Whether NIS is to be used.

Defaults can be specified; to modify the parameters later, use the command

```
# /sbin/set_parms
```

which will display help on how to change the parameters.

5.3 Cold Install

Each system is shipped with two CDs (or other media): Install and Core OS. The Install CD is bootable and contains a very basic HP-UX kernel. Core OS contains bundles of software that make up a complete HP-UX installation. Core OS is in swinstall format; it also contains additional operating system software that can be installed at a later time using the swinstall command. Cold install should be done when the system is purchased without instant ignition. The steps are:

- Switch on the system. The system will load firmware.
- Just after firmware is loaded and some hardware tests are performed, the system will prompt:

```
Processor is starting autoboot process.
To discontinue, press any key within 10 seconds.
```

Press a key to enter console mode.
- Mount the Install CD (or other media) in the drive.
- The goal now is to boot from the Install CD, which will cause the screen in Fig. 5.1 to be displayed. To find the hardware path of the CD-ROM drive, enter the SEA (search) command to search for bootable devices. To boot from the CD-ROM, enter a command like:

```
Boot 10/12/5.2.0
```

- The Install HP-UX option should be selected from the first installation screen, shown in Fig. 5.1.
- You will be prompted to specify if the system is to be connected to a network. As a beginner, do not specify connect to the network at this stage, as you want to get the system up and running quickly; you will be prompted

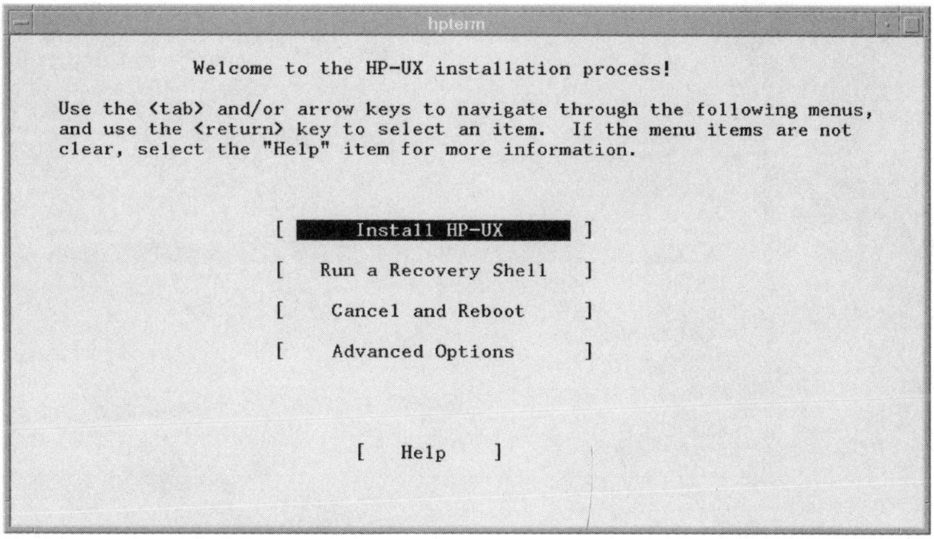

```
 hpterm
             Welcome to the HP-UX installation process!

   Use the <tab> and/or arrow keys to navigate through the following menus,
   and use the <return> key to select an item.  If the menu items are not
   clear, select the "Help" item for more information.



                    [          Install HP-UX          ]

                    [      Run a Recovery Shell        ]

                    [      Cancel and Reboot           ]

                    [      Advanced Options            ]



                           [    Help    ]
```

Figure 5.1   The main Install screen.

to enter networking information when the system boots for the first time after the installation.

- A list of disks will be displayed, as shown in Fig. 5.2. Choose one disk where HP-UX will reside.

- The next screen, Fig. 5.3, will prompt for logical volume information. The VxFS file system has some advantages, like support for on-line backups, over the standard HFS file system. However, for best use of VxFS, additional software may have to be purchased.

- The next screen, Fig. 5.4, prompts for assorted configuration parameters. Defaults work fine, usually.

- The next screen, Fig. 5.5, is a verification that you really want to wipe the specified disk and load the operating system in it.

- The next screen, Fig. 5.6, prompts if the swinstall utility should be run so that you can load products other than the one for the core operating system. As a beginner, do not run swinstall; you can install products after a successful install using the swinstall utility.

At this stage, essentially all install questions have been asked. The install process will load the HP-UX OS from the Install CD. After some initializations, a screen will ask that the Install CD be replaced with the Core OS CD. Software bundles from the Core OS CD are then loaded on the hard disk. At this stage, the operating system is loaded on the hard disk. The system will automatically reboot. This time, the operating system on the hard disk will boot. Figures 5.7, 5.8, and 5.9 show questions which have fairly simple answers.

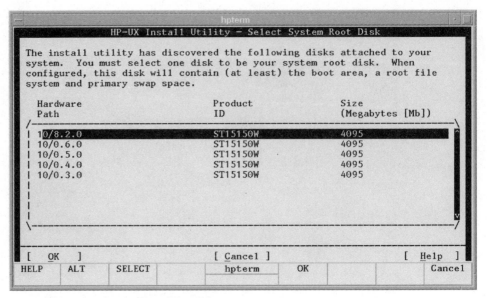

Figure 5.2 Section of operating system disk.

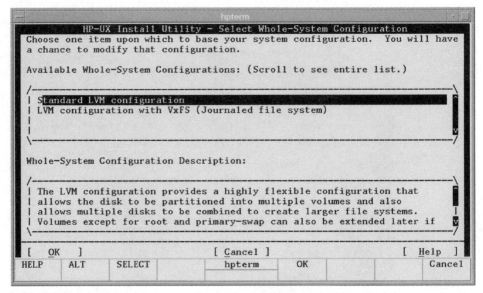

Figure 5.3 Choosing disk format: LVM or VxFS.

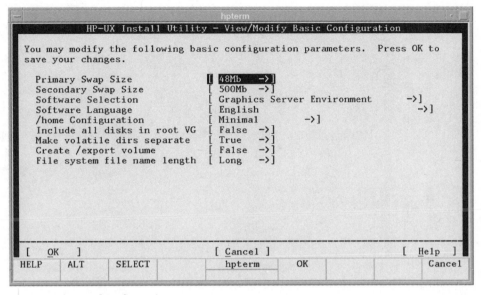

Figure 5.4   Assorted configuration parameters.

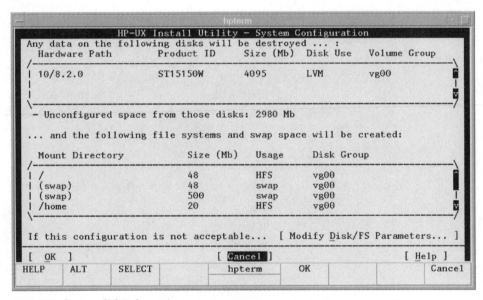

Figure 5.5   System disk information.

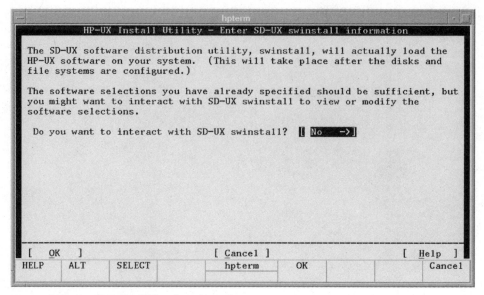

Figure 5.6   Option install additional products.

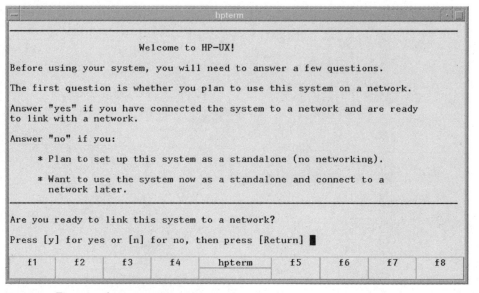

Figure 5.7   First-time boot screen.

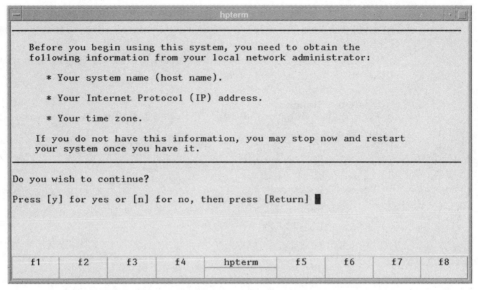

Figure 5.8 More first-time boot prompts.

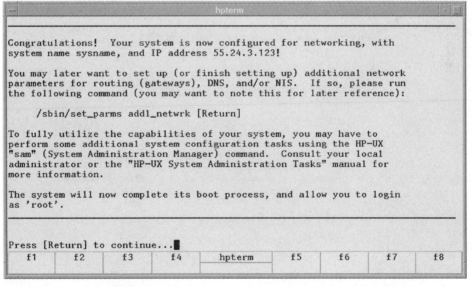

Figure 5.9 More first-time boot prompts.

After this initial configuration, the console Login prompt is displayed. The system is ready for use. A 2-user license is initially installed; additional purchased licenses may now be installed.

Here is a sample installation session, abridged to highlight the important ideas.

(System switched on)
(Note system info: two 100-MHz CPUs, and 256-Mbyte main memory)

```
Duplex Console IO Dependent Code (IODC) revision 4
--------------------------------------------------------------------------
   (c) Copyright 1990-1994, Hewlett-Packard Company, All rights reserved
--------------------------------------------------------------------------
   Processor   Speed          State        CoProcessor State  Cache Size
   ---------   -------   ------------------- ----------------  ----------
       0       100 MHz   Active              Functional        256 KB
       1       100 MHz   Idle                Functional        256 KB

   Central Bus Speed (in MHz)  :         100
   Available Memory (bytes)    :   268435456
   Good Memory Required (bytes):    11886592
   Primary boot path:      10/8.2     (dec)
   Alternate boot path:    10/12/5.0  (dec)
   Console path:           10/4/0.0   (dec)
   Keyboard path:          10/12/7.0  (dec)

Processor is starting autoboot process.
To discontinue, press any key within 10 seconds.
```

(Enter key pressed to interact with console)

```
Boot terminated.

------- Main Menu --------------------------------------------------------
        Command                         Description
        -------                         -----------
        BOot [PRI|ALT|<path>]           Boot from specified path
        PAth [PRI|ALT] [<path>]         Display or modify a path
        SEArch [DIsplay|IPL] [<path>]   Search for boot devices

        COnfiguration menu              Displays or sets boot values
        INformation menu                Displays hardware information
        SERvice menu                    Displays service commands

        DIsplay                         Redisplay the current menu
        HElp [<menu>|<command>]         Display help for menu or command
        RESET                           Restart the system
-------
```

(Booting from an alternate device. Device paths are described in Chapter 7, on backplanes.)

```
Main Menu: Enter command or menu > boot 10/12/5.2.0
Interact with IPL (Y or N)?> n
Booting...
Boot IO Dependent Code (IODC) revision 0
HARD Booted.
ISL Revision A.00.38 OCT 26, 1994
```

(Kernel being booted now)

```
ISL booting hpux (;0):INSTALL
Boot
: disk(10/12/5.2.0.0.0.0.0;0):INSTALL
3639476 + 323584 + 288928 start 0x1743e8

Networking memory for fragment reassembly is restricted to 24264704 bytes
    Swap device table: (start & size given in 512-byte blocks)
        entry 0 - auto-configured on root device; ignored - no room
WARNING: No dump device configured.  Dump is disabled.
netisr real-time priority reset to 100
Starting the STREAMS daemons.
    9245XB HP-UX (B.10.01) #1: Sat May 13 04:11:58 PDT 1995
Memory Information:
    physical page size = 4096 bytes, logical page size = 4096 bytes
    Physical: 262144 Kbytes, lockable: 202436 Kbytes, available: 232604 Kbytes

=======  HP-UX Installation Initialization. (Sun Dec 10 16:49:06 EST 1995)
        @(#) install/init (opt) $Revision: 5.6 $
    * EISA configuration has completed. Following the completion of a
      successful HP-UX installation, please check the "/etc/eisa/config.err"
      file for any EISA configuration messages.
    * Scanning system for IO devices...
    * Setting keyboard language.
```

(Figures 5.1 to 5.6 displayed here)

```
* Starting system configuration...
        * Creating LVM physical volume: /dev/rdsk/c2t2d0 (10/8.2.0)
        * Creating volume group: vg00
        * Creating logical volume: vg00/lvol1 (/)
        * Extending logical volume: vg00/lvol1 (/)
        * Creating logical volume: vg00/lvol2 (swap)
        * Extending logical volume: vg00/lvol2 (swap)
        * Creating logical volume: vg00/lvol3 (swap)
        * Creating logical volume: vg00/lvol4 (/home)
        * Creating logical volume: vg00/lvol5 (/opt)
        * Creating logical volume: vg00/lvol6 (/tmp)
        * Creating logical volume: vg00/lvol7 (/usr)
        * Creating logical volume: vg00/lvol8 (/var)
        * Making HFS filesystem for: /, (/dev/vg00/rlvol1)
        * Making HFS filesystem for: /home, (/dev/vg00/rlvol4)
        * Making HFS filesystem for: /opt, (/dev/vg00/rlvol5)
        * Making HFS filesystem for: /tmp, (/dev/vg00/rlvol6)
        * Making HFS filesystem for: /usr, (/dev/vg00/rlvol7)
        * Making HFS filesystem for: /var, (/dev/vg00/rlvol8)
        * Loading mini-system to hard disk...
x ./sbin/fs/hfs/mkfs, 200704 bytes, 392 tape blocks
x ./sbin/fs/hfs/newfs, 106496 bytes, 208 tape blocks
x ./sbin/fs/vxfs/mkfs, 159744 bytes, 312 tape blocks
x ./sbin/fs/vxfs/newfs, 106496 bytes, 208 tape blocks
```

(About 200 lines deleted)

```
x ./dev/config, 0 bytes, 0 blocks, character device
x ./dev/null, 0 bytes, 0 blocks, character device
x ./dev/console, 0 bytes, 0 blocks, character device
x ./dev/kmem, 0 bytes, 0 blocks, character device
x ./dev/mem, 0 bytes, 0 blocks, character device
x ./dev/rroot, 0 bytes, 0 blocks, character device
x ./dev/root, 0 bytes, 0 blocks, character device
```

```
x ./dev/tty, 0 bytes, 0 blocks, character device
x ./dev/syscon, 0 bytes, 0 blocks, character device
x ./dev/systty, 0 bytes, 0 blocks, character device
        * Installing boot area on disk.
        * Backing up LVM configuration for: vg00
```

(All devices are auto-configured)

```
insf: Installing special files for sdisk instance 0 address 10/0.3.0
insf: Installing special files for sdisk instance 1 address 10/0.4.0
insf: Installing special files for sdisk instance 2 address 10/0.5.0
insf: Installing special files for sdisk instance 3 address 10/0.6.0
insf: Installing special files for mux2 instance 0 address 10/4/0
insf: Installing special files for tape2 instance 0 address 10/4/8.1.0
insf: Installing special files for sdisk instance 4 address 10/8.2.0
insf: Installing special files for CentIf instance 4 address 10/12/0
insf: Installing special files for stape instance 1 address 10/12/5.0.0
insf: Installing special files for sdisk instance 5 address 10/12/5.2.0
insf: Installing special files for lan2 instance 0 address 10/12/6
insf: Installing special files for ps2 instance 0 address 10/12/7
insf: Installing special files for pseudo driver cn
insf: Installing special files for pseudo driver mm
insf: Installing special files for pseudo driver ptym
insf: Installing special files for pseudo driver ptys
```

(About 13 lines deleted)

```
insf: Installing special files for pseudo driver root
```

```
==================================================================
```

(Now installing OS components)

```
                    USER INTERACTION REQUIRED:
To complete the installation you must now remove the HP-UX installation
CD and insert the HP-UX Core Operating System CD.
Once this is done, press the <Return> key to continue: <Return>
        * Starting swinstall:
WARNING: The software specified contains a kernel fileset. It may be
         necessary to reconfigure and reboot the system to make the
         kernel software functional.

        * Beginning Analysis Phase.
        * Source:          localhost:/SD_CDROM
        * Target:          loopback:/
        * Target logfile:  loopback:/var/adm/sw/swagent.log
        * Options:
              loglevel                 1
              create_target_path       true
              use_alternate_source     false
              mount_all_filesystems    true
              autoreboot               true
              enforce_dsa              true
              install_setup_cmd        /usr/lbin/sw/install_setup
              system_prep_cmd          /usr/lbin/sysadm/system_prep
              system_file_path         /stand/system
              kernel_build_cmd         /usr/sbin/mk_kernel
              kernel_path              /stand/vmunix
              install_cleanup_cmd      /usr/lbin/sw/install_clean
              uncompress_cmd           /usr/contrib/bin/gunzip

              autorecover_product      false
              reinstall                false
```

```
                allow_downdate              false
                allow_multiple_versions     false
                allow_incompatible          false
                enforce_dependencies        true
                enforce_scripts             true
                enforce_kernbld_failure     true
                defer_configure             false

                reinstall_files             true
                reinstall_files_use_cksum   true
                write_remote_files          false
                compress_files              false
```

```
        * Reading source for product information.
        * Reading source for file information.
        * Checking mounted filesystems.
        * Checking existing products and filesets.
        * Running any "checkinstall" scripts.
        * Running "checkinstall" script for fileset "OS-Core.KERN-RUN".
        * Running "checkinstall" script for fileset "OS-Core.CORE-KRN".
        * Running "checkinstall" script for fileset "SW-DIST.SD-AGENT".
        * Running "checkinstall" script for fileset "SW-DIST.SD-CMDS".
        * Checking product and fileset dependencies.
        * Checking disk space requirements.
NOTE:     The used disk space on filesystem "/" is estimated to increase
          by 8002 Kbytes.
          This will leave 30431 Kbytes of available user disk space
          after the installation.
NOTE:     The used disk space on filesystem "/usr" is estimated to
          increase by 145841 Kbytes.
          This will leave 106359 Kbytes of available user disk space
          after the installation.
NOTE:     The used disk space on filesystem "/var" is estimated to
          increase by 3127 Kbytes.
          This will leave 58170 Kbytes of available user disk space
          after the installation.
NOTE:     The used disk space on filesystem "/opt" is estimated to
          increase by 16712 Kbytes.
          This will leave 72981 Kbytes of available user disk space
          after the installation.
        * Checking bundle version and security restrictions.
        * Checking for orphan bundles.
        * Summary of Analysis Phase:
```

(About 700 lines totally deleted in New Install section)

```
        New Install   B3920AA, r = B.10.01
        New Install   HPUXEngGS800, r = B.10.01
        New Install   SUPPORT-TOOLS.SUPPORT-INFO, r = B.10.01
        New Install   OS-Core.CORE-SHLIBS, r = B.10.01
        New Install   OS-Core.C-KRN, r = B.10.01
        New Install   OS-Core.KERN-RUN, r = B.10.01
        New Install   OS-Core.CORE-KRN, r = B.10.01
...
        New Install   Networking.LAN-KRN, r = B.10.01
        New Install   Networking.NET-KRN, r = B.10.01
        New Install   Networking.NETTL-MIN, r = B.10.01
        New Install   Networking.NETTL-RUN, r = B.10.01
        New Install   Networking.LAN-PRG, r = B.10.01
        New Install   Networking.LAN-RUN, r = B.10.01
...
        New Install   X11.X11R5-SHLIBS, r = B.10.01
        New Install   X11.MKFONTDIR, r = B.10.01
        New Install   X11.X11-FONTSRV, r = B.10.01
```

```
                    New Install   X11.AGRM, r = B.10.01
                    New Install   X11.DDX-ADVANCED, r = B.10.01
  . . .
                    New Install   TextEditors.EDIT-ENG-A-MAN, r = B.10.01
                    New Install   TextEditors.EDITORS, r = B.10.01
                    New Install   TextFormatters.TEXT-ENG-A-MAN, r = B.10.01
                    New Install   TextFormatters.TEXT-FMT, r = B.10.01
                    New Install   UUCP.UUCP, r = B.10.01
                    New Install   UUCP.UUCP-ENG-A-MAN, r = B.10.01
                    New Install   Upgrade.UPG-TLINK, r = B.10.01
                    New Install   X11BMS.BMS, r = B.10.01
             * The Analysis Phase succeeded.


             * Beginning the Install Execution Phase.
             * Filesets:          215
             * Files:             14699
             * Kbytes:            185616
             * Installing bundle "B3920AA, r = B.10.01" because it is a
               "reference" bundle and one or more of its contained filesets
               is being installed.
             * Installing bundle "HPUXEngGS800, r = B.10.01" .
  NOTE:        Creating the initial "/stand/system" file using the
               "/usr/lbin/sysadm/create_sysfile" command.
  Creating your system file in the file /stand/system
             * Running "preinstall" script for fileset
               "SUPPORT-TOOLS.SUPPORT-INFO".
  WARNING:  POTENTIAL SYSTEM PROBLEM - For Series 800 Machines
               System Diagnostics & Error Logging programs and HP Predictive Support
               have NOT been installed on your system. Without these tools installed,
               HP's memory board resiliency mechanism will not function and informa-
               tion
               that could help predict and prevent a system or peripheral failure will
               be lost. In addition, if a failure occurs, HP will not have the tools
               or data to diagnose the cause of the problem in a timely manner. This
               MAY CAUSE INCREASED DOWNTIME and possible future failures. HP strongly
               suggests that you load these tools, which are provided on the Support
               Media included with your installation or update software.
             * Installing fileset "SUPPORT-TOOLS.SUPPORT-INFO, r = B.10.01" (1
               of 215).
             * Installing fileset "OS-Core.CORE-SHLIBS, r = B.10.01" (2 of 215).
             * File "/usr/lib/dld.sl" could not be removed. It was renamed
               and added to the cleanup file "/var/adm/sw/cleanupfile".
```

(About 700 lines deleted)

```
             * Running "configure" script for fileset "TextEditors.EDITORS".
             * Running "configure" script for fileset "UUCP.UUCP".
             * Running "configure" script for fileset "X11BMS.BMS".
  NOTE:        A valid "sharedtmpdir" does not exist. If remote execution to this
               host is desired, then please follow the instructions in
               /usr/bms/README.sharedtmpdir to create the appropriate file.
             * Beginning the Batch Swmodify Phase
             * Ending the Batch Swmodify Phase
             * Summary of Execution Phase:
                    Configured B3920AA, r = B.10.01
                    Configured HPUXEngGS800, r = B.10.01
                    Configured SUPPORT-TOOLS.SUPPORT-INFO, r = B.10.01
                    Configured OS-Core.CORE-SHLIBS, r = B.10.01
                    Configured OS-Core.C-KRN, r = B.10.01
                    Configured OS-Core.KERN-RUN, r = B.10.01
```

(About 200 lines deleted)

```
                  Configured TerminalMngr.TERM-ENG-A-MAN,r = B.10.01
                  Configured TerminalMngr.TERM-MNGR-MIN,r = B.10.01
                  Configured TerminalMngr.TERM-MNGR-NHP,r = B.10.01
                  Configured TextEditors.EDIT-ENG-A-MAN,r = B.10.01
                  Configured TextEditors.EDITORS,r = B.10.01
         * Software installation & configuration complete.
         * Saving the list of software loaded.
         * Tuned kernel for large swap space: maxswapchunks 274
         * Building a new kernel using the command: "/usr/sbin/mk_kernel -o
           /stand/vmunix"
Compiling /stand/build/conf.c...
Loading the kernel...
         * Setting primary boot path to: 10/8.2.0
======= Install process complete. (Sun Dec 10 17:34:06 EST 1995)
NOTE:    System rebooting...
sync'ing disks (433 buffers to flush): 433 394 356 321 282 243 205 160 124 87
42 2
0 buffers not flushed
0 buffers still dirty
```

(System automatically rebooted here)
(This is what a reboot displays during normal course of operation)

```
Duplex Console IO Dependent Code (IODC) revision 4
-------------------------------------------------------------------------
    (c) Copyright 1990-1994, Hewlett-Packard Company, All rights reserved
-------------------------------------------------------------------------
```

Processor	Speed	State	CoProcessor State	Cache Size
0	100 MHz	Active	Functional	256 KB
1	100 MHz	Idle	Functional	256 KB

```
    Central Bus Speed (in MHz)  :       100
    Available Memory (bytes)    :   268435456
    Good Memory Required (bytes):   12386304
     Primary boot path:     10/8.2   (dec)
     Alternate boot path:   10/12/5.0   (dec)
     Console path:          10/4/0.0   (dec)
     Keyboard path:         10/12/7.0   (dec)

Processor is starting autoboot process.
To discontinue, press any key within 10 seconds.
10 seconds expired.
Proceeding...

Trying Primary Boot Path
------------------------
Booting...
Boot IO Dependent Code (IODC) revision 7
HARD Booted.
ISL Revision A.00.38 OCT 26, 1994
ISL booting hpux
Boot
: disc3(10/8.2.0;0)/stand/vmunix
3142428 + 311296 + 294080 start 0x16d768
inet_clts:ok inet_cots:ok Networking memory for fragment reassembly is
restricted to 24313856 bytes

Logical volume 64, 0x1 configured as ROOT
Logical volume 64, 0x2 configured as SWAP
Logical volume 64, 0x2 configured as DUMP
Logical volume 64, 0x3 configured as DUMP
    Swap device table: (start & size given in 512-byte blocks)
```

```
        entry 0 - major is 64, minor is 0x2; start = 0, size = 98304
Checking root file system.
Root check done, starting up init.
netisr real-time priority reset to 100
Starting the STREAMS daemons.
    9245XB HP-UX (B.10.01) #1: Mon May 22 23:35:19 PDT 1995
Memory Information:
    physical page size = 4096 bytes, logical page size = 4096 bytes
    Physical: 262144 Kbytes, lockable: 201660 Kbytes, available: 234052 Kbytes
/sbin/ioinitrc
insf: Installing special files for pseudo driver cn
insf: Installing special files for pseudo driver mm
insf: Installing special files for pseudo driver ptym
insf: Installing special files for pseudo driver ptys
insf: Installing special files for pseudo driver diag0
insf: Installing special files for pseudo driver dev_config
insf: Installing special files for pseudo driver strlog
insf: Installing special files for pseudo driver sad
insf: Installing special files for pseudo driver echo
insf: Installing special files for pseudo driver dlpi
insf: Installing special files for pseudo driver ptm
insf: Installing special files for pseudo driver pts
insf: Installing special files for pseudo driver beep
insf: Installing special files for pseudo driver klog
insf: Installing special files for pseudo driver sy
insf: Installing special files for pseudo driver kepd
insf: Installing special files for pseudo driver root
/sbin/bcheckrc:

Checking for LVM volume groups and Activating (if any exist)
Volume group "/dev/vg00" has been successfully changed.
/sbin/fsclean: /dev/vg00/lvol1 (root device) ok
/sbin/fsclean: /dev/vg00/lvol4 clean
/sbin/fsclean: /dev/vg00/lvol5 clean
/sbin/fsclean: /dev/vg00/lvol6 clean
/sbin/fsclean: /dev/vg00/lvol7 clean
/sbin/fsclean: /dev/vg00/lvol8 clean
File system is OK, not running fsck
mountall: /dev/vg00/lvol1 is already mounted
mountall: diagnostics from fsck
fsck: sanity check, /dev/vg00/lvol1 is already mounted
(c)Copyright 1983-1995 Hewlett-Packard Co., All Rights Reserved.
(c)Copyright 1979, 1980, 1983, 1985-1993 The Regents of the Univ. of California
(c)Copyright 1980, 1984, 1986 Novell, Inc.
(c)Copyright 1986-1992 Sun Microsystems, Inc.
(c)Copyright 1985, 1986, 1988 Massachusetts Institute of Technology
(c)Copyright 1989-1993 The Open Software Foundation, Inc.
(c)Copyright 1986 Digital Equipment Corp.
(c)Copyright 1990 Motorola, Inc.
(c)Copyright 1990, 1991, 1992 Cornell University
(c)Copyright 1989-1991 The University of Maryland
(c)Copyright 1988 Carnegie Mellon University


                    RESTRICTED RIGHTS LEGEND
Use, duplication, or disclosure by the U.S. Government is subject to
restrictions as set forth in sub-paragraph (c)(1)(ii) of the Rights in
Technical Data and Computer Software clause in DFARS 252.227-7013.



                    Hewlett-Packard Company
                    3000 Hanover Street
                    Palo Alto, CA 94304 U.S.A.


Rights for non-DOD U.S. Government Departments and Agencies are as set
forth in FAR 52.227-19(c)(1,2).
```

(Figures 5.7 to 5.9 displayed here)

```
HP-UX Start-up in progress
```

```
Mount file systems ...................................... [ OK  ]
Setting hostname ........................................ [ OK  ]
Set privilege group ..................................... [ OK  ]
...
Start system message logging daemon ..................... [ OK  ]
Start pty allocator daemon .............................. [ OK  ]
Start network tracing and logging daemon ................ [ N/A]
Configure HP Ethernet interfaces ........................ [ OK  ]
...
Start NFS server subsystem .............................. [ OK  ]

The system is ready.

Generic-Sys (generic) [HP Release B.10.01]

Console Login:
```

5.4 Updates

Once HP-UX is installed, updates to higher versions are performed with the swinstall utility. Refer to Chapter 17, on software installation, for a description of swinstall.

6

System Startup
and Shutdown

6.1 Introduction

HP-UX system startup and shutdown commands are typical of Unix systems. The startup procedure before the operating system is loaded is unique to HP 9000 systems. We will study this initial startup procedure. The startup procedure just after the operating system is loaded involves reading the file /etc/inittab and executing startup scripts, known as *rc scripts,* from etc/rc#.d. We will study the startup model.

6.2 Booting the System

Typically, after an HP 9000 system is configured, it boots the operating system automatically on power on. The sequence of events is:

- The Processor Dependent Code (PDC) is run from firmware. It performs hardware checks and initializations.

- The Initial System Loader (ISL) is loaded by the PDC. ISL resides on the first few blocks of disk.

- The *hpux* utility, part of ISL, is then run. *hpux* loads the kernel /stand/vmunix.

- Control passes to the operating system, which sets up the kernel tables and performs other initializations.

- The first process created is *swapper,* which handles swapping. This process has PID 0. The next process is the *init* daemon, which has a PID of 1. init reads the file /etc/inittab and creates a number of processes, many of them daemons.

We will elaborate on the startup steps later. Here is a sample output, with minor modifications, from an HP-UX boot. My annotations are in parentheses.

(PDC is in control here.)
(The PDC shows that the system has two CPUs, and that the system has 256 Mbytes of memory.
The ISL will be booted from the disk at primary boot path, 10/0.6.)

```
Firmware Version n.n
Duplex Console IO Dependent Code (IODC) revision n
-------------------------------------------------------------------------------
   (c) Copyright 1990-1994, Hewlett-Packard Company, All rights reserved
-------------------------------------------------------------------------------
  Processor   Speed            State        CoProcessor State  Cache Size
  ---------   -------     --------------     -----------------  ----------
       0      100 MHz     Active             Functional         256 KB
       1      100 MHz     Idle               Functional         256 KB

  Central Bus Speed (in MHz)   :        100
  Available Memory (bytes)     :    268435456
  Good Memory Required (bytes):     12156928

   Primary boot path:      10/0.6    (dec)
   Alternate boot path:    10/12/5.0    (dec)
   Console path:           10/4/0.0    (dec)
   Keyboard path:          10/12/7.0    (dec)

Processor is starting autoboot process.
To discontinue, press any key within 10 seconds.
```

(If a key is pressed, control returns to PDC. PDC access is required for changing boot paths, running processor diagnostics, and the like. PDC was accessed in a previous boot session to set the autoboot flag in nonvolatile memory.)
(ISL is booted after a 10-second time-out.)

```
10 seconds expired.
Proceeding...

Trying Primary Boot Path
------------------------
Booting...
Boot IO Dependent Code (IODC) revision 7
HARD Booted.
```

(ISL in control here. ISL passes control to the auto-execute file, which was created with the entry hpux (;0)/stand/vmunix.)

```
ISL Revision A.00.38 OCT 26, 1994
ISL booting hpux (;0)/stand/vmunix
(hpux utility in control here)
Boot
```

(The hpux utility loads the operating system from disc3(10/0.6.0;0). The .0;0 refers to SCSI disk 0, partition 0, which represents the complete disk.)

```
: disc3(10/0.6.0;0)/stand/vmunix
```

(The operating system, unix kernel, gains control and displays its text, data, and stack sizes: 340970, 311296, and 301216. Various kernel initializations are performed.)

```
3409700 + 311296 + 301216 start 0x177268
Logical volume 64, 0x1 configured as ROOT
Logical volume 64, 0x2 configured as SWAP
    Swap device table: (start & size given in 512-byte blocks)
        entry 0 - major is 64, minor is 0x2; start = 0, size = 98304
```

(The root disk , from which /stand/vmunix was loaded, is a logical volume. Dump space is checked. In most cases, core dumps of the kernel portion are sufficient for debugging; hence, the next message can be ignored.)

```
WARNING: Insufficient space on dump device to save full crashdump.
    Only 50331648 of 268435456 bytes will be saved.

Checking root file system.
Root check done, starting up init.
```

(init displaying following messages.)

```
netisr real-time priority reset to 100
Starting the STREAMS daemons.
    9245XB HP-UX (B.10.01) #1: Mon May 22 23:35:19 PDT 1995
Memory Information:
    physical page size = 4096 bytes, logical page size = 4096 bytes
    Physical: 262144 Kbytes, lockable: 201200 Kbytes, available: 233560 Kbytes
```

(Control passes to init, which performs hardware initializations and displays main memory information. init then executes commands from /etc/inittab. The basic commands from /etc/inittab are:)

/sbin/ioinitrc	**initialize I/O**
/sbin/bcheckrc	**ensure file systems are mountable**
cat/etc/copyright	**legalese**
/sbin/rc	**run startup scripts)**

```
/sbin/ioinitrc
/sbin/bcheckrc:
Checking for LVM volume groups and Activating (if any exist)
Volume group "/dev/vg00" has been successfully changed.
Volume group "/dev/sysvg01" has been successfully changed.
/sbin/fsclean: /dev/vg00/lvol1 (root device) ok
/sbin/fsclean: /dev/vg00/lvol3 clean
/sbin/fsclean: /dev/vg00/lvol4 clean
/sbin/fsclean: /dev/sysvg01/users clean
File system is OK, not running fsck
mountall: /dev/vg00/lvol1 is already mounted
mountall: diagnostics from fsck
fsck: sanity check, /dev/vg00/lvol1 is already mounted
```

(Copyright notice is from file /etc/copyright.)

```
(c)Copyright 1983-1995 Hewlett-Packard Co., All Rights Reserved.
(c)Copyright 1979, 1980, 1983, 1985-1993 The Regents of the Univ. of California
(c)Copyright 1980, 1984, 1986 Novell, Inc.
(c)Copyright 1986-1992 Sun Microsystems, Inc.
(c)Copyright 1985, 1986, 1988 Massachusetts Institute of Technology
(c)Copyright 1989-1993 The Open Software Foundation, Inc.
(c)Copyright 1986 Digital Equipment Corp.
(c)Copyright 1990 Motorola, Inc.
(c)Copyright 1990, 1991, 1992 Cornell University
(c)Copyright 1989-1991 The University of Maryland
```

(init now executes script file /sbin/rc, which is mentioned in /etc/inittab.)

```
        HP-UX Start-up in progress
        _____
```

(about 15 lines removed)

```
        Mount file systems ...................................... OK
        Setting hostname ....................................... OK
        Enable auxiliary swap space ............................ OK
        Start syncer daemon .................................... OK
        Configure LAN interfaces ............................... OK
        Start Software Distributor agent daemon ................ OK
        Configuring all unconfigured software filesets ......... OK
        Recover editor crash files ............................. OK
        Clean UUCP ............................................. OK
        List and/or clear temporary files ..................... OK
        Clean up old log files ................................ OK
        Start system message logging daemon .................... OK
        Start pty allocator daemon ............................. OK
        Start network tracing and logging daemon ............... OK
        Configure HP Ethernet interfaces ....................... OK
        Configure LAN interfaces ............................... OK
        Start name server daemon ............................... N/A
        Start NFS core subsystem ............................... OK
        Start NIS server subsystem ............................. OK
        Start NIS client subsystem ............................. OK
        Start NFS client subsystem ............................. OK
        Start Internet services daemon ......................... OK
        Starting mail daemon ................................... OK
        Start NCS broker daemons ............................... OK
        Start Gradient License Server Daemon ................... N/A
        Start time synchronization ............................. N/A
        Start accounting ....................................... N/A
        Start print spooler .................................... OK
        Start clock daemon ..................................... OK
        Support Tools Informational Fileset .................... OK
        Start diagnostic subsystem ............................. OK
        Start environment monitoring daemon .................... OK
        Start auditing subsystem ............................... N/A
        Starting the Performance Collection Software scopeux daemon ........ N/A
        Installing software to diskless nodes .................. OK
        Start NFS server subsystem ............................. OK

The system is ready.

Acme Corp (nodepqr/daisy) [HP Release B.10.01]
Console Login:
```

6.3 PDC: Processor Dependent Code

When the system boots, the primary CPU runs instructions from firmware called PDC. The PDC waits 10 seconds before loading ISL. If a key is pressed during the 10-second time-out, the console interacts with PDC. The PDC can be used to boot from alternate disks.

(Enter key pressed during 10-second wait period.)

```
Boot terminated.

------- Main Menu ------------------------------------------------------------

        Command                            Description
        -------                            -----------

        BOot [PRI|ALT|<path>]              Boot from specified path
        PAth [PRI|ALT] [<path>]            Display or modify a path
        SEArch [DIsplay|IPL] [<path>]      Search for boot devices

        COnfiguration menu                 Displays or sets boot values
        INformation menu                   Displays hardware information
        SERvice menu                       Displays service commands

        DIsplay                            Redisplay the current menu
        HElp [<menu>|<command>]            Display help for menu or command
        RESET                              Restart the system
-------
Main Menu: Enter command or menu >
```

The PDC would normally be accessed to change boot paths, enable auto-boot, or enter hardware maintenance mode. Here are some informational displays produced by PDC. The BOot command continues normal booting of ISL.

```
Main Menu: Enter command or menu > SEA

Searching for potential boot device(s)
This may take several minutes.
To discontinue search, press any key (termination may not be immediate).
    Path Number        Device Path (dec)      Device Type
    -----------        -----------------      -----------
      P0               10/0.6                 Random access media
      P4               10/4/16.0              LAN Module
      P5               10/12/5.2              Random access media
      P6               10/12/5.0              Sequential access media
      P7               10/12/6.0              LAN Module

Main Menu: Enter command or menu > IN

------- Information Menu ------------------------------------------------------

        Command                            Description
        -------                            -----------
        ALL                                Display all system information
        BootInfo                           Display boot-related information
        CAche                              Display cache information
        COprocessor                        Display coprocessor information
        IO                                 Display I/O interface information
        MEmory                             Display memory information
        FwrVersion                         Display firmware version
```

```
        PRocessor                        Display processor information

        BOot [PRI|ALT|<path>]            Boot from specified path
        DIsplay                          Redisplay the current menu
        HElp [<command>]                 Display help for specified command
        RESET                            Restart the system
        MAin                             Return to Main Menu
-------
Information Menu: Enter command > ALL

PROCESSOR INFORMATION
                        HVERSION  SVERSION                  Processor
     Processor   Speed   Model    Model/Op  CVERSION          State
     ---------   -----  -------   --------  --------     -------------
         0      100 MHz  0x058b    0x0491      12        Active
         1      100 MHz  0x058b    0x0491      12        Idle

     Central Bus Speed (in MHz) :        100
     Software ID (dec)          :     46651331
     Software ID (hex)          :  0x02c7d7c3
     Software Capability        :  0xf1
```

(Floating-point unit is also known as the coprocessor.)

```
COPROCESSOR INFORMATION

                 Coprocessor   Coprocessor   Coprocessor
     Processor      Model        Revision       State
     ---------   -----------   -----------   ------------------
         0      0x0000000b          1        Functional
         1      0x0000000b          1        Functional

CACHE INFORMATION

     Processor   Instruction Cache Size   Data Cache Size
     ---------   ----------------------   ---------------
         0             256 KB                 256 KB
         1             256 KB                 256 KB

MEMORY INFORMATION

MEMORY STATUS TABLE

     Carrier     Slot    Size(a + b)   Status
     -------     ----    -----------   ------
        0        0a/b      128MB       Configured
        0        1a/b      128MB       Configured

                           ----------
     TOTAL                   256MB

DETAILED MEMORY CONFIGURATION TABLE

     SPA          GROUP  SMC  SMC Status  Bank  Bank Status  Size  Slot/Carrier
     ---          -----  ---  ----------  ----  -----------  ----  ------------
     0x00000000     0     0   Configured   3    Configured   64MB  0a/b : 0
                          1   Configured   3    Configured   64MB  1a/b : 0
                          2   Configured   0    Configured   64MB  0a/b : 0
                          3   Configured   0    Configured   64MB  1a/b : 0

Group 0 interleaved 4 ways over 4 banks
Active, Installed Memory (bytes)  : 268435456 of Standard DRAM's
Deallocated Pages (bytes)          -          0
```

```
                                    ---------
Available Memory (bytes)          : 268435456
Good Memory Required by OS (bytes):  12156928


      Memory
HVERSION  SVERSION
--------  ----------
 0x0530   0x00000900
```

(See Chapter 7, on backplanes, for device path information.)

```
I/O MODULE INFORMATION
                                                                     IODC    IODC
     Path (dec)  Type            Bus Slot Mod  HVERSION  SVERSION    Vers    Dep
     ----        ----            --- ---- ---  --------  ----------  ------  ------
     8           I/O Adapter      0   2   0    0x5807    0x00000b50  0x00    0x00
     10          I/O Adapter      0   2   2    0x5807    0x00000b50  0x00    0x00
     10/0        A DMA I/O        2   0   0    0x0150    0x00008980  0x07    0x00
     10/4        Bus Converter    2   1   0    0x5000    0x00000c00  0x00    0x00
     10/4/0      A Direct I/O     7   0   0    0x0150    0x00000d00  0x04    0x00
     10/4/8      A DMA I/O        7   2   0    0x0040    0x00003980  0x04    0x00
     10/4/9      A Direct I/O     7   2   1    0x0040    0x00003a80  0x00    0x00
     10/4/16     B DMA I/O        7   4   0    0x0040    0x00005f80  0x00    0x00
     10/8        A DMA I/O        2   2   0    0x0140    0x00008980  0x07    0x00
     10/12       Bus Adapter      2   3   0    0x0150    0x00008100  0x00    0x00
     10/12/5     Foreign Module  13   1   1    0x0150    0x00008280  0x00    0x00
     10/12/6     Foreign Module  13   1   2    0x0150    0x00008a80  0x00    0x00
     10/12/0     Foreign Module  13   0   0    0x0150    0x00007400  0x00    0x00
     10/12/7     Foreign Module  13   1   3    0x0150    0x00008400  0x00    0x00
     10/12/8     Foreign Module  13   2   0    0x0150    0x00008400  0x00    0x00
```

(Boot parameters can be modified.)

```
BOOT INFORMATION

     Processor          Boot ID
     ---------          -------
        0                  2
        1                  2

     Autoboot:           ON
     Autosearch:         OFF
     Fastboot:           OFF

     Primary boot path:    10/0.6    (dec)
                           0a/0.6    (hex)
     Alternate boot path:  10/12/5.0   (dec)
                           0a/0c/05.0  (hex)
     Console path:         10/4/0.0    (dec)
                           0a/04/0.0   (hex)
     Keyboard path:        10/12/7.0   (dec)
                           0a/0c/07.0  (hex)

     LAN Station Address:  080009-b1cb8e

     Tue Nov 14 23:18:23 GMT 1995 (19:95:11:14:23:18:23)

FIRMWARE INFORMATION

Firmware Version: 2.0

     Information Menu: Enter command > main
```

```
------- Main Menu -----------------------------------------------------------
        Command                        Description
        -------                        -----------
        BOot [PRI|ALT|<path>]          Boot from specified path
        PAth [PRI|ALT] [<path>]        Display or modify a path
        SEArch [DIsplay|IPL] [<path>]  Search for boot devices

        COnfiguration menu             Displays or sets boot values
        INformation menu               Displays hardware information
        SERvice menu                   Displays service commands

        DIsplay                        Redisplay the current menu
        HElp [<menu>|<command>]        Display help for menu or command
        RESET                          Restart the system
-------
Main Menu: Enter command or menu > SER

------- Service Menu --------------------------------------------------------
        Command                        Description
        -------                        -----------
        MemRead <address> [<len>]      Read memory and I/O locations
        PIM [<proc>] [HPMC|LPMC|TOC]   Display PIM information
        PDT [CLEAR]                    Display or clear the Page Deallocation
                                       Table
        ChassisCodes [<proc>]          Display chassis codes

        BOot [PRI|ALT|<path>]          Boot from specified path
        DIsplay                        Redisplay the current menu
        HElp [<command>]               Display help for specified command
        RESET                          Restart the system
        MAin                           Return to Main Menu
-------
Service Menu: Enter command > main
------- Main Menu ───────────────────────────────
        Command                        Description
        -------                        -----------
        BOot [PRI|ALT|<path>]          Boot from specified path
        PAth [PRI|ALT] [<path>]        Display or modify a path
        SEArch [DIsplay|IPL] [<path>]  Search for boot devices
        COnfiguration menu             Displays or sets boot values
        INformation menu               Displays hardware information
        SERvice menu                   Displays service commands

        DIsplay                        Redisplay the current menu
        HElp [<menu>|<command>]        Display help for menu or command
        RESET                          Restart the system

Main Menu: Enter command or menu > BO
```

(Load ISL.)

6.4   ISL: Initial System Loader

The ISL is loaded from disk by the PDC. ISL can easily be changed by HP to accommodate different operating systems on HP 9000 hardware or to create different boot options for HP-UX. In a normal boot, PDC boots ISL, which in turn uses the hpux utility to boot the HP-UX kernel. To interact with ISL from the console,

- Boot system. During the PDC 10-second time-out period, enter a key. Console interacts with PDC.

- Enter the boot command to PDC. A question will be asked:

```
Interact with IPL (Y or N)?>
Answer Y.
```

- IPL will boot, display a menu, and wait for input from console.

The initial IPL display will be as shown here:

(Next line is from PDC.)

```
Main Menu: Enter command or menu > BO
Interact with IPL (Y or N)?> y
Booting...
Boot IO Dependent Code (IODC) revision 7
HARD Booted.
ISL Revision A.00.38 OCT 26, 1994
ISL> HELp

    HELP          Help Facility
    LS            List ISL utilities
    AUTOBOOT      Set or clear autoboot flag in stable storage
    AUTOSEARCH    Set or clear autosearch flag in stable storage
    PRIMPATH      Modify primary boot path in stable storage
    ALTPATH       Modify alternate boot path in stable storage
    CONSPATH      Modify system console path in stable storage
    DISPLAY       Display boot and console paths in stable storage
    LSAUTOFL      List contents of autoboot file
    FASTSIZE      Sets or displays FASTSIZE
    800SUPPORT    Boots the s800 Support Kernel from the boot device
    700SUPPORT    Boot the s700 Support Kernel from the boot device
    READNVM       Displays contents of one word of NVM
    READSS        Displays contents of one word of stable storage
    LSBATCH       List contents of batch file
    BATCH         Execute commands in batch file
    LSEST         List contents of EST (Extended Self Test) file
    EST           Execute commands in EST (Extended Self Test) file
Enter 'LS' to see a list of the ISL utilities.
ISL>
```

ISL can be used to modify boot path, boot flags, and the like. Many of the tasks can be performed from PDC also. Booting of the kernel can be initiated by entering

```
ISL> hpux
```

6.5 The init Process

The kernel /stand/vmunix creates the first process, swapper (PID 0), and the second process, *init* (PID 1). *init* performs hardware-specific initializations and checks and then runs commands from /etc/inittab. The /etc/inittab file can be accessed after system boots—for example, when the run level changes—as explained in Section 6.6. An example /etc/inittab file is

```
init:4:initdefault:
ioin::sysinit:/sbin/ioinitrc >/dev/console 2>&1
tape::sysinit:/sbin/mtinit > /dev/console 2>&1
muxi::sysinit:/sbin/dasetup </dev/console >/dev/console 2>&1      # mux init
stty::sysinit:/sbin/stty 9600 clocal icanon echo icrnl ignpar </dev/systty
brc1::bootwait:/sbin/bcheckrc </dev/console >/dev/console 2>&1   # fsck, etc.
link::wait:/sbin/sh -c "/sbin/rm -f /dev/syscon;      /sbin/ln
/dev/systty
                        /dev/syscon" >/dev/console 2>&1
cprt::bootwait:/sbin/cat /etc/copyright >/dev/syscon          # legal req
sqnc::wait:/sbin/rc </dev/console >/dev/console 2>&1          # system init
powf::powerwait:/sbin/powerfail >/dev/console 2>&1           # powerfail
cons:123456:respawn:/usr/sbin/getty console console          # system console
vue :4:respawn:/usr/vue/bin/vuerc                            # VUE invocation
#ttp5:234:respawn:/usr/sbin/getty -h tty0p5 9600
#ups::respawn:rtprio 0 /usr/lbin/ups_mond -f /etc/ups_conf
```

The first line specifies boot-time run level, 4 in this case. Run levels are explained in the next section. Each remaining entry has the format:

```
id:runlevel:action:command
```

where

- *id* is any one- to four-character unique value. Not used by init.
- *runlevel* is a number between 0 and 6. It specifies the run level in which the command is to be executed. If no run level is specified, the command is run at all run levels.
- *action* specifies when the command is to be executed. *boot* means the command is executed at system boot time only. *bootwait* means the command is executed at boot time only; *init* continues only after the command terminates. *off* means the process created by the command is killed. This is not relevant at system boot, but only when the inittab file is scanned during normal operation. The *powerwait* entries are executed when init receives a power-fail signal (SIGPWR). *respawn* means the command is executed if it does not exist (as a process); if the process terminates, execute the command again. This means the process will restart automatically if it is killed. *sysinit* entries are executed before init interacts with the console. *wait* means run the command and wait for the process to terminate.
- *command,* also known as *process,* is the command to be run depending on the runlevel and action fields.

6.6   Run Levels

A run level determines what default processes should be running on the system. When the system boots, the init command reads the init entry in /etc/inittab and brings the system up to the specified run level. Each line in /etc/inittab is scanned and commands are executed from all entries valid for the run level. Possible run levels are s, 0, 1, 2, 3, 4, 5, 6. The s run level is single-user mode and cannot be specified in /etc/inittab.

Run levels are also used by /sbin/rc, as described in Section 6.9.1, to determine what startup scripts to run. Typically, networking, NFS client, and most of the system features are started in run level 2. NFS server is enabled at run level 3. HP-VUE is enabled in run level 4. Site-specific startup processes should be in run levels greater than 3, since at lower run levels some subsystems may not be up by the time the site-specific startup commands execute. Current system run level can be determined by

```
# who -r
. run-level 4 Feb 5 11:32 4 0 S
```

6.7   Rescanning /etc/inittab by the init Process

init scans /etc/inittab at system boot, processes each line, and then sleeps. The file can be modified and *init* can be requested to reprocess it by:

```
# /sbin/init -q        Reprocess /etc/inittab at current run level.
```

init will scan and process /etc/inittab when the run level is changed by, for example,

```
# /sbin/init 5        Change to run level 5 and rescan /etc/inittab.
```

6.8   The rc Startup Paradigm

Until recently, many Unix systems, including HP-UX, had a startup script /etc/rc, which was modified as required at each site. There were a few problems with this method of startup:

- System upgrades had to be done carefully so as not to overlay startup customizations.
- Startup scripts were strewn in various locations referenced by /etc/rc.
- Startup parameters and commands were intermixed.
- Scripts for one run level were not easily differentiated from scripts for other run levels.

The current startup model addresses these problems.

6.9   Start and Stop Scripts

Startup and shutdown scripts are located in the directory /sbin/init.d. An example script is /sbin/init.d/acct, which starts and stops the accounting subsystem. Each script must accept four command line parameters:

start   Start the product.

stop   Shut down use of the product.

start_msg   Print summary startup message.

stop_msg   Print summary stop message.

Here are excerpts from /sbin/init.d/acct:

```
#!/sbin/sh
#
# @(#) $Revision: 72.5 $
#
#            Copyright (C) 1993 Hewlett-Packard Company
#                     ALL RIGHTS RESERVED.
#
# NOTE:    This script is not configurable! Any changes made to this
#          script will be overwritten when you upgrade to the next
#          release of HP-UX.
#
# Descr:
#    This script will start or stop process accounting.
#
# Args:
#    start : start up process accounting
#    stop : stop process accounting
#    start_msg : only print message indicating what 'start' action does
#    stop_msg : only print message indicating what 'stop' action does
#
# External Influences:
#    The environment variable START_ACCT can control the behavior of the
#    'start' action. If it is not set or set to anything but "1", then
#    the 'start' action will be skipped.
#
# Return Values:
#    0 : successful completion of task
#    1 : failure to complete task
#    2 : request was to start, but did not start process accounting
#        because control variable, START_ACCT, was not set to one.

PATH=/usr/sbin/acct:/usr/sbin:/usr/bin:/sbin
export PATH

rval=0

if [ -f /etc/rc.config ]
then
     . /etc/rc.config
else
     echo "ERROR: /etc/rc.config defaults file MISSING"
     exit 1
fi

case "$1" in
start_msg)
     echo "Start accounting"
     ;;

stop_msg)
     echo "Stop accounting"
     ;;

'start')
     if [ "$START_ACCT" -eq 1 ]
     then
             /usr/sbin/acct/startup

             if [ $? -eq 0 ]
```

```
                then
                        echo "Accounting started"
                else
                        echo "Unable to start accounting"
                        rval=1
                fi
        else
                # skip activation of process accounting
                rval=2
        fi
        ;;

'stop')
        if [ "$START_ACCT" -eq 1 ]
        then
                /usr/sbin/acct/shutacct

                if [ $? -eq 0 ]
                then
                        echo "Accounting stopped"
                else
                        echo "Unable to stop accounting"
                        rval=1
                fi
        else
                # skip termination of process accounting
                rval=2
        fi
        ;;

*)
        echo "usage: $0 {start|stop|start_msg|stop_msg}"
        rval=1
        ;;
esac

exit $rval
```

Note that the accounting subsystem is started only if the environment variable START_ACCT is set to 1 and the script is called by

```
#/sbin/init.d/acct start
```

For each start/stop script, environment shell variables are defined in a corresponding file in the directory /etc/rc.config.d. The accounting script environment variables file is /etc/rc.config.d/acct:

```
#!/sbin/sh
# @(#) $Revision: 72.5 $
# Process accounting. See acct(1m)
#
# START_ACCT: Set to 1 to start process accounting
#
START_ACCT=0
```

Each start/stop script must have an exit value, typically defined like the following:

0   Exited without error. OK will show on the display (with /sbin/rc).

1   Error exit. FAIL will appear on the display.

2   Script skipped because the /etc/rc.config.d configuration file environment variable overrides action. N/A will appear on the display.

3   Exited without errors, but with system reboot required.

6.9.1   Run levels and the start/stop scripts

The init daemon runs /sbin/rc as specified in /etc/inittab. /sbin/rc is a shell script calling other scripts. Relevant startup files are

`/sbin/init.d/*`	Contains all startup and shutdown scripts.
`/etc/rc.config.d/*`	Contains parameters for startup scripts. Typically, shell variable assignments.
`/sbin/rc#.d/*`	Contains startup and shutdown scripts for the run level. Startup script names start with S; shutdown (kill) script names start with K. The scripts are actually links to files in /sbin/init.d.
`/etc/rc.config`	A convenient script for sourcing all files in /etc/rc.config.d.

When /sbin/rc runs at system boot, it runs /etc/rc.config so that all parameters are defined as shell variables within the current process; then it executes all /sbin/rc#d/* startup scripts for all run levels starting from 1 up to the run level defined in /etc/inittab. For example, if the run level in inittab is 4, all files starting with S in /sbin/rc1.d, /sbin/rc2.d, /sbin/rc3.d, and /sbin/rc4.d are executed. Each script is given the command line parameter *start*.

Once the system is up,

- If the run level is changed to a higher number, all start scripts from the current level plus 1 up to (including) the new run level are executed.

- If the run level is changed to a lower number, the stop scripts from the current run level minus 1 up to (including) the new run level are executed.

Stop scripts start with K (for kill). Actually, for a product, the start and stop scripts are links to the same file in /etc/init.d; the start or stop parameter is specified when the script is called. Typically, the start script is one run level above the stop script. Example start and stop scripts for acct are

```
/sbin/rc2.d/S700acct -> /sbin/init.d/acct
/sbin/rc1.d/K300acct -> /sbin/init.d/acct
```

The scripts are invoked with commands like

```
/sbin/rc2.d/S700acct start
/sbin/rc1.d/K300acct stop
```

Here are the start/stop scripts, in /sbin/rc#.d, and the config files, in /sbin/init.d, on one system:

```
/sbin/rc0.d:
K480syncer K800killall K900hfsmount
```

```
/sbin/rc1.d:
K100hpnpd          K300acct          K435SnmpHpunix    K570nfs.client    K780syslogd
K190scope          K340xntpd         K435SnmpMib2      K580nis.client    K900swagentd
K230audio          K370vt            K440SnmpMaster    K590nis.server    S100hfsmount
K240auditing       K380xfs           K450ddfa          K600nfs.core      S320hostname
K250envd           K390rbootd        K460sendmail      K630named         S400set_prvgrp
K258diagnostic     K400i41md         K470rwhod         K660net           S420set_date
K270cron           K410ncs           K480rdpd          K684token         S440savecore
K280lp             K420dfs           K490gated         K700nettl         S500swap_start
K290hparray        K430dce           K500inetd         K770ptydaemon     S520syncer

/sbin/rc2.d:
K900nfs.server     S300nettl         S510gated         S590ncs           S740supprtinfo
S008net.sd         S316token         S520rdpd          S600i41md         S742diagnostic
S100swagentd       S320hpether       S530rwhod         S610rbootd        S750envd
S120swconfig       S340net           S540sendmail      S620xfs           S760auditing
S200clean_ex       S370named         S550ddfa          S630vt            S770audio
S202clean_uucp     S400nfs.core      S560SnmpMaster    S660xntpd         S800spa
S204clean_tmps     S410nis.server    S565SnmpHpunix    S700acct          S810scope
S206clean_adm      S420nis.client    S565SnmpMib2      S710hparray       S880swcluster
S220syslogd        S430nfs.client    S570dce           S720lp            S900hpnpd
S230ptydaemon      S500inetd         S580dfs           S730cron          S900laserrx

/sbin/rc3.d:
S100nfs.server

/sbin/rc4.d:
/sbin/init.d:
SnmpHpunix    cron         hpether      net           rwhod         swcluster
SnmpMaster    dce          hpnpd        nettl         savecore      swconfig
SnmpMib2      ddfa         hptoken      nfs.client    scope         syncer
acct          dfs          i41md        nfs.core      sendmail      syslogd
audio         diagnostic   inetd        nfs.server    set_date      template
auditing      envd         killall      nis.client    set_prvgrp    vt
clean_adm     gated        laserrx      nis.server    spa           xfs
clean_ex      hfsmount     lp           ptydaemon     supprtinfo    xntpd
clean_tmps    hostname     named        rbootd        swagentd
clean_uucp    hparray      ncs          rdpd          swap_start

/etc/rc.config.d:
LANG          clean        envd         lp            nfsconf       swcluster
SnmpHpunix    clean_tmps   hparray      mailservs     ptydaemon     swconfig
SnmpMaster    clean_uucp   hpetherconf  namesvrs      savecore      syncer
SnmpMib2      cron         hptokenconf  ncs           scope         vt
acct          dce          i41md        netconf       set_date      xfs
audio         dfs          laserrx      netdaemons    spa
auditing      diagnostic   list_mode    nettl         supprtinfo
```

6.9.2 Script-naming rationale

The files in /sbin/rc#d have the format TnnnNAME, where

- T is sequencing type, S for start and K for stop (kill) scripts.

- nnn is sequence number. In a run level, scripts are run in numeric order. Notice that the K scripts have reverse order from S scripts.

- NAME is the script name, typically, the name of the actual script in /sbin/init.d.

6.9.3   The startup rc log file: /etc/rc.log

During system boot, a log of rc files executed is placed in /etc/rc.log.

6.9.4   Creating startup scripts

A custom start/stop script can be created in /sbin/init.d. The file /etc/init.d/template can be copied and modified for this purpose. Environment variable parameters can be specified in a corresponding file in /etc/rc.config.d.

In the corresponding /sbin/rc#.d directories, an S and K file will have to be created with links to the actual script in /sbin/init.d. While any of the unused K and S numbers can be used for custom start/stop scripts, HP may use the numbers in the future, or third-party vendors may already be using the numbers. Two "don't care" numbers are assigned by HP: the number 900 for an S script at run level 900, and the number 100 for use as a K script at run level 1. These numbers should be used for custom applications.

6.10   Shutdown and Reboot

Shutdown and reboot commands are fairly typical of Unix systems. /sbin/shutdown terminates all processes in an orderly manner and brings the system to single-user mode. *shutdown* will prompt for a message to be sent to all logged-on terminals. It will give users 60 seconds to log out before starting by terminating processes. Options are

-h	Shutdown and halt.
-r	Shutdown and reboot automatically.
-y	No confirmation prompts are displayed.
grace time	Number of seconds to allow users to log out before proceeding with shutdown.

/usr/sbin/reboot terminates nonessential processes, syncs disks, shuts down the system, and reboots. Options are:

-h	Shutdown and halt
-m message	Displays the message on all logged-on terminals before shutdown

Both shutdown and reboot write a time-stamped message to /etc/shutdownlog. Here is a sample shutdown session; note the output of rc scripts:

```
# shutdown -h

SHUTDOWN PROGRAM
11/14/95 18:40:46 EST
Waiting a grace period of 60 seconds for users to logout.
Do not turn off the power or press reset during this time.

Broadcast Message from john321 (console) Tue Nov 14 18:41:46...
SYSTEM BEING BROUGHT DOWN NOW ! ! !
Do you want to continue? (You must respond with 'y' or 'n'.): y
```

```
System shutdown in progress
─────────────────────────────
Stop NFS server subsystem ...................................... OK
Stopping the Performance Collection Software scopeux daemon .... N/A
Stopping audio server daemon .................................. OK
Stop auditing subsystem ....................................... OK
Stop environment monitoring daemon ............................ OK
Stop diagnostic subsystem ..................................... OK
Stop clock daemon ............................................. OK
Stop print spooler ............................................ OK
(about 20 lines removed)
Stop Software Distributor agent daemon ........................ OK
Stop syncer daemon ............................................ OK
Killing user processes ........................................ OK
Unmount file systems .......................................... OK
```

```
Transition to run-level 0 is complete.
Executing "/sbin/reboot        ".
Shutdown at 18:43 (in 0 minutes)

        *** FINAL System shutdown message from john321@nodepqr ***
System going down IMMEDIATELY
System shutdown time has arrived
sync'ing disks (13 buffers to flush): 13
0 buffers not flushed
0 buffers still dirty
(shutdown complete)
```

6.11 Forgotten Root Password

If the system password is not known for any reason, the system must be booted in single-user mode and the password file manipulated. To bring the system into reboot mode,

- Physically power up the system. The PDC will run and you can interact with it by entering a key during the 10-second time-out period.
- Enter Boot at the PDC prompt.
- Enter Y to the question

```
Interact with IPL (Y or N)?>
```

- At the ISL prompt, enter *hpux -is,* to boot to single-user mode:

```
ISL> hpux -is
```

- At this stage, a minimal system is available and you are logged on. Try changing root password with

```
# passwd root
```

- Reboot system to normal multiuser mode.

7

Backplanes, Buses, and Devices

7.1 Introduction

Currently, the HP 9000 series of systems mainly consists of the J and 700 series workstations, and the D, E, K, and T series servers. Each series has its own backplane design. The device addressing technique is common to all systems, allowing HP-UX to be configured fairly easily across all systems. In this chapter, we will see how a system configures peripherals. On HP 9000s, drivers for most HP devices are included in the shipped kernel. Moreover, devices are sensed and configured automatically on power-up. However, a good understanding of the I/O subsystem helps in troubleshooting and configuring third-party devices.

7.2 The HP 9000 E Series System Backplane

The E series systems have an HP-PB (HP Precision Bus) based backplane. SCSI, Ethernet, Centronics Parallel, and terminal interfaces are built in. Two disk drives, a CD-ROM, and a DAT drive can be configured inside the cabinet. In addition, the backplane has four expansion slots. Figure 7.1 shows the E series system backplane. Examples of E series systems are the Models E25, E35, E45, and E55. They differ mainly in CPU speed and cache memory.

7.3 The HP 9000 K Series System Backplane

The K series systems also have an HP-PB based backplane. The Core I/O card is built in with Fast/Wide SCSI, Ethernet, and Centronics Parallel terminal and modem interfaces. Two CPUs can be plugged into the backplane; two CPUs are plugged into the front of the system cabinet. The expansion I/O card can be used for high-resolution graphics terminals, additional SCSI ports, and

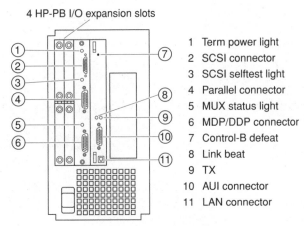

Figure 7.1   HP 9000 E series backplane.

so on. The backplane also accommodates four double-height and four single-height HP-PB cards. Bus and device addressing is discussed in the next sections. Figure 7.2 shows the K series system backplane.

7.4   Device Addressing

Peripheral devices are typically plugged into cards called *adapters,* which in turn are on buses (or bus converters). Each bus, adapter, and device combination is specified as an integer number. A device is represented by the numbers of the buses and adapters in its path, each followed by a slash (/). Additionally, when an adapter can support multiple devices (as can, for example, a SCSI adapter), the path to a particular device is represented with dots between the intermediate elements, like targets. Also, in expansion slots, the adapters are assigned numbers in increments of four starting with zero: 0, 4, 8, and so on. Here are some examples:

10/8   Represents bus 10, bus converter 8

10/16/4   Represents bus 10, bus converter 16, and device 4 (an FDDI card)

10/8.2   Represents bus 10, Fast/Wide SCSI bus 8, target 2

10/8.2.0   Represents bus 10, Fast/Wide SCSI bus 8, target 2, whole disk (disk type HP35480A)

Figure 7.3 shows the bus architecture of a K series system. In particular, it shows the interfaces of the K400 system discussed in the next section.

7.5   ioscan

The *ioscan* command sniffs the I/O subsystem and displays bus and device information. If the -k option is specified, kernel information is displayed; the hardware is not scanned. The -f option indicates full information, and the -u option displays usable devices. The -f option shows the corresponding device

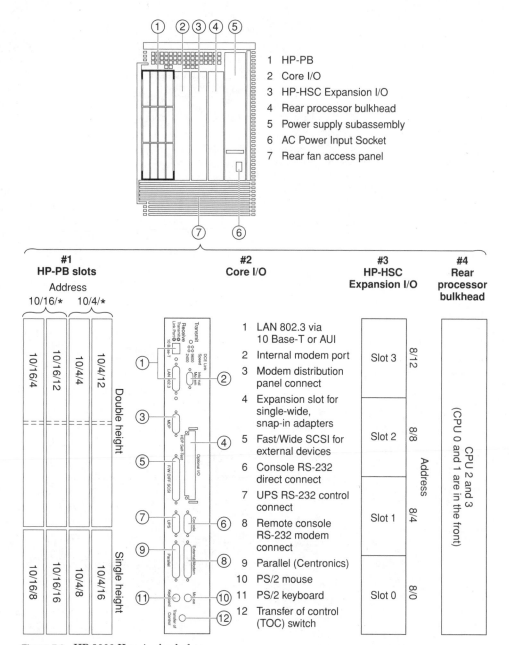

1 HP-PB
2 Core I/O
3 HP-HSC Expansion I/O
4 Rear processor bulkhead
5 Power supply subassembly
6 AC Power Input Socket
7 Rear fan access panel

Figure 7.2 HP 9000 K series backplane.

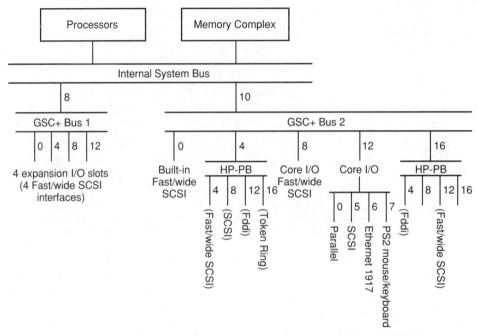

Figure 7.3 The K series bus architecture. Interfaces in parentheses are from the K400 system.

driver in the kernel and has an S/W State column, where the value CLAIMED means a kernel driver is configured and controlling the peripheral. Here are a sample command and output from an E25 system with

- One internal SCSI disk (56/52.6.0)
- One internal DAT tape drive (56/52.0.0)
- One built-in Ethernet connection (60/6)
- One Token connection (56/36)
- One built-in mux connection for eight RS232 TTYs (56/56)
- One built-in Centronics line printer connection (56/53)

```
# ioscan
```

(Lists all devices and their hardware addresses)

```
H/W Path   Class           Description
========================================
           bc
56         bc              Bus Converter
56/36          lan         HP J2166A - 802.5 Token Ring LAN
56/52          ext_bus     HP 28655A - SCSI Interface
56/52.0          target
56/52.0.0          tape    HP      HP35470A
56/52.6          target
56/52.6.0          disk    HP      C2490AM
```

```
56/53          ext_bus        HP 28655A - Parallel Interface
56/56          tty            MUX
60        ba                  Core I/O Adapter
60/6           lan            Built-in LAN
62        processor           Processor
63        memory              Memory
```

Here are some sample commands and corresponding output from a K400 system with

- One internal SCSI disk (10/0.6.0)
- Five external SCSI disks (8/0.1.0 to 8/0.5.0) on an SCSI interface on the expansion I/O slot
- Five additional external SCSI disks (10/8.1.0 to 10/8.5.0) on an SCSI interface on an HP-IB slot
- An SCSI CD-ROM drive (10/12/5.2.0)
- Three external DAT tape drives (10/4/8.5.0, 10/4/8.6.0, and 10/12/5.0.0)
- One mux connection (10/4/0)
- A token ring interface (10/4/16)
- Two FDDI interfaces (10/4/12 and 10/16/4)
- A built-in Ethernet connection (10/12/6)
- A Centronics parallel interface (10/12/0)

```
# ioscan -u
```

(Lists all usable devices, those with configured drivers in the kernel)

```
H/W Path      Class           Description
==============================================
8/0           ext_bus         GSC add-on Fast/Wide SCSI Interface
8/0.1.0            disk        HP      C2490WD
8/0.2.0            disk        HP      C2490WD
8/0.3.0            disk        HP      C2490WD
8/0.4.0            disk        HP      C2490WD
8/0.5.0            disk        HP      C2490WD
8/4           ext_bus         GSC add-on Fast/Wide SCSI Interface
8/8           ext_bus         GSC add-on Fast/Wide SCSI Interface
8/12          ext_bus         GSC add-on Fast/Wide SCSI Interface
10/0          ext_bus         GSC built-in Fast/Wide SCSI Interface
10/0.6.0           disk        HP      C2490WD
10/4/0        tty             MUX
10/4/8.5.0         tape        HP      HP35480A
10/4/8.6.0         tape        HP      HP35480A
10/4/12       lan             HP      J2157A - FDDI Interface
10/4/16       lan             HP      J2166A - 802.5 Token Ring LAN
10/8          ext_bus         GSC add-on Fast/Wide SCSI Interface
10/8.1.0           disk        HP      C2490WD
10/8.2.0           disk        HP      C2490WD
10/8.3.0           disk        HP      C2490WD
10/8.4.0           disk        HP      C2490WD
10/8.5.0           disk        HP      C2490WD
10/12/0       ext_bus         Built-in Parallel Interface
10/12/5       ext_bus         Built-in SCSI
```

```
10/12/5.0.0              tape    HP        C1533A
10/12/5.2.0              disk    TOSHIBA   CD-ROM XM-4101TA
10/12/6          lan             Built-in LAN
10/12/7          ps2             Built-in Keyboard/Mouse
10/16/4          lan             HP        J2157A - FDDI Interface
```

 # ioscan

```
H/W Path     Class              Description
===========================================
             bc
8            bc                 I/O Adapter
8/0              ext_bus        GSC add-on Fast/Wide SCSI Interface
8/0.1            target
8/0.1.0              disk       HP        C2490WD
8/0.2            target
8/0.2.0              disk       HP        C2490WD
8/0.3            target
8/0.3.0              disk       HP        C2490WD
8/0.4            target
8/0.4.0              disk       HP        C2490WD
8/0.5            target
8/0.5.0              disk       HP        C2490WD
8/4              ext_bus        GSC add-on Fast/Wide SCSI Interface
8/8              ext_bus        GSC add-on Fast/Wide SCSI Interface
8/12             ext_bus        GSC add-on Fast/Wide SCSI Interface
10           bc                 I/O Adapter
10/0             ext_bus        GSC built-in Fast/Wide SCSI Interface
10/0.6           target
10/0.6.0             disk       HP        C2490WD
10/4         bc                 Bus Converter
10/4/0           tty            MUX
10/4/4           ext_bus        HP        28696A - Fast/Wide SCSI Interface
10/4/8           ext_bus        HP        28655A - SCSI Interface
10/4/8.5             target
10/4/8.5.0               tape   HP        HP35480A
10/4/8.6             target
10/4/8.6.0               tape   HP        HP35480A
10/4/9           unknown        HP        28655A - Parallel Interface
10/4/12          lan            HP        J2157A - FDDI Interface
10/4/16          lan            HP        J2166A - 802.5 Token Ring LAN
10/8             ext_bus        GSC add-on Fast/Wide SCSI Interface
10/8.1           target
10/8.1.0             disk       HP        C2490WD
10/8.2           target
10/8.2.0             disk       HP        C2490WD
10/8.3           target
10/8.3.0             disk       HP        C2490WD
10/8.4           target
10/8.4.0             disk       HP        C2490WD
10/8.5           target
10/8.5.0             disk       HP        C2490WD
10/12        ba                 Core I/O Adapter
10/12/0          ext_bus        Built-in Parallel Interface
10/12/5          ext_bus        Built-in SCSI
10/12/5.0            target
10/12/5.0.0              tape   HP        C1533A
10/12/5.2            target
10/12/5.2.0              disk   TOSHIBA CD-ROM XM-4101TA
10/12/6          lan            Built-in LAN
10/12/7          ps2            Built-in Keyboard/Mouse
10/16        bc                 Bus Converter
10/16/4          lan            HP        J2157A - FDDI Interface
10/16/12         ext_bus        HP        28696A - Fast/Wide SCSI Interface
32           processor          Processor
34           processor          Processor
```

```
36             processor           Processor
38             processor           Processor
49             memory              Memory
```

 # ioscan -f

(Lists all devices; full listing includes device driver names)

```
Class       I   H/W Path    Driver      S/W State H/W Type Description
=============================================
bc          0               root        CLAIMED   BUS_NEXUS
bc          1   8           ccio        CLAIMED   BUS_NEXUS I/O Adapter
ext_bus     0   8/0         c720        CLAIMED   INTERFACE GSC add-on Fast/
                                                            Wide SCSI Interface
target      0   8/0.1       tgt         CLAIMED   DEVICE
disk        4   8/0.1.0     sdisk       CLAIMED   DEVICE    HP      C2490WD
target      1   8/0.2       tgt         CLAIMED   DEVICE
disk        5   8/0.2.0     sdisk       CLAIMED   DEVICE    HP      C2490WD
target      2   8/0.3       tgt         CLAIMED   DEVICE
disk        6   8/0.3.0     sdisk       CLAIMED   DEVICE    HP      C2490WD
target      3   8/0.4       tgt         CLAIMED   DEVICE
disk        7   8/0.4.0     sdisk       CLAIMED   DEVICE    HP      C2490WD
target      4   8/0.5       tgt         CLAIMED   DEVICE
disk        8   8/0.5.0     sdisk       CLAIMED   DEVICE    HP      C2490WD
ext_bus     1   8/4         c720        CLAIMED   INTERFACE GSC add-on Fast/Wide
                                                            SCSI Interface
ext_bus     2   8/8         c720        CLAIMED   INTERFACE GSC add-on Fast/Wide
                                                            SCSI Interface
ext_bus     3   8/12        c720        CLAIMED   INTERFACE GSC add-on Fast/Wide
                                                            SCSI Interface
bc          2   10          ccio        CLAIMED   BUS_NEXUS I/O Adapter
ext_bus     4   10/0        c720        CLAIMED   INTERFACE GSC built-in Fast/
                                                            Wide SCSI Interface
target      5   10/0.6      tgt         CLAIMED   DEVICE
disk        1   10/0.6.0    sdisk       CLAIMED   DEVICE    HP      C2490WD
bc          3   10/4        bc          CLAIMED   BUS_NEXUS Bus Converter
tty         0   10/4/0      mux2        CLAIMED   INTERFACE MUX
ext_bus     5   10/4/4      scsi3       CLAIMED   INTERFACE HP 28696A - Fast/
                                                            Wide SCSI Interface
ext_bus     6   10/4/8      scsi1       CLAIMED   INTERFACE HP 28655A - SCSI
                                                            Interface
target      6   10/4/8.5    target      CLAIMED   DEVICE
tape        1   10/4/8.5.0  tape2       CLAIMED   DEVICE    HP      HP35480A
target      7   10/4/8.6    target      CLAIMED   DEVICE
tape        2   10/4/8.6.0  tape2       CLAIMED   DEVICE    HP      HP35480A
unknown    -1   10/4/9                  UNCLAIMED UNKNOWN   HP 28655A - Parallel
                                                            Interface
lan         1   10/4/12     fddi        CLAIMED   INTERFACE HP      J2157A -
                                                            FDDI Interface
lan         3   10/4/16     token2      CLAIMED   INTERFACE HP      J2166A-802.5
                                                            Token Ring LAN
ext_bus     7   10/8        c720        CLAIMED   INTERFACE GSC add-on Fast/Wide
                                                            SCSI Interface
target      8   10/8.1      tgt         CLAIMED   DEVICE
disk        9   10/8.1.0    sdisk       CLAIMED   DEVICE    HP      C2490WD
target      9   10/8.2      tgt         CLAIMED   DEVICE
disk       10   10/8.2.0    sdisk       CLAIMED   DEVICE    HP      C2490WD
target     10   10/8.3      tgt         CLAIMED   DEVICE
disk       11   10/8.3.0    sdisk       CLAIMED   DEVICE    HP      C2490WD
target     11   10/8.4      tgt         CLAIMED   DEVICE
disk       12   10/8.4.0    sdisk       CLAIMED   DEVICE    HP      C2490WD
target     12   10/8.5      tgt         CLAIMED   DEVICE
disk       13   10/8.5.0    sdisk       CLAIMED   DEVICE    HP      C2490WD
ba          0   10/12       bus_adapter CLAIMED   BUS_NEXUS Core I/O Adapter
```

```
ext_bus      9  10/12/0      CentIf    CLAIMED   INTERFACE Built-in Parallel
                                                             Interface
ext_bus      8  10/12/5      c700      CLAIMED   INTERFACE Built-in SCSI
target      13  10/12/5.0    tgt       CLAIMED   DEVICE
tape         0  10/12/5.0.0  stape     CLAIMED   DEVICE    HP        C1533A
target      14  10/12/5.2    tgt       CLAIMED   DEVICE
disk         3  10/12/5.2.0  sdisk     CLAIMED   DEVICE    TOSHIBA CD-ROM XM-
                                                             4101TA
lan          0  10/12/6      lan2      CLAIMED   INTERFACE Built-in LAN
ps2          0  10/12/7      ps2       CLAIMED   INTERFACE Built-in
                                                             Keyboard/Mouse
bc           4  10/16        bc        CLAIMED   BUS_NEXUS Bus Converter
lan          2  10/16/4      fddi      CLAIMED   INTERFACE HP        J2157A -
                                                             FDDI Interface
ext_bus     10  10/16/12     scsi3     CLAIMED   INTERFACE HP 28696A - Fast/
                                                             Wide SCSI Interface
processor    0  32           processor CLAIMED   PROCESSOR Processor
processor    1  34           processor CLAIMED   PROCESSOR Processor
processor    2  36           processor CLAIMED   PROCESSOR Processor
processor    3  38           processor CLAIMED   PROCESSOR Processor
memory       0  49           memory    CLAIMED   MEMORY    Memory
```

7.6   Configuring Peripheral Devices: insf

Traditionally, a new device is configured in Unix by

- Building the kernel with the corresponding driver.
- Using the *mknod* command to make a device special file in the /dev directory with major and minor numbers as specified by the device manufacturer. Optional files like *raw* or *block mode access* files and subdirectories may have to be created.
- Setting appropriate ownership and access rights on the special file.

HP-UX has the command *insf* (install special file), which automates the last two steps. insf is effectively an intelligent form of mknod. In the simplest form,

```
# insf
```

installs and sets up device special files for all new devices connected to the system. Hence, to add a new device to an HP-UX system,

- Check that the device is connected to the system by using the ioscan command.
- Check that the device driver is in the kernel. If not, see Chapter 18, on kernel reconfiguration, for adding the device driver.
- Enter the insf command.

insf has options to install devices with a specific driver or in a specific hardware path. For example,

```
# insf -d disc3
```

will create special files for all new type disc3 disks connected to the system.
For each disk, the following two files will be created (as an example):

`dsk/c2t3d7 protection mask: rw-r---, owner: bin, group: sys`	Block mode special file
`rdsk/c2t3d7 protection mask: rw-r---, owner: bin, group: sys`	Character mode special file

insf has built-in information for all HP devices; third-party devices may
require appropriate options to be specified to insf, or mknod may have to be
used.

7.7 Getting Device Special File Information: lssf and lsdev

The *lssf* (list special file) command displays device special file information
such as major and minor numbers and the hardware path of the device. Here
is the edited output of the command

```
# lssf *
```

executed in the /dev and the /dev/rdsk directories of the K400 used in the
ioscan examples:

```
# lssf *

(Command executed in /dev directory)

CentIf card instance 9 handshake mode 2 at address 10/12/0 c9t0d0_1p
mux2 card instance 0 port 7 callout at address 10/4/0 cua0p7
mux2 card instance 0 port 7 callout at address 10/4/0 cul0p7
lan2 card instance 0 ether at address 10/12/6 ether0
lan2 card instance 0 ieee at address 10/12/6 lan0
fddi card instance 1 ieee at address 10/4/12 lan1
fddi card instance 2 ieee at address 10/16/4 lan2
token2 card instance 3 ieee at address 10/4/16 lan3
CentIf card instance 9 handshake mode 2 at address 10/12/0 lp
mux2 card instance 0 transparent hardwired at address 10/4/0 mux0
(command executed in /dev/rdsk directory)
sdisk card instance 0 SCSI target 1 SCSI LUN 0 section 0 at address 8/0.1.0
c0t1d0
sdisk card instance 0 SCSI target 2 SCSI LUN 0 section 0 at address 8/0.2.0
c0t2d0
sdisk card instance 0 SCSI target 3 SCSI LUN 0 section 0 at address 8/0.3.0
c0t3d0
sdisk card instance 0 SCSI target 4 SCSI LUN 0 section 0 at address 8/0.4.0
c0t4d0
sdisk card instance 0 SCSI target 5 SCSI LUN 0 section 0 at address 8/0.5.0
c0t5d0
sdisk card instance 4 SCSI target 1 SCSI LUN 0 section 0 at address ??? c4t1d0
sdisk card instance 4 SCSI target 6 SCSI LUN 0 section 0 at address 10/0.6.0
c4t6d0
sdisk card instance 4 SCSI target 8 SCSI LUN 0 section 0 at address ??? c4t8d0
sdisk card instance 7 SCSI target 1 SCSI LUN 0 section 0 at address 10/8.1.0
c7t1d0
sdisk card instance 7 SCSI target 2 SCSI LUN 0 section 0 at address 10/8.2.0
c7t2d0
```

```
sdisk card instance 7 SCSI target 3 SCSI LUN 0 section 0 at address 10/8.3.0
c7t3d0
sdisk card instance 7 SCSI target 4 SCSI LUN 0 section 0 at address 10/8.4.0
c7t4d0
sdisk card instance 7 SCSI target 5 SCSI LUN 0 section 0 at address 10/8.5.0
c7t5d0
sdisk card instance 8 SCSI target 2 SCSI LUN 0 section 0 at address 10/12/5.2.0
c8t2d0
```

The lsdev command lists the major and minor number of drivers configured in the kernel:

```
# lsdev
Character      Block        Driver         Class
        0       -1            cn            pseudo
        3       -1            mm            pseudo
       16       -1            ptym          ptym
       17       -1            ptys          ptys
       27       -1            dmem          pseudo
       28       -1            diag0         diag
       46       -1            netdiag1      unknown
       52       -1            lan2          lan
       56       -1            ni            unknown
       60       -1            netman        unknown
       64       64            lv            lvm
       69       -1            dev_config    pseudo
       72       -1            clone         pseudo
       73       -1            strlog        pseudo
       74       -1            sad           pseudo
      101       -1            asyncdsk      pseudo
      103       -1            token2        lan
      116       -1            echo          pseudo
      119       -1            dlpi          pseudo
      122       -1            inet_cots     unknown
      122       -1            inet_cots     unknown
      156       -1            ptm           strptym
      157       -1            pts           strptys
      159       -1            ps2           ps2
      164       -1            pipedev       unknown
      168       -1            beep          graf_pseudo
      177       28            disc3         disk
      188       31            sdisk         disk
      189       -1            klog          pseudo
      191       -1            fddi          lan
      193       -1            mux2          tty
      203       -1            sctl          pseudo
      205       -1            stape         tape
      207       -1            sy            pseudo
      212       -1            tape0         tape
      216       -1            CentIf        ext_bus
      227       -1            kepd          pseudo
      232       -1            diag2         diag
```

8

LVM:
Logical Volume
Manager

8.1 Introduction

LVM is a tool for managing disk space with more flexibility than was available with previous techniques based on disk partitioning or slicing. Before LVM, disks used to be carved out into contiguous partitions. Each partition was used as a separate file system. Increasing the size of a partition usually affected other partitions; hence, to increase the size of a file system, it was moved to an existing larger partition and the original partition was used for some other purpose.

LVM allows much finer control over allocation of space on disks. A disk is carved out into logical volumes (which are replacements for partitions), and space is allocated in multiples of a small fixed-size logical block, 4 Mbytes by default. Allocation is not necessarily contiguous; hence, logical volume sizes can easily be increased by allocating free blocks. LVM goes a step further: multiple disks can be treated as a single larger disk called a *volume group*. This is the rationale behind the popularity of LVM on many Unix systems today. HP-UX systems now use LVM, even for root file systems, though the older, partitioned disks are also supported.

When planning for LVM, drawing diagrams and visualizing helps in understanding and troubleshooting a complex setup.

8.2 LVM Basics: Physical Volumes, Volume Groups, and Logical Volumes

Physical volume is the LVM name for a physical disk initialized for LVM use. LVM uses complete disks; partitions are not used. The *pvcreate* command initializes physical disks. The physical volume must then be added to a volume

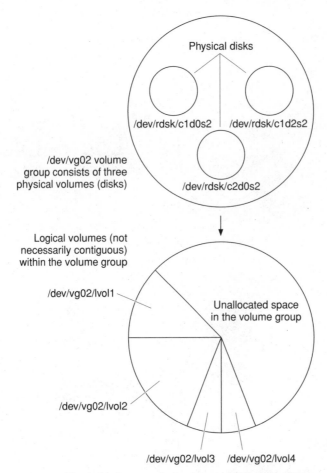

Figure 8.1 Physical volumes, volume groups, and logical volumes.

group. A volume group is thus effectively a large disk consisting of one or more physical volumes. The *vgcreate* command creates a volume group and adds a physical volume to it; the *vgextend* command adds a physical volume to an existing volume group.

By using the *lvcreate* command, a logical volume of a predetermined size can then be created on the volume group. The *newfs* command can be used to create a file system on this logical volume. Multiple logical volumes and corresponding file systems can be created on the volume group, provided, of course, there is sufficient free space.

Figure 8.1 illustrates these concepts.

8.2.1 Naming conventions

To a user program, logical volumes look like disks. Hence, the LVM device files reside under /dev. Volume groups reside under /dev, for example, /dev/vg02. Logical volumes reside under the corresponding volume group directory, for example, /dev/vg02/lvol3. Names for volume groups and logical volumes can be any valid file name; however, for clarity, the string *vg* should be present in volume names and *lvol* should be present in logical volumes mounted as file systems. Logical volumes not having file systems and used in raw mode—for example, for Sybase database use—should be identified by an appropriate name. This is because LVM cannot determine the use of these logical volumes.

When creating volume groups, if LVM were allowed to determine volume name, the names would be /dev/vg00, /dev/vg01, and so on. If LVM were allowed to *name* logical volumes, the names would be /dev/vgxx/lvol1, /dev/vgxx/lvol2, and so on. (Here vgxx is the volume group in which the logical volume is being created.)

8.3   Logical Extents and Physical Extents

When a new logical volume is created, it is allocated some number of the basic 4-Mbyte blocks. Four Mbytes is actually the default value for the unit of allocation; another value can be specified when creating the volume group (but not the logical volume). This unit of allocation is called an *extent*. Allocation units on physical volumes (disks) are called *physical extents*. Each logical volume consists of zero or more *logical* extents. Physical and logical extents are the same size for a volume group. LVM maps logical extents of a logical volume to physical extents of physical volumes in the volume group. This mapping information is stored on the physical volumes and loaded into memory when a volume group is activated.

Figure 8.2 illustrates these concepts with a volume group that has two logical volumes and two physical volumes.

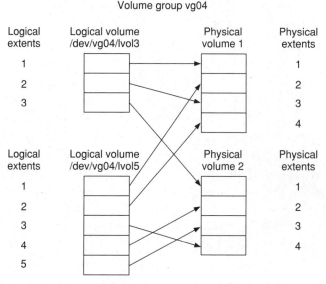

Figure 8.2   Mapping of logical extent to physical extent.

8.4   Using SAM to Analyze an LVM Setup

Given an HP system using LVM, how can we map out its LVM setup? We need to know

- The names of all volume groups
- The physical volumes (disks) in each volume group
- The logical volumes in each volume group
- File systems, if present, in each logical volume
- Logical volumes used as swap space

Bring up SAM and double-click the *disks and file systems* icon to go to the area of that name. Double-clicking on the *volume groups* icon displays a list of volume groups, as shown in Fig. 8.3. Double-clicking the *Disk Devices* icon displays the volume groups and corresponding disks. The disks are identified by hardware connection; disks can be better identified with their device names if the *vgscan -pv* command is used:

```
# /sbin/vgscan -pv

/dev/sysvg1
/dev/dsk/c0t1d0

/dev/dbvg1
/dev/dsk/c0t2d0
```

```
┌──────────────── Disks and File Systems (mcf11u12) ────────────────┐
│ File  List  View  Options  Actions                          Help  │
│                                                                   │
│                                                                   │
│ Volume Groups                                    0 of 9 selected  │
│                                                                   │
│         Mbytes          Physical    Logical                       │
│ Name    Available       Volumes     Volumes                       │
│ vg00       232 of 2028      1           8                         │
│ sysvg1    1432 of 2032      1           3                         │
│ dbvg1        0 of 2032      1           1                         │
│ dbvg2     1916 of 2032      1           3                         │
│ dbvg3      508 of 2032      1           2                         │
│ dbvg4     2032 of 2032      1           0                         │
│ dbvg5     2032 of 2032      1           0                         │
│ dbvg6     2032 of 2032      1           0                         │
│ dbvg7     1916 of 2032      1           3                         │
│                                                                   │
└───────────────────────────────────────────────────────────────────┘
```

Figure 8.3   Volume groups on a system.

```
/dev/dbvg4
/dev/dsk/c0t3d0

/dev/dbvg6
/dev/dsk/c0t4d0

/dev/vg00
/dev/dsk/c4t6d0

/dev/dbvg2
/dev/dsk/c7t1d0

/dev/dbvg3
/dev/dsk/c7t2d0

/dev/dbvg5
/dev/dsk/c7t3d0

/dev/dbvg7
/dev/dsk/c7t4d0

Scan of Physical Volumes Complete.
```

The logical volumes can be displayed, as shown in Fig. 8.4, by double-clicking the *Logical Volumes* icon under SAM. The file systems can be displayed,

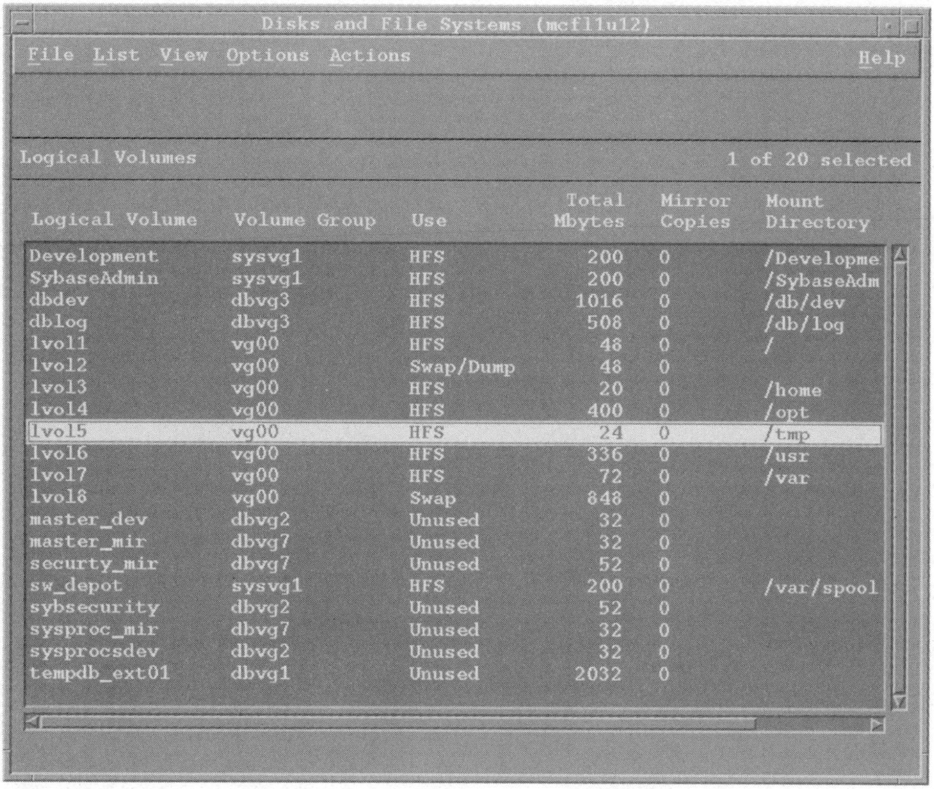

Figure 8.4 Logical volumes.

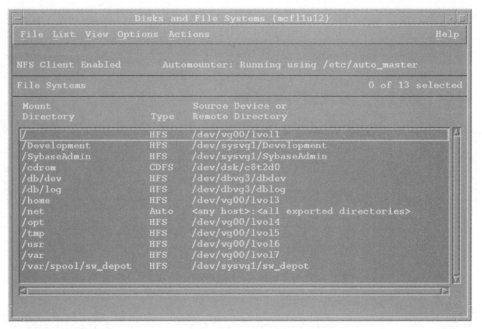

Figure 8.5 File systems.

as shown in Fig. 8.5, by double-clicking the *File Systems* icon, and the swap space allocated volumes can be displayed, as shown in Fig. 8.6, by double-clicking the *swap* icon.

From all the information displayed, we know that there are 9 volume groups, each volume group is on only one physical volume, there are 20 logical volumes, 11 logical volumes have mounted file systems, 2 logical volumes are used for swapping, and 7 logical volumes either have file systems that are not mounted or are being used as raw devices. In this case, the seven unmounted logical volumes are used as Sybase database raw devices. Figure 8.7 shows this pictorially.

8.5   Commands to Analyze an LVM Setup

While SAM is convenient to use, not all LVM operations are possible with SAM; some operations have to be done from the command line. Hence, any serious system administrator should know how to perform LVM tasks via the command line. LVM commands are in the /sbin directory. The command names begin with *lv, vg,* or *pv.* To analyze an existing system, the following commands can be used:

- *vgscan -pv* displays mapping of volume group to physical volume.

- *vgdisplay* displays volume group information. *vgdisplay -v* displays volume

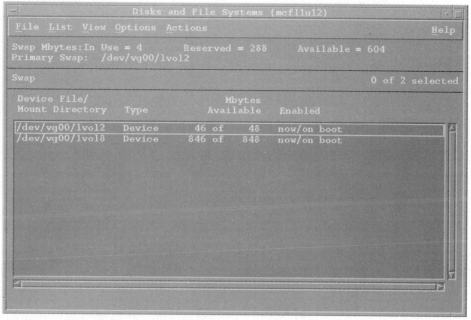

Figure 8.6   Swap space logical volumes.

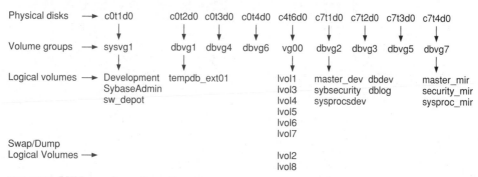

Figure 8.7   LVM sample configuration.

group information in verbose mode. Logical volume information is also displayed.

- *bdf* or *df* displays mounted file systems.
- */etc/swapinfo* displays swap logical volumes.

vgscan use was shown in the previous section. vgdisplay -v output is shown here partially:

```
# vgdisplay -v
```

```
--- Volume groups ---

VG Name                    /dev/vg00
VG Write                   Access read/write
VG Status                  available
Max LV                     255
Cur LV                     8
Open LV                    8
Max PV                     16
Cur PV                     1
Act PV                     1
Max PE per PV              1016
VGDA                       2
PE Size (Mbytes)           4
Total PE                   507
Alloc PE                   449
Free PE                    58
Total PVG                  0

   --- Logical volumes ---

   LV Name                 /dev/vg00/lvol1
   LV Status               available/syncd
   LV Size (Mbytes)        48
   Current LE              12
   Allocated PE            12
   Used PV                 1

   LV Name                 /dev/vg00/lvol2
   LV Status               available/syncd
   LV Size (Mbytes)        48
```

(Truncated)

Each volume group is displayed followed by all logical volumes in the
group. A simple way to display just the volume groups and the logical volumes is to use egrep, as here:

 # /sbin/vgdisplay -v | egrep "VG Name|LV Name"

```
VG Name /dev/vg00
   LV Name /dev/vg00/lvol1
   LV Name /dev/vg00/lvol2
   LV Name /dev/vg00/lvol3
   LV Name /dev/vg00/lvol4
   LV Name /dev/vg00/lvol5
   LV Name /dev/vg00/lvol6
   LV Name /dev/vg00/lvol7
   LV Name /dev/vg00/lvol8
VG Name /dev/sysvg1
   LV Name /dev/sysvg1/Development
   LV Name /dev/sysvg1/SybaseAdmin
   LV Name /dev/sysvg1/sw_depot
VG Name /dev/dbvg1
   LV Name /dev/dbvg1/tempdb_ext01
VG Name /dev/dbvg2
   LV Name /dev/dbvg2/master_dev
   LV Name /dev/dbvg2/sysprocsdev
   LV Name /dev/dbvg2/sybsecurity
VG Name /dev/dbvg3
   LV Name /dev/dbvg3/dbdev
   LV Name /dev/dbvg3/dblog
```

```
VG Name /dev/dbvg4
VG Name /dev/dbvg5
VG Name /dev/dbvg6
VG Name /dev/dbvg7
    LV Name /dev/dbvg7/security_mir
    LV Name /dev/dbvg7/sysproc_mir
    LV Name /dev/dbvg7/master_mir
```

The *bdf* and *swapinfo* commands provide the remaining information:

 # bdf

```
Filesystem          kbytes     used    avail %used Mounted on
/dev/vg00/lvol1      47829    28748    14298   67% /
/dev/vg00/lvol7      71765    59364     5224   92% /var
/dev/sysvg1/sw_depot
                    199381    24229   155213   14% /var/spool/sw_depot
/dev/vg00/lvol6     335061   220255    81299   73% /usr
/dev/vg00/lvol5      23893      283    21220    1% /tmp
/dev/vg00/lvol4     398869   281940    77042   79% /opt
/dev/vg00/lvol3      19861     1519    16355    8% /home
/dev/sysvg1/SybaseAdmin
                    199381    41570   137872   23% /SybaseAdmin
/dev/sysvg1/Development
                    199381       16   179426    0% /Development
/dev/dsk/c8t2d0     207702   207702        0  100% /cdrom
/dev/dbvg3/dbdev   1017681   233641   682271   26% /db/dev
/dev/dbvg3/dblog    508523    65601   392069   14% /db/log
```

 # /etc/swapinfo

```
              Kb       Kb       Kb   PCT  START/      Kb
TYPE       AVAIL     USED     FREE  USED  LIMIT RESERVE  PRI  NAME
dev        49152     1880    47272    4%      0       -    1  /dev/vg00/lvol2
dev       868352     1852   866500    0%      0       -    1  /dev/vg00/lvol8
reserve        -   297376  -297376
memory    413676   238616   175060   58%
```

Here, RESERVE is space that could be needed by running processes. PRI represents priority; space is taken from lower-priority devices first. All the above information can be used to derive Fig. 8.7.

8.6   Creating Volume Groups and Logical Volumes

To create a new volume group, at least one physical disk must be available. Commands can be entered at the command line to create the volume group; however, there are quite a few commands with a number of options. Hence, SAM should be used to create volume groups and logical volumes as it takes care of details and is convenient. Using SAM, the *Create or Extend* action can be selected from the menu of the Volume Groups display. SAM displays a list of available disks, one of which must be selected for the new volume group. The volume group name must then be entered. The volume group is created. SAM performs the following steps:

- Creates the device file for the physical disk, such as /dev/dsk/c7t5d0 and /dev/rdsk/c7t5d0.

- Executes *pvcreate* to initialize the volume. Example:

```
/sbin/pvcreate -f /dev/rdsk/c7t5d0
```

- Creates the volume group directory, such as /dev/vg02.
- Creates a character special file for the volume group "device." Example:

```
mknod /dev/vg02/group c 64 0x030000
```

- Uses *vgcreate* to create the volume group. Example:

```
/sbin/vgcreate /dev/vg02 /dev/dsk/c7t5d0
```

The volume group is now available for use. The vgcreate command makes an entry in /etc/lvmtab so that the volume group will be "seen" whenever the system reboots. More physical disks can be added to the volume group by the same SAM menu item. Logical volumes can now be created on the volume group. The *Create* action can be selected from SAM's Logical Volumes display. The following information can be entered:

- One of the listed volume groups where the new logical volume will be created
- The new logical volume name
- Size of the logical volume
- Whether the logical volume is to be mounted as a file system or as swap space
- Mount point if volume will be a new file system

SAM performs the following steps:

- Uses lvcreate to create the logical volume. Example with a volume size of 12 Mbytes:

```
/sbin/lvcreate -L 12 -n /lvol31 /dev/vg02
```

- As specified to SAM, if the logical volume will contain a file system, then commands like the following are executed:

```
mkdir /home/uservol
/usr/sbin/newfs /dev/vg02/lvol31
/usr/sbin/mount -u /dev/vg02/lvol31 /home/uservol
```

8.7 Advantage of Using a Single Disk Type in a Volume Group

Disks with different geometries (layout information, such as number of platters or sectors per cylinder) can be mixed in volume groups. However, this is not recommended, because only one disk type can be specified to newfs. (newfs is used to create a file system on a raw logical volume.) If a logical volume spans multiple physical volumes in a volume group, only the first volume's geometry will be used by newfs to perform layout of disk data structures. The other volumes may not perform efficiently.

8.8 Extending Logical Volumes

To increase the size of a logical volume it has to be unmounted. The *lvextend* command is then used. If the volume contains a file system, the file system command *extendfs* has to be run on the volume. The volume can then be mounted. SAM should be used to perform this task. The *Increase size* action should be selected from the menu of the Logical Volumes display. The new size can be specified. Given a new logical volume size of 32 Mbytes, SAM executes commands like the following internally:

```
/usr/sbin/umount /dev/vg02/lvol31
/sbin/lvextend -L 32 /dev/vg02/lvol31
/sbin/extendfs /dev/vg02/lvol31
/usr/sbin/mount -u /dev/vg02/lvol31 /home/uservol
```

8.9 Root Volume Considerations

Without LVM, a single disk typically contained boot information, the root file system and the primary swap file. The boot information consisted of a LIF volume (actually a separate file system in the first few blocks of the disk), which in turn contained a small program to load the operating system and the path to the operating system, somewhat like

```
hpux (52.4.0;0)/stand/vmunix
```

where (52.4.0;0) specifies the hardware path to the disk.

With LVM on the root disk, there must be LVM information before the actual root file system. LIF programs should know how to get to the root file system. Also, the volume group in which the root file system is can contain multiple disks. SAM cannot be used to create bootable volume groups. The following steps are needed to create a root volume group:

1. The disk is initialized with the *pvcreate -B* command. The -B makes the disk bootable; the LIF volume is created with the boot utilities and a BDRA (Boot Data Reserve Area). The BDRA is where information on all the logical volumes in the volume group is maintained. This information will be used during boot to access the primary swap file, if it is on another disk in the volume group. For example,

```
pvcreate -B /dev/rdsk/c2t1d0
```

creates the volume group directory, such as /dev/vg00, and creates a character special file for the volume group "device." Thus,

```
mknod /dev/vg00/group c 64 0x030000
```

uses vgcreate to creates the volume group; for example,

```
/sbin/vgcreate /dev/vg00 /dev/dsk/c2t1d0
```

2. Use *mkboot* to create LIF utilities:

```
mkboot /dev/rdsk/c2t1d0
```

mkboot knows the disk is part of a volume group from the information already stored on the disk by LVM; mkboot sets up LIF to point to the file system directly. The actual LIF boot command can be stored on the disk by creating the LIF AUTO file:

```
mkboot -a "hpux (52.3.0;0)/stand/vmunix /dev/rdsk/c2t1d0
```

3. Create a logical volume on the volume group. It must be the first logical volume on the bootable disk. The lvcreate command can be used with options to specify contiguous allocation of extents and to disable bad block relocation:

```
lvcreate -C y -r n -n root /dev/vg00
```

4. Extend the logical volume to, for example, 300 Mbytes and force the allocation on the boot disk (in case the volume group contains multiple disks):

```
lvextend -L 300 /dev/vg00/root /dev/dsk/c2t1d0
```

5. Specify that the logical volume is to be used as a root volume. This will write appropriate information in the BDRA area of all physical volumes of the volume group mentioning that the logical volume is the bootable root volume:

```
lvlnboot -r /dev/vg00/root
```

6. The root file system must now be created in the logical volume. The volume group is then bootable.

8.10   Contiguous Allocation

If a logical volume is the root volume, it must be contiguous on disk, since the boot program that loads the operating system assumes that given a starting block, the root file system is contiguous on disk. Also, for efficiency of access, data may be stored contiguously on disk. The -C y option to lvcreate creates a contiguous logical volume, as in

```
lvcreate -C y -n uservol /dev/vg03
```

8.11 Striping

Striping is a configuration where consecutive blocks or sets of blocks of a logical volume are allocated on different physical volumes. Hence, if a logical volume consists of three physical volumes, logical blocks 1 to 10 could be on disk 1, blocks 11 to 20 on disk 2, blocks 21 to 30 on disk 3, blocks 31 to 40 on disk 1, and so on. Striping improves I/O performance because many programs access files sequentially and, with striping, disk head movement is minimized for such accesses. However, reliability decreases because any one disk failure renders the striped logical volume useless. Another consideration is that today's RAID disk arrays offer striping in firmware on the disk hardware.

The number of disks to be used for the striped logical volume and the stripe size must be specified in the lvcreate command when creating the striped logical volume. In the following example, the logical volume spans three volumes (i 3) and the stripe size is 16 Kbytes (-I 16):

```
lvcreate -i 3 -I 16 -L 100 -n stripevol /dev/vg02
```

The logical volume size is specified as 100 Mbytes. Because the volume will be striped across three physical volumes, each volume's allocation is $33\frac{1}{3}$ Mbytes, which is rounded off to 36 Mbytes because allocation is in terms of extents that are multiples of 4 Mbytes. In the above example, the first 16 Kbytes of data is placed on one physical volume, the next 16 Kbytes on a second volume, the next 16 Kbytes on a third volume, the next 16 Kbytes on the first volume, and so on.

8.12 Mirroring

One or two mirror copies of a logical volume can be created. Mirroring improves read performance and can allow data access even when disks and controllers have failed. Mirroring commands are integrated with LVM; however, the mirroring software, MirrorDisk/UX, has to be purchased separately from HP. With RAID disk arrays available with mirroring firmware, LVM mirroring may be of limited use.

A logical volume to be mirrored is created and allocated space with the usual use of lvcreate and lvextend commands. The volume is then mirrored on another physical volume, not necessarily in the same volume group, with a command like:

```
lvextend -m 1 /dev/vg02/lvol4 /dev/dsk/c2t3d0
```

-m 1 specifies a single mirror, the original logical volume is /dev/vg02/lvol4, and the mirror logical volume will be allocated on the physical volume /dev/dsk/c2t3d0, which must be in the same volume group.

8.12.1 Strict allocation

Mirrored logical volumes should be on separate physical volumes, for then a single physical disk failure cannot affect data access. Such a policy is called *strict allocation*. The physical volumes can be in the same or different volume groups. This is the default policy which is specified as the -s y option when the logical volume is created, as in

```
lvcreate -s y -n lvol4 /dev/vg02
```

The -s g option is volume group–strict; mirrors of a logical volume must be on a separate physical volume in a separate volume group. The -s n option allows mirrors to be on the same physical volume and would not protect against disk failures.

8.12.2 Mirror Write Cache and Mirror Consistency Recovery

Two methods to synchronize disk contents after a system crash can be specified when creating mirrored logical volumes: Mirror Write Cache (MWC) and Mirror Consistency Recovery (MCR). If the MWC method is used, the system maintains a cache which contains information on pending writes to mirrored volumes during normal operation. During recovery after a crash, only the pending writes are performed to synchronize the contents of mirrored volumes. If the MCR method is used, no checks are performed during normal operations. During recovery after a crash, each logical extent in the mirrored logical volumes is examined and updated if required. MWC is the default method. The -M and -C flags to lvcreate determine the recovery method:

-M y	Use MWC.
-M n and -C y	Use MCR.
-M n and -C n	No recovery.

The last option can be used on swap volumes.

8.12.3 Splitting and merging mirrored logical volumes

A logical volume can be split for backup. When a volume is split, the original volume can be used as is and the second (mirrored) volume is called by the same name as the original but with the character b (for backup) added to the end. Hence,

```
lvsplit /dev/vg02/lvol5
```

leaves the original volume as /dev/vg02/lvol5 and renames the second volume /dev/vg02/lvol5b. The backup volume then must be *fsck*ed and *mount*ed:

```
fsck /dev/vg02/lvol5b
mount /dev/vg02/lvol5b /tmp/backup
```

While the two volumes are separate, LVM keeps track of extents updated on the original volume. The two volumes can be merged together into the original mirror state by a command like

```
lvmerge /dev/vg02/lvol5b /dev/vg02/lvol5
```

9

Networking:
TCP/IP and
Internet Services

9.1 Introduction

The networking features of HP-UX are typical of the offerings from the major Unix vendors. Hardware interfaces can be Ethernet, Fast Ethernet, Token Ring, FDDI, or serial line. Protocols supported are TCP/IP, SNA, X.25, and OSI, though, as expected, TCP/IP support is the most comprehensive. Protocols are not discussed in detail here; there are many books available that describe industry standard protocols. Network File System (NFS) and Network Information Services (NIS) can be considered networking components; they are covered separately in Chapters 11 and 10, respectively. Network programmers can use sockets or the Link Level Access (LLA) routines. Network programming issues are beyond the scope of this book.

9.2 What Is the Networking Hardware in My System?

SAM can be used to check what network cards are on a system. Double-click on the Networks and Communications icon and then, when a submenu of icons is displayed, double-click on Network Interface cards. The list of network cards and the addresses assigned to them is displayed. Figure 9.1 is the SAM display on an HP-UX system with four network cards.

Network hardware information can also be displayed from the command line with the *lanscan* and *ifconfig* commands. lanscan displays the card names and ifconfig displays the IP addresses (if assigned).

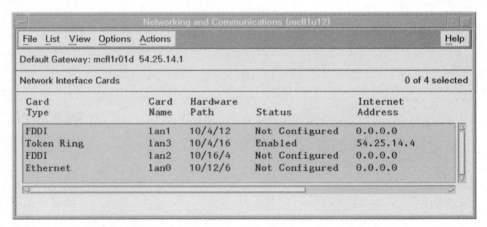

Figure 9.1 SAM display of network connections.

```
# lanscan
Hardware Station       Crd Hardware Net-Interface NM  MAC     HP DLPI Mjr
Path     Address       In# State    NameUnit State ID  Type    Support Num
10/4/12  0x080009C41364 1  UP       lan1     DOWN  4   FDDI    Yes     191
10/4/16  0x100090DC2AC1 3  UP       lan3     UP    5   802.5   Yes     103
10/16/4  0x080009C43344 2  UP       lan2     DOWN  6   FDDI    Yes     191
10/12/6  0x080009B16B5C 0  UP       lan0     DOWN  7   ETHER   Yes     52

# ifconfig lan0
lan0: flags=862<BROADCAST,NOTRAILERS,RUNNING>
# ifconfig lan3
lan3: flags=863<UP,BROADCAST,NOTRAILERS,RUNNING>
         inet 54.25.14.4 netmask ffffff00 broadcast 54.25.14.255
```

The lanscan output shows that three interfaces are present in the system. However, the Net-Interface State field shows that only one is connected to a network.

9.3   Supported Protocols and Products

HP-UX supports the following link-level and higher-level protocols:

- *Ethernet:* Ethernet is a bus network using the access method Carrier-Sense, Multiple Access with Collision Detection (CSMA/CD). Both the variants, Ethernet LAN and IEEE 802.3 LAN, are supported simultaneously. Speed is 10 Mbits/s.

- *Fast Ethernet:* There are two industry standards for Fast Ethernet. HP has adopted the 100VG-AnyLAN standard; the corresponding standard is IEEE 802.12. Speed is 100 Mbits/s. 100VG-AnyLAN has support for setting a higher priority for time-critical applications.

- *Token Ring:* Adheres to the IEEE 802.5 standard. Speed is 16 Mbits/s.

- *FDDI:* Adheres to the ANSI X3T9.5 standard. Speed is 100 Mbits/s.

- *Fiber Channel:* Corresponding standard is ANSI X3T9.3. Speed is 266 Mbits/s.

- *X.25:* Packet switch networks.

- *SNA:* An HP-UX system can act as a PU type 2.1 on an SNA network. LU6.2 application programming interface, 3270 and 3179G terminal emulation, and RJE are supported. The SNA transport will run over X.25 or Token Ring links.

- *Point-to-point connections:* These are Serial Line IP (SLIP) connections. Note that at this time, point-to-point protocol (PPP) is not supported on HP-UX.

- *OSI:* The OSI transport is OTS. Application layer support includes X.400 and FTAM. The transport runs over X.25 or Token Ring links.

TCP/IP can run over any link mentioned above.

9.4   Networking Hardware

An HP-UX system networks with other systems via the following hardware and link-level software:

- *LAN/9000:* This is the Ethernet card and corresponding software. On most systems, Ethernet connectivity is built into the system and offered as a standard product. The interface is usually *lan0*.

- *Token Ring/9000:* The Token Ring card occupies a single-height slot.

- *FDDI/9000:* The FDDI card occupies a double-height slot. FDDI is not supported on the small E series servers.

- *X-25:* Can be run over a serial line interface. Software has to be installed.

- *Fiber Channel:* This card connects the system to a hardware device called a Fiber Channel Switch.

- *100VG-AnyLAN:* This card connects the system to a 100VG-AnyLAN hub. Both standard and Fast Ethernet speeds are supported.

- *SLIP:* This is a serial line interface. The software is bundled with the operating system.

- *SDLC link:* Allows SNA connectivity. The transport runs over an X.25 or Token Ring card. Typically, an HP-UX system is on the same Token Ring as an IBM mainframe network. The HP-UX system behaves as a PU2.1 node. For mainframe access, other Unix systems access the HP-UX PU2.1 system via Token Ring, Ethernet, or other network connections.

9.5   Configuring an Ethernet, Token Ring, or FDDI Card

Most systems have one or more of the three interfaces: Ethernet, Token Ring, and FDDI. The hardware and software are called LAN/9000, Token Ring/9000, and FDDI/9000 correspondingly. They are very similar to install and configure. The basic steps are:

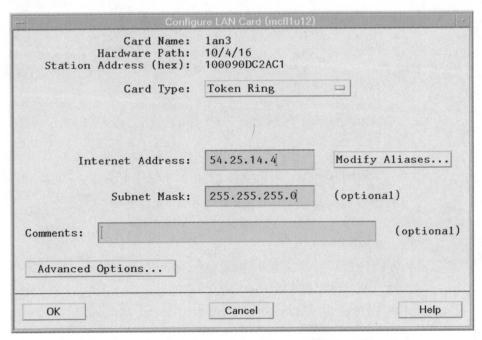

Figure 9.2 Sample SAM window for Ethernet, Token Ring, and FDDI configurations.

- Install the software using the *swinstall* command.
- Check whether the kernel, /stand/vmunix, has the device drivers configured. For Ethernet, the drivers are *lan0, lan1, lan2, lan3*; for Token Ring, the drivers are *token2*; for FDDI, the driver is *fddi*.
- Shut down the system and install the LAN card. When the card is properly installed and connected to an appropriate network, the LED on the card will be lit. If the LED is blinking, the hardware is not properly set up.
- Reboot the system and configure the card using SAM. Select the Networking and Communications area and then, when a subwindow with icons shows up, select Networking Interface Cards. Choose a card and select the *configure* action. Fill in appropriate information. An example screen to be filled out is show in Fig. 9.2. Two key fields must be entered: the Internet Address and the Subnet Mask. The installation process creates an IP name and address entry in /etc/hosts; if DNS is being used, the name server databases will have to be updated outside SAM.

9.5.1 Configuration details and system startup commands

When SAM configures the network interface card, it performs the following tasks:

- Device special files are created. The *insf* command is more convenient than the *mknod* command. Assume a device instance of 2 (which can be displayed with the lanscan command). For Ethernet, the files are /dev/lan2 and /dev/ether2; for Token Ring, the file is /dev/lan2; and for FDDI, the file is /dev/lan2. The *lssf* command displays details about the interfaces.

```
# lssf lan*
lan2 card instance 0 ieee at address 10/12/6 lan0
fddi card instance 1 ieee at address 10/4/12 lan1
fddi card instance 2 ieee at address 10/16/4 lan2
token2 card instance 3 ieee at address 10/4/16 lan3
# lssf ether*
lan2 card instance 0 ether at address 10/12/6 ether0
```

- One system startup file is created or updated: /etc/rc.config.d/netconf. This contains entries like

```
INTERFACE_NAME[0]=lan3
IP_ADDRESS[0]="54.25.14.4"
SUBNET_MASK[0]="255.255.255.0"
BROADCAST_ADDRESS[0]="54.25.14.255"
LANCONFIG_ARGS[0]=""
#
ROUTE_DESTINATION[0]="default"
ROUTE_MASK[0]=""
ROUTE_GATEWAY[0]="54.25.14.1"
ROUTE_COUNT[0]="1"
ROUTE_ARGS[0]=""
```

- Another startup file contains interface-specific information. It is one of /etc/rc.config.d/hpetherconf, /etc/rc.config.d/hptokenconf, and /etc/rc.config.d/hpfddiconf. These contain entries like these for two FDDI interface cards:

```
HP_FDDI_INTERFACE_NAME[0]=lan2
HP_FDDI_STATION_ADDRESS[0]=0x080009C43344
HP_FDDI_MTU[0]=4352
# The HP_FDDI_INIT_ARGS are reserved by HP. They are NOT user changable.
HP_FDDI_INIT_ARGS="HP_FDDI_STATION_ADDRESS HP_FDDI_MTU"
HP_FDDI_INTERFACE_NAME[1]=lan1
HP_FDDI_STATION_ADDRESS[1]=0x080009C41364
HP_FDDI_MTU[1]=4352
```

Once these tasks are performed by SAM, the system executes commands like these during a reboot:

```
# /sbin/init.d/hptoken start
# /sbin/init.d/net start
```

The two scripts pick up parameters from /etc/rc.config.d/hptokenconf and /etc/rc.config.d/netconf and apply them to the *ifconfig, route, lan_admin,* and *lanconfig* commands.

9.6   Troubleshooting Tips: lanscan, linkloop, lanadmin, netstat, and ping

- If a card is physically installed, the lanscan command will display information about it.

- Link-level loopback testing can be done by the linkloop command. The input is the station address of a local card or a card on another system on the LAN. The network management ID number is also required. The information can be displayed using lanscan. A sample use is

```
# linkloop -i 5 0x100090abd33b
-- OK
```

- Network-level connectivity can be tested using the *ping* command.

- The ifconfig command displays valuable information:

```
# ifconfig lan3
lan3: flags=863<UP,BROADCAST,NOTRAILERS,RUNNING>
        inet 65.33.27.6 netmask ffffff00 broadcast 65.33.27.255
```

FDDI has additional commands, *fddiinit, fddiinet, fddisetup, fddistat,* and *fddistop,* which should be studied. The lanadmin command displays interesting statistics on the card:

```
# lanadmin
            LOCAL AREA NETWORK ONLINE ADMINISTRATION, Version 1.0
                    Tue , Nov 7,1995 20:43:11
              Copyright 1994 Hewlett Packard Company.
                    All rights are reserved.

Test Selection mode.
          lan      = LAN Interface Administration
          menu     = Display this menu
          quit     = Terminate the Administration
          terse    = Do not display command menu
          verbose  = Display command menu

Enter command: lan

LAN Interface test mode. LAN Interface Net Mgmt ID = 4
          clear    = Clear statistics registers
          display  = Display LAN Interface status and statistics registers
          end      = End LAN Interface Administration, return to Test Selection
          menu     = Display this menu
          nmid     = Network Management ID of the LAN Interface
          quit     = Terminate the Administration, return to shell
          reset    = Reset LAN Interface to execute its selftest

Enter command: nmid

Enter Network Management ID.  Currently 4: 5

LAN Interface test mode. LAN Interface Net Mgmt ID = 5
          clear    = Clear statistics registers
          display  = Display LAN Interface status and statistics registers
          end      = End LAN Interface Administration, return to Test Selection
```

```
       menu     = Display this menu
       nmid     = Network Management ID of the LAN Interface
       quit     = Terminate the Administration, return to shell
       reset    = Reset LAN Interface to execute its selftest

Enter command: display

                    LAN INTERFACE STATUS DISPLAY
                     Tue , Nov 7,1995 20:43:22
Network Management ID              = 5
Description                        = lan3 Hewlett-Packard LAN Interface Hw Rev64
Fw rev 24448
Type (value)                       = iso88025-tokenRing(9)
MTU Size                           = 4170
Speed                              = 16000000
Station Address                    = 0x100090dc2ac1
Administration Status (value)      = up(1)
Operation Status (value)           = up(1)
Last Change                        = 12021
Inbound Octets                     = 529557544
Inbound Unicast Packets            = 1720033
Inbound Non-Unicast Packets        = 365909
Inbound Discards                   = 2925461
Inbound Errors                     = 0
Inbound Unknown Protocols          = 0
Outbound Octets                    = 461121427
Outbound Unicast Packets           = 1879324
Outbound Non-Unicast Packets       = 98132
Outbound Discards                  = 0
Outbound Errors                    = 0
Outbound Queue Length              = 0
Specific                           = 655369


Token Ring-like Functional Group
Index                              = 5
Commands                           = 1
Ring Status                        = 0
Ring State                         = 1
Ring Open Status                   = 11
Ring Speed                         = 4
Up Stream Node Address             = 0x000000000000
Active Monitor Participation       = 1
Functional Address Mask            = 0xc00000000000


Token Ring-like Statistics Group
Index                              = 5
Line Errors                        = 1
Burst Errors                       = 29
AC Errors                          = 0
Abort Transmission Errors          = 0
Internal Errors                    = 0
Lost Frame Errors                  = 0
Receive Congestions                = 0
Frame Copied Errors                = 0
Token Errors                       = 127
Soft Errors                        = 0
Hard Errors                        = 0
Signal Loss                        = 0
Transmit Beacons                   = 0
Ring Recovery                      = 0
Lobe Wire Faults                   = 0
Remove Station                     = 0
Single Station on Ring             = 0
Frequency Errors                   = 0
```

9.7   NetTL: Network Tracing and Logging

The NetTL subsystem is a tool for capturing network packets, events, and states. Logging sends the information to a file, and tracing allows snapshots to be studied. NetTL is a powerful troubleshooting tool particularly helpful when there are insidious network problems.

9.7.1   nettl: Logging network information

Logging is started by

```
# /usr/sbin/nettl  -start
```

The command can be run automatically at system startup by entering NETTL = 1 in /etc/rc.config.d/nettl. The command initializes the logging and tracing facility and starts logging binary information to the file /var/adm/nettl.LOG00. The file nettl.Log00 has a maximum size, determined in nettlgen.conf, and if it is full, messages are logged to nettl.LOG01. The two files are used alternately. The nettl -status command displays information on whether the subsystem is up, and on log files, logged networking components, and so on.

What information will be logged in nettl.LOG00 is determined by /etc/nettl-gen.conf. The *nettlconf* command should be used to change contents of this file. nettl.LOG00 also determines whether messages are sent to the console. The configuration in /etc/nettlgen.conf can be seen in the following:

```
# nettlgenconf -status
========== LOG CONFIGURATION ==========
Start by startup script : Yes
Console logging         : Yes
Log port size           : 8 Kbytes
Maximum log file space  : 1000 Kbytes
Log file                : /var/adm/nettl.LOG00
Console log option file : /var/adm/conslog.opts

========== SUBSYSTEM CONFIGURATION ==========

ID    NAME               LOG CLASS    GROUP NAME
----  ----------------   ---------    ------------------------------
   0  NS_LS_LOGGING      D E          ARPA/9000 NETWORKING
   1  NS_LS_NFT          D E          ARPA/9000 NETWORKING
   2  NS_LS_LOOPBACK     D E          ARPA/9000 NETWORKING
   3  NS_LS_NI           D E          ARPA/9000 NETWORKING
   4  NS_LS_IPC          D E          ARPA/9000 NETWORKING
   5  NS_LS_SOCKREGD     D E          ARPA/9000 NETWORKING
   6  NS_LS_TCP          D E          ARPA/9000 NETWORKING
   7  NS_LS_PXP          D E          ARPA/9000 NETWORKING
   8  NS_LS_UDP          D E          ARPA/9000 NETWORKING
   9  NS_LS_IP           D E          ARPA/9000 NETWORKING
  10  NS_LS_PROBE        D E          ARPA/9000 NETWORKING
  11  NS_LS_DRIVER       D E          LAN/9000 NETWORKING
  12  NS_LS_RLBD         D E          ARPA/9000 NETWORKING
  13  NS_LS_BUFS         D E          ARPA/9000 NETWORKING
  14  NS_LS_CASE21       D E          ARPA/9000 NETWORKING
  15  NS_LS_ROUTER21     D E          ARPA/9000 NETWORKING
  16  NS_LS_NFS          D E          ARPA/9000 NETWORKING
  17  NS_LS_NETISR       D E          ARPA/9000 NETWORKING
```

```
 19 NS_LS_NSE        D E        ARPA/9000 NETWORKING
 20 NS_LS_STRLOG     D E        ARPA/9000 NETWORKING
 21 NS_LS_TIRDWR     D E        ARPA/9000 NETWORKING
 22 NS_LS_TIMOD      D E        ARPA/9000 NETWORKING
 23 NS_LS_ICMP       D E        ARPA/9000 NETWORKING
 26 FILTER           D E        ARPA/9000 NETWORKING
 27 NAME             D E        ARPA/9000 NETWORKING
 29 NS_LS_IGMP       D E        ARPA/9000 NETWORKING
 31 TOKEN            D E        TOKEN RING/9000 Networking
127 FORMATTER        D E        FORMATTER
129 STREAMS          D E        STREAMS/UX

LOG CLASS:  (D)isaster, (E)rror, (W)arning, (I)nformative
```

Note the following regarding logging:

- Console logging is an option in etc/nettlconf. Obviously, all messages logged should not be sent to the console. The file /var/adm/conslog.opts is a filter file which determines what subset of messages are sent to the console.

- The log class indicates what level of messages are logged. In the example, disaster and error messages are logged; warning and informative messages are not logged.

- The subsystem IDs and names are determined by convention. Programmers logging information by means of NetTL can use arbitrary unused IDs and names for their specific networking components.

9.7.2   netfmt: Reporting on logged network information

The netfmt command is used to format and display the binary data in nettl log or trace files. The binary file must be specified with the -f option. Here are two example uses of the command; one shows the status of the binary log file, and the other displays some messages from the log file:

```
# netfmt -s -f/var/adm/nettl.LOG00 # log file status
============================= LOG File Summary =============================
          Node: mcf11u15
          HP-UX Version: B.10.01 B    Machine Type: 9000/829

          Total number of messages: 79
          Messages dropped: 0              Data dropped(bytes): 0
          First Message                    Last Message
                  Time: 10:39:42.200102        Time: 15:22:00.720146
                  Date: 10/11/95               Date: 11/08/95
          Message distribution:
                  Disaster:      78                  Error:        1
                  Warning:        0            Informative:        0
          ~~~~~~~~~~~~Message distribution by Subsystem~~~~~~~~~~~~
          Subsystem Name: NS_LS_PROBE       Group Name: ARPA/9000 NETWORKING
                  Disaster:       0                  Error:        1
                  Warning:        0            Informative:        0
          Subsystem Name: NS_LS_DRIVER      Group Name: LAN/9000 NETWORKING
                  Disaster:      75                  Error:        0
                  Warning:        0            Informative:        0
          Subsystem Name: TOKEN             Group Name: TOKEN RING/9000 Netw
                  Disaster:       3                  Error:        0
                  Warning:        0            Informative:        0
```

```
# netfmt -t 3 -f/var/adm/nettl.LOG00 # display last 3 message

***************************LAN/9000 NETWORKING**************************@#%
   Timestamp              : Wed Oct 11 EDT 1995 10:39:42.200102
   Process ID             : 5              Subsystem      : NS_LS_DRIVER
   User ID ( UID )        : 0              Log Class      : DISASTER
   Device ID              : -1                  Path ID    : 0
   Connection ID          : 0             Log Instance    : 0
   Location               : 01027
   ~~~~~~~~~~~~~~~~~~~~~~~~~~~~~~~~~~~~~~~~~~~~~~~~~~~~~~~~~~~~~~~~~~~~~~~~~~
Network NS_LS_DRIVER Disaster 1027, pid 5
   82596 failed to pass its internal loopback test.


**************************TOKEN RING/9000 Networking********************@#%
   Timestamp              : Mon Oct 16 EDT 1995 13:17:23.183887
   Process ID             : [ICS]          Subsystem      : TOKEN
   User ID ( UID )        : -1             Log Class      : DISASTER
   Device ID              : 1                   Path ID    : 0
   Connection ID          : 0             Log Instance    : 0
   ~~~~~~~~~~~~~~~~~~~~~~~~~~~~~~~~~~~~~~~~~~~~~~~~~~~~~~~~~~~~~~~~~~~~~~~~~~
<2305> Token Ring driver has detected a lobe wire fault or deinserted
       from the ring on interface unit <1>.


**************************TOKEN RING/9000 Networking********************@#%
   Timestamp              : Mon Oct 16 EDT 1995 13:21:41.074690
   Process ID             : [ICS]          Subsystem      : TOKEN
   User ID ( UID )        : -1             Log Class      : DISASTER
   Device ID              : 1                   Path ID    : 0
   Connection ID          : 0             Log Instance    : 0
   ~~~~~~~~~~~~~~~~~~~~~~~~~~~~~~~~~~~~~~~~~~~~~~~~~~~~~~~~~~~~~~~~~~~~~~~~~~
<2305> Token Ring driver has detected a lobe wire fault or deinserted
       from the ring on interface unit <1>.
```

A filter file can be specified to display specific message types. Filter specifications are put in a file and the file is specified with the -c option to netfmt.
An example filter file is

```
formatter filter subsystem      TOKEN
formatter filter time_from      2/18/96
formatter filter time_through  3/15/96
```

When the command

```
# netfmt -c filterfile -f /var/adm/nettl.LOG00
```

is entered, the only messages displayed will be those that were logged
between February 18, 1996, and March 15, 1996, and are part of the Token
Ring subsystem. Other filters are described in the netfmt man pages.

9.7.3 Tracing

In troubleshooting specific network problems—for example, a network card
malfunction—the logged information may not be sufficient. In particular, contents of packets may have to be dumped; however, they are not logged. Rather
than permanently enabling extensive logging for the subsystem related to the

card, tracing can be enabled to collect binary data on the card. Tracing can be disabled after resolving the problem. Tracing is started with the *traceon* option to nettl. The following command starts tracing on the TOKEN subsystem and sends trace output to the file toktmp.TRC0:

```
# nettl -entity TOKEN -traceon all -f toktmp
```

The *all* parameter to traceon captures all possible information including packet data and protocol headers. The .TRC0 file will fill up fast if any Token Ring interface on the system is in use. If the file fills up, binary data is sent to .TRC1 (the process is similar to the way information is sent to the logging files .LOG00 and .LOG01).

The netfmt command can be used to format and display contents of the binary trace file:

```
# netfmt -f toktmp.TRC0

vvvvvvvvvvvvvvvvvvvvvvvvvvvTOKEN RING/9000 Networkingvvvvvvvvvvvvvvvvvvvvvvvvvv@#%
Timestamp              : Sun Nov 12 EST 1995 11:08:33.481905
  Process ID           : [ICS]              Subsystem        : TOKEN
  User ID ( UID )      : -1                 Trace Kind       : PDU IN TRACE
  Device ID            : 1                  Path ID          : -1
  Connection ID        : 0
  Location             : 00123
~~~~~~~~~~~~~~~~~~~~~~~~~~~~~~~~~~~~~~~~~~~~~~~~~~~~~~~~~~~~~~~~~~~~~~~~~~~~~~~~~~
Received 62 bytes via 802.5 Sun Nov 12 11:08:33.048190 EST 1995
        pid=[ICS]    interface=[lan1]
        Dest: 10-00-90-cb-d4-4a  Source: 00-00-30-ac-a2-02   AC: 18  FC: 40
  14: aa aa 03 00 00 00 08 00 45 00 00 28 dd 3a 00 00   ........E..(.:..
  30: 3e 06 22 47 36 19 03 17 36 19 0e 06 02 01 03 f6   >."G6...6.......
  46: 14 3c 5e 13 07 91 80 95 50 10 04 00 2e 19 00 00   .<^.....P.......

vvvvvvvvvvvvvvvvvvvvvvvvvvvvTOKEN RING/9000 Networkingvvvvvvvvvvvvvvvvvvvvvvvvvv@#%
Timestamp              : Sun Nov 12 EST 1995 11:08:35.418830
  Process ID           : 28169              Subsystem        : TOKEN
  User ID ( UID )      : 0                  Trace Kind       : PDU OUT TRACE
  Device ID            : 1                  Path ID          : -1
  Connection ID        : 0
  Location             : 00123
~~~~~~~~~~~~~~~~~~~~~~~~~~~~~~~~~~~~~~~~~~~~~~~~~~~~~~~~~~~~~~~~~~~~~~~~~~~~~~~~~~
Transmitted 142 bytes via 802.5 Sun Nov 12 11:08:35.041883 EST 1995
        pid=28169    interface=[lan1]
        Dest: 00-00-30-ac-a2-02  Source: 00-00-00-00-00-00   AC: xx  FC: 40
  14: aa aa 03 00 00 00 08 00 45 00 00 78 7b 1d 40 00   ........E..x{.@.
  30: 40 06 3a 00 36 19 0e 06 36 19 0b 2b 10 5a 17 71   @.:.6...6..+.Z.q
  46: 28 13 24 b1 9e 02 9d f2 50 18 80 00 70 9a 00 00   (.$.....P...p...
  62: 38 01 00 05 00 80 00 0d 00 00 00 0c 00 00 00 11   8..............
  78: 00 00 00 0d 4c 01 00 05 00 80 00 1c 00 80 00 0d   ....L..........
  94: 00 02 01 c6 20 02 00 15 4c 01 00 05 00 80 00 1c   .... ...L.......
 110: 00 80 00 0d 00 02 01 c6 23 0b 00 13 4c 01 00 05   ........#...L...
 126: 00 80 00 1c 00 80 00 0d 00 0d 01 c6 20 02 00 15   ............ ...
```

If the -F option is specified, as in

```
# netfmt -F -f toktmp.TRC0
```

netfmt keeps the trace file open and displays events as they are logged to the file. Effectively, this allows monitoring in real time. Tracing data collection can be stopped by

```
# nettl -entity TOKEN -traceoff
```

9.7.4 nettladm: Screen-oriented logging and tracing

Most of the NetTL subsystem commands shown so far can be performed via the point-and-click nettladm interface. An X-window display or a character mode terminal like hpterm or VT100 is required. The startup command is

```
# /opt/nettladm/bin/nettladm
```

Figure 9.3 is the initial nettladm screen. Menu options allow looking at status information, stopping logging, modifying trace options, and so on. Although nettladm is convenient to use, a good understanding of underlying commands and operations helps in troubleshooting network problems.

9.8 TCP/IP Functionality

Components of the TCP/IP slew of commands and features which are supported in basic HP-UX are briefly discussed here. Section 9.10 considers configuration issues relevant to these products.

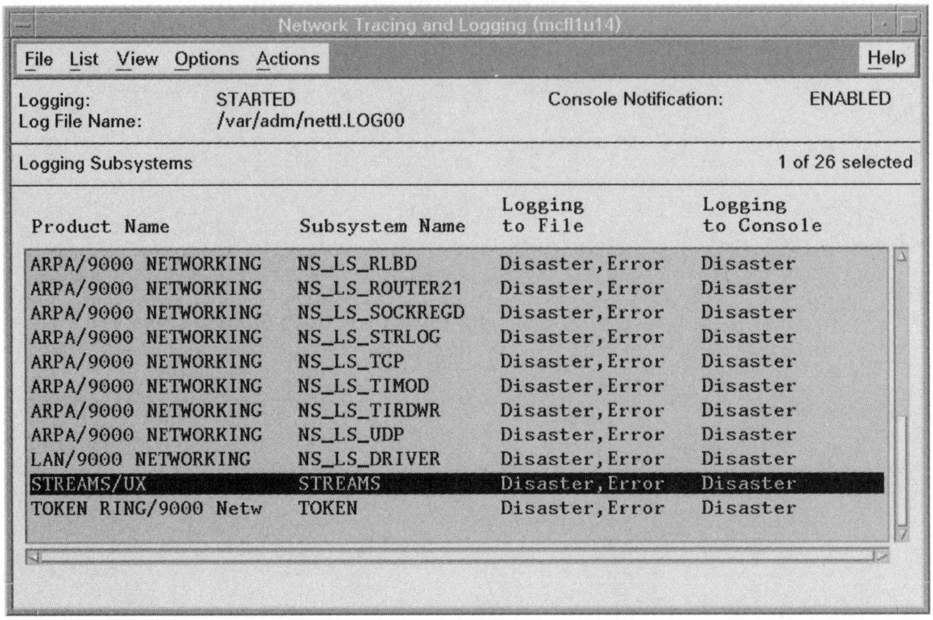

		Network Tracing and Logging (mcfl1u14)		

File List View Options Actions   Help

Logging: STARTED   Console Notification: ENABLED
Log File Name: /var/adm/nettl.LOG00

Logging Subsystems   1 of 26 selected

Product Name	Subsystem Name	Logging to File	Logging to Console
ARPA/9000 NETWORKING	NS_LS_RLBD	Disaster,Error	Disaster
ARPA/9000 NETWORKING	NS_LS_ROUTER21	Disaster,Error	Disaster
ARPA/9000 NETWORKING	NS_LS_SOCKREGD	Disaster,Error	Disaster
ARPA/9000 NETWORKING	NS_LS_STRLOG	Disaster,Error	Disaster
ARPA/9000 NETWORKING	NS_LS_TCP	Disaster,Error	Disaster
ARPA/9000 NETWORKING	NS_LS_TIMOD	Disaster,Error	Disaster
ARPA/9000 NETWORKING	NS_LS_TIRDWR	Disaster,Error	Disaster
ARPA/9000 NETWORKING	NS_LS_UDP	Disaster,Error	Disaster
LAN/9000 NETWORKING	NS_LS_DRIVER	Disaster,Error	Disaster
STREAMS/UX	STREAMS	Disaster,Error	Disaster
TOKEN RING/9000 Netw	TOKEN	Disaster,Error	Disaster

Figure 9.3 Network troubleshooting with nettladm: initial window.

9.8.1   telnet

telnet is used to log into another system on the network. A sample session is

```
$ telnet hpnode
Trying...
Connected to hpnode.mycomp.com.
Escape character is '^]'.
Local flow control on
Telnet TERMINAL-SPEED option ON

HP-UX mynode B.10.01 B 9000/819 (ttyp1)

login: p544jns
Password:
Last    successful login for p544jns: Sun Nov 12 16:41:05 GMT 1995 on ttyp1
Last unsuccessful login for p544jns: Thu Nov 9 21:59:55 GMT 1995 on ttyp2
Please wait...checking for disk quotas
(c)Copyright 1983-1995 Hewlett-Packard Co., All Rights Reserved.
(c)Copyright 1979, 1980, 1983, 1985-1993 The Regents of the Univ. of
California
...
  (c)Copyright 1988 Carnegie Mellon University

                    RESTRICTED RIGHTS LEGEND
Use, duplication, or disclosure by the U.S. Government is subject to
restrictions as set forth in sub-paragraph (c)(1)(ii) of the Rights in
Technical Data and Computer Software clause in DFARS 252.227-7013.


                    Hewlett-Packard Company
                    3000 Hanover Street
                    Palo Alto, CA 94304 U.S.A.

Rights for non-DOD U.S. Government Departments and Agencies are as set
forth in FAR 52.227-19(c)(1,2).

THIS IS A RESTRICTED COMPUTER. ANYONE GAINING
UNAUTHORIZED ACCESS WILL BE SUBJECT TO PROSECUTION

$
$logout
Connection closed by foreign host.
```

9.8.2   rlogin

rlogin is another TCP/IP command for logging into another system on the network. Unlike telnet, it has a mechanism, described in Sec. 9.10.2, whereby a login name and password do not have to be entered.

9.8.3   FTP: File Transfer Protocol

The File Transfer Protocol is used to transfer one or more files to or from the current system from or to another system on the network. A sample session is

```
$ ftp
ftp> open othernode
Connected to othernode.comp.com.
```

```
220 othernode FTP server (Version 1.7.19.1 Mon Apr 17 20:14:33 GMT 1995)
ready.
Name (othernode:p544jns):
331 Password required for p544jns.
Password:
230 User p544jns logged in.
Remote system type is UNIX.
Using binary mode to transfer files.
ftp> ls #      list files in home directory of othernode
200 PORT command successful.
150 Opening ASCII mode data connection for /usr/bin/ls.
total 1378
-r--r--r--   1 p544jns  users       446 Nov  9 11:52 .profile
-rw-------   1 p544jns  users       918 Nov 12 12:29 .sh_history
-rw-rw-rw-   1 root     sys      650922 Nov  9 11:53 allfiles
-rw-r--r--   1 root     sys        1366 Nov 10 14:30 tmp
-rw-------   1 p544jns  users      3973 Nov  9 13:25 tmptest
226 Transfer complete.
ftp> get tmp    # copy a file from othernode to current system
200 PORT command successful.
150 Opening BINARY mode data connection for tmp (1366 bytes).
226 Transfer complete.
1366 bytes received in 0.00 seconds (1357.05 Kbytes/s)
ftp> put tlog tmplog   # copy tlog on current node as file tmplog on othernode
200 PORT command successful.
150 Opening BINARY mode data connection for tmpb.
226 Transfer complete.
50066 bytes sent in 0.02 seconds (2488.78 Kbytes/s)
ftp> quit
221 Goodbye.
$
```

9.8.4 rcp

The *rcp* command is also used to transfer one or more files to or from the current system from or to another system on the network. The other system must trust your ID on the current node. This is elaborated on in Section 9.10.2. An example use of rcp is

```
# rcp tlog othernode:tmplog      Copy tlog from current node as file tmplog on othernode.
```

rcp is more convenient than ftp in command files. rcp also allows complete directory trees to be copied from one system to another. However, ftp has more options and is more secure.

9.8.5 remsh

The *remsh* command is used to execute a shell command on another system on the network. The other system must trust your ID on the current node. This too is elaborated on in Section 9.10.2. An example use of remsh is

```
# remsh othernode ls -a
.profile
allfiles
tmp
tmplog
```

9.8.6   rexec

The *rexec* command is also used to execute a shell command on another system on the network. The command differs from remsh in that a password must be entered. At many sites, remsh is disabled for security reasons; rexec can be used as a replacement.

9.8.7   rwho

The *usr/bin/rwho* command displays information on all users logged on all systems in the local network. The command output is like that of *who,* except that the node name is also displayed for each user. The rwhod daemon must be running on all the systems.

9.8.8   ruptime

The */usr/bin/ruptime* command displays uptime information on all systems in the local area network. The command output is like that of *uptime* except that a node name is also displayed. The rwhod daemon must be running on all the systems. A single line of the output may look like

```
nodepqr    up    14:23,    3 users,    load 0.10, 0.26, 0.12
```

9.8.9   finger

The *finger* command displays information on users logged on current or other systems. An example use is

```
$ finger p544jns@nodepqr
Login name: p544jns    (messages off) In real life: Shah Jay
Bldg: secaucus, Work phone: 222-333-4444
Directory: /home/p544jns              Shell: /usr/bin/sh
On since Nov 12 09:48:22 on ttyp2 from hpnode:1:0
No Plan.
```

The information is for user p544jns logged on node nodepqr. The form

```
$ finger @nodepqr
```

displays summary information on all logins on node nodepqr. The fingerd daemon must be running on the remote systems. Many system administrators do not run the daemon because of security concerns.

9.8.10   sendmail

sendmail is the mail subsystem on most Unix installations. It handles mail on the local system and with other systems on the network. Users access their messages by using a mail agent like *elm, mailx,* or *mail.* The default sendmail setup on HP-UX runs adequately for most installations; however, sendmail can be extensively customized. sendmail administration is not discussed in this book.

9.8.11   Domain Name Service (DNS) or BIND

DNS, also known as BIND, is basically a TCP/IP name and address lookup mechanism. Another node on the network can always be referred to by its IP address, as in

```
$ telnet 23.54.1.65
```

It is more convenient if the nodes have a mnemonic name. Names and addresses can be stored in /etc/hosts. A telnet command may then look like:

```
$ telnet  nodepqr
```

The telnet program issues a name-to-address translate call to the local system, which looks up the name in the /etc/hosts file, retrieves the network address, and returns it to telnet. This works very well in a small network; when there are many nodes on the network, maintaining all the /etc/hosts files—especially, maintaining consistency—can be a chore. DNS is a mechanism whereby maintaining the node name and network address information is centralized. If a node maintains a DNS database, other nodes can refer to this database. This way, when there are network changes, only one file needs to be updated. DNS configuration is described in many books on the market.

9.8.12   ntp: Network Time Protocol

The Network Time Protocol is used to synchronize all the systems on the network. The *xntpd* daemon continuously and automatically updates current system time by polling time servers specified in /etc/ntp.conf. If the daemon is not running, time can be also be set by *ntpdate,* which polls time servers once and sets the local time. *ntpdate* can be used in a cron job which runs, for example, every day.

9.8.13   route, arp, and gated

What happens when you issue a telnet to a host that is not defined in the route tables on the local system? If the IP address for a destination node is unknown, the system sends out a broadcast request on the local network asking for the node that has the address to return its Ethernet, Token Ring, or other hardware address. The protocol used for this step of IP-to-hardware address translation is the Address Resolution Protocol (arp). If a node responds with its hardware address, the local node keeps this in a location called the *arp cache*. The system uses the arp cache to translate IP addresses to hardware addresses. Once the hardware address for a node is known, packets are sent to the node by supplying the hardware address as the destination address. The arp cache can be inspected by *arp -A*.

If the destination node is in the local network, the above procedure works. What if the destination node is on a wide-area network? For example, the node can be on a network that is connected to a router connected in turn to the local network. In this case, the arp technique is not used, because, potentially, the broadcast request can travel over many networks around the world and the destination node may not exist. A route to the destination node must be specified in the routing tables of the local node. For example, if the local area network is connected to a router that is in turn connected to other networks, a route to the router can be added as

```
# /usr/sbin/route add destnode router
```

Now all packets for the destination node are sent to the router, which in turn will have routing table entries to forward the packet appropriately. Such a router is also known as a *gateway.* Adding routes this way requires that all nodes that will be accessed by the current node be defined in the route table. This can be tedious. A solution is provided: if the destination node is specified as the word *default,* all packets for unknown destinations are sent to the router:

```
# route add default router
```

A route entry can be removed with a command like

```
# route delete destnode router
```

The routing table can be displayed using the netstat command with the -r option:

```
# netstat -r
Routing tables
Destination     Gateway         Flags  Refs      Use  Interface  Pmtu PmtuTime
node1.comp.com  localhost       UH        9   220667  lo0        4608
hp324.tmp.com   routr.comp.com  UGHD      0        4  lan1       4170
aws.pop.org     routr.comp.com  UGHD      0     2957  lan1       4170
localhost       localhost       UH        0       68  lo0        4608
default         routr.comp.com  UG       22  1997266  lan1       4170
34.25.11        34.25.11.99     U         0       63  lan0       1500
34.25.14        node1.comp.com  U         1  3272287  lan1       4170
```

Note the following points regarding the routing table:

- Current node is node1. It has two interfaces, lan0 and lan1. It is connected to two local networks, 34.25.11 and 34.25.14. A router (routr) on one of the local networks is connected to other networks. node1 uses the router for all destinations not on the local network.

- The flags are:

  U: Route to a local network directly from the local node

UH: Route to a remote host directly through the local network. Destination is on LAN.

- *UG or UGH:*   Route to a remote host via the gateway (router).

- *UGHD:*   Nodes discovered by the router.

The router mentioned above is the gateway to other nodes not on the local network. The gateway could be a hardware device like, for example, a CISCO router; or it could be another HP-UX system. The hardware router can be configured on the basis of manufacturer-supplied information. The HP-UX system must also be configured using the Unix-standard *gated* mechanism. The gated daemon performs routing from one network to another. It supports a number of routing protocols, such as RIP, BGP, EGP, HELLO, and OSPF. gated uses configuration information from /etc/gated.conf. Configuring an HP-UX system as a gateway basically requires proper setup of gated.conf. The *gdc* command has options to manipulate gated.conf and the gated daemon. *gated* replaces older routing programs like *routed* and *egpup*.

9.8.14   ping

ping is typically used to

- Determine if a node is reachable.

- Determine round-trip packet time to a node.

- Determine intermediate nodes (the route) a packet passes through before reaching a destination node. The -o qualifier is used for this.

Here are two sample pings from a local system, mynode, to another system, nodepqr. The pings were stopped by ctrl-c.

```
# ping nodepqr
PING nodepqr.acme.com: 64 byte packets
64 bytes from 54.25.47.27: icmp_seq=0. time=7. ms
64 bytes from 54.25.47.27: icmp_seq=1. time=7. ms
64 bytes from 54.25.47.27: icmp_seq=2. time=7. ms
64 bytes from 54.25.47.27: icmp_seq=3. time=7. ms
(ctrl-c)
----nodepqr.acme.com PING Statistics----
4 packets transmitted, 4 packets received, 0% packet loss
round-trip (ms) min/avg/max=7/7/7
#
# ping -o nodepqr
PING nodepqr.acme.com: 64 byte packets
64 bytes from 54.25.47.27: icmp_seq=0. time=10. ms
64 bytes from 54.25.47.27: icmp_seq=1. time=10. ms
64 bytes from 54.25.47.27: icmp_seq=2. time=11. ms
64 bytes from 54.25.47.27: icmp_seq=3. time=10. ms
64 bytes from 54.25.47.27: icmp_seq=4. time=10. ms
(ctrl-c)
----nodepqr.acme.com PING Statistics----
5 packets transmitted, 5 packets received, 0% packet loss
round-trip (ms)  min/avg/max=10/10/11
5 packets sent via:
```

```
       23.25.254.1      - routr1.acme.com
       34.23.47.1       - routr6.acme.com
       34.12.47.27      - nodepqr.acme.com
       23.11.254.2      - routr1.acme.com
       32.32.14.1       - routr3.acme.com
       32.14.14.6       - mynode.acme.com
  #
```

9.8.15   tftp and bootp

Small systems with little or no disk space can boot from a boot server on the local network. The small system will know its local hardware address (12 hex digits); however, it many not know its IP address or from which boot server it can load the operating system. The bootp protocol is used to get the necessary information, and then the tftp protocol is used by the small system to load the operating system.

The small system can send out a *bootpquery* broadcast on the local network. A boot server configured to recognize the hardware address will respond with the system's IP address and load file. The bootpquery command can be used to test this:

```
#/usr/sbin/bootpquery  02608c32ef2d
```

A response from nodepqr that can service a small system, clientbaby, might be:

```
Received BOOTREPLY from nodepqr (23.44.11.24)

Hardware Address:     02:60:8c:32:ef:2d
Hardware type:        ethernet
IP Address:           23.44.11.106
Boot file:            /export/tftpboot/clientbaby/stand/uxbootlf
```

How does nodepqr know it should respond to the bootpquery? The bootpd daemon must be running on nodepqr. The bootpd daemon reads /etc/bootptab for information on clients it will send information to. bootptab might have an entry like:

```
clientbaby: ht=ether: ha=02608c32ef2d: ip:23:44:11:106: \
            bf:/export/tftpboot/clientbaby/stand/uxbootlf
```

The bootpd daemon listens to bootp requests and sends a reply if a matching hardware address is found in one of the /etc/bootptab entries.

Once clientbaby gets the bootp reply, it knows which file to load and from what system (nodepqr, in this example). It then uses the trivial file transfer protocol (tftp), which is a stripped-down version of ftp. ftp is not used, because normally ftp requires a login name and password. Moreover, ftp has a lot of code that cannot be accommodated in a small system's nonvolatile memory or firmware. The client can load the load file by

```
tftp nodepqr
tftp> get /export/tftpboot/clientbaby/stand/uxbootlf
```

Note that any system on the local network can pull off files from nodepqr. Boot servers will typically allow only a certain set of files to be accessible via tftp. This is done by starting the tftpd daemon with a path name as in:

```
/usr/lbin/tftpd  /export/tftpboot
```

This will allow systems on the network to access any file under the tree /export/tftpboot; all other files will not be accessible via tftp. Note that the tftp directory tree should be write-protected from others, since the tftp put command can be used by a malicious user to change files.

9.9   IP Network Addressing

An IP address is a 4-byte integer. For convenience of notation, the addresses are referred to as n.n.n.n, where n represents one of the four bytes. Each interface has an address and an associated subnet (or network) mask. The mask determines whether a destination node is within the same network or in another. For example, if a node has the address 104.21.103.4 and a subnet mask of 255.255.255.0, all nodes 104.21.103.* are in the same network. Typically, nodes (actually, the interfaces) on the same LAN are configured to have the same subnet masks. Subnetting is required to determine routing; network identifiers, like 104.21.103, are used by networking software like the route command.

Within a subnet, all-zeros and all-ones addresses are reserved and cannot be assigned to interfaces.

9.10   TCP/IP Configuration Issues

9.10.1   inetd: The Internet superserver

ftp, telnet, bootp, and other TCP/IP applications accept connections from other systems on the network. They can do this by running a process that continuously monitors corresponding TCP/IP ports. These processes are called daemons. Rather than running all the daemons at system startup, only one daemon, inetd, is run. This may reduce the number of processes in the system and centralizes some configuration issues. The inetd daemon monitors ports and runs appropriate daemons when requests come in. inetd reads the file /etc/inetd.conf to determine commands to be executed for running the daemons. Here is an excerpted inetd.conf:

```
##
#
# @(#)inetd.conf $Revision: 1.21.111.1 $ $Date: 94/11/04 14:51:52 $
#
# Inetd reads its configuration information from this file upon execution
# and at some later time if it is reconfigured.
```

```
#
# A line in the configuration file has the following fields separated by
# tabs and/or spaces:
#
#         service name         as in /etc/services
#         socket type          either "stream" or "dgram"
#         protocol             as in /etc/protocols
#         wait/nowait          only applies to datagram sockets, stream
#                              sockets should specify nowait
#         user                 name of user as whom the server should run
#         server program       absolute pathname for the server inetd will
#                              execute
#         server program args. arguments server program uses as they normally
#                              are starting with argv[0] which is the name of
#                              the server.
##
ftp            stream tcp nowait root /usr/lbin/ftpd ftpd -l
telnet         stream tcp nowait root /usr/lbin/telnetd telnetd

# Before uncommenting the "tftp" entry below, please make sure
# that you have a "tftp" user in /etc/passwd. If you don't
# have one, please consult the tftpd(1M) manual entry for
# information about setting up this service.
#tftp          dgram  udp wait    root /usr/lbin/tftpd    tftpd
bootps         dgram  udp wait    root /usr/lbin/bootpd   bootpd
#finger        stream tcp nowait bin  /usr/lbin/fingerd fingerd
login          stream tcp nowait root /usr/lbin/rlogind rlogind
shell          stream tcp nowait root /usr/lbin/remshd   remshd
exec           stream tcp nowait root /usr/lbin/rexecd   rexecd
#uucp          stream tcp nowait root /usr/sbin/uucpd    uucpd

time           stream tcp nowait root internal
time           dgram  udp nowait root internal
echo           stream tcp nowait root internal
echo           dgram  udp nowait root internal
```

Note that entries like finger and tftp have been commented at the local site for security reasons. The -l option to ftpd is for logging events to the syslog facility.

9.10.2 The r-commands security bypass

As mentioned previously, rlogin, rcp, and remsh do not require a password to access another system, provided the other system is set up to trust the current system. This can be done in one of two ways:

- Create /etc/host.equiv on the other system and put entries in it like

```
node23      kathy
hpnodeq     +
```

   In the first case, a user with login name Kathy from system node 23 can issue r-commands on this system. In the second case, all users from node hpnodeq can log onto this system.

- A user can create an .rhosts file in his or her home directory on the remote node. Contents of these files will be similar to /etc/hosts.equiv contents.

The file /etc/hosts.equiv can be managed by the root user only; however, the .rhosts file can be created by individual users. A user can then compromise system security if, for example, he or she has access to confidential files and has an .rhosts entry allowing access to his or her account from any system. A privileged user on another system can create a suitable account on his or her system and then use rlogin to get into the other sensitive systems. That is why many sites do not allow .rhosts-based access. To disable access validation via .rhosts, the r-entries in /etc/inetd.conf should be modified to include the -l option as in this example:

```
login  stream tcp nowait root /usr/lbin/rlogind rlogind -l
```

9.10.3 /etc/services

Application daemons like ftpd and telnetd listen for incoming requests on previously defined (well-defined) ports on the network. Clients can access the application by specifying the node's IP address and the proper port number. While high-number ports can be used for custom network applications, the low-number ports are defined as a standard in /etc/services. A custom application using ports must have an entry in this file, since networking components perform lookups on this file. Excerpts from this file are:

```
# @(#)services $Revision: 1.26.111.4 $ $Date: 95/02/17 16:32:46 $
#
# This file associates official service names and aliases with
# the port number and protocol the services use.
#
# Some of the services represented below are not supported on HP-UX.
# They are provided solely as a reference.
#
# The form for each entry is:
# <official service name>  <port number/protocol name> <aliases>
#
# See the services(4) manual page for more information.
# Note: The entries cannot be preceded by a blank space.
#
tcpmux          1/tcp                       # TCP port multiplexer (RFC 1078)
echo            7/tcp                       # Echo
echo            7/udp                       #
discard         9/tcp   sink null           # Discard
discard         9/udp   sink null           #
systat          11/tcp  users               # Active Users
daytime         13/tcp                      # Daytime
daytime         13/udp                      #
qotd            17/tcp  quote               # Quote of the Day
chargen         19/tcp  ttytst source       # Character Generator
chargen         19/udp  ttytst source       #
ftp-data        20/tcp                      # File Transfer Protocol (Data)
ftp             21/tcp                      # File Transfer Protocol (Control)
telnet          23/tcp                      # Virtual Terminal Protocol
smtp            25/tcp                      # Simple Mail Transfer Protocol
time            37/tcp  timeserver          # Time
time            37/udp  timeserver          #
rlp             39/udp  resource            # Resource Location Protocol
whois           43/tcp  nicname             # Who Is
domain          53/tcp  nameserver          # Domain Name Service
```

```
domain        53/udp   nameserver    #
bootps        67/udp                 # Bootstrap Protocol Server
bootpc        68/udp                 # Bootstrap Protocol Client
tftp          69/udp                 # Trivial File Transfer Protocol
#
# PV performance tool services entries
pvserver     382/tcp    # PV server
pvalarm      383/tcp    # PV alarm management
#
# UNIX services
#
biff         512/udp   comsat        # mail notification
exec         512/tcp                 # remote execution, passwd required
login        513/tcp                 # remote login
who          513/udp   whod          # remote who and uptime
```

9.10.4   IP name-to-addresses translation

The IP layer and lower layer networking software require IP addresses; node names are not used, though system users would rather use names than IP addresses. Most networking products will accept names from users and perform lookups to retrieve IP addresses. Name and address tables can be in /etc/host, NIS, or DNS. The file /etc/nsswitch.conf determines which lookup technique to use. For example, if the file contains

```
hosts: dns nis files
```

dns is used if configured; otherwise, nis is used if configured; and if neither of these is configured, /etc/host is used. Note that only one lookup method is used and an error is returned if the name is not found by that method. nsswitch.conf can be configured to use all three methods with

```
hosts: dns [NOTFOUND=continue] nis [NOTFOUND=continue] files
```

Sample entries in /etc/hosts are:

```
12.14.43.55       nodepqr dbnode
32.1.43.22        hpdb
```

Here, each address is followed by one or more node names the user can use for that node. Node names beyond the first are called aliases.

10

NIS:
Network Information
Services

10.1 Introduction

Network Information Services (NIS) centralizes the management of similar files that normally exist on multiple systems. For example, a network can contain 20 HP-UX systems, which can have a single password file if NIS is used; without NIS, 20 different /etc/passwd files would have to be maintained. NIS was previously called Yellow Pages (YP) and was developed by Sun Microsystems, Inc.

Not every network is suitable for NIS conversion:

- If your network has very few systems, centralized management of NIS databases may be relatively time-consuming. NIS involves additional software components, which will have to be learned and troubleshot.

- Different systems administration staff may be responsible for different groups of systems. NIS typically centralizes management of password and files and the like, though NIS domains can be exploited to distribute the management of NIS databases.

- NIS will not work on HP-UX systems that have been converted to trusted (secure) systems.

- If NIS authentication is not used, as is the case at many sites because of the additional maintenance burden, snoopers on the network can monitor sensitive information.

- Customization can be tricky. For example, if the password file is under NIS, a user can log into any system that is using NIS. Hence, for example, a user cannot be restricted to using a few systems and not others. In the case where password files are on individual systems, simply removing a user's entry from a system will disable access for the user on that system.

- NIS is not officially supported over a wide area network (WAN), because of potential timing problems. However, I have been able to use NIS over a WAN without any problems.

NIS+ is an enhanced version of NIS that is not supported on HP-UX.

10.2   NIS Terminology: Servers, Domains, Maps, and Databases

One system on the network stores NIS information. This system is called the *master server*. For redundancy and better performance, other systems can be designated *slave servers*. A slave server gets database information from the master server. All other systems on the network, called NIS clients, can query the master or slave servers. High-availability environments should have one master server and at least one slave server; two slave servers are recommended.

A database served by NIS is called a *map*. A network is divided into *domains*. A domain is simply the set of maps. The maps are stored under the directory /var/yp/domainname in the NIS server systems. The same set of master and slave servers can serve maps for multiple domains. In reality, most networks will have only one domain.

Maps are NIS internal-format databases created from ASCII files. For example, NIS can maintain a *group* database for all the systems in a network. This alleviates the need to maintain the file /etc/group on each node. The default source ASCII file for creating the group map files is /etc/group.

Here is a list of NIS maps that are built by default on HP-UX. User-defined ASCII files can be converted to maps, which are then served; a good understanding of NIS scripts is required to do this.

Map name	ASCII source file	Map file name
aliases	/etc/mail/aliases	mail.aliases
		mail.byaddr
group	/etc/group	group.byname
		group.bygid
hosts	/etc/hosts	hosts.byname
		hosts.byaddr
netgroup	/etc/netgroup	netgroup
		netgroup.byhost
		netgroup.byuser
netid	/etc/netid	netid.byname
networks	/etc/networks	network.byaddr
		network.byname
passwd	/etc/passwd	passwd.byname
		passwd.byuid
protocols	/etc/protocols	protocols.byname
		protocols.bynumber
publickey	/etc/publickey	publickey.byname

rpc	/etc/rpc	rpc.byname
		rcp.bynumber
services	/etc/services	servi.bynp
		services.byname
automounter	/etc/auto_master	auto.master
vhe_list	(Obsolete)	
ypservers	(No ASCII file)	ypservers

10.3   Setting Up a Master Server

10.3.1   Domain name

Choose a powerful system as the NIS master server. Define the domain name
first with a command like

```
$ domainname mydom
```

The existing domain name can be listed with

```
$ domainname
```

10.3.2   ypinit -m

The next step is to build the NIS database. Run ypinit specifying the -m parameter indicating that this will be master server:

```
$ ypinit -m
```

The prompts ask for other master servers. Then the ASCII files mentioned in
the previous section are read and the corresponding maps are created under
/var/yp/mydom. The ASCII files must contain information for your entire network, since all nodes will be using the created maps. Here is a sample session
where we also specify a slave server, nodepqr.

```
#
# domainname mydom
#
# domainname
mydom
#
# ypinit -m
You will be required to answer a few questions to install the Network
Information Service.
All questions will be asked at the beginning of this procedure.

Do you want this procedure to quit on non-fatal errors? [y/n: n] y


At this point, you must construct a list of the hosts which will be
NIS servers for the "mydom" domain.
This machine, nismast, is in the list of Network Information Service servers.
Please provide the hostnames of the slave servers, one per line.
```

When you have no more names to add, enter a <ctrl-D> or a blank line.

```
        next host to add: nismast
        next host to add: nodepqr
        next host to add:
```

The current list of NIS servers looks like this:

```
nismast
nodepqr
```

Is this correct? [y/n: y] **y**

There will be no further questions. The remainder of the procedure should take 5 to 10 minutes.

Building the ypservers database... ypservers build complete.

```
Running make in /var/yp:
updated passwd
updated group
updated hosts
updated networks
updated rpc
updated services
updated protocols
updated netgroup
/var/yp/mydom/mail.aliases: 7 aliases, longest 17 bytes, 120 bytes total
/etc/mail/rev-aliases: 0 aliases, longest 0 bytes, 0 bytes total
updated aliases
updated publickey
updated netid
updated vhe_list
updated auto.master
```

nismast has been set up as a master Network Information Service server without any errors.
If there are running slave NIS servers, run yppush(1M) now for any databases which have been changed. If there are no running slaves, run ypinit on those hosts which are to be slave servers.
#

The *make* scripts use the *makedbm* command to convert an ASCII file to a map file. The map database is shown here:

```
# ls /var/yp/mydom
aliases.time          netgroup.byuser.pag    protocols.time
auto.master.dir       netgroup.dir           publickey.byname.dir
auto.master.pag       netgroup.pag           publickey.byname.pag
auto_master.time      netgroup.time          publickey.time
group.bygid.dir       netid.byname.dir       rpc.byname.dir
group.bygid.pag       netid.byname.pag       rpc.byname.pag
group.byname.dir      netid.time             rpc.bynumber.dir
group.byname.pag      networks.byaddr.dir    rpc.bynumber.pag
group.time            networks.byaddr.pag    rpc.time
hosts.byaddr.dir      networks.byname.dir    servi.bynp.dir
hosts.byaddr.pag      networks.byname.pag    servi.bynp.pag
hosts.byname.dir      networks.time          services.byname.dir
hosts.byname.pag      passwd.byname.dir      services.byname.pag
hosts.time            passwd.byname.pag      services.time
mail.aliases.dir      passwd.byuid.dir       vhe_list.dir
mail.aliases.pag      passwd.byuid.pag       vhe_list.pag
```

```
mail.byaddr.dir          passwd.time              vhe_list.time
mail.byaddr.pag          protocols.byname.dir     ypservers.dir
netgroup.byhost.dir      protocols.byname.pag     ypservers.pag
netgroup.byhost.pag      protocols.bynumber.dir
netgroup.byuser.dir      protocols.bynumber.pag
#
```

Although a second master server is specified, information is not sent to it yet. The *.time files are used by *make* to determine which maps are to be rebuilt when in the future some of the source ASCII files are updated. The *.dir and *.pag files are the index and data files for each map. It is not important to know the internal format of these files. Multiple maps are produced for each ASCII file for lookup convenience; for example, the input ASCII file /etc/passwd produces two maps: passwd.byname, and passwd.byuid.

10.3.3   Serving the NIS maps

The master server is not yet serving the NIS databases. Serving is enabled by setting the following parameters in /etc/rc.config.d/namesvrs:

```
NIS_MASTER_SERVER = 1
NIS_CLIENT = 1
NIS_DOMAIN = mydom
```

and then running the startup scripts, nis.server and nis.client, as in:

```
# cd /sbin/init.d
# ./nis.server start
starting NIS SERVER networking
    starting up the portmapper
        portmap already started, using pid: 531
        domainname mydom
    starting up the Network Information Service
        starting up the ypserv daemon
        /usr/lib/netsvc/yp/ypserv
        starting up the ypxfrd daemon
        /usr/sbin/ypxfrd
        starting up the rpc.yppasswdd daemon
        /usr/lib/netsvc/yp/rpc.yppasswdd /etc/passwd -m passwd PWFILE=
/etc/passwd
        starting up the rpc.ypupdated daemon
        /usr/lib/netsvc/yp/rpc.ypupdated
        starting up the keyserv daemon
        /usr/sbin/keyserv
# ./nis.client start
```

The following processes are started:

- *ypserv:* This is the process that serves the NIS maps to other systems.

- *ypxfrd:* This process transfers map information to slave servers.

- *rpc.yppasswdd:* This daemon allows users to change their password using $ yppasswd.

- *rpc.ypupdated:* This daemon allows programmatic updates to the maps.

■ *keyserv:*   This daemon supports authenticated NIS exchanges.

Note that the startup files are modified so that NIS will automatically start when the system boots.

To verify what maps are served, issue a ypwhich command:

```
# ypwhich -m
auto.master nismast
vhe_list nismast
netid.byname nismast
publickey.byname nismast
mail.byaddr nismast
netgroup.byhost nismast
netgroup.byuser nismast
mail.aliases nismast.acme1.com
netgroup nismast
protocols.byname nismast
protocols.bynumber nismast
servi.bynp nismast
services.byname nismast
rpc.byname nismast
rpc.bynumber nismast
networks.byaddr nismast
networks.byname nismast
hosts.byaddr nismast
hosts.byname nismast
group.bygid nismast
group.byname nismast
passwd.byuid nismast
passwd.byname nismast
ypservers nismast
#
```

10.4   Slave Servers

At this stage, slave server systems can be set up. We entered the name of a slave server, nodepqr, during ypinit. If slave servers are added later, the ypservers map on the master server has to be manually updated to add the slave servers:

```
# cd /var/yp/mydom
```

```
# makedbm -u ypserver > asciifile    Map to ASCII. Edit ASCII file and add a line with
                                      the slave server node name.
```

```
# makedbm asciifile ypservers         ASCII to map.
```

Log into the slave server and remove all entries from /etc/passwd except for root and other entries which are required for the system to boot. Add the following at the end:

```
+::-3:35001:::
```

The plus sign means that if a password entry is not found in /etc/passwd, check NIS. /etc/passwd may look like this:

```
root:jpdOLM1PX37Y6:0:3::/:/sbin/sh
daemon:*:1:5::/:/sbin/sh
bin:*:2:2::/usr/bin:/sbin/sh
sys:*:3:3::/:
adm:*:4:4::/var/adm:/sbin/sh
uucp:*:5:3::/var/spool/uucppublic:/usr/lbin/uucp/uucico
lp:*:9:7::/var/spool/lp:/sbin/sh
nuucp:*:11:11::/var/spool/uucppublic:/usr/lbin/uucp/uucico
hpdb:*:27:1:ALLBASE:/:/sbin/sh
+::-3:35001:::
```

Similarly, the group file should contain only the essential groups, and then a +:*:*. /etc/group may look like this:

```
root::0:root
other::1:root,hpdb
bin::2:root,bin
sys::3:root,uucp
adm::4:root,adm
daemon::5:root,daemon
mail::6:root
lp::7:root,lp
tty::10:
nuucp::11:nuucp
+:*:*
```

The slave server is initialized with the ypinit -s command. Here is a sample session:

```
# cd /var/yp
# domainname mydom
# ypinit -s nismast
You will be required to answer a few questions to install the Network
Information Service.
All questions will be asked at the beginning of this procedure.

Do you want this procedure to quit on non-fatal errors? [y/n: n] n
OK, but please remember to correct anything which fails.
If you don't, some part of the system (perhaps the NIS itself) won't work.

Can the existing directory "/var/yp/mydom"
and its contents be destroyed? [y/n: n] y
There will be no further questions. The remainder of the procedure, copying
the databases from nismast, will take a few minutes.

Note that if your master NIS server, nismast, is an HP machine, it is
expected that the NIS databases ethers.byaddr, and ethers.byname
will not exist for you to copy. As a result, you may ignore any "no such map"
error messages produced when those maps are attempted to be transferred.
This may also be true if nismast is not an HP machine.
If your master NIS server, nismast, is not an HP machine, it is expected
that the NIS database vhe_list will not exist for you to copy, and you may
ignore any "no such map" error messages seen when it is attempted to be
transferred. This may also be true if nismast is an HP machine and
its ypmake(1M) is from an older release.

Transferring group.bygid for domain mydom from nismast...
Transferring group.byname for domain mydom from nismast...
Transferring hosts.byaddr for domain mydom from nismast...
```

```
Transferring hosts.byname for domain mydom from nismast...
Transferring netgroup for domain mydom from nismast...
Transferring netgroup.byhost for domain mydom from nismast...
...
Transferring servi.bynp for domain mydom from nismast...
Transferring ethers.byaddr for domain mydom from nismast...
ypxfr: can't get order number for map ethers.byaddr from ypserv at nismast
        reason: no such map in server's NIS domain
Transferring ethers.byname for domain mydom from nismast...
ypxfr: can't get order number for map ethers.byname from ypserv at nismast
        reason: no such map in server's NIS domain
Transferring netmasks.byaddr for domain mydom from nismast...
ypxfr: can't get order number for map netmasks.byaddr from ypserv at nismast
        reason: no such map in server's NIS domain
Transferring bootparams for domain mydom from nismast...
ypxfr: can't get order number for map bootparams from ypserv at nismast
        reason: no such map in server's NIS domain
Transferring ypservers for domain mydom from nismast...

nodepqr has been set up as a slave Network Information Service server with
errors.
Please remember to correct the errors, and run ypinit again.

At this point, make sure that /etc/passwd, /etc/hosts, /etc/networks,
/etc/group, /etc/protocols, /etc/services, /etc/rpc and /etc/netgroup have
been edited so that when the Network Information Service is activated, the
databases you have just created will be used in addition to or instead of the
/etc ASCII files.
#
```

The slave server is now set up; information from the master server, nis-mast, has copied over. Note that some maps were not present on the master server; these maps are not being used on this network.

The slave server must now be started. The following variables are set as shown in /etc/rc.config.d/namesvrs:

```
NIS_SLAVE_SERVER=1
NIS_CLIENT=1
NIS_DOMAIN=mydom
```

The following commands start the slave server and the bind service to connect the client to the server:

```
# /sbin/init.d/nis.server start
# /sbin/init.d/nis.client start
```

10.5   Setting Up a Client

Every system that will use NIS will have the modifications. /etc/passwd and /etc/group must be modified as shown in the slave servers section above. The + entry must be present at end. The file /etc/rc.config.d is modified to contain

```
NIS_CLIENT=1
NIS_DOMAIN=mydom
```

and the script nis.client is run as in

```
# /sbin/init.d/nis.client start
starting NIS CLIENT networking
    starting up the portmapper
        portmap already started, using pid: 807
        domainname mydom
    starting up the Network Information Service
        starting up the ypbind daemon
        /usr/lib/netsvc/yp/ypbind
        Checking NIS binding.
    Bound to NIS server using domain mydom.
        starting up the keyserv daemon
```

The script will run automatically at system boots. Note that none of the servers or client systems can be a trusted system. See SAM to find out how to convert to or from a trusted system.

10.6 Updating the Maps

If a map has to be updated, the corresponding ASCII file is changed and a make issued, as in

```
# cd /var/yp
# make
```

The maps are updated and the changed maps are *yppush*ed to the slave servers.

10.7 yppasswd

Users will have to use the yppasswd command instead of passwd to change passwords. The password will be changed in the NIS /etc/passwd file and the NIS maps. The slaves are updated and then an update is sent over to all slave servers. On a client, if the account—for example, root—is defined in /etc/passwd before the + line, the local /etc/passwd is updated, not the NIS files.

10.8 ypxfr, yppush, and Regular Slave Server Updates

When maps in the master server are updated, they are not automatically sent to the slave servers, as this can create a lot of network traffic. The yppush command issued on the master server sends a map to all slave servers (defined in the map ypservers):

```
# yppush passwd.byname        Push to slaves.
```

The ypxfr command is an equivalent command which is executed on a slave server to pull a map from the master server:

```
# ypxfr passwd.byname        Pull to slave.
```

The master may be updated frequently; hence a cron job should be set up to update the slaves at regular intervals. Some of these maps, like the passwd maps, should be pulled hourly; and some other maps, like the group maps, should be pulled daily. Scripts to perform pulls of all maps are provided in three files—one to transfer some maps every hour, one to transfer some maps every day, and one to transfer some maps twice a day.

```
# cat /var/yp/ypxfr_1perday
#       @(#)ypxfr_1perday: $Revision: 1.21.111.1 $    $Date: 94/11/04 11:35:34 $
#
# (c) Copyright 1987, 1988 Hewlett-Packard Company
# (c) Copyright 1985 Sun Microsystems, Inc.
#
# ypxfr_1perday - Do daily Network Information Service map check/updates

/usr/sbin/ypxfr group.bygid
/usr/sbin/ypxfr group.byname
/usr/sbin/ypxfr networks.byaddr
/usr/sbin/ypxfr networks.byname
/usr/sbin/ypxfr protocols.byname
/usr/sbin/ypxfr protocols.bynumber
/usr/sbin/ypxfr rpc.bynumber
/usr/sbin/ypxfr services.byname
/usr/sbin/ypxfr ypservers
/usr/sbin/ypxfr vhe_list

# cat /var/yp/ypxfr_1perhour
#       @(#)ypxfr_1perhour: $Revision: 1.20.111.1 $    $Date: 94/11/04 11:35:36 $
#
# (c) Copyright 1987 Hewlett-Packard Company
# (c) Copyright 1985 Sun Microsystems, Inc.
#
# ypxfr_1perhour - Do hourly Network Information Service map check/updates

/usr/sbin/ypxfr passwd.byname
/usr/sbin/ypxfr passwd.byuid

# cat /var/yp/ypxfr_2perday
#       @(#)ypxfr_2perday: $Revision: 1.21.111.1 $     $Date: 94/11/04 11:35:37 $
#
# (c) Copyright 1987 Hewlett-Packard Company
# (c) Copyright 1985 Sun Microsystems, Inc.
#
# ypxfr_2perday - Do twice-daily Network Information Service map check/updates

/usr/sbin/ypxfr ethers.byaddr
/usr/sbin/ypxfr ethers.byname
/usr/sbin/ypxfr hosts.byaddr
/usr/sbin/ypxfr hosts.byname
/usr/sbin/ypxfr mail.aliases
/usr/sbin/ypxfr netgroup
/usr/sbin/ypxfr netgroup.byhost
/usr/sbin/ypxfr netgroup.byuser
```

The three scripts should run as cron jobs. The cron entries may appear as

```
0 2 * * *      /var/yp/ypxfr_1perday
0 8,14 * * *   /var/yp/ypxfr_2perday
30 * * * *     /var/yp/ypxfr_1perhour
```

Of course, you can be creative and determine your own transfer schedule for each map. Note that the cron jobs must be running on each slave server.

10.9   The Name Server Switch File: /etc/nswswitch

Programs like telnet and ftp perform host name-to-address translation by using routines like *gethostbyname*(). The host name table can be

- The /etc/hosts file
- Served by Domain Name Service (DNS)
- Served by NIS

The file /etc/nsswitch determines which lookup method should be used. Example entries are

- *hosts: nis dns files:*   Use NIS. If NIS is not maintaining the host tables, use DNS. If DNS is not running, use /etc/hosts. Note that if a product is running and returns an error, the lookup does not continue searching other products; an error is returned to the calling program.
- *hosts: dns [NOTFOUND =continue] nis [NOTFOUND =continue] files:* Use DNS. If the host is not found in DNS or DNS is not running, try NIS. If the host is not found in NIS or NIS is not running or NIS is not maintaining the hosts table, try /etc/hosts.

Note that /etc/hosts should contain some basic entries and /etc/nswswitch should be set up to look at these entries in case DNS or NIS fails.

10.10   ypcat: Displaying Map Contents

The contents of a map can be displayed using the ypcat command from any node, server, or client:

```
# ypcat group.byname
root::0:root
other::1:root,hpdb
bin::2:root,bin
sys::3:root,uucp
adm::4:root,adm
daemon::5:root,daemon
mail::6:root
lp::7:root,lp
tty::10:
nuucp::11:nuucp
users:: 30:john423,shah564, pina543,anand234,tulsi434
sybase:*:203:sybase
```

11

NFS:
Network File System
and the
Automounter

11.1 Introduction

Network File System (NFS) allows users on one system to transparently access a directory tree on another system. Effectively, a system can have file systems that are not only on local disks but also on other systems. NFS was originally developed by Sun Microsystems. However, today it is supported on most Unix implementations. NFS is the basis for implementing diskless HP-UX cluster nodes.

NFS is usually maintained using SAM. However, we will be using the command line to gain a better understanding of NFS internals. Normally, SAM's *networking and communications* area should be used. Note that the Virtual Home Environment (vhe) feature of pre-V10.0 HP-UX, which used NFS, is obsolete. *nfsstat* is a useful command for monitoring NFS; however, for lack of space, I choose not to discuss it. You may want to study the Distributed File System (DFS) and Andrew File System (AFS), which are competing file systems with some better functionality. NFS is bundled with HP-UX; DFS and AFS are not.

11.2 Quick Start

To allow remote systems to mount directories on the local system, the local system must be set up as an NFS server and must export the directories. To set up the local system as an NFS server, /etc/rc.config.d/nfsconf must contain:

```
NFS_SERVER=1
START_MOUNTD=1
```

The system must then be rebooted or the following command must be issued:

```
/sbin/init.d/nfs.server start
```

NFS uses RPC's portmapper to allow connections from other systems. A client can check whether a system has an NFS server setup by getting all RPC service names from the server with the command *rpcinfo -p hostname*. Two processes, rpc.lockd and rpc.statd, support NFS file locking operations. Each NFS request from a client is serviced by a process *nfsd*. As nfsd is single-threaded, multiple nfsd processes are usually started to service multiple simultaneous NFS requests. By default, four nfsd processes are started. The nfsstat command displays NFS operation counts; nfsstat can be used for troubleshooting problems.

11.2.1 Exporting directories

Just as /etc/fstab contains information on file systems available locally, /etc/exports contains information on all file systems (or directories) exported from the local system. The directory to be exported must be entered in the file /etc/exports either manually or by using SAM. An example export file is

```
/home/testpak
/home/prods  -anon=65535
/dev/progs -anon=65534, access=nodepqr
```

A directory is exported with the exportfs command. The directory must exist in /etc/exports.

```
# exportfs /home/prods
```

Various options can be specified to exportfs or can be placed in /etc/exports. The anon and access options are shown in the above /etc/exports file; example use on the command line is

```
# exportfs -o access=nodepqr /dev/progs
```

The options are:

anon=uid	Requests from unknown users are treated as coming from uid. If anon is not specified, requests are assumed to be from user *nobody*. If uid is set to 65535, anonymous access is disabled.
async	Writes will be asynchronous.
ro	Export directory read-only.
rw=hostname,...	Export directory read-write to specified hosts, read-only to others.
access=hostname,...	Give access to specified hosts or netgroups only. Default is to allow any host to mount the exported directory.

Directories can be unexported with commands like

```
# exportfs -u /dev/progs
```

All directories mentioned in /etc/exports can be exported with

```
# exportfs -a
```

Currently exported directories are mentioned in /etc/xtab.

11.2.2   Mounting remote directories

To set up the local system as an NFS client, /etc/rc.config.d/nfsconf must contain

```
NFS_CLIENT=1
```

The system must then be rebooted, or the following command must be issued:

```
/sbin/init.d/nfs.client start
```

The mount command used for local mounts is also used for remote mounts; the host name has to be specified, as in

```
# mount nodepqr:/dev/progs  /home/test/programs
```

11.2.3   showmount: Listing exported and remotely mounted directories

showmount has the following options:

- *-a:* List all mounts issued on other systems to mount directories exported by the local system.
- *-d:* List exported directories that are currently mounted by clients.
- *-e:* List exported directories.

An example output is

```
$ showmount -a
nodepqr.acme.com:/home/userfiles
host231.acme.com:/usr/local/binaries
```

To find what directories are mounted by the current system over directories exported by other systems, display /etc/mnttab, which shows all local and remote mounts; directories that are remote will have a node name in their entry.

11.3   automounter and the Master Auto Map

The *automounter* is a component of NFS that mounts directories when access to them is requested and unmounts them after 5 minutes (default) of idle time. It reduces resource consumption on systems and the network. No automounter setup is required on an NFS server; the client must be set up with the following line in /etc/rc.config.d/nfsconf:

```
AUTOMOUNT=1
```

The automount process will run when */sbin/init.d/nis.client start* is executed, normally at system boot. *automount* reads the master map, /etc/auto_master. Each line in auto_master has the form:

```
local-mount-point-start              map-name          mount-options
```

An example entry is

```
/dev/progs                           /etc/auto_file nosuid
```

Mount options are similar to those specified in /etc/exports or the exportfs command. The local-mount-point-start specifies the directory tree that will be handled by the map file. For example, if the user attempts to mount /home/progs/dev and the local-mount-point-start is /home/progs, the entry is used to process the remote mount. *map-name* specifies a map file containing information on each subdirectory under the local-mount-point-start that can be processed. An example map file is

```
dev        nosuid        nodepqr:/home/progs/dev
```

Here, if the user attempts to access /home/prog/dev, automount will mount /home/progs/dev from nodepqr to a temporary directory, /tmp_mnt, and link /home/progs/dev to this directory. Effectively, automount executes the following commands:

```
# mkdir /tmp_mnt/home/progs/dev
# mount nodepqr:/home/progs/dev /tmp_mnt/home/progs/dev
# ln -s /tmp_mnt/home/progs/dev /home/progs/dev
```

Two kinds of map files can be mentioned in the master map: direct maps, and indirect maps.

11.3.1 Direct and indirect maps

A direct map is specified in the master file as

```
/-                              /etc/auto_direct        [mount_options]
```

Note that the entry starts with /-. /etc/auto_direct contains entries like

```
/home/progs/dev     -nosuid        nodeabc:/home/progs/dev
/home/progs/test    -nosuid        nodepqr:/dev/test/test2
```

When any of the directories or a subdirectory of the directory specified at the start of a line in /etc/auto_direct is accessed, the corresponding remote directory is mounted under /tmp_mnt and a symbolic link is established.

An indirect map is specified in the master file as, for example,

```
/home/prog          /etc/auto_progs     -nosuid
```

The indirect map will contain entries like

```
dev                 -nosuid             nodeabc:/home/progs/dev
test                -nosuid             nodepqr:/dev/test/test2
```

Effectively, the top-level directory is specified in the master map while subdirectories are specified in the indirect map file. Indirect map files are generally more efficient because the client automounter will mount the top level directory only once for all subdirectory requests.

11.3.2   Redundant mount servers

In the direct and indirect map files, the remote directory to be mounted can actually be specified as two directories; if the first one does not mount, the second one is tried. An example entry is

```
/home/progs/dev     -nosuid             nodeabc:/home/progs/dev \
                                        nodepqr:/progs/devback
```

11.3.3   The * and & wildcards for the local subdirectory and the remote host

The asterisk (*) can be used to represent the remote subdirectory that is the same as the local subdirectory. It can be used in indirect maps only. The ampersand (&) is replaced by the local subdirectory name when used in the remote directory or node name (right-hand side). It can be used in direct or indirect maps. Example uses of these are the following:

/etc/auto_master contains:

```
/home               /etc/auto_progs     -nosuid
```

/etc/auto_progs contains:

```
*                   -nosuid             nodepqr:/home/userfiles/&
```

If the user accesses /home/john231, the asterisk represents john231 and the ampersand represents john231, so /home/john231 will be mounted over nodepqr:/home/allfiles/john231. Note that this becomes a convenient way to mount all users' home directories automatically.

12

HP VUE
and the
Common Desktop
Environment (CDE)

12.1 Introduction

HP VUE is a window manager and desktop based on Motif and the X-protocol. It provides point-and-click functionality to manage files, send and receive mail, access on-line help, edit files, and access terminal emulators. It provides mechanisms to run any program by clicking icons and to develop graphics environments for applications.

CDE is also a window manager and desktop. CDE is a joint industry effort, mainly, to counter the threat of dominance by Microsoft Windows and to provide a consistent look and feel across Unix platforms. X/OPEN licenses CDE, and most of the major companies such as DEC, IBM, HP, and SUN, have adopted it. CDE will likely be the dominant Unix graphics front end in the coming years. HP's CDE has VUE functionality incorporated in it. Perhaps the most interesting component of CDE is dtksh, the Desktop KornShell. dtksh implements K-shell functionality and supports building of GUI applications by simply writing scripts. Hence, Motif widgets, pushbuttons, Check boxes, Xlib functions, menus, and similar X11 programming features typically available to C programmers can now be used in shell scripts. dtksh is described further in Appendix A.

Because the look and feel of CDE are basically those of VUE, most of the discussion of VUE here is applicable to CDE also.

12.2 Starting VUE

A VUE session starts with the logon screen shown in Fig. 2.1 in Chapter 2. The terminal must be an X-station: an X-terminal, a PC running X-software,

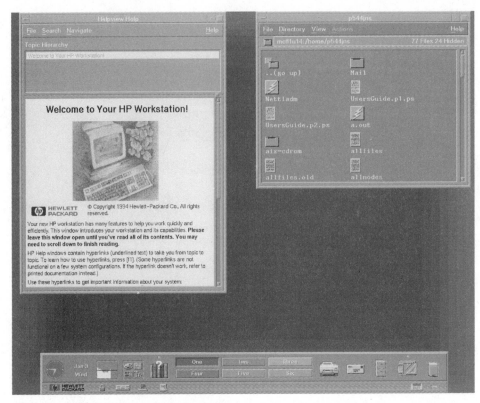

Figure 12.1 VUE main screen, just after login.

or a graphics terminal attached to a system that supports the X-protocol. The HP system can be set up to display the logon screen automatically when the system boots; or the logon screen can be displayed by using the X Display Management Communications Protocol (XDMCP), which can be initiated from the X-station by a line mode command such as *X -query hpsystem* or by menu choices from PC X-software packages.

Figure 12.1 shows a typical new-user screen after successful logon. The screen shows a help viewer window, a file manager window, and the front panel.

12.3   The Front Panel: Using VUE Features

The front panel is the key window on HP VUE. See the CDE front panel in Fig. 12.5 which is similar. The front panel is always present on the screen and has

- An area on the left where date, time, and system load are displayed.
- Icons in the top area, such as Style Manager and Help, which perform actions integrated with VUE.
- Icons in the bottom area, such as mail, which represent system or user applications.

- A row of arrows at the top pointing upward. When clicked, they pop up subpanels. These subpanels can be customized for user applications.

- A set of buttons, six in the picture, representing workspaces. A workspace is like a separate desktop.

- A trash can. A file can be deleted by dragging the file icon from another window such as the File Manager window to the trash can. Actually, the files are not immediately removed; they remain in the trash can until the VUE session is terminated.

- An EXIT button to log off VUE.

12.4   Workspaces: Simulating Multiple Desktops

Workspaces are a means of organizing icons, windows, and such into separate display areas to organize tasks and to avoid screen clutter. Consider a small organization where the system administrator is also a programmer. The two sets of tasks would be fairly independent of each other. It would be convenient to display system administration–related windows on one display while displaying compiler, debugger, profiler, and similar windows on another display. This can be achieved on one screen by using VUE and putting the two sets of windows on two different workspaces. Only one workspace is displayed at a time; all the others are hidden behind. Any workspace can be brought to the foreground by clicking the corresponding workspace button on the front panel.

12.5   The Desktop

The VUE screen display is considered a desktop. The desktop has a number of workspaces. The desktop always displays at least the front panel and a workspace. Related icons are typically grouped together in windows. Many icons can be dragged from the original window and put on the desktop for easy access. Figures 12.2 shows a desktop with two icons on the desktop dragged from the two windows: File Manager and Personal Toolbox, which are also displayed. The windows can be closed; however, the icons will remain on the desktop.

The background color of the desktop is the background color of the workspace on top. The background color and design are called a *backdrop*. The backdrop can be changed by clicking the Backdrop icon from the Style Manager, the fourth big icon from the left on the front panel.

On logging out of a VUE session, the complete state of the desktop including the workspaces is saved in files under your home directory. The state is restored on the next login.

12.6   File Management

The File Manager is a poor cousin of Microsoft Windows File Manager. The File Manager window is brought up by clicking on the file cabinet on the front panel. Figure 12.1 and 12.2 showed the File Manager on the top right. One

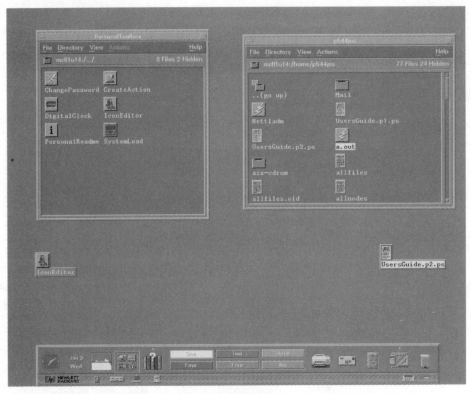

Figure 12.2   VUE with two icons dragged onto the desktop.

file per icon was displayed. The icon depends on what type of file it represents. The file type classification is based on a method similar to what the *file* command on the system uses, based on /etc/magic contents. (Sometimes the file's type is not guessed correctly.) Double-clicking on an icon causes an action appropriate for the file's type. For example, clicking on a.out causes the program to run, clicking on ascii256.0 causes the symbols in the object file to be displayed, and clicking on logo.l.pm invokes the *icon editor* with the file as a parameter.

A file icon can be dragged from the File Manager window and placed on the desktop workspace. A copy of the icon is created on the workspace. This icon will remain even after the File Manager window is closed. This way commonly used files and programs can be accessed quickly.

A file icon can be dragged onto the trash can in the front panel. The file is removed from the current directory and will be deleted after logout. In the interim, the file can be retrieved from the trash can if required.

The menu items allow the common functions of renaming and copying files in addition to one interesting item: Annotate, under the file menu. *File Annotation* allows a note to be attached to files. The note can be text or voice.

12.7   Toolboxes: Personal, General, and Network

One way to run applications or programs is to create icons for them on the front panel and define actions to be performed when an icon is clicked. This limits the number of applications and also clutters the front panel. Another method for running applications would be to create action icons and place them in a separate window. Such a window along with the icons and actions acts as a container called a *toolbox*. Figure 12.2 shows a toolbox on the top left of the screen. An application is invoked by double-clicking on its icon. Toolbox windows are similar to File Manager windows. Toolboxes are also similar to Microsoft Windows Program Groups. VUE has three toolboxes:

- *Personal toolbox:*   For applications customized by you.

- *General toolbox:*   For VUE and system-related applications. Cannot be user updated.

- *Network toolbox:*   For applications on other systems. Cannot be user updated.

The personal toolbox is accessed by clicking on the corresponding icon on the front panel. Other toolboxes are accessed from the subpanel, which is brought up by clicking the up-arrow above the personal toolbox on the front panel. Items can be moved (by dragging the mouse) or copied (by pressing the control key and dragging the mouse) from any toolbox to the personal toolbox.

12.7.1   Icons and actions

You can start your program by double-clicking a corresponding icon in the personal toolbox. To set up the icon, double-click the CreateAction icon in the utilities subdirectory of the general toolbox. The CreateAction window pops up and a few fields have to be entered. The command to be run is entered in the command line field. A single parameter can be specified with $1, which will then be prompted for when the icon is double-clicked. The prompt is entered in the field Filename Prompt. If the icon fields are left blank, default icons are used. Once all the fields are entered and the OK button is clicked, a new icon is created in the personal toolbox. Double-clicking on the icon causes the parameter, if any, to be prompted for and the command line to be executed in a terminal emulation window.

For those familiar with Microsoft Windows, creating a new icon in the personal toolbox is like creating a new program group icon in Windows. The CreateAction popup is like the Properties popup in the Microsoft Windows Program Manager menu.

12.8   The Style Manager

VUE's colors, fonts, and similar features or resources can be customized using the Style Manager. Each user's customizations are stored in files under

Figure 12.3 The Style Manager for customizing VUE.

his or her home directory; hence, the changes are reflected in future sessions. Figure 12.3 shows the style menu. The icons are

- *Color:* VUE uses eight colors for displaying window frames, menus, and so on. These colors are called a palette. The set of colors can be changed by selecting one of the palettes listed in this popup.
- *Font:* Changes size of fonts used by VUE.
- *Backdrop:* Used to change current workspace background color. *Nobackdrop* can be used to display X's background color set by *xsetroot.*
- *Keyboard:* Select whether autorepeat is enabled, and click volume.
- *Mouse:* Used to select rates for double-click and acceleration.
- *Audio:* Speaker volume, tone, and duration of sound.
- *Screen:* Screen saver and lock settings.
- *Window:* Whether current window is selected by clicking or location of mouse pointer, and whether window icons are placed on the desktop or in a separate icons window.
- *Startup:* Determines whether, after login, a standard home session is used to set up workspaces or the workspace should look as it did just before the previous logout.

12.9   Helpview

The HP help system is used by VUE. The viewer is called Helpview. It supports keyword searches and hyperlink navigation. The F1 key can be used to get context-sensitive help. HP's help system is somewhat similar to the Microsoft Windows help system.

12.10   VUE Startup and Internals

VUE is installed under /usr/vue. The directories are

- */usr/vue/app-defaults:* Contains resource settings for VUE applications and VUE window manager. Similar to X11 app-defaults directory, which contains X application defaults. For example, the file /usr/vue/app-defaults/Vuefile contains resource information for the VUE File Manager. A sample line is:

```
Vuefile*fileMenu.find.accelerator: ctrl<key>f
```

which declares ctrl-f as equivalent to the FIND menu item. VUE customizations such as front panel customizations or number of workspaces are stored in /usr/vue/app-defaults/vuewm.

- */usr/vue/bin:* Contains all the VUE executables such as vuestyle, which pops up the Style Manager, and Helpview, which displays the help viewer.

- */usr/vue/config:* Contains VUE configuration information. Xaccess contains information on who can log in using XDMCP. Xconfig contains VUE Login Manager resources. Xserver contains one line per X server to be started on the local system. Entries in this file will cause the VUE login prompt to be displayed on each local display when the system reboots.

- */usr/vue/icons:* Contains all the VUE icons. The files *.pm are pixmaps (color icons), and the files *.bm are bitmaps (black and white icons).

- */usr/vue/palettes:* Contains information on the palettes listed under the Color option of the Style Manager.

When the system boots, /etc/inittab contains an entry to start VUE by executing the command /usr/vue/bin/vuerc. (Current system run level must be the same as that specified in the vuerc entry of the inittab file.) The file basically runs /usr/vue/bin/vuelogin. When this file executes, all the local displays mentioned in /use/vue/bin/xservers have a corresponding X server started and the VUE login prompt is displayed. Each VUE session has a corresponding process, *vuelogin,* on the system. Other users can log into the system by an XDMCP command such as *X -query hpsys.*

vuelogin is called the Login Manager. It reads the initial configuration file (/usr/vue/config/Xresources), starts the X server, displays the login screen (by running /usr/vue/bin/vuegreet), validates login, and then calls the VUE Session Manager (by running /usr/vue/bin/vuesession).

12.11   Customization of VUE and VUE Resources

VUE stores user-specific information under the directory .vue in the user's home directory. During startup, VUE executes .vueprofile in the user's home directory. When a new user logs in, VUE does not find .vue or .vueprofile; hence, it creates these from template files under /usr/vue. Startup scripts such as .profile are not executed by VUE login. If .profile should be executed, it should be sourced in .vueprofile. When a user logs out, complete session information is noted in files under .vue so that the desktop can be restored when the user logs in again.

The VUE window manager startup resources are in /home/.vue/vuewmrc. This is where you can customize the front panel and can mouse right button popup menus and other window manager features.

VUE does not read any X resource files. Instead, resources are read in from /home/.vue/sessions/current/vue.resources   or /home/.vue/sessions/home/vue.resources. *current* or *home* depends on the startup options selection in the Style Manager startup section. These files can be modified to customize resources; however, beware that during logout, VUE writes these files.

The general toolbox has a subdirectory, System_Admin, which has icons for editing the resource files and /home/.vue/vuewmrc.

12.12   HP VUE Lite

VUE Lite refers to a scaled-down version of VUE. It consumes fewer resources on the host and the X-station. The front panel has fewer icons, and applications like File Manager are not brought up. Session information is stored under /home/.vue/sessions/lite.

12.13   Other VUE Features

Alt-TAB can be pressed to go to the next window on the screen.

The VUE logon screen has a *fail-safe session* option which can be selected from the menu displayed by clicking *option* on the logon menu. This brings up a simple terminal emulation window after the user name and password are entered. This can be useful if the VUE session hangs or is unusable because of some bad settings. The problem can be corrected from the terminal session; the user then logs out and logs back in.

The mail icon invokes the *elm* mail package. The text editor icon invokes /usr/vue/bin/vuepad. This editor is somewhat like Microsoft Windows Notepad editor. It has a spelling checker.

12.14   The Common Desktop Environment (CDE)

CDE consists of components adopted from products developed by various vendors. For example, the user interface is derived from HP's VUE; and ToolTalk; the underlying messaging mechanism, is derived from Sun Microsystem's *ToolTalk* for Solaris OpenWindows. Because the user interface is derived from HP VUE, the look and feel of CDE are very much those of HP VUE. Figure 12.4 shows the CDE screen just after login. Note how similar the front panel is to HP's VUE front panel.

At the time of writing this book, CDE was still being worked on by HP. Hence, expect minor differences from what is described here. In particular,

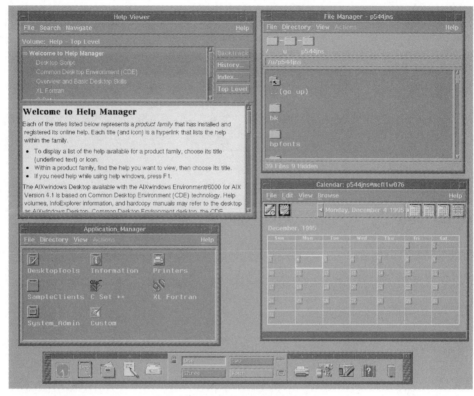

Figure 12.4   Common Desktop Environment (CDE) main screen.

note the top-level directories like /etc and /usr which may not be the same as mentioned here.

12.15   The CDE Front Panel

Figure 12.5 shows the CDE front panel with three subpanels. Note that workspaces are supported just as in HP VUE. Though the front panel behaves very much like HP VUE's front panel, the applications, such as Calendar and Mail, are not the same as in HP VUE.

12.16   Starting CDE

The Login Manager displays a login screen somewhat like the VUE login screen. The CDE session manager can be started from an X server with a command like:

```
# xinit /usr/dt/bin/Xsession
```

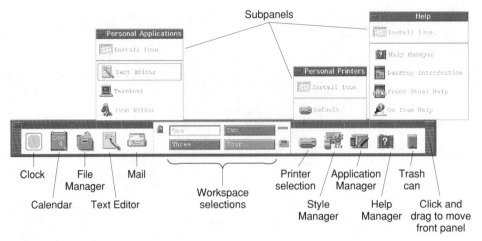

Figure 12.5 CDE front panel and subpanels.

The login server process displays the CDE login window on specified X-terminals. The login server daemon either can be started at system boot or can be started with

```
# /usr/dt/bin/dtlogin -daemon
```

The login server reads the configuration file /etc/dt/config/Xconfig, which contains lines like these:

```
#   Configuration file for the Login Manager
#
#   (c) Copyright 1993, 1994 Hewlett-Packard Company
#   (c) Copyright 1993, 1994 International Business Machines Corp.
#   (c) Copyright 1993, 1994 Sun Microsystems, Inc.
#   (c) Copyright 1993, 1994 Unix System Labs, Inc., a subsidiary of
#   Novell, Inc.
#
#   This file contains behaviour resources for the CDE DT Login Manager.
#   It also specifies the location of other configuration files used by
#   the Login Manager.
#
#   Appearance resources for the login screen are contained in the file
#   specified by the "*resources" resource below.
#
#   Most resources can be limited to a single display by including the
#   display name in the resource. If the display name is not included, the
#   resource will apply to all displays managed by the Login Manager. When
#   specifying the display name, replace the ":" character in the name
#   with an underscore "_". If the name is fully qualified, also replace
#   dot "." characters with underscores.
#
#   Example:
#
#   Dtlogin*machine_domain_name_0*startup: /etc/dt/Xstartup.aa
#
#   For more information see the man page, Dtlogin(1X).
#
############################################################################
```

```
Dtlogin.errorLogFile:          /var/dt/Xerrors
Dtlogin.pidFile:               /var/dt/Xpid
Dtlogin.accessFile:            /usr/dt/config/Xaccess
Dtlogin.servers:               /usr/dt/config/Xservers
Dtlogin*resources:             /usr/dt/config/%L/Xresources
Dtlogin*startup:               /usr/dt/config/Xstartup
Dtlogin*reset:                 /usr/dt/config/Xreset
Dtlogin*setup:                 /usr/dt/config/Xsetup
Dtlogin*failsafeClient:        /usr/dt/config/Xfailsafe
############################################################################
# To specify the system env vars to be exported to the users session
Dtlogin.exportList:        ODMDIR NLSPATH TZ ...
# To specify the maximum size of the Login Manager error log file in
# kilobytes.
Dtlogin.errorLogSize:     50
```

The Xservers file specifies terminals on which the login window should automatically be displayed on system boot. A login window can be displayed on X-terminals via the XDMCP protocol.

The Xsetup script runs after the X-server has started but before the login screen is displayed. The Xstartup script file is run after a user logs in but before the session starts.

The Session Manager executes $HOME/.dtprofile. Normally, .profile or .login is not executed. The default Workspace Manager is /usr/dt/bin/dtwm. Applications to be started, such as Help Manager and File Manager, are declared in /etc/dt/config/C/sys.session.

Resources are made available via the X server RESOURCE MANAGER property. Default resources are loaded from /usr/dt/config/C/sys.resources. These are augmented by resources in $HOME/.Xdefaults. Hence, customizations can be stored in .Xdefaults in your home directory.

When logging in the first time, files will be created under $HOME/.dt. Errors can be found in $HOME/.dt/startlog.

12.17   The CDE HELP Subsystem

The *dthelp* facility is available to C language and dtksh script programmers. Help can be made available in the following forms:

- *Menubar:* Help can be supplied with an application. In this case, the rightmost item in the main window menu bar should be the help menu.

- *F1 key:* This is typically used in applications to display context-sensitive help.

- *Standalone:* This type of help is invoked by the *dthelpview* command. Typical information is tutorials and references.

Help is written in SGML markup language. Both formal and shorthand markups are supported. Backtracking, history of visited pages, and index searches are supported. An SGML source file is called a HelpTag file, and by convention it has the extension .htg. An example tag is

```
<book>HP-UX Programmer's Guide<\book>
```

The run-time help file is created by a compilation command like

```
# dthelptag prog.htg
```

The output file has the extension .sdl, for Semantic Delivery Language. If the file is a standalone help volume, the help can be accessed by a command like

```
# dthelpview -helpVolume prog.sdl
```

A sample Helpview window is displayed in the CDE main screen of Fig. 12.4. That window shows the Helpview Browser, which displays all help topics registered in the system.

12.18   ToolTalk

ToolTalk is a service that allows applications running under CDE to deliver messages to other applications without the applications knowing (much) about each other. The ToolTalk daemon, *ttsession,* is started by the Session Manager, just after logging in. ttsession enables independent applications in the X environment to communicate with each other via ToolTalk messages.

The ToolTalk API functions are used by applications to communicate with the ToolTalk service. Applications can also use the ToolTalk Messaging Toolkit, which is a higher-level interface to the ToolTalk API. Applications that will accept messages register with the ToolTalk service. For each message the application will accept, the application registers a *message pattern* with ToolTalk service. Messages can be *notices* or *requests*. A notice is an informational message (event notice) which is read and discarded. A request message requires an operation to be performed and a reply to be sent to the requester.

An example of the use of ToolTalk is in a CASE environment where an application running the compiler can call the ToolTalk service when there is a compilation error, to run an editor which will open the source file for editing. ToolTalk is extensively used by most of the standard applications, like File Manager and Calendar.

Chapter

13

Security Issues

13.1 Introduction

The default installation of HP-UX is not secure compared with other major Unixes. For example, passwords are stored in /etc/passwd, which can be read by any user on the system. The solution is to convert the system to a trusted system. Additionally, useful security-auditing functionality is available on a trusted system.

Access Control Lists (ACLs) are available for the standard High-Performance File System (HFS). ACLs provide more fine-grain access modes to files than available using the standard Unix access control mechanisms.

We will mainly be discussing HP-UX–specific security issues. Security administration is a complex topic. There are many books and articles available on Unix security issues; most of these issues are not covered here. We will briefly mention some products available on the Internet which may address security administration concerns at your site.

13.2 Trusted Systems

SAM must be used to convert a nontrusted HP-UX system to a trusted system: go to the Auditing and Security area; double-click on any of the security display icons, for example, the Audited Events icon; and confirm the conversion to a trusted system. A trusted system has the following enhancements over standard Unix security features:

- Encrypted passwords are not kept in /etc/password; they are moved to a separate set of directories which cannot be read by ordinary users.

- Passwords are made more secure; for example, users can be forced to enter passwords with a minimum length of six characters.

- User access can be restricted based on time of day.

- Security auditing is enabled; user activity on the system can be monitored more effectively.

- Access to hardwired terminals, including those on muxes, and modem ports can be controlled.

Network Information Services (NIS) is not supported on a trusted system, partly because NIS has some security limitations.

13.2.1 The trusted database

In a nontrusted system, an entry in /etc/passwd may look like this:

```
john321:eRskyrejstYwE:212:432:John Doe,New City, 321-435-
3242:/home/john321:/usr/bin/sh
```

The entry in a trusted system will look like this:

```
john321:*:212:432:John Doe,New City,321-435-3242:/home/john321:/usr/bin/sh
```

The password is moved to the file /tcb/files/auth/j/john321. *tcb* and *auth* are mnemonics for *trusted computing base* and *authorized*. Each user's password file is in /tcb/files/auth/L/username, where L is the first letter of the user name. The files are also known as a protected password database. It is claimed that this arrangement is more efficient than merely placing each user's file, for example, directly in /tcb/files/auth. All files under /tcb are non-readable by world users.

There are two other files under the /tcb tree: /tcb/files/devassign and /tcb/files/ttys. devassign has an entry for each terminal on the system; each entry has a field which lists users' allowed system access from that terminal device. ttys provides last login and related information on each terminal device.

13.2.2 Protected password database

An example of a protected password database file is /tcb/files/m/mary531. Each protected password file contains the encrypted password and a number of other authentication entries, some of which are

- A unique audit ID

- Password expiration time

- Password lifetime

- Time of last successful and unsuccessful password change

- Time when the account will expire

- Maximum time between logins before account expires

- Number of days before expiration when warning messages will start appearing

- Whether passwords are user- or system-generated
- Whether user-generated passwords are to be checked if they are easily guessable
- Time periods when the account can be logged into
- Terminal or remote host of last successful and unsuccessful logins
- Number of unsuccessful login attempts; cleared when successfully logged in
- Maximum number of login attempts before account is locked

An example protected password file is

```
puser1:u_name=puser1:u_id#513:\
      :u_pwd=eRtEtkSyukKxk:\
      :u_auditid#17:\
      :u_auditflag#1:\
      :u_pswduser=puser1:u_suclog#816914231:u_suctty=ttyp7:
u_unsuclog#816914224:\
      :u_unsuctty=ttyp6:u_lock@:chkent:
```

The entries are

u_name	Username
u_id	User ID
u_pwd	Encrypted password
u_auditid	Audit ID
u_auditflag	Whether the user's activities will be audited
u_pswduser	User name
u_suclog	Binary time of last successful login
u_suctty	Tty of last successful login
u_unsuclog	Binary time of last unsuccessful login
u_unsuctty	Tty of last unsuccessful login
u_lock	Account lock field

When a user attempts login, the login program authenticates the login with the fields in the user's protected password file and updates fields on successful and unsuccessful login attempts.

13.3 Auditing

Auditing can be enabled by setting AUDITING=1 in /etc/rc.config.d/auditing and rebooting the system. It can also be enabled from SAM's Auditing and Security area. The auditing subsystem is started or stopped by the *audsys* command. Auditing can be enabled only if the system is in the trusted-system mode. Essentially, when auditing is enabled, a log of certain system calls is maintained in a binary audit file. The primary audit file is /.secure/etc/audfile1, and in case this file is full, a secondary audit file, /.secure/etc/audfile2, is used. Example system calls that can be audited are fork(), kill(), reboot(), open(), and mount(). For convenience, the system calls are grouped into events (except for a few like login). For example, the *process* event consists of the system calls fork(), exit(), kill(), vfork(), and nsp_init(). The *audevent* command displays currently audited events and system calls. audevent is also used to change what events and system calls are to be logged to the audit file. Logging a lot of events and system calls can fill up the audit log file quickly. Here is a list of normally audited events and the associated system calls:

Event type	Audit on success	Audit on failure	Associated system calls
admin	Yes	Yes	audctl, audswitch, stime, reboot, setaudid, setaudproc, setdomainname, setevent, sethostid, setprivgrp, settimeofday, swapon
close	No	No	close
create	No	No	creat, mkdir, mknod, msgget, pipe, semget, shmat, shmget
delete	No	No	msgctl, rmdir, semctl
ipcclose	No	No	shutdown
ipccreat	No	No	bind, socket
ipcdgram	No	No	sendto, recvfrom
ipcopen	No	No	accept, connect
login	Yes	Yes	
modaccess	No	No	chdir, chroot, link, setgid, setuid, rename, setgroups, setresgid, setresuid, shmctl, shmdt, unlink
moddac	Yes	Yes	chmod, chown, fchmod, fchown, fsetacl, setacl, umask
open	No	No	open, execv, execve, ptrace, truncate, ftruncate
process	No	No	fork, exit, kill, vfork, nsp_init
removable	No	No	mount, umount, vfsmount
uevent1	No	No	
uevent2	No	No	
uevent3	No	No	

Note that uevent1, uevent2, and uevent3 can be used by programmers writing audit entries. The audisp command is used to display the audit log file. Here is a sample edited output. The major fields are

PID   Process identification
E   Event success/failure
EVENT Event identification code
PPID   Parent PID
AID   Audit identification, typically unique for each user
RUID   Regular user ID
RGID   Regular user group ID
EUID   Effective user ID
EGID   Effective group ID

```
# audisp /.secure/etc/aufile1
(edited output)
users and aids:
puser1
17
All events are selected.
All ttys are selected.
Selecting successful & failed events.
start time :
Nov 20 17:50:00 1995
TIME               PID E  EVENT   PPID    AID   RUID   RGID   EUID   EGID TTY

~~~~~~~~~~~~~~~~~~~~~~~~~~~~~~~~~~~~~~~~~~~~~~~~~~~~~~~~~~~~~~~~~~~~~~~~~~~~~~~~~~~~~~~~~~
951120 20:37:04   7131 S  10242   6437     17      0      3      0      3 ttyp7
[ Event=admin; User=puser1; Real Grp=sys; Eff.Grp=sys; ]

SELF-AUDITING TEXT: audisp -u puser1 -t 11201750 /.secure/etc/audfile1
~~~~~~~~~~~~~~~~~~~~~~~~~~~~~~~~~~~~~~~~~~~~~~~~~~~~~~~~~~~~~~~~~~~~~~~~~~~~~~~~~~~~~~~~~~
951120 20:37:04   7131 S    247   6437     17      0      3      0      3 ttyp7
[ Event=audswitch; User=puser1; Real Grp=sys; Eff.Grp=sys; ]

      RETURN_VALUE 1 = 0;
      PARAM #1 (int) = 0
~~~~~~~~~~~~~~~~~~~~~~~~~~~~~~~~~~~~~~~~~~~~~~~~~~~~~~~~~~~~~~~~~~~~~~~~~~~~~~~~~~~~~~~~~~
951120 20:38:35   7188 S   9218   7186     17      0     20      0     20 ttyp8
[ Event=login; User=puser1; Real Grp=users; Eff.Grp=users; ]

SELF-AUDITING TEXT: User=puser1 uid=513 audid=17 Successful login
~~~~~~~~~~~~~~~~~~~~~~~~~~~~~~~~~~~~~~~~~~~~~~~~~~~~~~~~~~~~~~~~~~~~~~~~~~~~~~~~~~~~~~~~~~
951120 20:38:35   7188 S    247   7186     17      0     20      0     20 ttyp8
[ Event=audswitch; User=puser1; Real Grp=users; Eff.Grp=users; ]

      RETURN_VALUE 1 = 0;
      PARAM #1 (int) = 0
~~~~~~~~~~~~~~~~~~~~~~~~~~~~~~~~~~~~~~~~~~~~~~~~~~~~~~~~~~~~~~~~~~~~~~~~~~~~~~~~~~~~~~~~~~
951120 20:38:35   7188 S    243   7186     17      0     20      0     20 ttyp8
[ Event=setaudproc; User=puser1; Real Grp=users; Eff.Grp=users; ]

      RETURN_VALUE 1 = 0;
      PARAM #1 (int) = 1
~~~~~~~~~~~~~~~~~~~~~~~~~~~~~~~~~~~~~~~~~~~~~~~~~~~~~~~~~~~~~~~~~~~~~~~~~~~~~~~~~~~~~~~~~~
951120 20:38:35   7204 S     60   7188     17    513     20    513      6 ttyp8
[ Event=umask; User=puser1; Real Grp=users; Eff.Grp=mail; ]

      RETURN_VALUE 1 = 0;
      PARAM #1 (int) = 7
~~~~~~~~~~~~~~~~~~~~~~~~~~~~~~~~~~~~~~~~~~~~~~~~~~~~~~~~~~~~~~~~~~~~~~~~~~~~~~~~~~~~~~~~~~
```

Selected records can be displayed by the following options to audisp:

-u (username)	Display records for specified user.
-e (eventname)	Display records of specified event.
-c (syscall)	Display records of specified system call.
-p	Display successful operations.
-f	Display failed operations.
-l (ttyname)	Display operations from tty name.
-t (start-time)	Display records logged since specified time.
-s (stop-time)	Display records logged before specified time.

The audusr command can be used to restrict logging for a specified set of users, possibly to keep the audit log file from growing too quickly. All auditing functionality can be accessed via SAM windows.

13.4   ACLs: File Access Control Lists

For controlling access to files, Unix defines three access modes—read, write, and execute (rwx)—and assigns these modes to three classes of users: owner, group, and others. Suppose access to a file is to be granted to the owner, the owner's group, and two other users only: john342 and mary543 (neither in the owner's group). This access requirement cannot be handled by the standard Unix file access control method. HP has extended the Unix access control method by means of Access Control Lists (ACLs). A file has an associated ACL which consists of Access Control Entries (ACEs). Each ACE has the format

```
(user.group, mode)
```

An example entry is

```
(john342.developer, rwx)
```

A percent sign (%) in the user or group field means no specific user or group. In fact, the default Unix access modes can be represented as three ACEs as shown here, where the lsacl command lists each file's ACL:

```
# ls -l tmp
-rwxrw-r--    1 root      sys        3655 Nov 20 20:39 tmp
# lsacl tmp
(root.%,rwx)(%.sys,rw-)(%.%,r--) tmp
```

An ACL on a file is manipulated by the *chacl* command. Here are some sample commands. *lsacl -l* lists ACEs one per line. Note that access control modes are specified as in the *chmod* command:

```
# ls -l tmp1            # show file access mode
-rw-rw-rw-  1 root      sys 3655 Nov 20 21:27 tmp1
# lsacl tmp1            # show file ACEs
(root.%,rw-)(%.sys,rw-)(%.%,rw-) tmp1
# lsacl -l tmp1         # show ACEs in long format
tmp1:
rw- root.%
rw- %.sys
rw- %.%
#
# chacl  "mary434.%=rw" tmp1 # user mary434 does not exist
chacl: invalid ACL: invalid user name in ACL entry: "mary434.%=rw"
#
# chacl  "mary433.%=rw" tmp1  # grant read and write access to mary433
#
# ls -l tmp1 # Note the + sign for ACEs present
-rw-rw-rw-+ 1 root      sys        3655 Nov 20 21:27 tmp1
#
# lsacl -l tmp1
```

```
tmp1:
rw- root.%
rw- mary433.%
rw- %.sys
rw- %.%
#
# lsacl tmp1
(root.%,rw-)(p544tn1.%,rw-)(%.sys,rw-)(%.%,rw-) tmp1
#
# chacl "john215.users=r" tmp1        # only read access for John
# lsacl -l tmp1
tmp1:
r— john215.users
rw- root.%
rw- mary433.%
rw- %.sys
rw- %.%
#
# chacl "john215.users + rw" tmp1     # add read and write access for John.
# chacl "john215.users-w" tmp1        # remove write access for John.
# lsacl -l tmp1
tmp1:
r— john215.users
rw- root.%
rw- mary433.%
rw- %.sys
rw- %.%
# chacl -d "mary433.%=rw" tmp1        # delete an ACE
#
# lsacl tmp1
(john215.users,rw-)(root.%,rw-)(%.sys,rw-)(%.%,rw-) tmp1
#
# chacl -d "john215.users=r" tmp1    # ACE delete requires exact match
chacl: file "tmp1": no matching ACL entry to delete for "john215.users-r"
```

To check access to a file, ACEs are checked in the following order against the accessor's user and group IDs:

(u.g, rwe)	Use entry if user and group match those of file accessor.
(u,%, rwe)	Use entry if user matches and group is specified as not specific.
(%.g, rwe)	Use entry if group matches and user is specified as not specific.
(%,%, rwe)	Use entry if both user and group are specified as not specific.

Note that the -A option must be specified when the chmod command is used; otherwise the file's ACE information is removed.

13.5 Assorted Security Products

Here is a biased list of products I have found useful to monitor and deter intruders from my systems and the network. All the products are freely available on the Internet.

■ *Satan* (*Security Administrator Tool for Analyzing Networks*): This is a tool which runs on a Unix system and pokes IP ports on other systems on the network to determine vulnerabilities. It will help you find holes intruders may use to compromise your systems. The software requires Mosaic and Perl to be installed. In the current version, V1.1.1, scripts can be written to scan the systems; however, printing of the reports is via a point-and-click GUI interface (based on X), which can be tedious.

- *COPS (Computer Oracle and Password System):*   This software checks for a few potential security problems on the system; however, its main feature is to show possible file protection problems. For example, it will flag a file which is owned by root, and yet it is writable by world.

- *Crack:*   This software attempts to guess passwords by looking at the password fields in the file /etc/passwd. Of course, when HP-UX is set up as a trusted system, the passwords are stored in different files under /tcb, which is not normally accessible to most users. However, I feel that the passwords should be checked in case someone can get to them, for example, by looking at backup tapes. I have a shell/awk script to extract the passwords and present them to crack in the /etc/passwd format.

- *Tripwire:*   This software package can be used to ensure that files on your system are not replaced by an intruder. Files may be replaced to have commands perform tasks which they should not be performing. For example, the /bin/ls command file can be replaced to perform the normal listing function and, if the user is root, to modify the protections on some password files which the intruder can then access. Tripwire basically keeps a checksum of the contents of each file on the system. When tripwire is run in the future, it runs the checksum program and compares the output with previous checksums. If there is a mismatch for a particular file, the file is not the same as when tripwire was run the first time. The checksum includes i-node and modification time information.

- *Tcpwrapper:*   This program logs information whenever a network service is requested on a node from another node. Network services are those defined in /etc/inetd.conf. The program also allows services to be denied to specified hosts or sets of hosts. Some of this functionality is available in HP-UX via the file /var/adm/inetd.sec, which allows and denies services to specified hosts or networks.

- *SSH (secure shell):*   Passwords and similar information flow on the network when you log into another system on your network. Snoopers can grab this information via simple programs. SSH allows you to do an equivalent of rlogin from one system to another; your session information is encrypted when it goes out to the network (and decrypted at the other end). All the steps are transparent once SSH is properly configured. The package supports other "r" commands.

14

Accounting: Monitoring and Charging for Resource Use

14.1 Introduction

HP-UX accounting facility is similar to that found on most Unix systems. It is an inelegant hotchpotch of files and commands. Per-user daily or monthly reports can be generated for disk, memory, and CPU use, login date and time, connect minutes, and per-process resource use. While the final reports are useful, most sites do not enable accounting because of its complexity. Hopefully the discussion here will be sufficient to allow you to exploit this useful subsystem. Accounting programs and scripts are in /usr/sbin/acct, and data files are under /var/adm. Note that System Activity Reporter (sar) is a separate facility from accounting.

14.2 Accounting Procedure Overview

Three basic kinds of accounting reports can be generated: user login and logout information, per-process resource use information, and per-user disk use information. The sources of information for these reports are:

- When a user logs in and logs out, a binary entry is made by the login process in /var/adm/wtmp. Accounting programs fetch data from this file.

- No specific disk information is gathered. Disk utilization reports are generated by scanning file systems.

- Per-process information is stored by the system in /var/adm/pacct. A record is written to the file when a process terminates. Because this file can grow

fast, process accounting is not enabled by default. To start process accounting, execute

```
/usr/sbin/acct/startup
```

To start process accounting every time the system boots, enter START_ACCT=1
in the startup configuration file /etc/rc.config.d/acct.

14.3 Generating Reports

14.3.1 Daily reports

Report creation involves going through a number of steps, described later.
The shell scripts *dodisk* and *runacct* encapsulate these steps.

# /usr/sbin/acct/dodisk	Creates disk usage binary data file, /var/adm/acct/nite/disktacct.
# /usr/sbin/acct/runacct	Processes wtmp, pacct, and disktacct files.

runacct effectively retrieves data from wtmp, pacct, and disktacct and creates various files under the directory /var/adm/acct. In particular, a summary
report is generated in the file, /var/adm/acct/sum/rprtmmdd, where mmdd is
current month and date. The *prdaily* command displays this file. See the
notes which follow output of the commands shown here.

```
# /usr/sbin/acct/prdaily 1113 # display report for November 13th.
```

(Edited and truncated output.)

```
Nov 14 12:41 1995  DAILY REPORT FOR HP-UX Page 1
from Mon Nov 13 19:48:40 1995
to   Tue Nov 14 04:00:01 1995
1       runacct
1       acctcon1
TOTAL DURATION IS 491 MINUTES
LINE        MINUTES PERCENT # SESS  # ON    # OFF
tty0p2      0       0       0       0       2943
tty0p3      0       0       0       0       2943
tty0p4      0       0       0       0       2943
tty0p5      0       0       0       0       2943
ttyp1       12      2       1       1       2
ttyp3       5       1       1       1       2
TOTALS      17      —       2       2       11776
```

```
Nov 14 12:41 1995  DAILY USAGE REPORT FOR HP-UX Page 1
```

UID	LOGIN NAME	CPU (MINS) PRIME	NPRIME	KCORE-MINS PRIME	NPRIME	CONNECT (MINS) PRIME	NPRIME	DISK BLOCKS	# OF PROCS	# OF SESS	# DISK SAMPLES
0	TOTAL	0	3	0	16	0	17	769444	12077	2	20
0	root	0	3	0	5	0	0	238710	11987	0	1
1	daemon	0	0	0	0	0	0	304	16	0	1
2	bin	0	0	0	0	0	0	408094	0	0	1
4	adm	0	0	0	11	0	0	3620	52	0	1
5	uucp	0	0	0	0	0	0	912	0	0	1
9	lp	0	0	0	0	0	0	408	0	0	1
514	test123	0	23	0	12	0	12	10	21	2	1

```
516    john321  0    12      0     4      0     15     10     4      0   1
1002   mary211  0    3       0     2      0     2004   28396  8      0   1

Nov 14 04:00 1995   DAILY COMMAND SUMMARY Page 1
                                 TOTAL COMMAND SUMMARY
```

COMMAND NAME	NUMBER CMDS	TOTAL KCOREMIN	TOTAL CPU-MIN	TOTAL REAL-MIN	MEAN SIZE-K	MEAN CPU-MIN	HOG FACTOR
TOTALS	12077	15.70	3.17	2038.41	4.96	0.00	0.00
diskusg	1	10.31	0.07	0.30	140.26	0.07	0.25
getty	11768	1.47	2.94	1965.64	0.50	0.00	0.00
rlogind	2	0.97	0.01	19.41	126.09	0.00	0.00
sh	22	0.83	0.02	37.97	53.76	0.00	0.00
more	5	0.72	0.00	2.21	143.20	0.00	0.00
runacct	1	0.70	0.01	0.11	124.24	0.01	0.05
rlogin	2	0.22	0.00	8.14	144.00	0.00	0.00
nulladm	10	0.20	0.00	0.02	46.77	0.00	0.20
dodisk	1	0.11	0.00	0.30	128.00	0.00	0.00
cat	25	0.06	0.00	0.01	15.04	0.00	0.53
pr	10	0.06	0.00	0.53	13.92	0.00	0.01
dmesg	1	0.02	0.00	0.00	74.00	0.00	0.40
crontab	7	0.02	0.00	1.27	13.60	0.00	0.00

(Monthly command summary deleted; similar to daily command summary.)

```
Nov 14 04:00 1995   LAST LOGIN Page 1

00-00-00   adm        00-00-00   john123     95-11-12   root
00-00-00   bin        00-00-00   mary321     95-11-14   test123
00-00-00   daemon     00-00-00   lp          00-00-00   uucp
```

Regarding the preceding output,

- The prdaily report has five tables: tty line information, per-user resource use statistics, per-command resource use statistics (daily and monthly), and last login information for each user.

- The tty line information may not be of much use, since, nowadays, tty line numbers are dynamically assigned when users log in over the network.

- The per-user resource use table can be the basis for a fee-charging algorithm. Note that the information in the DISK BLOCKS column is from the dodisk command output file, disktacct.

- The per-command resource use statistics can be used to optimize heavily used programs.

- If the last login information for a user is "zero," then the user logged in before the report time and has processes running on the system.

- Prime and nonprime times are defined in /usr/sbin/acct/holidays, which is described later.

- Hog factor is total CPU time divided by elapsed time.

- The file /var/adm/wtmp is the source for tty line use and user login and logout information. The records processed by runacct are removed from the file. Similarly, the file /var/adm/pacct is the source for command and process information. Processed records are removed from the file. The information is presented as reports and also stored in daily binary files described later.

runacct creates a number of files in /var/adm/acct/sum which are used for monthly reporting.

14.3.2 Monthly reports

Typically, daily reports are created by running dodisk and runacct each night. The daily data can be summarized into a monthly report by *monacct:*

```
# /usr/sbin/acct/monacct      Generate monthly accounting report.
```

The report generated is similar to the daily report shown above except that no table of tty line information is created. The monthly report is stored in the file /var/adm/acct/fiscal/fiscrptmm, where mm is the month, 01 to 12. The file can be printed, as an example, by

```
# lp -d laserlp /var/adm/acct/fiscal/fiscrpt11      Print November accounting report.
```

monacct reads files created by runacct in /var/adm/acct/sum. The files are processed and removed. Monthly files are created in /var/adm/acct/fiscal.

The following sections describe accounting steps in greater detail for troubleshooting, generating custom reports, and charging.

14.4   Total Accounting Files

There are various sources of data for the accounting commands. As an initial step in the accounting scripts, such as runacct, the source data is converted to a standard format called *total accounting records*. The records are stored in files called tacct files. These files are then used by other commands for further processing. The binary contents of a total accounting record are those shown in the per-user section of the report above. The fields are

UID	User ID.
Login name	User name.
CPU	Minutes of CPU time used. Prime and nonprime time values are recorded.
Kcore	CPU time (in seconds) times average Kbytes of main memory used divided by 60. This is a measure of amount of memory and the length of time it was used. Prime and nonprime time values are recorded.
Connect	Session elapsed time. Prime and nonprime time values are recorded.
Disk blocks	Information gathered by dodisk.
# of procs	Total number of processes spawned by the user. Information gathered from pacct file.
# of sess	Number of logins.

disk samples   Number of times disk accounting was run to obtain average infor-
mation displayed.

fee   Fee units charged. Fees are described later.

The steps that follow show how tacct files are created. The contents of a
tacct file can be displayed by a command like

```
# prtacct tacctfile
```
     ASCII display of binary tacct file

14.5 Disk Accounting Steps

The dodisk command reports on each user's disk use on all the file systems in
/etc/fstab. The dodisk script, in turn, uses three key commands: *diskusg, acctdusg,* and *acctdisk.*

diskusg takes device file names (corresponding to file systems) and produces a report on disk use by each report:

```
# /usr/sbin/acct/diskusg /dev/vg00/lvol1
```
     Report blocks used on disk by each user.

```
0       root     38434
2       bin      32342
9       lp       20
213     john21   2135
```

The reports shows user ID, user name, and disk blocks occupied by the user's
files. diskusg reporting is based on inode use. acctdusg produces a similar
report; however, its input is file names. Typically, the *find* command is used
to pipe file names to it:

```
# find /home | acctdusg
```
     Report blocks used under /home by each user.

diskusg is more accurate and faster than acctdusg. The output of these
commands can be piped to acctdisk to create a total accounting records file:

```
# diskusg /dev/vg00/lvol1 | acctdisk > disktacct
```

14.6 User Connect Session Accounting Steps

As mentioned before, user login, logout, and tty information is recorded in the
binary file, var/adm/wtmp, whenever a user logs in and out. acctcon converts
this file to a total accounting record file:

```
# acctcon</var/adm/wtmp>ctacct
```

14.6.1 Process accounting steps

When process accounting is started by /usr/sbin/acct/startup, the kernel will
enter a binary record in var/adm/pacct when a process on the system terminates. The command *acctprc1* produces an ASCII report by reading the pacct
records and adding login names corresponding to user IDs in the pacct file.

The command *acctprc2* accepts output from *acctprc1,* sorts and summarizes the data, and produces a total accounting records file:

```
# acctprc1</var/adm/pacct | acctprc2>ptacct
```

14.7 Merging tacct Files

The above steps show how individual total accounting record files are created. The files have to be merged to produce per-user reports. The following command merges disk, user connect session, and process total accounting files to produce a "complete" total accounting records file:

```
# acctmerg disktacct ctacct < ptacct > tacct
```

runacct creates the tacct file /var/adm/acct/sum/daytacct. monacct creates the tacct file /var/adm/acct/nite/fiscal/tacctmm, where mm represents the month.

14.8 Charging for Resource Use

The *chargefee* command allows the system administrator to enter an amount to be charged to a user. For example,

```
# chargefee john243 240
```

charges $2.40 to user john243. A total accounting entry is made in /var/adm/fee. The accounting file is merged with other tacct files when runacct runs. The total fee for a particular user is displayed in the "charge fee" column of the prdaily report.

To charge for resource use, awk scripts can be created and run on tacct files. Here is an example script where arbitrary costs are associated with various resources and the billing amount is printed for each user in the daily total accounting record file, /var/adm/acct/nite/daytacct.

```
acctmerg -a < daytacct > ascii_tacct        create ASCII form of daily tacct file
awk 'BEGIN  {
             # per unit charges
             cpu_pr = 0.08        Prime time charge for 1 min CPU time
             cpu_np = 0.03        Nonprime time CPU use
             mem_pr = 0.002       Prime time kilocore CPU minutes charge
             mem_np = 0.0001      Nonprime time memory use
             con_pr = 0.0003      Prime time charge for session connect time
             con_np = 0.0001      Nonprime time connect time
             dskblk = 0.001       Charge per disk block
             procs  = 0.01        Charge per process created
             sess   = 0.15        Charge per session created
             fee    = 0.01        Cents of fee charged
             }
      {
```

```
        totalamt 5 cpu_pr * $3 1 cpu_np * $4 1 mem_pr * $5 \
          + mem_np * $6 + con_np * $7 + con_np * $8 \
          + dskblk * $9 + procs * $10 + sess * $11 \
          + fee * $13
        # display username and amount billed
        printf "%s %10.2f\n", $2, totalamt
}' ascii_tacct
```

15

Backup and Recovery

15.1 Introduction

Disk-to-tape backups and restores can be performed with the following utilities: fbackup and frecover, tar, dump and restore, cpio, dd, and OmniBack II. OmniBack II has to be purchased separately; the other utilities are bundled with the base operating system. For routine backups, fbackup and frecover are the best for system administrators. They can be used for incremental backups and backups across the network. The utilities, however, do not support multiple backups on a single tape. tar backups are portable to other Unix platforms, and tar supports multiple backups on a single tape. tar cannot perform incremental backups. dump and restore are traditional Unix utilities. They are slow and cannot handle Access Control Lists (ACLs) on files. Use fbackup and frecover instead; they have all the dump and restore functionality and more. cpio copies named files to tape. dd is used to copy data block by block from one medium to another. It handles ASCII to EBCDIC conversion. It is also useful for piping tape data on one system over to another system on the network.

OmniBack II is useful at sites that handle large backup volumes regularly. OmniBack II

- Supports backup of disks on one system to tape devices on another system

- Handles HP stacker and jukebox devices fairly well

- Keeps track of how many times tapes are used and warns if tapes are written to too many times

- Keeps track of backups performed and lists them for restores

- Supports encrypted and compressed backups

- Supports Netware, Windows NT, and SAP backups to HP systems

- Allows backup functions to be assigned to groups like systems administrators, operators, and users

While OmniBack II has the functionality required by major data centers, fbackup and frecover may be a sufficient backup solution for many sites. In fact, SAM has a Backup and Recovery area, which is essentially a GUI interface to fbackup and frecover. Scheduled backups, even network backups and incremental backups, can be set up by novice system administrators.

15.2   Backup Strategy

If all your disk data can fit in a single tape drive, daily backups are easy to perform; just put a tape in the drive every day before going home, and ensure that a cron job is set up to perform backups every night. The tape can be physically unmounted and the backup log can be checked in the morning.

More thought has to be given to backups when

- More data has to be backed up than can fit on one tape and human intervention is required during the backup process.
- Complete backups take a long time.
- There is very little time, daily or weekly, when files are not accessed by users.

Incremental backups can be a viable solution for many sites. An incremental backup is a backup of files modified since a previous backup. For example, a complete disk backup can be done on Saturday. Then, an incremental backup can be done on Tuesday to cover files modified since Saturday's backup. Hopefully, not many files will have changed since Saturday, and the Tuesday backup will finish quickly. If there is a disk crash on Wednesday, the Saturday full backup will have to be restored, followed by a restore of the Tuesday incremental backup. Modifications since the Tuesday backup will be lost.

To augment the Saturday and Tuesday backups, another incremental backup could be taken on Thursday. This incremental backup can be one of two types:

1. Backup of files modified since the Tuesday incremental backup. In this case, if the disk crashes on Friday, three restores will have to be done: the full Saturday backup will have to be restored, followed by the Tuesday backup restore, followed by the Thursday backup restore.

2. Backup of files modified since the Saturday complete backup. In this case, if the disk crashes on Friday, only two restores will have to be done: the full Saturday backup will have to be restored, followed by the Thursday backup restore. The disadvantage of this backup over the one mentioned above is that all files modified since Saturday are accounted for in this backup, while in the above backup, only files modified since Tuesday are accounted for.

fbackup, dump, and OmniBack II support 10 levels of backup, 0 to 9. A level 0 backup is a full backup. A database of files covered, the backup level of each file, and the backup date and time are maintained by the backup utility. When another backup is performed on the same set of files, the utility checks, for each file, the current backup level and the previous backup level noted in the database. If the current backup level is higher and the file has been modified since the last backup, a backup is made of the file. In the incremental backup illustration above, the Saturday backup could be at level 0, the Tuesday incremental backup at level 3, and the Thursday incremental backup at level 6. In the second illustration, the Saturday backup could be at level 0, the Tuesday backup at level 3, and the Thursday backup at level 3 (or 2 or 1).

A reasonable backup strategy could be a weekend full, level 0 backup and a daily incremental, level 3 backup over the weekend backup (not incremental over the previous day). This way, in case of file system corruption, only two backups need to be restored.

15.3   fbackup and frecover

fbackup backs up specified files or all files under one or more specified directory trees. fbackups can span more than one tape. The files and directories can be specified on the command line with the -i option, or they can be specified in a file, called a graph file, and this file can be specified with the -g option. The backup device can be specified with the -f option. The -v option is for verbose messages. An example is

```
# /usr/sbin/fbackup -f /dev/rmt/1m -i /home/p544jns/tmpdir -v
fbackup(1004): session begins on Fri Nov 17 21:11:41 1995
fbackup(3203): volume 1 has been used 4 time(s)
fbackup(3024): writing volume 1 to the output file /dev/rmt/1m
    1: /
    2: /home
    3: /home/p544jns
    4: /home/p544jns/tmpdir
    5: /home/p544jns/tmpdir/sessions
    6: /home/p544jns/tmpdir/sessions/swlist.last
    7: /home/p544jns/tmpdir/tmp
    8: /home/p544jns/tmpdir/tmpa
    9: /home/p544jns/tmpdir/typescript
fbackup(1005): run time: 51 seconds
```

Here, all files under the directory /home/p544jns/tmpdir are sent as backup to the DDS tape in /dev/rmt/1m. Note that fbackup displays the number of times the tape has already been used for fbackups. This information can be used to determine if the tape is worn out.

A graph file–based backup is

```
# /usr/sbin/fbackup -f /dev/rmt/1m  -g graph.bak -v
```

The content of the graph file can be:

```
i /home/p544jns
i /home/john215
```

Here, the two directory trees will be covered in backup. When many separate directories are to be covered, they can be specified on the command line with multiple -i options; however, specifying these directories in graph files may be more convenient. Graph files must be used for dumps of backup levels 0 to 9. Files can be restored with the frecover command. For example, the following command takes the files covered by the previously described backup and loads them back into their original locations:

```
# frecover -f /dev/rmt/1m -r -v
drwxr-xr-x      p544jns users   /home/p544jns/tmpdir
drwxr-xr-x      p544jns users   /home/p544jns/tmpdir/sessions
-rw-r--r--      p544jns users   /home/p544jns/tmpdir/sessions/swlist.last
-rw-r--r--      p544jns users   /home/p544jns/tmpdir/tmp
-rw-r--r--      p544jns users   /home/p544jns/tmpdir/tmpa
-rw-r--r--      p544jns users   /home/p544jns/tmpdir/typescript
```

If any file exists on disk with a later modification date than the one on the tape, the file is not restored.

The -I option is for creating an index of a backup tape. Hence it can used to check the contents of a tape:

```
# frecover -f /dev/rmt/1m -I tape.index        Create a tape contents file.
```

Normally, files are recovered to their original directory; however, the -X option specifies that files be restored relative to the current working directory:

```
# frecover -f /dev/rmt/1m -r -X        Restore files to current directory and below.
```

If files had been backed up using the relative path specification, ./, which is the current directory, then, during a restore, the files would be restored relative to the current working directory even if the -X option were not used. An example of a relative backup command is

```
# fbackup -f /dev/rmt/1m -i ./home/p544jns/tmpdir
```

15.3.1 Selective restores

A subset of files can be recovered by using the -i or the -g (graph file) option, as in

```
# frecover -f /dev/rmt/1m -r -i /home/p544jns/tmpdir/sessions
```

15.3.2 The graph file and backup levels

A backup level can be specified from among the options -0 to -9. The -u option specifies that the past backups database file be updated to note that the backup was done at this level. For example,

```
# fbackup -f /dev/rmt/1m -3 -u -g graph.bak
```

Note that when the -u option is used, the -i option cannot be used; a graph file must be specified. The past updates database file is /var/adm/fbackupfiles/dates, which may contain entries like

```
/etc/sam/br/graphCEAa15967 0 816461495 816461749
    STARTED: Wed Nov 15 13:51:35 1995    ENDED: Wed Nov 15 13:55:49 1995
graph.bak 3 816663820 816663871
    STARTED: Fri Nov 17 22:03:40 1995    ENDED: Fri Nov 17 22:04:31 1995
```

The line starting with STARTED is for human readability; it is not used by the system. The other lines note the graph file, backup level, and backup date and time in internal format. This information is used when an incremental backup is done with the same graph file. Note that the graph files tmp and ./tmp are not considered the same; also, two backups done on two different graph files with the same name would be mixed up in the dates file.

The next time a backup command like

```
# fbackup -f /dev/rmt/1m -5 -u -g graph.bak
```

is issued, the dates file is checked. Since the previous backup was at level 3, only files modified since the previous level 3 backup time will be backed up to tape. The level 5 backup information is inserted in the dates file.

15.3.3 Network backups

fbackup and frecover can be performed over the network by simply specifying the host name and a colon in the -f option, as in

```
# fbackup -f nodepqr:/dev/rmt/1m -3 -u -g graph.bak
```

Not all tape devices may be supported for network backups and restores; DDS and 9-track tape drives are supported.

15.3.4 Backups with SAM

The System Administration Manager has a Backup and Recovery area which has a GUI front end to fbackup and frecover. From SAM, backup jobs can be scheduled for regular execution via the cron facility. The features are convenient and useful. Figure 15.1 shows the initial scheduled backup setup window. The option Add an Automated Backup was selected from the Action menu. Figures 15.2 and 15.3 show the windows displayed when the Select Backup Scope and the Select Backup Times buttons are clicked. As can be seen, a full and incremental backup schedule can be set up for an arbitrary set of files and directory trees. Remote backups and "one-shot" interactive backups are also supported.

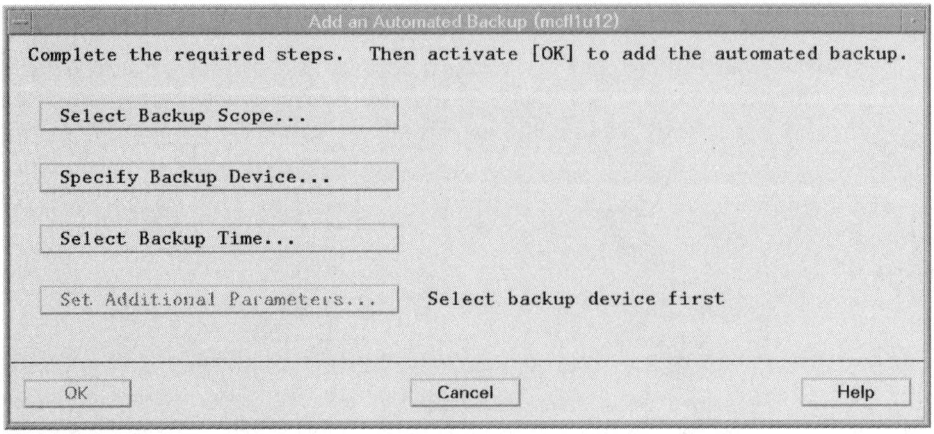

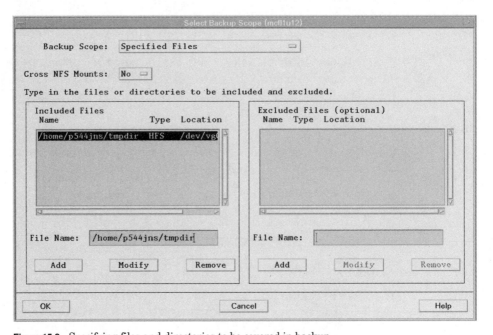

Figure 15.1   SAM window to set up scheduled backups via cron.

Figure 15.2   Specifying files and directories to be covered in backup.

15.4   tar

tar is the most popular standard Unix utility for backups and restores. Some pros and con of tar are:

- tar tapes are usually portable across Unix platforms.
- tar does not provide backup to Access Control List (ACL) information on files.
- Multiple tar backups can be made to a single tape.

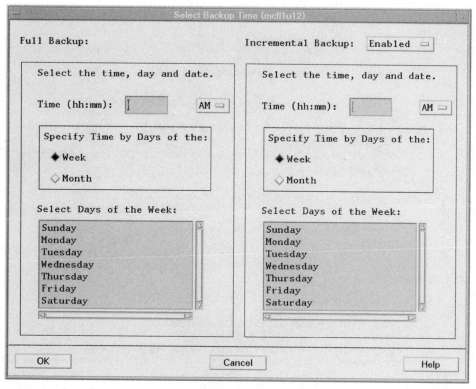

Figure 15.3 Specifying repeat frequency of full and incremental backups.

Tar backups are also known as archives. Common tar options are:

- *c:* Create a backup.
- *t:* List what is on the backup.
- *x:* Extract (restore) from backup.
- *f:* Backup tape or file name. If - is specified as a tape or filename, standard input (for restore) and standard output (for backup) are assumed.
- *v:* Verbose mode.

The following command creates backup for files under the directory tree /home/p544jns/tmpdir on the tape in drive /dev/rmt/1m. The dash in front of options is not required; I prefer to use it, for then the command is more consistent with other Unix commands. The *a* at the start of the output lines represents archive.

```
$ tar -cvf /dev/rmt/1m /home/p544jns/tmpdir
a /home/p544jns/tmpdir/sessions/swlist.last 1 blocks
a /home/p544jns/tmpdir/tmpb 1 blocks
a /home/p544jns/tmpdir/tmp 1 blocks
a /home/p544jns/tmpdir/tmpa 6 blocks
```

```
a /home/p544jns/tmpdir/typescript 1 blocks
$
```

The backup can be to a file, test.tar in this command:

```
$ tar -cvf test.tar /home/p544jns/tmpdir
```

The backup can specify multiple directories, as in:

```
$ tar -cvf test.tar /home/p544jns/tmpdir /home/john231 /var/spool
```

The files can be restored using the x option as shown here. The files are restored in their original location.

```
$ tar -xvf /dev/rmt/1m /home/p544jns/tmpdir
x /home/p544jns/tmpdir/sessions/swlist.last, 445 bytes, 1 tape blocks
x /home/p544jns/tmpdir/tmpb, 243 bytes, 1 tape blocks
x /home/p544jns/tmpdir/tmp, 23 bytes, 1 tape blocks
x /home/p544jns/tmpdir/tmpa, 2752 bytes, 6 tape blocks
x /home/p544jns/tmpdir/typescript, 88 bytes, 1 tape blocks
$
```

15.4.1   Listing backup contents

The -t option lists the contents of a backup:

```
$ tar -tvf /dev/rmt/1m /home/p544jns/tmpdir
x /home/p544jns/tmpdir/sessions/swlist.last, 445 bytes, 1 tape blocks
x /home/p544jns/tmpdir/tmpb, 243 bytes, 1 tape blocks
x /home/p544jns/tmpdir/tmp, 23 bytes, 1 tape blocks
x /home/p544jns/tmpdir/tmpa, 2752 bytes, 6 tape blocks
x /home/p544jns/tmpdir/typescript, 88 bytes, 1 tape blocks
$
```

15.4.2   Selective restores

To restore a subset of files held in backup, the restore command specifies only the directory trees to be restored:

```
$ tar -xvf /dev/rmt/1m /home/p544jns/tmpdir/sessions
x /home/p544jns/tmpdir/sessions/swlist.last, 445 bytes, 1 tape blocks
$
```

15.4.3   Restoring to other directories

The backup shown in the above example can be restored only to the original location. To restore a backup under a different tree, the backup must be taken with a relative file specification, as in

```
$ tar -cvf /dev/rmt/1m ./tmpdir
```

Note the dot in the directory name of the files which were backed up. The current directory must be /home/p544jns if files in the previous sample backups are to be backed up. A restore can be done to any directory by setting the current working directory to the new directory and issuing a command such as

```
$ tar -xvf /dev/rmt/1m ./tmpdir
x ./tmpdir/sessions/swlist.last, 445 bytes, 1 tape blocks
x ./tmpdir/tmpb, 243 bytes, 1 tape blocks
x ./tmpdir/tmp, 23 bytes, 1 tape blocks
x ./tmpdir/tmpa, 2752 bytes, 6 tape blocks
x ./tmpdir/typescript, 88 bytes, 1 tape blocks
$
```

15.4.4 Multiple backups to a tape

For a single backup, tar writes data to a tape and then writes a physical tape mark. If the rewind command is not issued to the tape, another tar backup could be written to the tape (followed by a tape mark). In the backup examples above, the tape drive rewinds the tape after the command completes. To support multiple backups, the tape device name should be of the no-rewind form. For example, /dev/rmt/1m is the rewind form of a tape drive, and /dev/rmt/1mn is the no-rewind form of the same tape drive. Here are two tar backups to a single tape drive:

```
$ tar -cvf /dev/rmt/1mn /home/p544jns/tmpdir
$ tar -cvf /dev/rmt/1mn /home/mary432/cfiles
```

The tape will contain tar backup for /home/p544jns/tmpdir followed by a tape mark, followed by a tar backup of /home/mary432/cfiles followed by a tape mark (actually, end-of-tape mark).

How can the second tar backup be restored? One way is to list the first tar backup with the no-rewind tape device—which will place the tape at the beginning of the second tar backup—and then to perform a tar extract:

```
$ tar -tvf /dev/rmt/1mn
$ tar -xvf /dev/rmt/1mn   /home/mary432/cfiles
```

Suppose the tape was put away and, after a few days, a third tar backup was to be written to the tape. The tape should be mounted and the two tar backups should be listed using the no-rewind tape drive name. This can be followed by the third tar backup.

```
$ tar -tvf /dev/rmt/1mn
$ tar -tvf /dev/rmt/1mn
$ tar -cvf /dev/rmt/1mn   /home/john452/tmps
```

You get the idea. Note that we used the tar listing command to skip tape marks. A more elegant way to skip tape marks is by using the mt utility. For example,

```
$ mt -t /dev/rmt/1mn fsf 1
```

will cause the tape to advance one tape mark. *fsf* is for file space forward. Some other mt commands are

```
$ mt -t /dev/rmt/1mn bsf 1      Backward-space one tape mark.
$ mt -t /dev/rmt/1mn fsf 2      Forward-space two tape marks.
$ mt -t /dev/rmt/1mn rewind     Rewind tape to beginning of tape.
```

Understanding the data format for tapes and visualizing how information is stored on a tar tape are key to manipulating multiple tar backups.

15.4.5   tar across the network

To make a backup of files in a local directory to a tape drive on a remote system, a command like this can be used:

```
$ tar -cvf - /var/spool | remsh nodepqr dd of=/dev/rmt/1m
```

Observe that

- The tar tape device name is given by a dash, meaning that the output will be sent to standard output.
- The tar output is sent to the remote system nodepqr, where the dd utility (described later in this chapter) writes the data to tape, block by block.

A restore can be done by executing the command

```
$ remsh nodepqr dd if=/dev/rmt/1m | tar -cvf - /var/spool
```

The *if* option to dd specifies the input data source.

15.5   dump and restore

dump and restore are traditional Unix utilities for full and incremental backups of file systems using dump levels 0 to 9. The utilities are similar to fbackup and frecover, though the latter are newer and have more functionality. *rdump* and *rrestore* support network backups and restores. Pros and cons of dump and restore are that

- Only complete file systems can be dumped, though selected directories can be restored.
- Access Control Lists (ACLs), are not dumped.

  Commonly used dump options are

- *0-9:*   Specifies a dump level. 0 is for a full dump.
- *u:*   Writes dump information in file /var/adm/dumpdates. This information is used for incremental dumps.
- *f:*   Tape drive name.

Commonly used restore options are:

- *r:* Restore complete dump to current directory.

- *x:* Extract (restore) named files.

- *t:* List files on tape.

- *i:* Interactive restore. File names are read from tape and then a shell prompt is displayed. Files to be extracted or excluded can then be entered interactively.

Here is a sample session:

```
# # backup the /home file system. Level 0 dump. Update /var/adm/dumpdates.
# /usr/sbin/dump -0uf /dev/rmt/1m /home
  DUMP: Date of this level 0 dump: Sun Nov 19 13:16:58 1995
  DUMP: Date of last level 0 dump: the epoch
  DUMP: Dumping /dev/vg32/rlvol6 (/home) to /dev/rmt/1m
  DUMP: This is an HP long file name filesystem
  DUMP: mapping (Pass I) [regular files]
  DUMP: mapping (Pass II) [directories]
  DUMP: estimated 6136 tape blocks on 0.16 tape(s).
  DUMP: dumping (Pass III) [directories]
  DUMP: dumping (Pass IV) [regular files]
  DUMP: DUMP: 6136 tape blocks on 1 tape(s)

  DUMP: DUMP: /dev/vg32/rlvol6 has 0 inodes with unsaved optional acl entries
  DUMP: DUMP IS DONE
  DUMP: level 0 dump on Sun Nov 19 13:16:58 1995
  DUMP: Tape rewinding
#
# # list files on tape
# /usr/sbin/restore -vtf /dev/rmt/1m
Verify tape and initialize maps
Tape block size is 10
Dump date: Sun Nov 19 13:16:58 1995
Dumped from: the epoch
Extract directories from tape
Initialize symbol table.
dir        2 .
dir        3 ./lost + found
...
leaf    1986 ./p544jns/typescript
leaf    1944 ./p544jns/.glancerc
leaf    1943 ./p544jns/nohup.out
...
leaf     780 ./sybase/.sh_history
leaf     775 ./sybase/.cshrc2
leaf    1191 ./synctime/.rhosts
dir     2736 ./tmp5dir
dir     3123 ./tmp5dir/p544jns
dir       43 ./tmp5dir/p544jns/tmpdir
dir      419 ./tmp5dir/p544jns/tmpdir/sessions
leaf     420 ./tmp5dir/p544jns/tmpdir/sessions/swlist.last
...
leaf      49 ./tmp5dir/p544jns/tmpdir/1file
#
# #restore selected files. Note that the files have a relative path
# #and they are restored in the current directory.
# /usr/sbin/restore -vxf /dev/rmt/1m ./p544jns/tmpdir
Verify tape and initialize maps
Tape block size is 10
```

```
Dump    date: Sun Nov 19 13:16:58 1995
Dumped from: the epoch
Extract directories from tape
Initialize symbol table.
Make node ./p544jns
Make node ./p544jns/tmpdir
Make node ./p544jns/tmpdir/sessions
Make node ./p544jns/tmpdir/tmp4.dir
Make node ./p544jns/tmpdir/tmp4dir
Extract requested files
You have not read any tapes yet.
Unless you know which volume your file(s) are on you should start
with the last volume and work towards the first.
Specify next volume #: 1
extract file ./p544jns/tmpdir/tmp4dir/4file
extract file ./p544jns/tmpdir/sessions/swlist.last
extract file ./p544jns/tmpdir/tmp
extract file ./p544jns/tmpdir/tmpa
extract file ./p544jns/tmpdir/typescript
extract file ./p544jns/tmpdir/tmpb
extract file ./p544jns/tmpdir/tmp.tar
extract file ./p544jns/tmpdir/1file
Add links
Set directory mode, owner, and times.
set owner/mode for '.'? [yn] n
#
```

15.6   cpio

cpio -o copies files whose names are specified in standard input to standard output as an archive. *cpio -i* accepts a previously created archive in standard input and extracts files to the current directory tree. Examples of uses of the commands are

```
$ # backup files in current directory to tape
$ ls | cpio -o > /dev/rmt/1m
```

(Using tape drive with immediate report mode enabled (reel #1).)

```
27 blocks
$
$ # restore all files from tape to current directory
$ cpio -i < /dev/rmt/1m
27 blocks
$
```

A pattern can be specified during restore to selectively restore files:

```
$ cpio -i < /dev/rmt/1m tmp*        Restore files whose names start with tmp.
```

The find command can be used to back up a directory tree:

```
$ find . -print | cpio -o > /dev/rmt/1m
```

The -d option can be specified during a restore to create directories if required:

```
$ cpio -id < /dev/rmt/1m
```

A table of contents can be produced with the -t option:

```
$ cpio -it < /dev/rmt/1m        Do not restore; just list files on tape.
```

15.7   dd

dd is a byte-by-byte copy utility. Typically it is used to get data from or send data to a tape when a command accepts input from standard input or sends output to standard output. It is also used to send data over the network to another system's devices. Some of its options are:

- *if=file:* Specifies input. If not specified, standard input is assumed.
- *of=file:* Specifies output. If not specified, standard output is assumed.
- *bs=n:* Specifies input and output block size.
- *conv=conv-option:* Converts input before writing output. Some conv-options are EBCDIC, ASCII, ucase, and lcase.

Example dd commands are:

```
$ dd if=/home/tmp of=/dev/rmt/1m                      Write file to tape.
$ tar -cvf - /home | remsh nodepqr dd of=/dev/rmt/1m  A tar on the current system
                                                      whose output is sent to dd on
                                                      another system where the
                                                      data is written to tape.
```

15.8   OmniBack II: Cells, Cell Manager, and Agents

OmniBack II is a centralized backup management tool. A large network is divided into logical subnetworks for OmniBack (short for OmniBack II). Such subnetworks are called *cells*. Many organizations may simply have one cell. Each cell has a Cell Manager which runs on multiple nodes. The Cell Manager consists of a Cell Server node and one or more Session Manager nodes. The Cell Server node is where the OmniBack software is installed; the Session Manager nodes are where OmniBack backup and restore commands can be issued.

Systems that have disks to be backed up and tape devices for backups will have processes called Disk Agents and Media Agents. As an example, a site can have three large HP 9000 S800 systems with disk and tape drives and 100 smaller HP 9000 S700 systems that have some disk drives but no tape devices. The complete environment can be considered one cell. The Cell Server will be one HP 9000 S800, and the Session Managers could be all three HP 9000 S800s. Disk Agents could be running on all 103 systems; Media Agents could be running on the three large systems. The complete environment has a single backup database shared by all the Session Managers; for example, a

Figure 15.4 OmniBack II main window.

scheduled backup set up by a Session Manager will be reflected in the displays of the other Session Managers.

15.8.1 OmniBack setup

OnniBack software has to be installed on one node in the cell. This node is called the Cell Server. The installation is with *swinstall* and is typical of other installs. An iFOR/LS license is required to use the product. iFOR/LS is described in Appendix B of this book. Omniback has a convenient GUI based on X-windows. All functionality is also supported via the command line mode. The X-windows interface is started by

```
# /opt/omni/bin/xomni
```

Figure 15.4 shows the window that pops up. The first step is to install the functionality required on each of the Session Manager nodes. Typically, the major nodes are configured for console operations, Disk Agents, and Media (tapes, ROMs and such) Agents; smaller nodes are configured at least for Disk Agents so that their disks can be backed up to the major nodes. The installation steps are:

- Click on the Install button. A Cell Administration window pops up displaying the nodes where OmniBack components are configured. Initially, there are no configured nodes.

- Click on the Edit menu and select the Install Host(s) option. A list of nodes and install options will have to be added. The three main install options are Cell Console, Disk Agent, and Media Agent. The Cell Console should be installed on all nodes from which OmniBack operations like backup and restores will be performed. Disk Agents should be installed on all systems having disks that will be backed up. Media Agents should be installed on systems that have backup devices.

Note that appropriate OmniBack software modules are copied from the Cell Server to the other nodes during installation. Once done, the backup media in the cell will have to be assigned to pools.

15.8.2 Media and pool setup

Clicking on the Media button in the main window displays the pools set up in the cell. A backup device must be a member of one and only one pool. Figure

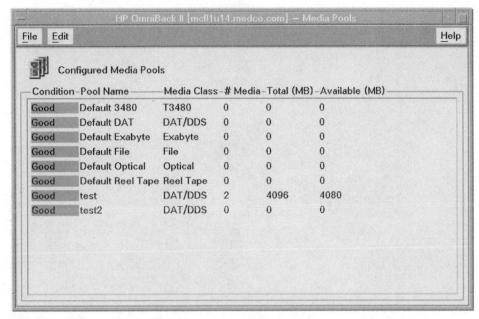

Figure 15.5 The media pools window.

15.5 shows a sample window. A pool can contain multiple backup devices. Pooling helps in media management; as an example, when devices are pooled, OmniBack determines which device to use for a backup to reduce tape aging. To create a new pool, click on the Edit menu and select Create Pool. A pool name has to be entered; optionally, media class, maximum number of overwrites, and similar information can be entered. Once a pool is created, backup devices are added to the pool.

To add a device to a pool, click on the Devices button of the OmniBack main window. A configured devices window will be displayed, as shown in Fig. 15.6. Select the Create Logical Device option from the Edit menu. Key information required is

- A logical device name, for example, nodepqr_tape
- Physical device name, for example, /dev/rmt/0m
- The pool to which the device will be assigned, for example, testpool
- Host name where the device is located, for example, nodepqr
- Description for documentation

Once the backup devices and pools are defined, OmniBack is ready for backups.

15.8.3 Quick start: Datalists

To perform a backup, click on the backup button in the OmniBack main window. A list of scheduled backups will be displayed. Click the Actions menu,

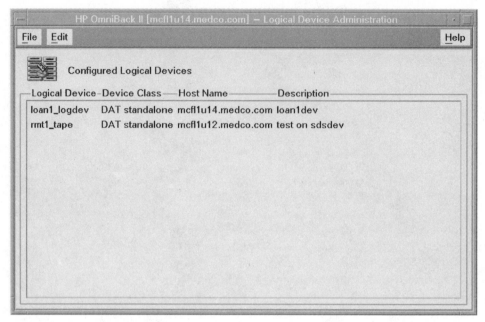

Figure 15.6   The backup devices window.

followed by the Backup submenu, followed by the Interactive option. A back-up editor window will show up. The objects (such as file systems or raw disks) to be backed up and the device where the objects should be backed up will have to be entered with the Add option in the Objects menu. Key information required is

- Host name of file system or other object to be backed up
- Files and directories to be backed up
- The logical name of the backup device
- File system options such as compression, encryption
- Pre- and postexecution scripts, if any
- How long the backup should be kept before the backup medium may be reused

The object and backup device information entered is called a *datalist*. The backup can be done immediately or the dataset can be saved for future use using the file menu Save as option. Figure 15.7 shows the window after the created datalist is saved as test2dataset. All saved datalists are displayed in the window that shows up when the backup button is clicked on the OmniBack main window.

If a new backup medium is used, it should be initialized by clicking on the Media button in the OmniBack main window, followed by clicking a pool, fol-

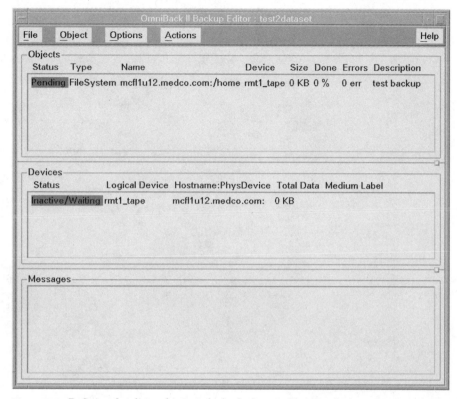

Figure 15.7 Defining datalists: objects to be backed up and backup devices.

lowed by selecting Manage Media from the Edit menu, followed in turn by selecting Initialize Medium from the Edit menu of the new window.

To perform the backup, click on Start Backup from the Actions menu in the Backup Editor window, shown in Fig. 15.7. A popup window will prompt for the type of backup, full or incremental. If incremental backup is to be performed, one of ten levels, 0 to 10, can be specified. The Messages area of the Backup Editor window will display backup progress and problems.

15.8.4 Restores

A list of backups is displayed in a window when the Restore button is clicked on the OmniBack main window. A backup can be selected, and the Restore option from the Actions menu will display a window where the restore option can be further specified. Figure 15.8 shows the restore options window where the full backup of /home is on tape and the /home/p544jns/tmpdir directory tree is to be restored. Once the required information is entered and the OK button is clicked, a Restore Monitor window, somewhat like the Backup Editor window, will be displayed. The Start Restore option from the Actions menu will start the restore operation. The Messages area displays progress and problems.

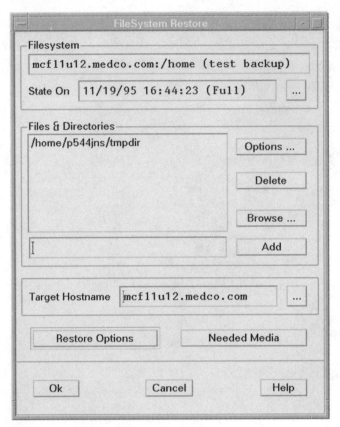

Figure 15.8 Restore options.

15.8.5 Monitoring backups and restores

All backups and restores initiated from all the Session Managers in the cell can be displayed by clicking on the Monitor button of the OmniBack main window. Figure 15.9 shows a sample Monitor window.

15.8.6 Scheduled backups

To create a scheduled backup, first create a datalist specifying what is to be backed up and to what devices. This is done by clicking on the Backup button in the OmniBack main window, followed by choosing Create from the Edit menu of the Backup window. The datalist is created as described in Section 15.8.3.

Once the datalist is created, select the datalist from the Backup window and choose Change Schedule from the Edit menu. Backup schedule, backup type (incremental or full), and similar information can then be entered.

Completion status of scheduled backups can be checked in the Messages area of the Backup Editor window where the datalist details are displayed.

Figure 15.9   Monitoring backups and restores in a cell.

15.8.7   Assigning roles to users: Security issues

Clicking on the Users button on the OmniBack menu displays user classes and users who belong to each class. There are four predefined classes:

- *Admin:*   Users in this class can configure OmniBack and perform backup restores and all other operations.

- *Senior-operator:*   Users in this class are allowed admin operations except configuring Omniback.

- *Operator:*   Users in this class can start backups and respond to mount requests.

- *End-user:*   Users in this class can restore their own data and respond to their own mount requests.

OmniBack can be customized to create new user classes that have a subset of the 16 or so OmniBack functions.

15.8.8   OmniBack command line interface

Complete OmniBack functionality is accessible via commands. All commands are in /opt/omni/bin and the command names start with omni. The main commands are:

omnib.	Back up a specified datalist.
omnicc.	Display license information.
omnicellinfo.	Display cell configuration such as objects, pools, and devices.
omnidb.	Query OmniBackup database.
omniminit.	Initialize a medium in a backup device.
omnimlist.	Display contents of a medium.
omnimm	Manage media and pool.
omnir	Perform a restore.
omnistat	Display active backup and restore sessions

Sample uses of these commands are shown here. My comments are in parentheses.

```
# omnicc -query
```

(Information on licensing and nodes configured in the cell)

```
            OmniBack II Licensing Summary
            ==============================
                     Total          Still available
       -------------------------------------------------
Client hosts          2500                    2498
Parallel backups       250                     250

Configured client hosts
-------------------------------------------------
     node2112.acme1.com
     node2114.acme1.com
#
# omnicellinfo -cell
```

(Nodes configured in the cell and OmniBack software versions of components on each node)

Host	OS	CC ORACLE	DA OST	MA SAP	OB NOVELL
node2112.acme1.com	hp s800 hp-ux-10.01	A.01.30	A.01.30	A.01.30	-
		-	-	-	-
node2114.acme1.com	hp s800 hp-ux-10.01	A.01.30	A.01.30	A.01.30	-
		-	-	-	-

```
Summary:
        2 configured host[s].
        2 installed Cell Console[s].
        2 installed Disk Agent[s].
        2 installed Media Agent[s].
        0 installed OmniBack I Agent[s].
        0 installed Oracle Integration Agent[s].
        0 installed OmniStorage Integration Agent[s].
        0 installed SAP Integration Agent[s].
        0 installed Novell Integration Agent[s].
#
# omnicellinfo -object
```

(Shows file system and raw disk backups configured in database)

Object	Label	Next Scheduled
(Edited)		
[FS] node2114.acme1.com:/var		Not scheduled
[FS] node2114.acme1.com:/usr/local		Not scheduled
[FS] node2114.acme1.com:/home/icpdev		Not scheduled
[FS] node2114.acme1.com:/home	test	11/21/95 04:30:00
[FS] node2114.acme1.com:/Development		Not scheduled

```
Altogether 27 object[s] found.
#
# omnicellinfo -dev
```

(Available backup devices/media)

```
Device name        Host               Device type        Pool
==============================================================================
loan1_logdev       node2114.acme1.c DAT standalone       test
rmt1_tape          node2112.acme1.c DAT standalone       test
==============================================================================
Together : 2 configured device[s].
#
# omnidb -object
```

(This command lists backed-up objects and similar information from the log database)

```
Object Name                                              Object type
==============================================================================
node2114.acme1.com:/home 'test'                          FileSystem
node2112.acme1.com:/home 'test backup'                   FileSystem
node2112.acme1.com:/home ''                              FileSystem
#
# omnib -filesystem node2112:/home -device rmt1_tape
```

(A backup from the command line)

```
[Normal] From: BMA@node2112.acme1.com "rmt1_tape"  Time: 11/19/95 17:54:11
        STARTING Medium Agent "rmt1_tape"

[Normal] From: VBDA@node2112.acme1.com ""  Time: 11/19/95 17:54:12
        STARTING Disk Agent for node2112.acme1.com ""

[Normal] From: VBDA@node2112.acme1.com ""  Time: 11/19/95 17:54:29
        COMPLETED Disk Agent for node2112.acme1.com ""

[Normal] From: BMA@node2112.acme1.com "rmt1_tape"  Time: 11/19/95 17:54:57
        COMPLETED Medium Agent "rmt1_tape"
#
# omniminit -init rmt1_tape # note the error
```

(Initialize a medium)

```
[Normal] From: IMA@node2112.acme1.com "rmt1_tape"  Time: 11/19/95 17:55:10
        STARTING Medium Agent "rmt1_tape"

[Warning] From: MSM@node2114.acme1.com "rmt1_tape"  Time: 11/19/95 17:54:46
         OmniBack II medium "test_5" in drive.
         Medium is still under protection => recycle medium.
         Initialization denied.
[Normal] From: IMA@node2112.acme1.com "rmt1_tape"  Time: 11/19/95 17:55:11
        ABORTED Medium Agent "rmt1_tape"
#
# omnimm -recycle test_5
```

(Omnimm performs media operations; -recycle is to allow reuse of the medium)

```
Medium test_5 successfully recycled.
#
# omniminit -init rmt1_tape -force
```

(Initialize a new medium)

```
[Normal] From: IMA@node2112.acme1.com "rmt1_tape"  Time: 11/19/95 17:55:42
        STARTING Medium Agent "rmt1_tape"
```

```
[Normal] From: MSM@node2114.acme1.com "rmt1_tape"  Time: 11/19/95 17:55:18
      OmniBack II medium "test_5" in drive.
      Initialization allowed.

[Normal] From: IMA@node2112.acme1.com "rmt1_tape"  Time: 11/19/95 17:55:43
      /dev/rmt/1m
      Initializing new medium: "test_6"

[Normal] From: MSM@node2114.acme1.com "rmt1_tape"  Time: 11/19/95 17:55:24
      New medium added to pool: test
         MediumID: 36190e06:30afb5d6:1ea6:0001
         Label:    test_6
         Location:

[Normal] From: IMA@node2112.acme1.com "rmt1_tape"  Time: 11/19/95 17:55:51
      COMPLETED Medium Agent "rmt1_tape"
#
```
 # omnistat

(Statistics)

```
No currently running sessions.
#
```
 # omnimlist -device rmt1_tape

(List contents of specified medium)

```
Scanning media...
Scanning of media successfully finished.
Medium : test_6 [36190e06:30afb5d6:1ea6:0001]
No query data found.
#
```

16

Performance
Monitoring, Analysis,
and Tuning

16.1   Introduction

Performance measurement and analysis on Unix platforms has become a critical operational issue only in the last few years, since Unix moved into the mainstream commercial market. Traditional tools like *vmstat* and *sar* are too simplistic and do not gather adequate data. Moreover, these tools do not produce professional-quality reports and graphs for capacity planning and management use. HP has augmented these tools by a series of performance products, available as separately licensed products (all those in the list that follows except for *top*). Many of the products run on other Unix platforms, like SUN Solaris and IBM AIX—an advantage that helps in developing a performance strategy in a heterogeneous environment. The performance products are:

- GlancePlus, also known as Glance, is an on-line performance monitoring and diagnostic tool.

- PerfRX is a performance analysis tool running on Unix Systems. It can be used to study historic data collected by Performance Collection Software (PCS) now known as MeasureWare.

- LaserRX is a performance analysis tool running on a Windows PC system. Its functionality is somewhat like that of PerfRX.

- Process Resource Manager can be used to allocate CPU time in a specified manner to groups of processes. Process groupings can be specified.

- Perfview is a centralized performance monitoring tool running under the

OpenView Management Framework. Multiple systems can be monitored from a single system.

■ *top* displays processes ranked by CPU use; very useful if no licensed performance products are installed.

We will study these products and briefly mention the usual Unix products. Data Source Integration is a software product that allows data from multiple sources to be collected in a single file. It does nothing that cannot be done with awk and similar utilities; the product will not be discussed.

Performance product binary, source, help, and other "constant" files are stored under /opt/perf; data files are stored under /var/opt/perf.

16.2   gpm and Glance

GlancePlus is useful for monitoring performance and troubleshooting in real time. We will briefly describe the character terminal interface; however, we will concentrate on the X-windows interface.

16.2.1   Character terminal interface

GlancePlus is started on an HP or a VT character-mode terminal with the *glance* command. Figure 16.1 shows the initial Glance screen on an HP terminal (emulator). Some comments:

■ The display is updated at 5-second intervals.

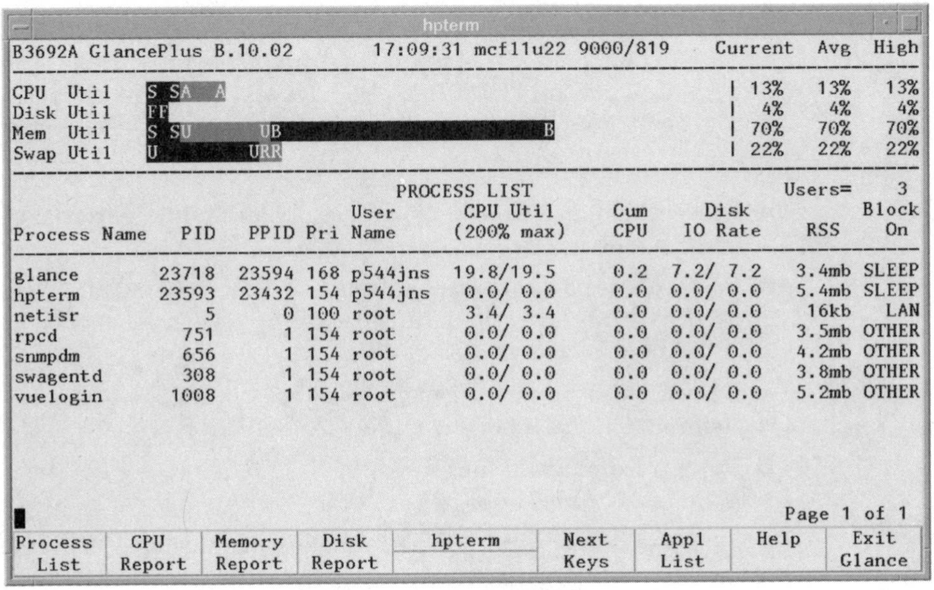

```
┌─────────────────────────── hpterm ───────────────────────────┐
│ B3692A GlancePlus B.10.02      17:09:31 mcf11u22 9000/819    Current  Avg  High │
│──────────────────────────────────────────────────────────────│
│ CPU  Util  S SA  A                                   |  13%   13%   13%│
│ Disk Util  FF                                        |   4%    4%    4%│
│ Mem  Util  S SU      UB                        B     |  70%   70%   70%│
│ Swap Util  U        URR                              |  22%   22%   22%│
│──────────────────────────────────────────────────────────────│
│                          PROCESS LIST                    Users=   3 │
│                              User    CPU Util   Cum    Disk        Block│
│ Process Name   PID  PPID Pri Name  (200% max)  CPU  IO Rate   RSS   On  │
│                                                                         │
│ glance        23718 23594 168 p544jns 19.8/19.5  0.2  7.2/ 7.2  3.4mb SLEEP│
│ hpterm        23593 23432 154 p544jns  0.0/ 0.0  0.0  0.0/ 0.0  5.4mb SLEEP│
│ netisr            5     0 100 root     3.4/ 3.4  0.0  0.0/ 0.0  16kb   LAN│
│ rpcd            751     1 154 root     0.0/ 0.0  0.0  0.0/ 0.0  3.5mb OTHER│
│ snmpdm          656     1 154 root     0.0/ 0.0  0.0  0.0/ 0.0  4.2mb OTHER│
│ swagentd        308     1 154 root     0.0/ 0.0  0.0  0.0/ 0.0  3.8mb OTHER│
│ vuelogin       1008     1 154 root     0.0/ 0.0  0.0  0.0/ 0.0  5.2mb OTHER│
│                                                                         │
│                                                        Page 1 of 1│
│ █                                                                       │
│┌───────┬───────┬───────┬───────┬──────────┬──────┬──────┬──────┬───────┐│
││Process│ CPU   │Memory │ Disk  │  hpterm  │ Next │ Appl │ Help │ Exit  ││
││ List  │Report │Report │Report │          │ Keys │ List │      │Glance ││
│└───────┴───────┴───────┴───────┴──────────┴──────┴──────┴──────┴───────┘│
└──────────────────────────────────────────────────────────────┘
```

Figure 16.1 Initial Glance screen on a character terminal.

- The top part of the screen displays four global bars:

  CPU Util: The codes displayed are S (system activity), R (real-time priority), U (user code at normal priority), N (user code at nice [low] priority).

  Disk Util: The codes displayed are F (file system activity), V (virtual paging activity).

  Mem Util: The codes displayed are S (system), U (User), B (buffer cache).

  Swap Util: The codes displayed are U (used—and reserved—swap space), R (reserved but unused swap space).

- The middle part of the screen displays per-process information. Resident Storage Size (RSS) is the total main memory including text, data, stack, and shared memory.

- The menu at the bottom has options to display other information in the middle part of the screen. The options can be clicked on or selected by the function keys on the terminal.

- h displays a help menu for Glance.

- To exit Glance, enter e.

Since the X-windows interface is more convenient to use, further description is based on that interface.

16.2.2   X-windows interface

The command *gpm*, or, using the full path, /opt/perf/bin/gpm, displays the GlancePlus main window shown in Fig. 16.2. Some comments on this summary (or global) window are:

- CPU use is scaled to 100 percent, and memory, disk, and network activity graphs are scaled to highest values seen by GlancePlus. The legend ps represents points. Each graph has stacked components. The legends are shown in the window displayed when Resource History is selected from the Reports menu.

- The Alarm, CPU, Memory, Disk, and Network buttons change color depending on conditions specified by Adviser, which is described later. Clicking the Alarm button displays a list of alarms. Clicking the other four buttons displays different graphs on the corresponding component.

- The ? button can be used to display help on various areas of the screen. Click the button, then click, say, on the CPU graph subwindow to display help on the graph.

A variety of detailed reports and graphs on CPU, memory, disk, swap, and overall system can be produced by selections from the reports menu. Figure 16.3 shows a network report. It indicates that only one (lan1) of the two net-

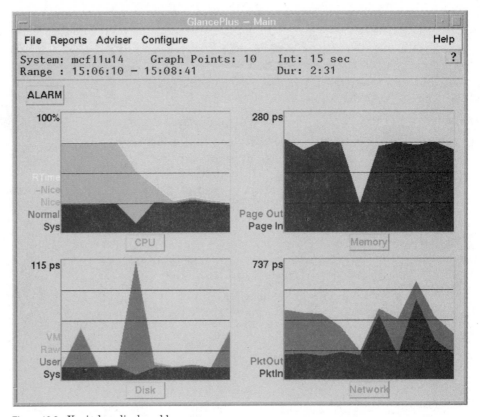

Figure 16.2 X-window displayed by gpm.

Interface Name	Network Type	Input Pkt	In Pkt Rate	Output Pkt	Out Pkt Rate	Colls	Coll Rate	Errors	Error Rate
ni0	Serial	0	0.0	0	0.0	0	0.0	0	0.0
ni1	Serial	0	0.0	0	0.0	0	0.0	0	0.0
lo0	Loop	0	0.0	0	0.0	0	0.0	0	0.0
lan1	Lan	649	309.0	336	160.0	0	0.0	0	0.0
lan0	Lan	0	0.0	0	0.0	0	0.0	0	0.0

GlancePlus — Network By Interface

File   Reports   Configure   Help

System: mcf11u14   Last Update: 19:15:53   Int: 2 sec   ?

LANs: All 5 Selected   Packet In Rate: 309.0 Packet Out Rate: 160.0

Figure 16.3 Example of a GlancePlus detail report: network interface use.

```
┌─────────────────────────────────────────────────────────────────┐
│ ─        GlancePlus – System Tables Report                        │
├─────────────────────────────────────────────────────────────────┤
│ File  Reports                                             Help    │
├─────────────────────────────────────────────────────────────────┤
│ System: mcf11u14     Last Update: 19:18:47     Int: 2 sec   ?     │
│                                                                   │
│ System Table                    Avail   Used   Util%  High%       │
│                                                                   │
│ Proc Table (nproc)                276    125    45%    46%        │
│ File Table (nfile)                800    251    31%    32%        │
│ Shared Mem Table (shmmni)         200     16     8%     8%        │
│ Message Table (msgmni)             50      6    12%    12%        │
│ Semaphore Table (semmni)           64      9    14%    14%        │
│ File Locks (nflocks)              200     23    12%    12%        │
│ Pseudo Terminals (npty)            60      8    13%    15%        │
│ Buffer Headers (nbuf)              na  46884     na     na        │
│                                                                   │
│ System Table                    Avail   Reqs   Used   High        │
│                                                                   │
│ Shared Memory              39.1gb178.3mb         na     na        │
│ Message Buffers                  56kb           0kb    0kb        │
│ Inode Cache (ninode)              476           476    476        │
│ DNLC Cache                        476                             │
│                                                                   │
│                     Min    Max    Avail   Used    High            │
│                                                                   │
│ Buffer Cache    32.0mb320.0mb320.0mb320.0mb320.0mb                │
│                                                                   │
│                          Avail    Used    Reserved                │
│                          Size     Size    Size   Util%            │
│                                                                   │
│ Swap Space               1.5gb   488mb    719mb   47%             │
└─────────────────────────────────────────────────────────────────┘
```

Figure 16.4 Example of a GlancePlus detail report: systemwide table use.

work interfaces (lan0 and lan1) is being used. Figure 16.4 shows systemwide information. The report indicates that no resource is heavily utilized.

16.2.3 Process details

The reports option in the GlancePlus main menu has three process-oriented selections: Application List, PRM Group List, and Process List. All these selections display per-process or per-process-group information. Application List displays overall CPU use and process counts by groups of processes; the groups are X-windows, network, memory management and other root, and others. The PRM Group List displays information on processes grouped by the Process Resource Manager, described later in this chapter. The Process List selection from the Reports menu displays per-process information in extensive detail.

Figure 16.5 shows the Process List window. The information is continuously updated. Some comments are:

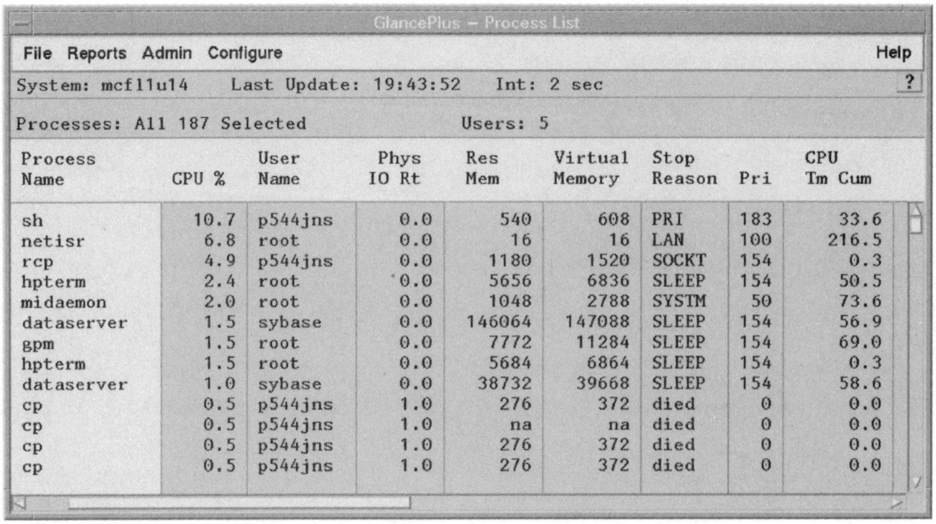

```
┌─────────────────────────────────────────────────────────────────────────┐
│ ─                    GlancePlus - Process List                            │
│  File  Reports  Admin  Configure                                    Help  │
│ ───────────────────────────────────────────────────────────────────────  │
│  System: mcf11u14    Last Update: 19:43:52    Int: 2 sec             ?    │
│ ───────────────────────────────────────────────────────────────────────  │
│  Processes: All 187 Selected                    Users: 5                  │
│ ───────────────────────────────────────────────────────────────────────  │
│  Process            User        Phys    Res   Virtual  Stop         CPU   │
│  Name       CPU %   Name        IO Rt   Mem   Memory   Reason  Pri  Tm Cum│
│                                                                           │
│  sh          10.7   p544jns     0.0      540      608  PRI     183   33.6 │
│  netisr       6.8   root        0.0       16       16  LAN     100  216.5 │
│  rcp          4.9   p544jns     0.0     1180     1520  SOCKT   154    0.3 │
│  hpterm       2.4   root        0.0     5656     6836  SLEEP   154   50.5 │
│  midaemon     2.0   root        0.0     1048     2788  SYSTM    50   73.6 │
│  dataserver   1.5   sybase      0.0   146064   147088  SLEEP   154   56.9 │
│  gpm          1.5   root        0.0     7772    11284  SLEEP   154   69.0 │
│  hpterm       1.5   root        0.0     5684     6864  SLEEP   154    0.3 │
│  dataserver   1.0   sybase      0.0    38732    39668  SLEEP   154   58.6 │
│  cp           0.5   p544jns     1.0      276      372  died      0    0.0 │
│  cp           0.5   p544jns     1.0       na       na  died      0    0.0 │
│  cp           0.5   p544jns     1.0      276      372  died      0    0.0 │
│  cp           0.5   p544jns     1.0      276      372  died      0    0.0 │
└─────────────────────────────────────────────────────────────────────────┘
```

Figure 16.5 Process List window.

- The columns to be displayed can be selected from a list of about 50 process metrics. The Choose Metrics selection from the configure menu displays the choices.

- Columns can be sorted. The sample window shown in Fig. 16.5 is sorted by percent CPU use. Multiple sort columns can be specified. The Sort Fields selection from the configure menu allows you to click on column headings of columns to be sorted.

- Column positions can be changed so that important metrics are displayed at the left. The Arrange Columns selection from the configure menu allows you to move columns.

- A subset of processes can be selected for display by the Filters selection on the Reports menu. An example selection criterion is Phys IO Rate > 2 and CPU % > 60.

Details on a particular process can be displayed by clicking on the process row in the Process List window and then selecting an option from the Reports menu. Figure 16.6 was created by clicking on the process name *dataserver* and then selecting Process Open Files from the Reports menu. Figure 16.7 was created by selecting the process *rcp* and then selecting Process Resources from the Reports menu. This display shows that the process has died; actually, the process is in a *zombie* state, about to be removed from the system.

16.2.4 Adviser

Adviser is the component of GlancePlus that generates alarms, which appropriately change the colors of the five buttons on the main window. An example Adviser language use is

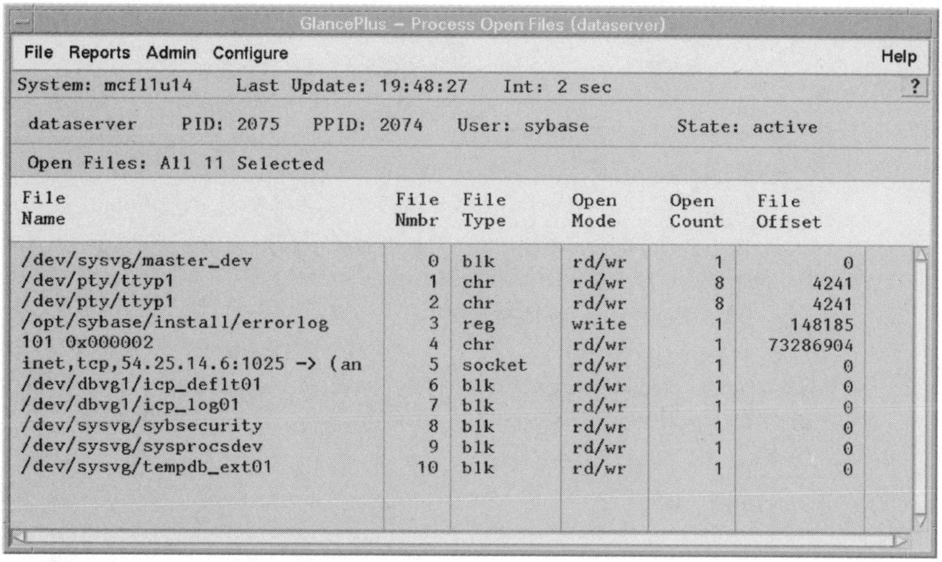

```
┌─┐                    GlancePlus - Process Open Files (dataserver)          ┌───┐
│─│  File  Reports  Admin  Configure                                    Help │   │
│   ├──────────────────────────────────────────────────────────────────────┤ ? │
│    System: mcf11u14      Last Update: 19:48:27     Int: 2 sec             └───┘
│
│    dataserver     PID: 2075    PPID: 2074    User: sybase        State: active
│   ┌──────────────────────────────────────────────────────────────────────────
│    Open Files: All 11 Selected
│   ┌──────────────────────────────────────────────────────────────────────────
│    File                                 File  File    Open    Open   File
│    Name                                 Nmbr  Type    Mode    Count  Offset
│   ─────────────────────────────────────────────────────────────────────────
│    /dev/sysvg/master_dev                  0   blk     rd/wr     1         0     │▲│
│    /dev/pty/ttyp1                         1   chr     rd/wr     8      4241     │ │
│    /dev/pty/ttyp1                         2   chr     rd/wr     8      4241     │ │
│    /opt/sybase/install/errorlog           3   reg     write     1    148185    │ │
│    101 0x000002                           4   chr     rd/wr     1   73286904   │ │
│    inet,tcp,54.25.14.6:1025 -> (an        5   socket  rd/wr     1         0    │ │
│    /dev/dbvg1/icp_deflt01                 6   blk     rd/wr     1         0     │ │
│    /dev/dbvg1/icp_log01                   7   blk     rd/wr     1         0     │ │
│    /dev/sysvg/sybsecurity                 8   blk     rd/wr     1         0     │ │
│    /dev/sysvg/sysprocsdev                 9   blk     rd/wr     1         0     │ │
│    /dev/sysvg/tempdb_ext01               10   blk     rd/wr     1         0     │▼│
│
└────────────────────────────────────────────────────────────────────────────────
```

Figure 16.6 Process details: open files.

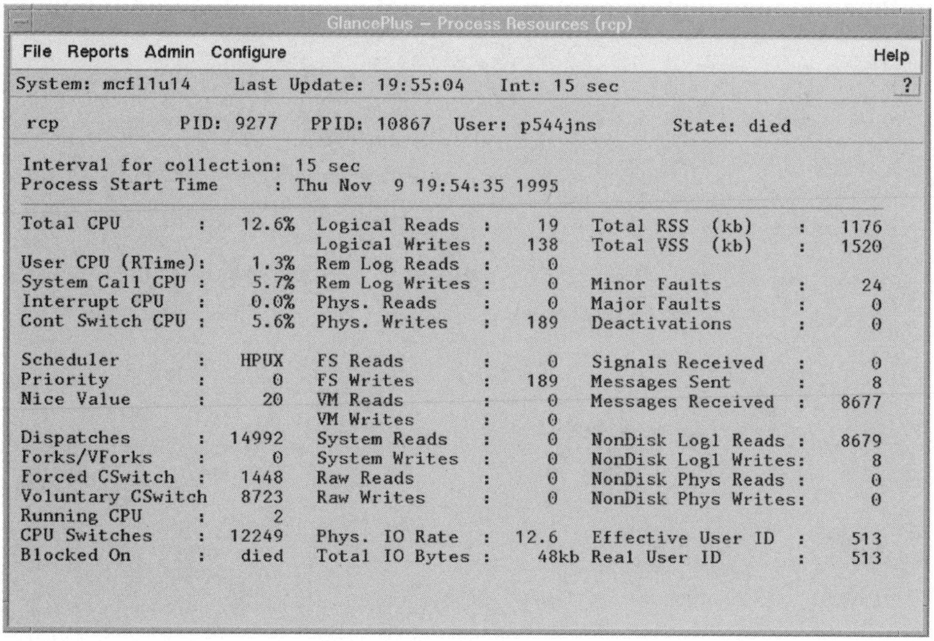

```
┌─┐                    GlancePlus - Process Resources (rcp)                  ┌───┐
│─│  File  Reports  Admin  Configure                                    Help │   │
│   ├──────────────────────────────────────────────────────────────────────┤ ? │
│    System: mcf11u14      Last Update: 19:55:04     Int: 15 sec            └───┘
│
│    rcp            PID: 9277    PPID: 10867  User: p544jns      State: died
│   ┌──────────────────────────────────────────────────────────────────────────
│    Interval for collection: 15 sec
│    Process Start Time     : Thu Nov  9 19:54:35 1995
│   ─────────────────────────────────────────────────────────────────────────
│    Total CPU        :  12.6%   Logical Reads  :     19   Total RSS  (kb)   :  1176
│                                Logical Writes :    138   Total VSS  (kb)   :  1520
│    User CPU (RTime):   1.3%   Rem Log Reads  :      0
│    System Call CPU :   5.7%   Rem Log Writes :      0   Minor Faults      :    24
│    Interrupt CPU   :   0.0%   Phys. Reads    :      0   Major Faults      :     0
│    Cont Switch CPU :   5.6%   Phys. Writes   :    189   Deactivations     :     0
│
│    Scheduler        :  HPUX   FS Reads       :      0   Signals Received  :     0
│    Priority         :     0   FS Writes      :    189   Messages Sent     :     8
│    Nice Value       :    20   VM Reads       :      0   Messages Received :  8677
│                               VM Writes      :      0
│    Dispatches       : 14992   System Reads   :      0   NonDisk Logl Reads :  8679
│    Forks/VForks     :     0   System Writes  :      0   NonDisk Logl Writes:     8
│    Forced CSwitch   :  1448   Raw Reads      :      0   NonDisk Phys Reads :     0
│    Voluntary CSwitch:  8723   Raw Writes     :      0   NonDisk Phys Writes:     0
│    Running CPU      :     2
│    CPU Switches     : 12249   Phys. IO Rate  :   12.6   Effective User ID :   513
│    Blocked On       :  died   Total IO Bytes :   48kb   Real User ID      :   513
│
└────────────────────────────────────────────────────────────────────────────────
```

Figure 16.7 Process details: resource use.

```
ALARM tbl_proc_table_util > 80 FOR 1 MINUTES
   START RED ALERT "PROC table is nearly full "
   END RESET ALERT "End of PROC table full condition "
```

A few comments:

- tbl_proc_table_util is one of the many metrics collected. The list of metrics is in the manual and in the on-line help.

- If the alarm condition is met, the START clause will turn the Alarm button red and will write the text quoted in the START clause into the alarm history window. The text can be displayed from the Adviser menu.

- When the value of tbl_proc_table_util goes below 80, the END clause is evaluated; the Alarm button changes to normal color and writes the text quoted in the END clause into the alarm history window.

The Adviser menu has a selection, Edit Adviser Syntax, that displays a window where alarms can be entered, syntax can be checked, and the alarms installed so that GlancePlus continuously evaluates the alarms. Alarms can be loaded from other files and stored into specified files. Writing alarms is fairly simple; studying metrics and deciding on what should be considered an alarm is the hard part. Practice will help. Here are other alarms.

```
//CPU_Bottleneck Alarms
//The next statement makes a variable from a metric.
CPU_RedAlert = CPU_RedAlert
ALARM CPU_Bottleneck > 50 FOR 2 MINUTES
   START IF CPU_RedAlert < 10 THEN
           YELLOW ALERT "CPU Bottleneck probability= ", cpu_bottleneck, "%"
   REPEAT EVERY 2 MINUTES
         IF CPU_RedAlert < 10 THEN
           YELLOW ALERT   "CPU Bottleneck probability= ", cpu_bottleneck, "%"
   END RESET ALERT  "End of CPU Bottleneck Warning Alert"

//Network_Bottleneck Alarms
NETWORK_RedAlert = NETWORK_RedAlert
ALARM Network_Bottleneck > 50 FOR 2 MINUTES
  START IF NETWORK_RedAlert > 10 THEN
           YELLOW ALERT "Network Bottleneck probability= ", network_bottleneck,
"%"
  REPEAT EVERY 2 MINUTES
        IF NETWORK_RedAlert < 10 THEN
           YELLOW ALERT "Network Bottleneck probability= ", network_bottleneck,
"%"
  END   RESET ALERT "End of Network Bottleneck Warning Alert"

ALARM Network_Bottleneck > 90 FOR 2 MINUTES
   START {
         RED ALERT "Network Bottleneck probability= ", network_bottleneck, "%"
         NETWORK_RedAlert = 10
         }
   REPEAT EVERY 2 MINUTES
         RED ALERT "Network Bottleneck probability= ", network_bottleneck, "%"
   END {
        RESET ALERT "End of Network Bottleneck Critical Alert"
        NETWORK_RedAlert = 0
        }

// SHARED MEMORY TABLE ALARM
```

```
ALARM tbl_shmem_table_util  > 90 FOR 1 MINUTES
   START RED ALERT "SHARED MEMORY table is nearly full "
   END RESET ALERT "End of SHARED MEMORY table full condition "
// GLOBAL SWAP ALARM

ALARM GBL_SWAP_SPACE_RESERVED_UTIL > 95
   START RED ALERT "GLOBAL SWAP space is nearly full "
   END RESET ALERT "End of GLOBAL SWAP space full condition"
```

Adviser also processes "nonalarm" statements such as:

```
if tbl_proc_table_util > 80 then
      exec "echo 'process table over 80 percent full' | mail root"
```

16.3   midaemon: The Measurement Interface Daemon

A number of products like GlancePlus and MeasureWare, previously known as Performance Collection Software (PCS), use system metrics. Rather than have each product probe memory kernel structures, a single daemon gathers kernel information and other products get the raw data from this daemon. This daemon process is the Measurement Interface. If it is not running, a product, like GlancePlus, starts it as one of the initialization steps. To start and stop the daemon explicitly, commands like these can be used:

```
# /opt/perf/bin/midaemon -p      Start midaemon.
# /opt/perf/bin/midaemon -T      Stop midaemon.
```

16.4   Data Collection: PCS and scopeux

Performance data can be collected in files for historical analysis. The data can be used by products like PerfRX and LaserRX. The collection process is called the *scopeux* daemon. Collection is started by

```
# /opt/perf/bin/scope.start      Data collector start script.
```

To start scopeux at system boot, edit /etc/rc.config.d/scope and change SCOPE_START=0 to SCOPE_START=1. The script also starts midaemon and pvserver if they are not started. pvserver is the Perfview Agent described later. Data metrics are logged every 5 minutes. The data is collected in five files in the directory /var/opt/perf/datafiles. The files are logappl, logdev, logglob, logindx, and logproc. This raw data can be used directly by analysis tools; however, the *extract* command converts this data into a format suitable for reporting, archiving, and compressing. The extract program is described in Section 16.4.4.

16.4.1   Data collection parameters

The file /var/opt/perf/parm can be modified to specify

- *Maximum sizes of the log files:*   This ensures that the files do not grow very large. If the file size is reached, older data is discarded.

- *Logging thresholds:* Because process data can quickly fill up log files, a threshold is needed to determine whether a process's metrics are logged. A process's metrics are logged only if one or more of the specified threshold values are exceeded for the process. This helps keep the log files from filling up with useless data. For example, disk = 5 specifies that a process's metrics will be logged only if the process does more than five I/Os per second in a 1-minute sample to be logged.

- *Application classification.*

Here is an excerpt from a parm file. Note how applications are grouped on the basis of files they access or user names.

```
size global = 10.0, application = 10.0, process = 20.0, device = 10.0
threshold cpu = 5.0, disk = 5.0, first = 5, response = 30
```

This example application may be appropriate for Motif environments:

```
application = xwindows
file = X*,xload,xclock,xterm,hpterm,grmd,softmsg*,vue*
```

This example application may be appropriate for networked environments:

```
application = network
file = nfs*,biod,automount,inetd,snmp*,rpc*,llbd,netfmt,nvsisr,ttisr,portmap
file = rbootd,strmem,strweld,vtdaemon,telnet*,ftp*,*rlogin*,remsh*,rcp,nktl*
```

This application could be used on systems that experience memory bottlenecks. The files used for memory management differ on different platforms.

```
application = memory management
file = swapper,vhand,syncer
```

Note: This entry should be near the end of your application definitions should you choose to keep it, because it will pick up all processes owned by root which were not included in preceding application definitions.

```
application = other user root
user = root
```

16.4.2 perfstat: Is MeasureWare running?

perfstat is a simple script that displays processes that should be running for data collection. If the output is as here, the data collector is running properly:

```
# /opt/perf/bin/perfstat
*****************************************************
** perfstat for nodetest on Fri Nov 10 21:34:08 EST 1995
*****************************************************
ps -ef list of performance tool processes:
    root 13445    1  1  Nov  9  ?        52:00 /opt/perf/bin/midaemon
    root 20416    1  0 19:19:40 ?         0:02 /opt/perf/bin/pvserver
    root 20417    1  0 19:19:40 ?         0:06 /opt/perf/bin/scopeux
************ (end of perfstat -p output) ***************
```

perfstat has other options to display system configuration and performance status files.

16.4.3   Data collector housekeeping: The utility command

The *utility* command displays information on the data collector log files and on scopeux status and performs similar housekeeping functions. Here is a sample session where the log file information is displayed:

```
# /opt/perf/bin/utility
800 B2663A PCS/UX Utility (B.02.00.60)
Fri Nov 10 10:09:16 1995                    (C) Hewlett Packard Co. 1990-1995

To get more information on a specific topic enter:
MENU or ?      To get a list of available commands
HELP TASKS     Information on different tasks you can perform
HELP commands  Information about a specific command
HELP           To enter the HELP subsystem for more detailed help

To use a simplified guided commands mode:
GUIDE

utility> Enter command: menu
Command    Parameters   Function
HELP       [topic]      Get information on commands and options
GUIDE      Enter guided commands mode for novice users
LOGFILE    [logname]    Specify a log file to be processed
LIST       [filename/*] Specify the listing file

START      [startdate time] Specify a starting date and time for SCAN
STOP       [stopdate  time] Specify an ending date and time for SCAN
DETAIL     [ON/OFF] Set level of detail in SCAN report
SHOW       [ALL]    Show the current program settings

SCAN       [logname] Read the logfile and produce a summary report
RESIZE     [GLOB/APPL/PROC/DEV][DAYS = ][EMPTY = ] Resize raw log files
PARM       [parmfile]      Check a PARM file for errors
ALARMS     [alarmfile/OFF/ON] Specify an Alarms Definition file
VERSIONS   Print the version numbers for Performance Programs
SCOPE      [status/start/kill]    Communicate with scopeux collector
TERSE      [ON/OFF] Set level of prompting and output details
! or SH    [command] Execute a system command
MENU or ? List the command menu (This listing)
EXIT or Q Terminate the program

utility> Enter command: scan
No LOGFILE has been specified
ENTER THE LOG FILE NAME (/var/opt/perf/datafiles/logglob)
```

(Collected data is stored in these files)

```
Global      file: /var/opt/perf/datafiles/logglob
Application file: /var/opt/perf/datafiles/logappl
Process     file: /var/opt/perf/datafiles/logproc
Device      file: /var/opt/perf/datafiles/logdev
Index       file: /var/opt/perf/datafiles/logindx
System ID: nodetest
System Type  9000/829 S/N 149831311 O/S HP-UX B.10.01 B
Data Collector: UX A.10.02
```

```
Data Covers:    2 days from 11/09/95 to 11/10/95
Shift is:       All Day
Global Application Process Disk Volume data records are available
Maximum file sizes: Global=10.0 Application=10.0 Process=20.0 Device=10.0 MB
```

(Here is the data collection interval)

```
Global      data covers 11/09/95 20:55:00 to 11/10/95 10:05:00
Application data covers 11/09/95 20:55:00 to 11/10/95 10:05:00
Process     data covers 11/09/95 20:51:00 to 11/10/95 10:09:00
Device      data covers 11/09/95 20:55:01 to 11/10/95 10:05:00
The  default  starting Date & Time = 11/09/95 12:00 AM (FIRST + 0)
The  default  stopping Date & Time = 11/10/95 11:59 PM (LAST - 0)
 Scanning the log files, Please wait ...
Logfile:  /var/opt/perf/datafiles/logglob
```

(Overall logging information including system configuration)

```
11/09/95 20:49 System ID="nodetest"
SCOPE/UX A.10.02.26 SAMPLE INTERVAL = 300,300,60 Seconds, Log version=D
Configuration: 9000/829  , O/S HP-UX      B.10.01 B CPUs=4
Logging Global Application=All Process
        Device= Disk Volume records
Thresholds: CPU= 5.00%, Disk=5.0/sec, First=5.0 sec, Resp=30.0 sec, Trans=100
            Nonew=FALSE, Nokilled= FALSE, Shortlived= FALSE (<1 sec)
HPUX Parms: Buffer Cache Size = 32767KB, NPROC = 276
Wait Thresholds: CPU=100.00%, Disk=100.00%, Memory=100.00%, Impede=100.00%
Optimize collector for increased accuracy
Memory: Physical = 640.0 MB,  Swap = 1530.0 MB, Available to users = 616.8 MB
There are 4 LAN interfaces: 464="ni0", 467="ni1", 474="lo0", 828="lan1"

11/09/95 20:49 There are 4 Disk Devices:
    Disk #1738="10/0.6.0"
    Disk #1720="10/0.3.0"
    Disk #1726="10/0.4.0"
    Disk #1732="10/0.5.0"
```

(Application classification, from parm file)

```
11/09/95 20:49 Application(1) ="other
 Comment=all processes not in user-defined applications

11/09/95 20:49 Application(2)="xwindows"
 File=X*,xload,xclock,xterm,hpterm,grmd,softmsg*,vue*
 11/09/95 20:49 Application(3)="network"

File=nfs*,biod,automount,inetd,snmp*,rpc*,llbd,netfmt,nvsisr
File=ttisr,portmap,rbootd,strmem,strweld

File=vtdaemon,telnet*,ftp*,*rlogin*,remsh*,rcp,nktl*

11/09/95 20:49 Application(4)="memory management"
 File = swapper,vhand,syncer

11/09/95 20:49 Application(5)="other user root"
User=root
```

(Collected data summary based on application classification)

Application	Records	Percent of Total CPU	Disk	Trans
other	159	90.1%	95.8%	100.0%
xwindows	159	0.1%	0.0%	0.0%
network	159	0.2%	0.0%	0.0%
memory management	159	0.4%	2.0%	0.0%
other user root	159	9.1%	2.2%	0.0%
All user applications	80.0%	9.9%	4.2%	0.0%

```
Process Summary Report:  11/09/95 08:51 PM to 11/10/95 10:09 AM
There were 13.3 hours of process data
Process records were logged for the following reasons:
```

Log Reason	Records	Percent	Recs/hr
New Processes	5	0.3%	0.4
Killed Processes	7	0.5%	0.5
CPU Threshold	1532	99.2%	114.9
Disk Threshold	8	0.5%	0.6
Wait on CPU	10	0.6%	0.8

```
NOTE: A process may be logged for more than one reason at a time.
Record counts and percentages will not add up to 100% of the process records.

Scan started on        11/09/95 08:51 PM
Scan stopped on        11/10/95 10:09 AM
*******************************************************************
Overall, user defined applications account for
      636 out of      795 records    ( 80.0%)
      0.3 out of      3.5 CPU hours   (  9.9%)
      0.0 out of      0.1 M disk IOs  (  4.2%)
      0.0 out of      0.0 M trans     (  0.0%)
*******************************************************************

The total time covered was          13:18:00 out of 13:18:00
Time lost when collector was off     00:00    0.00%
The scope collector was started       1 times
```

Type	------Total------ Records	MegaBytes	--Each Full Day-- Records	MegaBytes	-------Dates------ Start	Finish	Full Days
Global	160	0.04	289.4	0.081	11/09/95 to	11/10/95	0.6
Application	802	0.10	1450.9	0.175	11/09/95 to	11/10/95	0.6
Process	1545	0.26	2781.1	0.467	11/09/95 to	11/10/95	0.6
Disk	497	0.02	899.1	0.040	11/09/95 to	11/10/95	0.6
Volume	380	0.01	687.5	0.016	11/09/95 to	11/10/95	0.6
Overhead		0.03					
TOTAL	3384	0.47	6107.9	0.779			

```
The Global      file is now  0.5% full with room for 245 more full days
The Application file is now  1.0% full with room for 113 more full days
The Process     file is now  1.3% full with room for  84 more full days
The Device      file is now  0.4% full with room for 356 more full days
*******************************************************************
utility> Enter command: quit
```

16.4.4   Archiving: The extract command

The extract command accepts raw data from the original data collector files in /var/opt/perf/datafiles or from files created by the extract command itself and can

■ Create ASCII or spreadsheet format files. This is an *export* process.
■ Summarize the data and write it to a file, which can be archived or used by the analysis tools.
■ Produce simple reports.
■ Append the data to a previously created extract file.

The extract can be based on

■ Date and time ranges
■ Type of data to be extracted: global, process, volume, and so on

The types of data that can be extracted are global, application, process, disk, volume, and configuration. A detail or summary extract or both can be specified. Detail keeps the original data logged at 5-minute intervals. Summary produces hourly output, which could be useful for archiving as the size is reduced by a factor of 10. Here is a sample session that extracts all data from the standard data collector log files and produces rxlog, which can be used by the analysis tools.

```
$ /opt/perf/bin/extract
800 B2663A PCS/UX Extract (B.02.00.85)
Fri Nov 10 16:20:28 1995              (C) Hewlett Packard Co. 1990-1995

To get more information on a specific topic enter:
MENU or ?     To get a list of available commands
HELP TASKS    Information on different tasks you can perform
HELP commands Information about a specific command
HELP          To enter the HELP subsystem for more detailed help

To select guided command mode for the novice user, type
GUIDE

extract> Enter command: global both
Global: BOTH Detail & Summary records will be extracted
extract> Enter command: application both
Application: BOTH Detail & Summary records will be extracted
extract> Enter command: process detail
Process DETAIL records will be extracted
extract> Enter command: disk both
Disk Device: BOTH Detail & Summary records will be extracted
extract> Enter command: volume both
Volume: BOTH Detail & Summary records will be extracted
extract> Enter command: configuration both
CONFIG DETAIL records will be exported

extract> Enter command: extract
No LOGFILE has been specified
ENTER THE LOG FILE NAME (/var/opt/perf/datafiles/logglob) <Return>
```

(The extract process displays the following line as feedback)

```
Global file:       /var/opt/perf/datafiles/logglob
Application file: /var/opt/perf/datafiles/logappl
Process file:      /var/opt/perf/datafiles/logproc
Device file:       /var/opt/perf/datafiles/logdev
Index file:        /var/opt/perf/datafiles/logindx
System ID: nodetest
System Type  9000/829 S/N 149831311 O/S HP-UX B.10.01 B
Data Collector: UX A.10.02
Data Covers:  2 days from 11/09/95 to 11/10/95
Shift is:      All Day
Global Application Process Disk Volume data records are available

The first Global      record is on 11/09/95 at 08:55 PM
The first Application record is on 11/09/95 at 08:55 PM
The first Process     record is on 11/09/95 at 08:51 PM
The first Device      record is on 11/09/95 at 08:55 PM
The  default  starting Date & Time = 11/09/95 08:51 PM (LAST - 30)
The  default  stopping Date & Time = 11/10/95 11:59 PM (LAST - 0)
Enter the output file name (rxlog)
Output file "rxlog" was created
Logfile:  /var/opt/perf/datafiles/logglob
Output:   rxlog ** Extracted File **
Report:   Default
List:     "stdout"

The  default  starting Date & Time = 11/09/95 08:51 PM (LAST - 30)
The  default  stopping Date & Time = 11/10/95 11:59 PM (LAST - 0)
The  default  shift = 12:00 AM - 12:00 AM

Global..... BOTH detail & summary records will be extracted
Application BOTH detail & summary records will be extracted
Process.........DETAIL.......... records will be extracted
Disc Device BOTH detail & summary records will be extracted
Volume......BOTH detail & summary records will be extracted
Configuration....DETAIL.......... records will be exported

Extracting Global data          starting 11/09/95 08:55 PM
..100%
Extracting Application data      starting 11/09/95 08:55 PM
..100%
Extracting Process data          starting 11/09/95 08:51 PM
..100%
Extracting Disk and Volume data starting 11/09/95 08:55 PM
..100%

The extracted file contains 2 days of data from 11/09/95 to 11/10/95
```

Data Type	Examined Records	Extracted Records	Space
GLOBAL	235	235	0.07 MB
GLOBAL SUMMARIES		22	0.01 MB
APPLICATION	1177	1177	0.14 MB
APPLICATION SUMMARIES		112	0.01 MB
PROCESS	2576	2576	0.43 MB
DISK DEVICE	798	798	0.04 MB
DISK DEVICE SUMMARIES		86	0.00 MB
VOLUME	730	730	0.02 MB
VOLUME SUMMARIES		294	0.01 MB
OVERHEAD			0.14 MB

			0.87 MB

```
extract> Enter command: quit
```

Some other parameters can be specified for the extract utility:

- *Global summary:*   Only summary records should be extracted.

- *Extract month 6:*   Only data for June should be extracted.

- *Output rxlog, append:*   Extracted data is appended to the previously extracted data file, rxlog.

- *Start 02/14/96:*   Extract data starting date.

- *Stop today-2:*   Extract data end date, today minus 2 days.

- *Show all:*   Display current selection of extract options, report file, start and stop date, and such.

In addition, the following parameters can be specified for an export (instead of extract which generates internal format data), which generates an ASCII or a spreadsheet (WKS) output file:

- *Report /var/opt/perf/reptall:*   Export all metrics. Obviously, the output will be very wide. The report file can be copied to another location and fields can be removed. The report file also specifies report headings, whether column headings should be outputted, column separator, and so on.

- *Export:*   Instead of extract.

16.5   PerfRX: Performance Analysis

HP PerfRX analysis software is a graphing and reporting package. It uses data collected by PCS. It can read PCS log files directly, or it can read files created by the extract utility. An X-windows terminal is required. The command to start PerfRX is

```
# /opt/perf/bin/rx
```

The initial "splash" window has a File menu with the option Open Log File. The log files in the /var/opt/perf.datafiles directory can be specified. If the extract utility was run, the data could have been collected to a single file—for example, rxlog, which can be specified. Data collected on other systems can be run through the extract utility and either copied over or NFS-exported to the PerfRX system. The Draw option on the Graph menu on the initial window can then be selected to graph the data. When the option is selected, the window shown in Fig. 16.8 is displayed. One or more of the 20 or so available graphs can be selected.

The window shows other parameters that can be specified. Clicking on Draw displays the selected graph (or graphs). Figure 16.9 shows an example Global CPU Utilization graph.

A few comments on PerfRX graphs follow:

- The Format options are Line, Stacked, and Pie.

- The Zoom options are Time, Application, Process, and Numbers. Click and

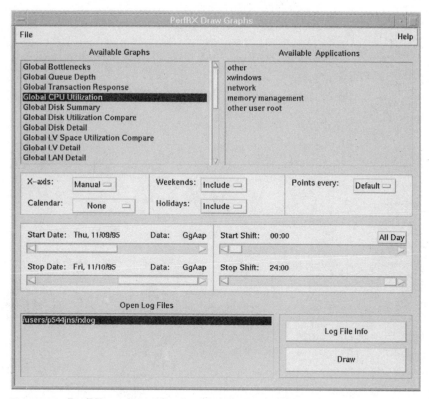

Figure 16.8   PerfRX graph specification window.

drag the mouse over the graph horizontally, starting and ending over the y-axis range for which details are required. Information from the selected range is displayed depending on the Zoom option selection. Figure 16.10 shows the window that popped up when the Zoom option was processed and the data near 12 noon was zoomed. As many fields are displayed, the Configure menu option can be used to select columns to be displayed at the left.

- Clicking on a legend at the left disables the display of the corresponding metric on the graph.

- The Configure menu can be used to change colors and legends.

- Graphs can be printed. Graph data can be exported to a file in ASCII or spreadsheet (WKS) format.

16.5.1   LaserRX: Performance analysis on a PC

PerfRX runs on HP-UX, whereas LaserRX runs on a Windows PC. Both have somewhat similar functionality, though PerfRX produces more graphs, allows columns to be rearranged in the process windows, and has more graph configuration options. LaserRX reads the same input data files PerfRX does. Data can

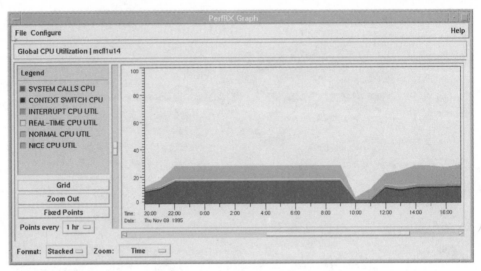

Figure 16.9 CPU use graph.

DATE AND TIME	PROCESS NAME	USER NAME	CPU UTIL	VIRTUAL MEM SIZE	LOGICAL DISK IO	RUN TIME	PRIORITY
11/10/95 12:31:01	ftpd	root	2.54	1808	7.0	520	154
11/10/95 12:32:01	netisr	root	7.41	16	0.0	64020	100
11/10/95 12:32:01	RUN_MCDBT02	sybase	0.00	540	0.0	9277	178
11/10/95 12:33:01	netisr	root	7.49	16	0.0	64080	100
11/10/95 12:33:01	RUN_MCDBT02	sybase	0.00	540	0.0	9336	178
11/10/95 12:33:01	ftpd	root	2.62	1808	7.1	640	154
11/10/95 12:34:01	netisr	root	7.07	16	0.0	64140	100
11/10/95 12:34:01	RUN_MCDBT02	sybase	0.00	540	0.0	9396	178
11/10/95 12:35:01	netisr	root	6.91	16	0.0	64200	100
11/10/95 12:35:01	RUN_MCDBT02	sybase	0.00	540	0.0	9457	178
11/10/95 12:36:01	netisr	root	8.27	16	0.0	64260	100
11/10/95 12:36:01	ftpd	root	3.78	1808	9.7	820	154
11/10/95 12:37:01	netisr	root	7.31	16	0.0	64320	100
11/10/95 12:37:01	RUN_MCDBT02	sybase	0.00	540	0.0	9576	178
11/10/95 12:38:01	netisr	root	7.38	16	0.0	64380	100
11/10/95 12:38:01	ftpd	root	3.13	1808	8.0	940	154
11/10/95 12:39:01	netisr	root	7.88	16	0.0	64440	100
11/10/95 12:39:01	RUN_MCDBT02	sybase	0.00	540	0.0	9696	178
11/10/95 12:39:01	ftpd	root	2.70	1808	7.1	1000	179
11/10/95 12:39:01	rcp	p544jns	0.58	1520	0.2	20	0
11/10/95 12:40:01	netisr	root	8.52	16	0.0	64500	100
11/10/95 12:40:01	RUN_MCDBT02	sybase	0.00	540	0.0	9756	178

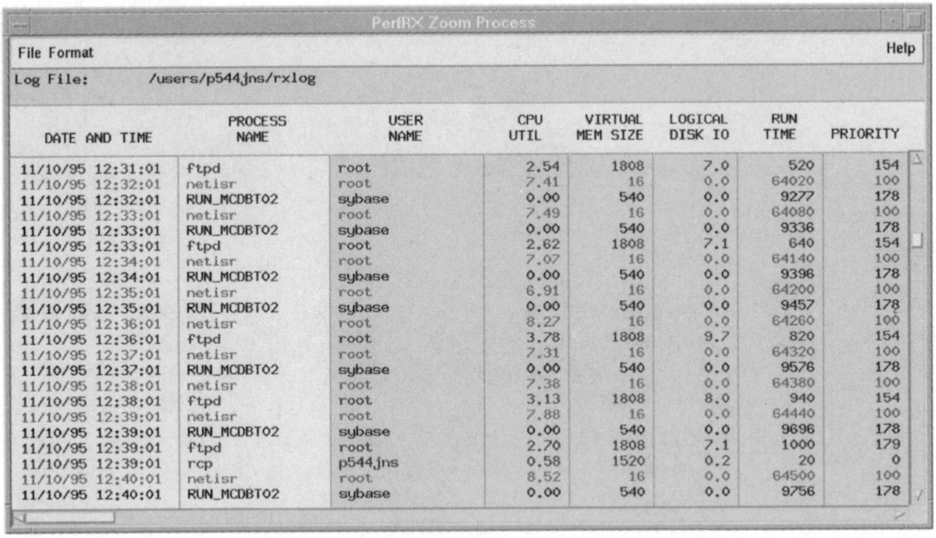

Figure 16.10 Processes in a time range selected on the CPU use graph.

be retrieved from a Unix system or from a local PC file that has been copied over from a Unix system.

Figure 16.11 shows a LaserRX window. Two graphs, Global CPU Utilization and Global LAN Detail, were selected.

16.6 Process Resource Manager

Process Resource Manager (PRM) is a software package that allows greater control over CPU allocation to processes than the standard HP-UX scheduler.

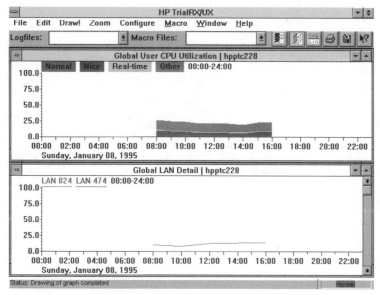

Figure 16.11 LaserRX graphs.

Processes can be classified into groups. A specified minimum percentage of CPU time can be assigned to a group. Total percentage allocation to all groups should not exceed 100.

In conventional process priority–based scheduling, a high-priority process can go into a CPU loop and not allow any other process to execute. PRM maintains the ratio of CPU time between two processes or two groups of processes. Process groups are defined in */etc/prmconf,* the information is loaded into the PRM scheduler with *prmconfig -i,* and the scheduler is enabled with *prmconfig -e.*

PRM is not much use if the CPU is not heavily used. A number of kernel and command changes have been made to accommodate PRM. GlancePlus reports information on PRM process groups along with the normal reports on CPU, memory, and disks.

16.7 Perfview: Centralized Performance Monitoring

Perfview runs under the OpenView management framework. It communicates with the process *pvserver* on each of the managed nodes. The midaemon must be running on the managed nodes; it is typically started by the Performance Collection Software startup command /opt/perf/bin/scope.start. pvserver reads an alarm file, /var/opt/perf/alarmdef, and sends messages to Perfview when an alarm condition is encountered. Perfview displays this information on the OpenView console and sends appropriate messages to the OpenView log and error-handling subsystem. Some lines from an alarmdef file are:

```
# File: /var/opt/perf/alarmdef
# ************************** Global alarms ***************************
# Sample alarm for CPU bottleneck.
# Note: Two IF conditions must both be true for alarm to go off.
#        The HOLDOFF statement will keep alarm from starting again
#        until 2 hours after the previous alarm start.
alarm = "total cpu is too high" type = "CPU busy" severity = 5
  holdoff = 120
  if "TOTAL CPU UTIL" > 95 for 10 minutes
# Note: The following "then" and "finish" actions are commented out
#        in this example to avoid sending unwanted email messages:
# then ! echo "Total CPU on 'uname -n' over 90% for 10 mins" | mail root
# finish ! echo "Excessive total CPU alarm on 'uname -n' ended"  mail root
# Sample user variable declarations
var PACKETS_PER_MINUTE = "PACKETS IO/SEC" * 60
var LAN_COLLISION_PERCENTAGE = "COLLISIONS/MIN" * 100 / PACKETS_PER_MINUTE
# Sample alarm for LAN problem based on user variables.
alarm = "LAN collisions over 5 percent of packets" type="LAN" severity=3
  if "PACKETS IO/SEC" > 10 for 5 minutes
  if LAN_COLLISION_PERCENTAGE > 5 for 5 minutes
# Sample alarm definition shows use of pvtrap in actions. This alarm
# if uncommented, will go off every thirty minutes.
#
# For HP-UX 10.X systems:
#alarm = "pvtrap Test Alarm" type = "test" severity = 2
# if "TOTAL CPU UTIL" >= 0 for 30
# then ! /opt/perf/bin/pvtrap mgrnode PVTRAP test

# *********************** Application alarms ************************
# Sample alarm definition for Network.
# Note: The application name must exactly match the name specified in
#        the active parm file. The metric name must match a valid name,
#        but is not case sensitive.
#alarm = "Network processes using > 30% of CPU" type="appl" severity=2
# if "prog dev:TOTAL CPU UTIL" > 30 for 10 minutes
# repeat = 30
```

pvtrap is a command to send snmp traps to an OpenView system.

16.7.1   top: Processes ranked by CPU use

The *top* command displays overall CPU use, overall memory use, and per-process information. The process listing is sorted by CPU use. The display is updated every 5 seconds (default value). Figure 16.12 shows a sample top display.

16.8   Traditional Unix Performance Tools

16.8.1   vmstat

vmstat displays CPU activity, free-memory information, paging, trap rates, and disk transfer information. If an integer parameter is specified, vmstat displays information continuously at the interval specified in seconds. For example, *vmstat -n 10* displays basic information every 10 seconds. Here are some sample *vmstat* commands. Note that the CPU display is for a four-CPU system.

```
┌──────────────────────────────────── hpterm ──────────────────────────────┐
│ System: mcf11u14                                      Fri Nov 10 20:00:59 1995 │
│ Load averages: 0.15, 0.12, 0.12                                            │
│ 141 processes: 139 sleeping, 1 running, 1 zombie                           │
│ Cpu states:                                                                │
│ CPU   LOAD   USER   NICE    SYS    IDLE  BLOCK  SWAIT   INTR   SSYS         │
│  0    0.15   0.0%   0.0%   4.4%   95.6%   0.0%   0.0%   0.0%   0.0%         │
│  1    0.00   0.2%   0.0%   1.6%   98.2%   0.0%   0.0%   0.0%   0.0%         │
│  2    0.14   0.2%   0.0%   0.4%   99.4%   0.0%   0.0%   0.0%   0.0%         │
│  3    0.32   0.6%   0.0%   0.2%   99.2%   0.0%   0.0%   0.0%   0.0%         │
│ ────   ────   ────   ────   ────    ────   ────   ────   ────   ────       │
│ avg   0.15   0.4%   0.0%   1.6%   98.0%   0.0%   0.0%   0.0%   0.0%         │
│                                                                            │
│ Memory: 29996K (11160K) real, 34300K (13804K) virtual, 52136K free  Page# 1/8 │
│                                                                            │
│ CPU  TTY    PID USERNAME   PRI NI   SIZE    RES  STATE    TIME %WCPU   %CPU COMMAND │
│  0    ?      5 root       100 20     0K     0K sleep  436:18  3.53   3.52 netisr  │
│  3    ?  16737 sybase     154 20  3036K   432K sleep    7:46  1.32   1.32 dataserv │
│  0    ?  16651 sybase     154 20  3052K   448K sleep    8:41  1.22   1.22 dataserv │
│  3    ?  20588 p544jns    154 20  4396K   584K sleep    0:00  0.60   0.60 hpterm  │
│  2   p2 20586 p544jns     178 20   236K   304K run      0:00  0.47   0.47 top     │
│  2    ?    296 root       154 20    20K    92K sleep   50:07  0.47   0.46 syncer  │
│  3    ?  13445 root        50 10   720K   476K sleep   51:40  0.42   0.42 midaemon │
│  2    ?      7 root       -32 20     0K     0K sleep   33:25  0.32   0.32 ttisr   │
│  0   p3 20584 p544jns     154 20  4424K   612K sleep    0:00  0.16   0.16 hpterm  │
│  1    ?      3 root       128 20     0K     0K sleep   16:58  0.15   0.15 statdaem │
│  2   p4 20594 p544jns     154 20    64K   168K sleep    0:00  0.12   0.12 rlogin  │
│  3   p4 20593 p544jns     156 20    60K   164K sleep    0:00  0.10   0.10 rlogin  │
│  0    ?  20153 p544jns    154 20  4928K  1124K sleep    0:03  0.07   0.07 vuewm   │
│  3    ?  20155 p544jns    154 20  5112K  1304K sleep    0:03  0.07   0.07 vuefile │
│  3    ?  20417 root       168 20   880K   780K sleep    0:01  0.06   0.06 scopeux │
│  1    ?   1053 root       168 20   136K   260K sleep   17:02  0.06   0.06 PSMON   │
│  2    ?      4 root       128 20     0K     0K sleep    2:30  0.05   0.05 unhashda │
│  2    ?  20416 root       154 20   628K   244K sleep    0:01  0.05   0.05 pvserver │
│  2    ?  20160 p544jns    154 20  4664K   848K sleep    0:00  0.02   0.02 helpview │
│  3    ?     16 root       138 20     0K     0K sleep    0:05  0.02   0.02 vx_logfl█│
└────────────────────────────────────────────────────────────────────────────┘
```

Figure 16.12 Output of the top command.

```
$ vmstat -n # format output for 80 column display.
VM
      memory                       page                        faults
      avm    free    re   at   pi   po   fr   de   sr    in    sy    cs
      3190  13241    7   12    0    0    0    0    0   734  1783   288
CPU
      cpu          procs
  us sy id    r    b    w
   3  6 91    0    2    0
   3  2 95
   4  3 93
   4  2 94
$
$ vmstat -s # paging information
0 swap ins
0 swap outs
0 pages swapped in
0 pages swapped out
28889223 total address trans. faults taken
14139784 page ins
0 page outs
19393 pages paged in
0 pages paged out
13899315 reclaims from free list
14136228 total page reclaims
21 intransit blocking page faults
```

```
13607636 zero fill pages created
7522828 zero fill page faults
13870151 executable fill pages created
19398 executable fill page faults
0 swap text pages found in free list
8875447 inode text pages found in free list
0 revolutions of the clock hand
5282 pages scanned for page out
0 pages freed by the clock daemon
208817379 cpu context switches
675555336 device interrupts
42259021 traps
1288618446 system calls
$
$ vmstat -Sn # so an si instead of re and at
VM
        memory                    page                      faults
      avm   free   si   so   pi   po   fr   de   sr   in   sy   cs
      3095  13241   0    0    0    0    0    0    0  734  1783  288
CPU
      cpu         procs
   us sy id    r    b    w
    3  6 91    0    0    0
    3  2 95
    4  3 93
    4  2 94
$
$ vmstat -f
438108 forks, 18616007 pages, average= 42.49
$
```

The fields are

- *memory:* avm = active virtual pages; free = size of free list.

- *page:* Paging activity. re = reclaims, at = address translation fault, si = processes swapped in, so = processes swapped out, pi = pages paged in, po = pages paged out, fr = pages freed per second, de = anticipated short-term memory shortfall, sr = pages scanned by clock algorithm per second.

- *faults:* Averaged over last 5 seconds. in = device interrupts per second, sy = system calls per second, cs = CPU context switches per second.

- *cpu:* us = user time, sy = system time, id = idle.

- *procs:* Processes. r = in run queue, b = blocked, w = runnable but swapped.

16.8.2 iostat

The command iostat displays I/O rate for each disk on the system, along with tty and CPU use information. Note that nowadays, logical volume rather than disk information would be more useful.

```
$ iostat -t
            tty              cpu
         tin tout      us   ni   sy   id
           0   41       3    0    3   93

   device    bps     sps     msps
```

```
c0t6d0      0    0.0    1.0
c0t4d0      1    5.0    1.0
c0t5d0      0    0.0    1.0
c0t3d0      0    0.0    1.0
```

The fields are

- *tty:* tin = characters read from terminals, tout = characters sent to terminals.

- *cpu:* us = percent of time spent in user mode, ni = nice (low-priority user processes) mode, sy = system mode, id = idle.

- *device:* bps = Kbytes/s transferred, sps = seeks/s, msps = milliseconds per average seek.

16.8.3   sar

sar is used to display or collect data on a number of metrics on CPU use, I/O rates, tty activity, system calls, swapping, process context switching, inode cache, semaphores, and so on. Here is a simple run of sar that displays CPU activity every second for 5 seconds:

```
$ sar 1 5
HP-UX mcf1lu10 A.09.04 E 9000/816     11/10/95
20:52:15    %usr    %sys    %wio    %idle
20:52:16       9       9       0      82
20:52:17      12       6       0      82
20:52:18       7       6       0      87
20:52:19       8       7       0      85
20:52:20       8       8       0      84
Average        9       7       0      84
```

The sar command in the above example is equivalent to

```
$ sar -u 1 5
```

The -u option displays CPU information. Various sar options are:

- *-u:* CPU information. -uM displays information on each CPU in a multiprocessor system.

- *-b:* Buffer activity–physical read/writes, cache read/writes, and character device I/O.

- *-d:* Device (disk and tape) information—busy, I/O rate, blocks per second, wait and service times.

- *-y:* tty activity.

- *-c:* System call information.

- *-w:* Swapping and switching activity.

- *-a:* Use of file access system routines.

- *-q:* CPU queue information. -qM displays information on each CPU on a multiprocessor system.
- *-v:* Process, inode, and system file table information.
- *-m:* Message and semaphore activity.

The -A option reports all data, equivalent to specifying all the above options. Obviously, it would be convenient if sar data could be collected and written to a file in binary form for use by the sar command later. The sa1 command is used to collect sar binary data. When the following command is issued:

```
# /usr/lbin/sa/sa1
```

an entry is made in the file /var/adm/sa/sadd, where dd is today's date. If a repeat interval is specified to sa1, data is written at every repeat interval. Effectively, the command

```
# /usr/lbin/sa/sa1 300
```

writes a binary sar record to /var/adm/sa/sadd every 5 minutes forever. Note that up to 31 /var/adm/sa/sadd files may be present. Such an sa1 command can be run at system startup, or an appropriate cron job can be set up. Then reports can be produced by specifying time intervals to sar. For example,

```
# sar -s 08:00:00 -e 17:00:00 -f /var/adm/sa/sa12
```

will generate the default CPU report from the 12th of this (or any other) month's collected data within the time interval 8 a.m. to 5 p.m. The -f option is not required if today's report is being generated.

Chapter

17

Installing Software with Software Distributor: SD-UX and OpenView SD

17.1 Introduction

Layered software products on HP-UX are managed by Software Distributor, which is significantly different from the older *update*. The interface to Software Distributor is a set of software management commands for installing, configuring, listing, and other software maintenance tasks. SD-UX is the version of Software Distributor that runs on HP-UX and can perform operations on the *local* computer. OpenView SD runs on HP-UX under the OpenView Network and Systems Management Framework and can perform operations on the local *and remote* computers—that is, all HP-UX computers on the network. Thus, SD-UX is effectively a crippled version of OpenView SD. The manuals contain sufficient information for third-party vendors to develop software for distribution with Software Distributor.

Software can be distributed on tape or CD-ROM. Software Distributor supports protected software; the software can be retrieved only when a codeword or a customer ID is entered.

17.2 Quick Start: Installing a Software Product

We will install GlancePlus, which is a performance monitoring tool. An applications CD-ROM is available from HP that contains GlancePlus and other products. Most of the products are codeword-protected; however, GlancePlus Trial is not. The CD-ROM should be mounted on the system. Here the assumption is that the CD-ROM is mounted at */cdrom*.

243

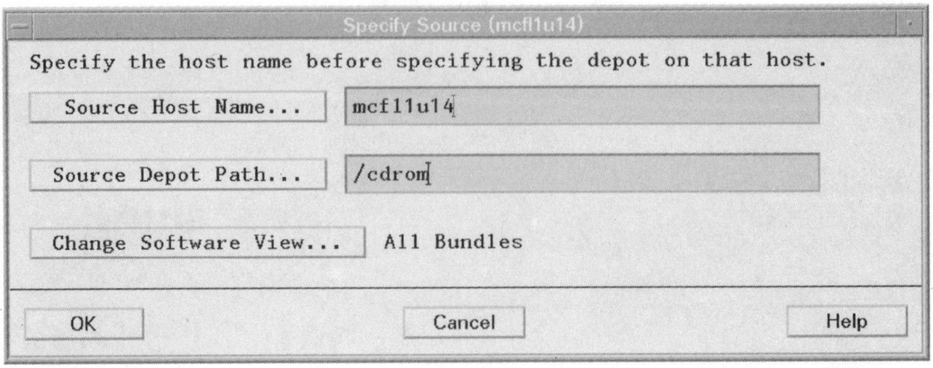

Figure 17.1 Prompt for software source mode and directory.

To install a product, Software Distributor's *swinstall* command is used. (The *swlist* command lists the software currently installed on the system. It can be used to check if GlancePlus Trial is installed.) swinstall can run in GUI mode if X-windows is running, otherwise, a TUI (Terminal User Interface) mode is used on HP and VT100 compatible terminals. Some Software Distributor commands are line-oriented. The GUI/TUI commands are available under System Administration Manager (SAM). All examples here assume that the GUI mode is used though SAM is not used.

When swinstall is entered, the SD Install main window shows up. In addition, a small popup window will prompt for the source of the software to be installed. Figure 17.1 shows this window. The Source Host Name field should contain the name of the local host, and the Source Depot Path field should contain the path of the CD-ROM, which is /cdrom in this example. More popup windows will prompt for customer ID and codewords. The Cancel button should be pressed on these windows.

The SD install main window then displays the list of products that can be accessed from the CD-ROM. This is not the complete list of products, since the proper codeword and customer ID were not entered. Figure 17.2 shows an example main window. To install Trial HP GlancePlus/UX for S800, select it by clicking on the row, and then select the Actions menu and click on Mark for Install. The Marked? column will display *yes* next to the product.

To install marked products, select the Actions menu and click on the Install Analysis submenu. A number of checks are performed and the result is displayed on the Install Analysis popup window, shown in Fig. 17.3. If the Status field displays Ready, as in this example, the OK button can be pressed. The Install window shown in Fig. 17.4 will pop up and display status information while the installation is going on. On successful completion, the window looks like the one shown in Fig. 17.4.

GlancePlus Trial is now installed. The *swlist* command will now display the products on the system including GlancePlus Trial. The command to start GlancePlus is

```
# /opt/perf/bin/gpm
```

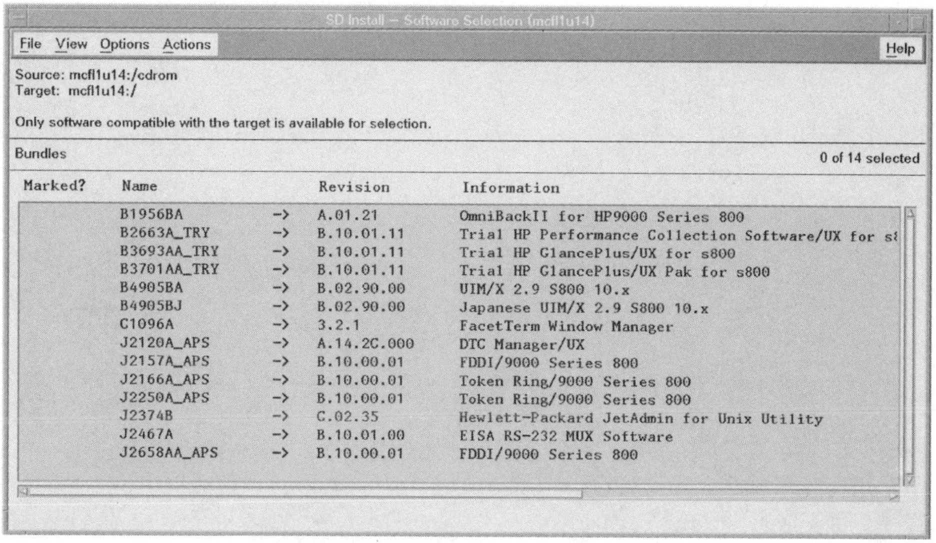

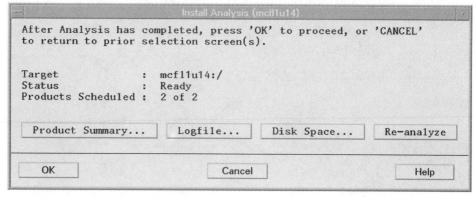

Figure 17.2   Products accessible on source media.

Figure 17.3   Install Analysis phase display.

17.3   Depots

In the above example, software was installed directly from the source CD-ROM. However, for installing software on multiple systems across the network, it is usually more convenient to load the software into a directory and install from this directory. Such a directory is called a depot. */var/spool/sw* is the default depot directory. The *swcopy* command copies software packages from the CD-ROM to a depot. When installing the software on another system, swinstall can be run on that system and the system and directory of the depot can be specified when prompted for the software source. Alternately, the depot directory can be NFS-mounted across the network onto a system where the software is to be installed. The NFS file locking feature must be enabled.

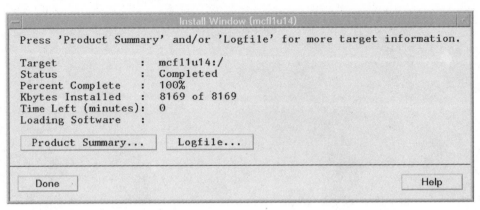

Figure 17.4   Installation phase display.

17.3.1 Registered depots

A depot can be registered with the *swreg* command. All registered depots are displayed when a depot is to be selected from a list. This is particularly useful when software is to be installed from a remote system that has multiple depots.

For example, if software from a CD-ROM is copied using swcopy to a directory /languages, the command

```
# swreg -l depot /languages
```

registers the depot /languages.

17.4 Bundles, Products, Subproducts, and Filesets

Distribution software is typically packaged as bundles or products. Bundles consist of products, which consist of subproducts consisting of filesets which in turn consist of files. For example, a developer's bundle may consist of a compiler, a debugger, and a profiler. A compiler product may consist of subproducts such as preprocessor, multiple versions of the compiler, and an optimizer. Filesets are a collection of related files pertaining to a subproduct.

17.5 Listing Software

The swlist command lists software installed on a system or software present in a depot. The -s option lists software in a specified directory, the -v option displays information in verbose mode, and the -l option displays information down to the specified level: depot, bundle, subproduct, fileset, or file. An example of the use of these commands is given here (the output is edited to remove some blank lines):

```
# swlist -l depot                 List all depots.
 Initializing...
  Target "mcfl1u14" has the following depot(s):
  /var/spool/sw
  /usr/netdist/products

# swlist                          List all software installed on current system.
  Initializing...
  Contacting target "mcfl1u14"...
  Target: mcfl1u14:/
  B2663A_TRY   B.10.01.11  Trial HP Performance Collection Software/UX for s800
  B3701AA_TRY  B.10.01.11  Trial HP GlancePlus/UX Pak for s800
  B3897A_AGM   B.10.01     HP-UX 16-User License
  B3900AA      B.10.01     HP C/ANSI C Developer's Bundle for HP-UX 10.0 (S800)
  J2250A_APS   B.10.00.01  Token Ring/9000 Series 800
  J2374B       C.02.35     Hewlett-Packard JetAdmin for Unix Utility
  OnlineDiag   B.10.01.00  HPUX 10.0 Support Tools Bundle

# swlist s /var/spool/sw          List all software under the directory.
  Initializing...
  Contacting target "mcfl1u14"...
  Target: mcfl1u14:/var/spool/sw
  B3693AA_TRY  B.10.01.11  Trial HP GlancePlus/UX for s800

# swlist -s /var/spool/sw -l product       List all products (not bundles).
Initializing...
  Contacting target "mcfl1u14"...
  Target: mcfl1u14:/var/spool/sw

  Glance             B.10.01.11    HP GlancePlus/UX
  MeasurementInt     B.10.01.11    HP-UX Measurement Interface

# swlist -s /var/spool/sw -l subproducts Glance     List all subproducts of product.
Glance
  Initializing...
  Contacting target "mcfl1u14"...
  Target: mcfl1u14:/var/spool/sw
  Glance                       B.10.01.11    HP GlancePlus/UX
  Glance.Runtime               Runtime Configuration

# swlist -s /var/spool/sw -l fileset Glance.Runtime   List fileset info within.
Glance.Runtime
  Initializing...
  Contacting target "mcfl1u14"...
 swlist   Depot Table of Contents
 For depot:  mcfl1u14:/var/spool/sw
 Date:  Sun Oct 29 17:06:37 1995
 Glance.Runtime
subproduct
tag                    Runtime
software_spec          Glance.Runtime,r=B.10.01.11,a=HP-UX_B.10.01_700/800,v=HP
size                   6927863
title                  Runtime Configuration
description            "
Vendor Name            Hewlett-Packard Company
SD-Product Name        Glance
Subproduct Name        Runtime

This is currently the only SD-subproduct for the Glance product.
"
contents               GLANCE GPM GPLIC

  Glance.Runtime.GLANCE
fileset
tag                    GLANCE
software_spec          Glance.GLANCE,r=B.10.01.11,a= HP-UX_B.10.01_700/800,v=HP
```

```
data_model_revision      2.10
instance_id              1
control_directory        GLANCE
size                     1374754
revision                 B.10.01.11
title                    HP GlancePlus files
description              "Vendor Name                     Hewlett-Packard Company

Product Name                              HP GlancePlus/UX
Fileset Name                              GLANCE

This fileset supports the entire Runtime file set to enable the
HP GlancePlus/UX character mode interface: /opt/perf/bin/glance.

    "
date                     10/29/95 14:57:47 EST
timestamp                814996667
state                    available
is_kernel                false
is_reboot                false
is_packaged_in_place     false
is_secure                false
ancestor                 HPUX9.GLANCE
media_sequence_number
prerequisite             MeasurementInt.MI,r>=B.10.01.11,a=HP-
UX_B.10.01_700/800,v=HP

   Glance.Runtime.GPM
fileset
tag                      GPM
software_spec            Glance.GPM,r=B.10.01.11,a=HP-UX_B.10.01_700/800,v=HP
data_model_revision      2.10
instance_id              1
control_directory        GPM
size                     5553109
revision                 B.10.01.11
title                    HP GlancePlus Motif interface files
description              "Vendor Name                     Hewlett-Packard Company

Product Name                              HP GlancePlus/UX
Fileset Name                              GPM

This fileset supports the Runtime file set to enable the HP
GlancePlus/UX Motif mode interface: /opt/perf/bin/gpm.

    "
date                     10/29/95 14:57:47 EST
timestamp                814996667
state                    available
is_kernel                false
is_reboot                false
is_packaged_in_place     false
is_secure                false
ancestor                 HPUX9.GPM
media_sequence_number
prerequisite             MeasurementInt.MI,r>=B.10.01.11,a=HP-
UX_B.10.01_700/800,v=HP
```

17.6   Software Distributor Commands and Interfaces

All Software Distributor commands start with *sw*. The commands are briefly
described here. All the commands can be invoked from the command line. In

addition, swinstall, swcopy, and swremove offer a graphic interface on X-stations and a screen-oriented interface on HP or VT100 compatible terminals.

- *swinstall:* Installs and configures software on local system. If OpenView SD-UX is being used, software can be installed on other systems with the *-t hostname* option.

- *swcopy:* Copies distribution software from a CD-ROM to a directory called a depot. Software can then be installed from the depot.

- *swremove:* Removes installed software.

- *swlist:* Displays information on installed software and software in depots.

- *swcluster:* Installs software for an NFS cluster by installing it in the server root file system and then linking the NFS clients to it.

- *swconfig:* Normally run automatically during swinstall; however, can be used later for reconfigurations.

- *swverify:* Compares original software files with those that were installed.

- *swreg:* Registers depots so that they are displayed when a depot list operation is performed.

- *swmodify:* Can be used to make minor modifications to catalog files.

- *swpackage:* Command to create software packages for distribution via Software Distributor.

- *swagentd:* Communicates with other nodes performing Software Distributor operations with local node.

- *swacl:* Manipulates access control lists on SD software objects. Enhances access security.

17.7 Installed Products Database (IPD) and Catalog Files

The IPD contains information on products and filesets present in the local system and an installation history. It consists of a set of files under /var/adm/sw/products. A similar database for products and filesets in a depot is called *catalog files*. The catalog files for a depot are under the *catalog* subdirectory of the depot, for example, /var/spool/sw/catalog. The swmodify command can be used to make minor changes in these files.

17.8 Codeword and Customer ID

When the swinstall command is run, the source information window, shown in Fig. 17.1, is displayed. Following that, a codeword and customer ID window, shown in Fig. 17.5, is displayed. The customer ID is required to access any software, even the unprotected software. If only the customer ID is entered without a codeword, the unprotected software is accessible. To access other software, a codeword is required. Codewords and customer IDs are sup-

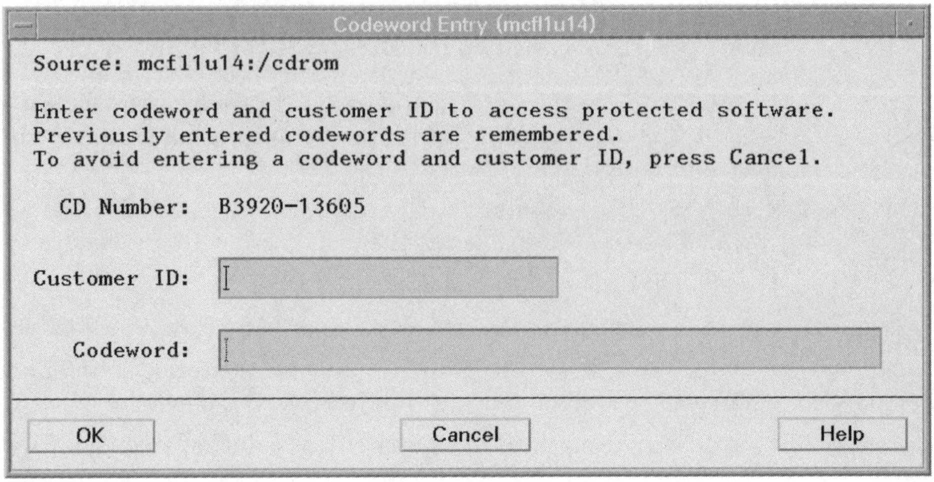

```
┌─────────────────────────────────────────────────────────────────────────┐
│  ─                    Codeword Entry (mcfl1u14)                         │
├─────────────────────────────────────────────────────────────────────────┤
│  Source: mcf11u14:/cdrom                                                  │
│                                                                           │
│  Enter codeword and customer ID to access protected software.            │
│  Previously entered codewords are remembered.                            │
│  To avoid entering a codeword and customer ID, press Cancel.             │
│                                                                           │
│    CD Number:   B3920-13605                                              │
│                                                                           │
│  Customer ID:  [                               ]                         │
│                                                                           │
│    Codeword:   [                                               ]         │
│                                                                           │
│  ┌──────────┐        ┌──────────┐              ┌──────────┐              │
│  │   OK     │        │  Cancel  │              │  Help    │              │
│  └──────────┘        └──────────┘              └──────────┘              │
└─────────────────────────────────────────────────────────────────────────┘
```

Figure 17.5 Protected software required fields.

plied on a license certificate when a product is purchased. Different codewords may be required for different products. Obviously, HP is serious about
stemming software piracy.

17.9 OpenView SD

The OpenView version of Software Distributor runs on systems that have the
OpenView Management Framework installed. For most SD commands, it
allows the *-t hostname* option, which effectively allows operations to be performed on other systems on the network. This way, software on multiple systems can be managed from a single system.

18

Configuring
the
HP-UX Kernel

18.1 Introduction

In Unix terminology, the kernel is the operating system including device drivers. The HP-UX kernel is in the file */stand/vmunix*. As a matter of fact, this is the standard kernel file on many Unix implementations. Not long ago, kernels had to be reconfigured often because main memory was at premium; internal table sizes were increased or device drivers were included only if absolutely required. Today, kernels are configured to accommodate future requirements; hence, reconfigurations are not that frequent. Here we will primarily discuss how to configure the kernel, how to load specific drivers into the kernel, and how to modify and tune kernel parameters. The kernel can be configured using SAM, however, the commands will also be discussed for a better understanding of the kernel configuration process.

18.2 How the Kernel Is Loaded into Main Memory

When the system boots, the goal of bootstrap programs is to load the kernel file and pass control to the kernel. On HP systems, the bootstrap programs consist of the primary bootstrap loader, which is in firmware, and the secondary bootstrap program, called the Initial System Loader (ISL), which is located in the initial few blocks of the disk. The ISL loads /stand/vmunix. Why the two-step bootstrap process? The primary bootstrap loader cannot be easily modified once the CPU is manufactured. The secondary bootstrap loader, ISL, can be customized or even completely changed to accommodate various booting situations:

- ISL may be different from one version of the operating system to the other.

- ISL can load the kernel from standard disk partitions or a Logical Volume Manager volume.

- ISL, in fact, can load an entirely different operating system.

To accommodate various bootstrapping requirements, the ISL is customized, not the primary bootstrap loader.

Once the kernel is loaded into memory and control is passed to it, the system is running HP-UX, though it may take a few minutes before users can log on because various initializations need to be performed.

18.3   Customizable Kernel Components

The kernel will have to be rebuilt if any one of four components requires changes: device drivers, subsystems, dump devices, or configurable parameters. Each device connected to the system must have a corresponding device driver in the kernel to handle I/O. The default kernel contains drivers for the common HP devices. Subsystems are components that handle a particular functionality within the kernel. Examples are the X.25 interconnect protocol and the Network File System (NFS). Dump devices are for storing kernel memory dumps when there is a panic condition—for instance, when the operating system cannot continue because some tables are in an inconsistent state. Configurable parameters are for changing sizes of data structures or tuning the system.

18.4   Quick Start: Changing a Parameter

To change a kernel parameter, the steps are:

- Get the current kernel configuration in a file.

- Change the parameter in this configuration file.

- Make a new kernel specifying the modified configuration file.

- Replace the existing kernel file, /stand/vmunix, with the new file.

- Reboot the system so that the new kernel with the modified parameter is used.

For this example, assume that the kernel parameter *maxdsiz* is to be increased to 128 Mbytes. maxdsiz specifies the maximum data segment size for a running process. Its default value is 64 Mbytes. If a program has a lot of large arrays, this value may be too low. Note that your kernel will not have the default value for the parameter if it has been reconfigured with a different value. To change the value of the maxdsiz kernel parameter,

- Go to /stand/build by

```
# cd /stand/build
```

As a convention, all builds should be performed in this directory.

- Create the configuration file from the current kernel. As a convention, the configuration file is called *system*. The command to create it is

```
# /usr/lbin/sysadm/system_prep -v -s system
```

The -v is for verbose mode. The file created is /stand/build/system. It is an ASCII text file showing the current kernel configuration. Items not listed have default values.

- Modify maxdsiz in the configuration file. Look for a line such as

```
maxdsiz     0x4000000
```

0x4000000 is 64 Mbytes written in hex. The value could be different on your system. If the line is found, replace it with

```
maxdsiz     0x8000000
```

If maxdsiz is not found, add the above line in the section of the configuration file headed "Tunable parameters."

- Create a new kernel with the command

```
# /usr/sbin/mk_kernel -v -s system
```

The -v is for verbose mode. The kernel is built using the configuration file, system, in the current directory. The kernel will be created in /stand/build/vmunix_test.

- Current kernel and configuration files are /stand/vmunix and /stand/system. They should be kept in case the new kernel does not work properly. These files should be renamed to /stand/vmunix.prev and /stand/system.prev:

```
# mv /stand/system  /stand/system.prev
# mv /stand/vmunix  /stand/vmunix.prev
```

The newly built kernel and the new configuration file should be copied to the current location:

```
cp /stand/build/system   /stand/system
cp /stand/build/vmunix_test  /stand/vmunix
```

- Now, when the system is rebooted, the new kernel with the updated maxdsiz value will be loaded.

Note that the file /stand/system is for documentation use; the kernel does not use it.

Conventionally, kernel builds are done in the directory /stand/build.

18.5   Kernel-Related Files and Directories

The directory /usr/conf/master.d contains files that specify information on drivers, subsystems, and configurable parameters. The file /usr/conf/master.d/core-hpux contains all the basic kernel definitions. Here is the file, heavily edited. *Block major* and *Char major* are small integers that represent the driver's entry number in the kernel tables. A -1 entry in the column indicates that the driver does not support block or character mode operations. (A driver can handle multiple devices that are identified with a minor device number.) The tunable parameters are briefly described at the end of the chapter.

```
$DRIVER_INSTALL
* Driver      Block major      Char major      Required for
*                                              minimal system
asio0           -1                1
pty0            -1               16                   1
lpr1            -1              181
mux0            -1                1
tape1           -1              212
disc1           26              214
disc2           27              175
netdiag         -1               46
scsi1           -1               -1


* Core drivers
lasi            -1               -1
asp             -1               -1


* WSIO drivers
stape           -1              205
schgr           29              231
sflop           23              106
$$$

$ALIAS
*
* The following entries form the alias table.
* field 1: product #     field 2: driver name
*
2213A           sdisk
Quantum_210S    sdisk
HP_2212A        sdisk

$TUNABLE
*
*range acctresume<=101
*range maxdsiz<=0x7b03a000
*range maxdsiz>=256*1024
*range maxfiles<=2048
*range maxfiles>=30


acctresume      ACCTRESUME      4
maxdsiz         MAXDSIZ         0x04000000
nfile           NFILE           (16*(NPROC+16+MAXUSERS)/10+32+2*(NPTY+NSTRPTY))
*
* LVM stuff
maxvgs          MAXVGS          10
no_lvm_disks    NO_LVM_DISKS    0
```

```
*
$$$
$DRIVER_DEPENDENCY
*
* Driver name    <dependency>  <dependency>.....
*
sdisk          sctl
stape          sctl
disc4          hpfll disc3
tape1          tape1_included sio
scsi1          sio
mux0           cio_ca0
$$$
$DRIVER_LIBRARY
*
* Driver handle   <libraries>
*
* subsystems first
uipc           libuipc.a
pfo            libpfo.a
* filesystem
ufs            libufs.a
nfs            libnfs.a
$$$
$LIBRARY
*
* The library table.  Each element in the library table describes
* one unique library.  The flag member is a boolean value, it is
* initialized to 1 if the library should *always* be included on
* the ld(1) command line, or 0 if the library is optional (i.e. it
* is only included when one or more drivers require it).  The order
* of the library table determines the order of the libraries on the
* ld(1) command line, (i.e. defines an implicit load order).  New
* libraries must be added to this table.
* Note: libhp-ux.a must be the last entry, do not place anything after it.
*
* Library    <required>
*
libuipc.a       0
libufs.a        1
libnfs.a        0
libcdfs.a       0
libpfo.a        0
libhp-ux.a      1
$$$
$SUBSYSTEMS_DEFINE
tape1_included
tape2_included
uipc
pfo
nfs
$$$
```

Note the information the file contains for the kernel-building program:

- Name of each driver and the drivers' major numbers
- Whether a driver must be included (required for minimal system)
- Aliases that can be used as driver names in /stand/build/system
- Tunable parameters and the range of values they can take

- Driver dependencies; when a driver is specified in /stand/build/system, the dependent drivers are included automatically by the build program

- Object libraries where the actual driver code resides

/usr/conf/master.d contains a few other files formatted like core-hpux. Examples are vxfs, which contains information on the optional journaled file system, and fddi, which contains FDDI interface–related device driver and library information.

The kernel-building process has the following internal steps:

- mk_kernel calls a program, /usr/sbin/config, which reads the file /stand/build/system, gathers the necessary driver and parameter information from the definition files /usr/conf/master.d/*, and produces two files, /stand/build/conf.c and /stand/build/config.mk. conf.c contains constants that specify the tunable parameter values. config.mk specifies which driver object files will be linked with the basic kernel.

- The basic kernel (locore.o) and device driver code is stored in object file format within libraries in /usr/conf/bin. When the kernel is built, the basic kernel and required driver objects are linked together by ld (the linker) to form the executable kernel. Hence, when the make utility is run on config.mk, conf.c is compiled and then conf.o, locore.o (basic kernel), and driver.o files are linked to form vmunix_test.

18.6   Using SAM to Configure the Kernel

SAM is very convenient for kernel reconfigurations. It has the following advantages over the command line mode:

- It lists all available drivers and subsystems and indicates which drivers and subsystems are present in the current kernel.

- It lists all configurable parameters, including parameters that have not been changed, and shows their current values.

- It validates configurable parameter ranges when a new value is being entered.

- It provides a short description of each configurable component.

To configure the kernel, run SAM and select the Kernel Configuration area. There are four icons corresponding to configurable parameters, drivers, dump devices, and subsystems. Figures 18.1, 18.2, and 18.3 show sample windows of parameters, drivers, and subsystems. The Actions menu has options to add and delete drivers and subsystems and to change parameter values. A new kernel can be created with the Create Kernel option in the Action menu. Essentially, SAM runs the mk_kernel command and creates /stand/build/vmunix_test, optionally moving it to /stand/vmunix and rebooting the system.

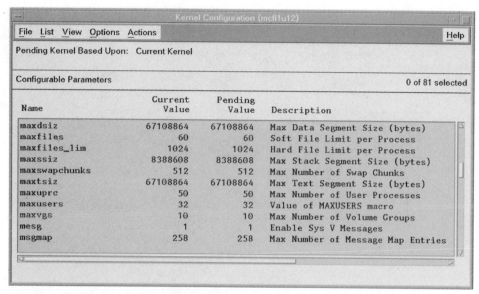

Figure 18.1 SAM window of configurable kernel parameters.

```
┌─────────────────────────────────────────────────────────────────────────┐
│                    Kernel Configuration (mcfl1u12)                        │
│  File  List  View  Options  Actions                               Help    │
│  Pending Kernel Based Upon:   Current Kernel                              │
│                                                                           │
│  Drivers                                                  0 of 73 selected │
│                                                                           │
│               Current    Pending                                         │
│    Name       State      State      Description                          │
│  ┌──────────────────────────────────────────────────────────────────┐   │
│   CentIf       In         In        Parallel Printer/Scanner Interface Module │
│   CharDrv      In         In        Simple character mode driver         │
│   asio0        Out        Out       Built-in Serial Interface Driver     │
│   asyncdsk     In         In        Asynchronous Disk Pseudo Driver      │
│   audio        Out        Out       Audio Driver                         │
│   autox0       Out        Out       MO Autochanger Hardware Driver (Series 800) │
│   beep         Out        Out       Non HIL Beeper Driver                │
│   c700         In         In        SCSI Interface Module                │
│   c720         In         In        SCSI Interface Module                │
│   ccio         In         In        Unknown CDIO                         │
│   cio_ca0      In         In        CIO Channel Adapter Module           │
│   core         In         In        Core IO CDIO                         │
│   diaghpib1    Out        Out       HP-PB HP-IB Diagnostics Module       │
│   disc1        Out        Out       HP-IB CS/80 Disk and Tape Drive Module │
│   disc2        Out        Out       HP-FL CS/80 Disks Module             │
│   disc3        In         In        SCSI Disk Module                     │
│   disc4        Out        Out       HP-PB HP-FL Disk Module              │
│   eeprom       Out        Out       EISA EEPROM Driver                   │
│   eisa         Out        Out       EISA CDIO                            │
│   etest        Out        Out       EISA Test Driver                     │
│   fdc          Out        Out       PC Floppy Controller Driver          │
│   fddi         In         In        EISA FDDI Interface Driver           │
│   graph3       Out        Out       Built-in Graphics Module             │
│   hil          Out        Out       HIL Keyboard Driver                  │
│  └──────────────────────────────────────────────────────────────────┘   │
└─────────────────────────────────────────────────────────────────────────┘
```

Figure 18.2 SAM window of kernel device drivers.

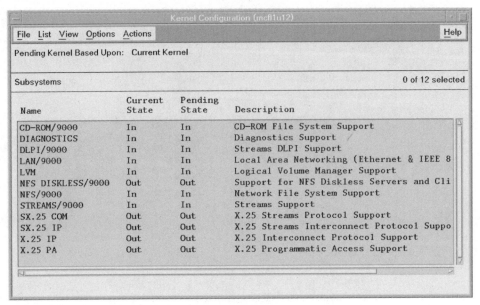

Figure 18.3 SAM kernel subsystem configuration.

18.7   Configurable Parameters

There are about 85 configurable parameters in the HP-UX kernel. Some parameters' values are dependent on some others'. The value specification is an
expression in /stand/build/system. If the values need to be constants, exercise
caution. In any case, any parameter changes must be done with careful
thought for the implications. Here is a broad and somewhat arbitrary classification of parameters:

- *Accounting parameters:*   These parameters are effective when process
  accounting is enabled. Process accounting normally consumes a lot of disk
  space. The parameters specify in terms of percent of disk space when to
  suspend or resume logging of accounting information.

- *File system parameters:* These parameters specify percent of memory to
  be used as file buffer cache, maximum number of files in the system and
  per process, number of file locks, and whether disk writes should be asyn-
  chronous.

- *IPC shared memory parameters:* These parameters specify number and
  sizes of messages, semaphores, and shared memory and whether the features should be disabled.

- *Logical Volume Manager (LVM) parameters:* These parameters specify
  maximum number of logical volumes and whether there are any LVM volumes on the system.

- *Network communications parameters:* One parameter, netisr_priority, specifies priority of network packet processing requests.

- *Swap parameters:* These parameters relate to file system swapping, pseudo-swap (free-memory swap), swap chunk size, and whether swapping is enabled over remote-mounted NFS disks.

- *Process management parameters:* These parameters determine maximum virtual memory size for process data, text, and stack; maximum number of processes per user; maximum number of processes on the system; and maximum number of time slices given to a process before it is preempted by another.

- *Miscellaneous parameters:* These parameters specify maximum users on the system, style of daylight saving time, time zone information, whether power failure features are to be enabled, and other information.

Table 18.1 lists the kernel parameters.

TABLE 18.1   HP-UX kernel parameters

NSTRBLKSCHED	Number of blockable streams scheduler daemons are to run
NSTREVENT	Maximum number of outstanding streams bufcalls
NSTRPUSH	Maximum number of streams modules in single stream
NSTRSCHED	Number of streams scheduler daemons to run
STRCTLSZ	Maximum size of streams message control (bytes)
STRMSGSZ	Maximum size of streams message data (bytes)
acctresume	Threshold to resume accounting
acctsuspend	Threshold to suspend accounting
allocate_fs_swapmap	Allocate Swapmap space at swapon
bootspinlocks	Number of spinlocks allocated before VM is initialized
bufpages	Number of buffer pages
create_fastlinks	Create Fast Symbolic Links
dbc_max_pct	Maximum Dynamic Buffer Cache size as % of system RAM size
dbc_min_pct	Minimum Dynamic Buffer Cache Size as % of system RAM size
default_disk_ir	Immediate report (with cache enable) behavior, SCSI disks
dskless_node	Diskless Node Flag
dst	Daylight saving time policy
eisa_io_estimate	Estimated number of I/O pages used by EISA cards
eqmemsize	Number of equivalent mapped memory pages on reserve list
file_pad	Number of file table entries reserved for superuser
fs_async	Select Asynchronous Writes
hpux_aes_override	Select strict OSF AES behavior
hz	Ticks per second (not tunable)
iomemsize	Maximum memory available to I/O subsystem
maxdsiz	Maximum data segment size (bytes)
maxfiles	Soft File Limit per process
maxfiles_lim	Hard File Limit per process
maxssiz	Maximum stack segment size (bytes)
maxswapchunks	Maximum number of swap chunks
maxtsiz	Maximum text segment size (bytes)
maxuprc	Maximum number of user processes

TABLE 18.1   HP-UX kernel parameters (*Continued*)

maxusers	Value of MAXUSERS macro
maxvgs	Maximum number of volume groups
mesg	Enable Sys V messages
msgmap	Maximum number of message map entries
msgmax	Message maximum size (bytes)
msgmnb	Maximum number of bytes on message queue
msgmni	Number of message queue identifiers
msgseg	Number of segments available for messages
msgssz	Message segment size
msgtql	Number of message headers
nbpg	Number of bytes per page (not tunable)
nbuf	Number of Buffer Cache Headers
ncallout	Maximum number of pending time-outs
ncdnode	Maximum number of open CDFS files
nclist	Number of cblocks for pty and tty data transfers
ndilbuffers	Number of DIL buffers
netisr_priority	Real-time process priority
netmemmax	Network Dynamic Memory Limit
netslop	Extra space for networking (not tunable)
nfile	Maximum number of open files
nflocks	Maximum number of file locks
ninode	Maximum number of open inodes
nni	Number of network interfaces supported by system
no_lvm_disks	Number of disks in LVM group
nproc	Maximum number of processes
npty	Number of ptys (pseudo-ttys)
nstrpty	Maximum number of streams-based PTYs
nswapdev	Maximum devices that can be enabled for swap
nswapfs	Maximum file systems that can be enabled for swap
num_clients	Approximate number of clients in an NFS diskless cluster
page_text_to_local	Enable/disable program text segments swap to local swap
pfail_enabled	Power failure enabled
public_shlibs	Public shared libraries
remote_nfs_swap	Enable swapping across NFS (for diskless clients)
rtsched_numpri	Number of POSIX.1b real-time priorities to support
scroll_lines	Number of ITE offscreen lines
sema	Enable Sys V semaphores
semaem	Maximum value for adjust on exit semaphores
semmap	Maximum number of semaphore map entries
semmni	Number of semaphore identifiers
semmns	Maximum number of semaphores
semmnu	Number of semaphore Undo structures
semume	Semaphore Undo entries per process
semvmx	Semaphore maximum value
shmem	Enable Sys V shared memory
shmmax	Maximum shared memory segment (bytes)
shmmni	Number of shared memory identifiers
shmseg	Shared memory segments per process
streampipes	Force all pipes to be streams-based
swapmem_on	Allow memory to exceed swap space
swchunk	Swap chunk size (1K blocks)
timeslice	Scheduling interval (10-ms ticks)
timezone	Minutes west of Greenwich
unlockable_mem	Nonlockable memory (bytes)

19

Programming on HP-UX

19.1 Introduction

HP-UX is supplied with a "crippled" K&R C compiler. This compiler is useful for kernel rebuilds and minor programming tasks but cannot be used for serious development work because of its numerous limitations. Most C code from other sources will not compile as is with this compiler. Except for this compiler, the *as* assembler, and the shells (such as POSIX, Korn, and dtksh), there are no programming facilities in bare-bones HP-UX. For high-level program development, HP offers

- Compilers for ANSI C, C++, FORTRAN, Pascal, and COBOL.

- A linker, *ld*, which is part of the operating system.

- Two language debuggers, *xdb* and *dde* (Distributed Debugging Environment). xdb is a line-oriented debugger that works in symbolic mode with all the languages. However, the standard debugger on HP-UX is dde; it has all the xdb functionality and more. Also, dde is GUI oriented; it exploits the Motif X-interface.

- HP/PAK programmer's analyzer kit. It consists of three tools: *dpat* for analyzing run-time behavior of programs, *hpc* for profiling, and *xps* for studying CPU use by multiple processes.

- *gprof* and *prof,* which are standard Unix program profiling tools that work on HP-UX. These tools are not discussed here.

- *make* and *sccs,* which are used for conditional compilations and maintaining source code.

- *SoftBench,* which is a GUI-based program development environment. SoftBench integrates most of the products mentioned here in visual framework. It will not be discussed here.

We will specifically discuss two programming languages, C and C++, though most of the chapter is relevant to all languages. No attempt is made to teach the languages.

19.2   C++ Overview

The HP C++ compiler is a full-fledged implementation of ANSI C++. Class and function templates along with exception handling (*try, catch,* and *throw*) are fully supported. The compiler code is derived from the AT&T and USL (Unix System Laboratories) C++ compiler, cfront. Initial versions of HP C++ acted as a translator, generating C code which was compiled with the HP C compiler. HP C++ can now directly compile source code.

The debugger, dde, fully supports C++; dde handles name demangling, overloaded functions and operators, and exception handling.

The C++ source file name must end with .c or .C. During normal compilation, the compiler has a number of phases, such as preprocessing and object file creation, that create intermediate files. These files are deleted before the compilation ends, unless appropriate options are specified on the command line.

Linking of C++ programs must be done with the CC command and not the ld command, although the C++ compiler internally calls ld. This is because C++ runs a pass after linking called the *c++patch* pass, which modifies the executable file.

19.3   Quick Start: Compiling a Simple C++ Program

Here is a rudimentary C++ program, hello.C:

```
#include <iostream.h>
void main()
{
  int x;
  cout << "Hello world!\n\n";
  cout << "Enter a number: ";
  cin >> x;
  cout << x << " squared is " << x*x << "\n";
}
```

The program can be compiled by

```
# CC hello.C
```

Note that CC refers to the C++ compiler and cc refers to the C compiler. No options are specified; the default action is to compile and link the program and create an executable file: a.out. Intermediate files are created by the preprocessor and the cfront compiler; however, these are deleted after use. The file a.out can be run as:

```
# a.out
Hello world!

Enter a number: 3
3 squared is 9
```

19.4 cpp.ansi: The Preprocessor

cpp.ansi handles preprocessor directives during compilation. Each directive starts with a "number" sign (#). Examples are

```
#define  sqr(x) x*x
#include <iostream>
```

The preprocessor accepts a C++ source file named *basename.c* or *basename.C* and creates an output file, *basename.i.* Normally this file is deleted; the -P option is specified to create and keep the intermediate file, as in:

```
CC -P hello.C      Create the preprocessor output file, hello.i.
```

19.5 cfront: Compiler and Translator

The component cfront accepts the output of the preprocessor and either compiles the C++ program to a relocatable object form or translates the program to C, depending on compilation options. The output object file is named *basename.o,* and the output C program file is named *basename..c.* As a default, cfront compiles the source; if the +T option is specified, the program is translated to C and then the C code is compiled.

```
# CC +T hello.C      Translate the C++ program to C. Compile and link the C program.
```

19.6 Intermediate Assembly Language

When the C++ program is compiled in translation mode, the -S option can be specified to create and keep assembly language output file:

```
# CC +T -S hello.C      Assembly language output in hello.s.
```

19.7 C++ Compiler Passes

A C++ program is compiled in multiple passes (or phases). The passes depend on whether the program is to be compiled or translated.

Figure 19.1 shows the passes for a compiled C++ program, and Fig. 19.2 shows the passes for a linked C++ program. In both cases, it is assumed that templates are not used; templates are stored in a template repository, and there are separate passes to handle templates.

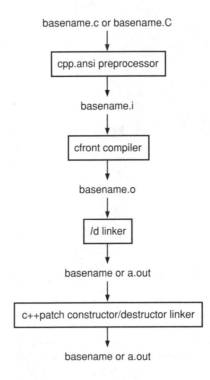

basename.c or basename.C

cpp.ansi preprocessor

basename.i

cfront compiler

basename.o

/d linker

basename or a.out

c++patch constructor/destructor linker

Figure 19.1 C++ compiler passes: compiler mode.

basename or a.out

19.8   Multiple C++ Compilation Modules

A C++ executable can be created by linking multiple object files corresponding to multiple source files. Multiple source files or compilation modules can be used to logically partition the application. Each file is compiled with the -c option to produce a .o file without linking. The CC command is once more run to link the files to produce an executable. When a source file is modified, that file only needs recompilation, followed by the CC command to link all the files. Example commands are

`# CC main.C -o main.o`	Compile a module. Output object file is main.o.
`# CC sub1.C -o sub1.o`	Compile a subroutine module. Output object file is sub1.o.
`# CC sub2.C -o sub2.o`	Compile another subroutine module. Output file is sub2.o.
`# CC main.o sub1.o sub2.o -o main`	Link all modules. Output executable file is main.

19.9   C++ Compiler Optimizations

The HP C++ compiler can perform extensive "behind-the-scenes" optimizations to produce efficient and compact code. Optimizations should be performed after code has been debugged. Any one of five levels of optimizations can be specified with the options +O0, +O1, +O2, +O3, or +O4. +O0 performs minimal optimizations, while +O4 performs all possible optimizations. Example use is

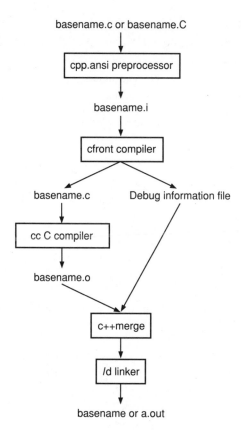

basename.c or basename.C

cpp.ansi preprocessor

basename.i

cfront compiler

basename.c   Debug information file

cc C compiler

basename.o

c++merge

/d linker

basename or a.out

Figure 19.2 C++ compiler passes: translation mode.

```
# CC +O4 hello.c
```

Additionally, for any specified optimization level, some optimizations can be disabled. For example, +O3 and +O4 perform in-lining of functions, among other optimizations. The +Onoinline option disables this particular optimization, as in:

```
# CC +O4 +Onoinline hello.C
```

The -O option is the equivalent of +O2.

19.10 C++ Profile-Based Optimization

The C++ optimizer can perform static optimizations when one of the options +O0 through +O4 is used. However, the optimizer can do an even better job if it knows the flow of the program during execution. To use this profile-based optimization, the program is compiled with the "Instrument" option, +I, which inserts special code in the executable. When the program is run, a file, flow.data by default, is created where program flow information is recorded as the program runs. After execution, the program is compiled again with the +P option; the compiler then studies the profile data in flow.data and performs optimizations. Example usage is

```
# CC +I +O4 hello.C -o hello.exe    Instrument the executable.
# hello.exe < sampledata            Run the program using realistic sample data.
                                    flow.data will be created.
# CC +P +O4 hello.C -o hello.exe    Recompile. flow.data is used to optimize code.
```

19.11   C++ Compiler Options

Here are the commonly used compiler options:

-c   Produce object file and do not link. Example:

```
# CC hello.C -c hello.o
```

    This is typically used when an executable is made from multiple compilation modules.

-g	Generate information for symbolic debugger. This option is required if xdb or dde is to be used to debug the program.
-lx	Search in library libx.sl or libx.a.
-Ldir	Causes the linker to search for libraries libx.sl or libx.a in dir before searching /lib and /usr/lib. This option must precede -l.
-ooutfile	Name of linker output file, a.out by default.
-O	Use optimizer at level 2. Same as +O2.
-P	Run only preprocessor; leave output in basename.i.
-S	Compile and leave assembly language output in basename.s.
-v	Enable verbose mode. Shows information on various compilation passes.
+eh	Enable C++ exception handling.
+I	Instrument application for profile-based optimization.
+On	Optimize at level n, where n is between 0 and 4. +O0 performs minimal optimization.
+P	Optimize on basis of profile data in flow.data created when executing the program created with the I option.
+T	Translator mode. C++ is converted to C and C is compiled.

19.12   The ANSI C Compiler and Linker

HP's ANSI C and C++ have similar command syntax. Read the preceding sections on C++, since some information will not be repeated here. The ANSI C compiler is under /opt/ansic. The following must be executed in KornShell to use the compiler:

```
# export PATH=/opt/ansic/bin:$PATH
```

The ANSI C compiler's default operation is to compile programs in non-ANSI mode. To use ANSI mode, the -Aa option must be used. For portability, always use the option.

19.13   Quick Start: Compiling a C++ Program

Here is a program, ascii.c, which prints all the 256 possible 1-byte characters:

```
/* output all 256 possible byte values */
#include <stdio.h>
main()
{
short int c;
 for (c=0; c<= 255; c++)
 { printf("%c\n",c);
 };
};
```

The program can be compiled by

```
# cc ascii.c
```

The output executable can be run by

```
# a.out
```

256 characters, one per line, are sent to the terminal.

19.14   C Compiler Passes

The source program file name must have .c as a suffix. The preprocessor, cpp.ansi, takes this file as input and produces an intermediate source file with the suffix .i in the name. The main compiler, ccom, converts this to an object file with the suffix .o in the name. Alternatively, the main compiler will produce an assembler file if the -S option is used. The linker, ld, then creates an executable, a.out, with the .o file as input. The process is depicted in Fig. 19.3.

19.15   Multiple C Compilation Modules

See Section 19.8. The principle is the same as for C++.

19.16   C Compiler Optimizations

See Section 19.9, for C++.

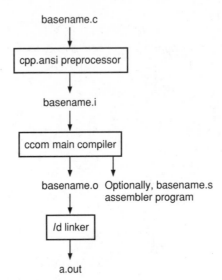

Figure 19.3 C compiler passes.

19.17 C Profile-Based Optimization

See Section 19.10, for C++.

19.18 ANSI C Compiler Options

Most of the C compiler options are held in common with the C++ compiler. Here are the commonly used compiler options:

-Aa   Compile in strict ANSI mode.

-c   Produce object file and do not link; for example,

```
# cc ascii.c -c ascii.o
```

  This is typically used when an executable is made from multiple compilation modules.

-g   Generate information for symbolic debugger. This option is required if xdb or dde is to be used to debug the program.

-lx   Search in library libx.sl or libx.a.

-Ldir   Causes the linker to search for libraries libx.sl or libx.a in dir before searching /lib and /usr/lib. This option must precede -l.

-ooutfile   Name of linker output file, a.out by default.

-O   Use optimizer at level 2. Same as +O2.

-P   Run only preprocessor; leave output in basename.i.

-S   Compile and leave assembly language output in basename.s.

-v   Enable verbose mode. Shows information on various compilation passes.

+I   Instrument application for profile-based optimization.

+On   Optimize at level n, where n is between 0 and 4. +O0 performs minimal optimization.

+P   Optimize on the basis of profile data in flow.data created when executing
              the program created with the I option.

19.19   dde: Distributed Debugging Environment

The debugger has a graphic and a line-oriented interface. All the commands
mentioned here are the same for either interface. The display format is different, however, and the graphic interface has point-and-click functionality. The
discussion assumes that the graphic interface is being used. A C language
program is used for illustrating debugger features; however, all HP languages (other than COBOL) are supported by the debugger. The debugger
understands language-specific syntax.

19.19.1   Quick start

To debug an executable, the source files must be compiled with the -g option,
as in

```
$ CC -g hello.C -o hello     C++ compiler
$ cc -g ascii.c -o ascii     C compiler
```

In the following discussion, the C program, ascii.c, is used to illustrate
debugger features. The program is run from a terminal emulation window
with the command

```
# dde ascii
```

If the program accepts parameters, the name of the executable should be preceded by a double dash; otherwise, else the program's parameters may be
treated as dde parameters:

```
# dde -- ascii -s20     Program ASCII has the option -s20.
```

Two windows pop up; the transcript display window, Fig. 19.4, is where you
interact with the debugger; and the source display window, Fig. 19.5, is
where you see the current location in the program. Your program output is
displayed in the terminal emulator window from which the debug session was
started. Commands can be entered in the transcript display window at the
dde> prompt. Most commands can be entered in multiple ways; for example,
the *step* command,which executes a single statement, can be entered by:

- Entering *step* at the dde> prompt.
- Clicking on the Step button on the left side of the transcript display win-
  dow.
- Using the Step item from the Execute menu in the transcript display win-
  dow.
- Entering the Alt-S key combination. This menu shortcut is displayed in the
  Execute menu.

Menu offering
debugger
features

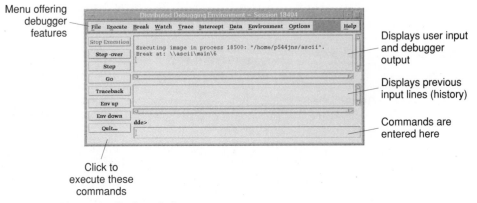

Displays user input
and debugger
output

Displays previous
input lines (history)

Commands are
entered here

Click to
execute these
commands

Figure 19.4   Transcript display window.

Double click on a line
number to set or cancel
a breakpoint

Clicking the three mouse
buttons here displays three
pop-up menus

Source line numbers

The arrow shows
current location

Start and end of
programs always
have a breakpoint

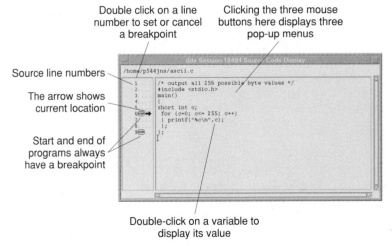

Double-click on a variable to
display its value

Figure 19.5   Source display window.

- Clicking the middle mouse button in the source display window, which will pop up a menu where *step* is one of the clickable buttons.

Most debugger commands can be abbreviated to the first three letters of the command.

19.19.2   Basic commands: step, go, print, set, and breakpoint

The step command executes a single instruction. Variations are

```
dde> step 5          Execute next five statements.
dde> step -until 8   Step until line number 8 is reached.
dde> step -over      Execute one statement including the functions called in the statement.
```

The go command executes a program until it completes or until an event occurs, such as encountering a breakpoint. Examples are

```
dde> go                    Run until an event has occurred.
dde> go -until 20          Run program until line 20 is reached or an event has occurred.
dde> go -until func2       Run program until func2 is reached or an event has occurred.
```

The print command prints values of variables or evaluates expressions. Examples are

```
dde> print c               Display value of c.
dde> print (c + 3)*2       Evaluate the expression and display the result.
dde> print myarray[2]      Display value of third element of array.
dde> print &(myarray[3])   Display address of location where the value of myarray[3] is
                           stored. Only in C and C++.
```

The set command assigns a value to a variable. Examples are

```
dde> set c = 5
dde> set c = (c+2)+4
dde> set game = 'football'   String assignment.
dde> set c += 3              Increment value of c by 3. This construct can be used only
                             when debugging C programs.
```

The breakpoint command is used to stop program execution at specified locations, possibly to check variable values, file contents, and so on. The program stops just before the breakpoint. Examples are

```
dde> breakpoint 7          Break at line 7.
dde> breakpoint func2      Break at location func2, possibly a function entry point.
```

Breakpoints can be deleted with commands like

```
dde> delete breakpoint func2
```

19.19.3 Scope: Specifying locations and variables in a large program

Variables can be in other program modules than the current one. Moreover, the program could have multiple functions using the same variable name for different variables. Similarly, the same function name can be used in different program modules. Object names are normally searched for in the current environment; to be specific, a fully qualified name can be used as \module\block... \object-name. Examples are

```
dde> set "ascii.c"\main\c = 5     Variable c in block main in file ascii.c.
dde> set \"ascii.c"\main\c = 5    Same as above.
dde> set \main\c = 5              Variable c in block main in current environment.
dde> breakpoint \main\7           Break at line 7 in block main.
dde> breakpoint \"tmp.c"\func2\3  Break at line 3 of program ascii.c. The line is in block
                                  func2.
```

Note how the debugger displays names as fully qualified names.

19.19.4   Monitors: Breakpoints, intercepts, traces, watchpoints

Breakpoints were described in the previous section.

Intercepts are program events. Examples are signals in C, like SIGIO. An event can be intercepted by the debugger with commands like

```
dde> intercept signal SIGIO
```

If the signal is raised when the program is running, control returns to the debugger. Intercepts can be deleted with commands like

```
dde> delete intercept signal SIGIO
```

Trace can be set by

```
dde> trace        Start trace.
```

Once set, line numbers of all statements executed by the program are displayed. Tracing can be canceled by

```
dde> delete trace
```

Watchpoints return control to the debugger when the values of specified variables change. For example,

```
dde> watchpoint c      Stop execution if the value of variable c changes.
```

A separate watchpoint variable window displays watchpointed variables. If the go command is issued, the debugger stops when the value of the variable changes. The new value of the variable is displayed in the watchpoint variable window. Watchpoints can be deleted with a command like

```
dde> delete watchpoint c
```

A set of common operations can be performed on breakpoints, intercepts, traces, and watchpoints; hence, a collective term is used for them: monitors. The following examples illustrate monitor commands:

```
dde> list monitors          Display all monitors, each identified by a number.
dde> suspend monitor 5      Monitor 5 is temporarily not effective.
dde> activate monitor 5     Monitor 5 is now effective.
dde> delete monitor 5       Remove the item.
```

19.19.5   Recording commands

Commands from a debugger session can be stored in a file. The file can be edited outside the debugger, if required, and then played back. Example commands are

```
dde> property record recfile      Start recording commands into file recfile.
dde> ...                          Various commands.
```

```
dde> property record -off          Stop recording.
dde>...
dde> <recfile                      Later on, the file can be played back.
```

19.19.6 Customization

When the debugger starts running, it will read commands from the file .dderc in your home directory. The .dderc file can contain customizations like

```
alias s step
property array_dim_max 20          Display only 20 elements if a long array is being printed.
```

Various X-windows–related parameters can be customized by copying /opt/langtools/dde/lib/nls/app-defaults/C/DDE to your home directory and editing the file. For example, the size of the history subwindow in the transcript display window can be increased from the default 3 to 12 by changing the appropriate line in dde:

```
DDE*MotifCommandArea.historyVisibleItemCount: 12
```

19.19.7 Other debugger commands and features

The alias command can be used to create shorthands for long commands:

```
dde> alias s step
```

Multiple commands can be entered on a single line, separated by a semicolon:

```
dde> print c; set c = 4
```

The -do option specifies an action for monitors:

```
dde> breakpoint 7 -do [print c; go]
```

The property command is used to change various debugger settings:

```
dde> property array_dim_max 20          Display only 20 elements if a long array is being printed.
```

The describe command displays the attributes of variables or functions:

```
dde> describe c     Displays that c is a short int.
```

19.19.8 Line-mode debugger interface

Line-mode debug mode can be used if an X-station is not available. An example of a command to start debugging is

```
# dde -ui line ascii
```

or

```
# dde -ui line -- ascii -s20    The program ASCII has an option -s20.
```

All the debugger commands mentioned above are available in line mode; however, the format of displayed output is different. An example session follows:

```
# dde -ui line ascii
Executing image in process 23887: "/home/p544jns/ascii".
Break at: \\ascii\main\6
Source File: /home/p544jns/ascii.c
    6 B>  for (c=0; c<= 255; c++)
dde> step
Stepped to: \\ascii\main\7
    7 >   { printf("%c\n",c);
dde> breakpoint 7
dde> go
Break at: \\ascii\main\7
    7 B>  { printf("%c\n",c);
dde> trace
dde> go
Trace at: \\ascii\main\6
Break at: \\ascii\main\7
Trace at: \\ascii\main\7
    7 B>  { printf("%c\n",c);
dde> quit
#
```

The view command can be used to display a block of lines:

```
dde> view -10 lines 20    Display 20 lines starting from 10 lines before current location.
dde> view 15 lines 10     Display 10 lines from line 15.
```

19.20   Program Performance and Profiling with HP/PAK

The Programmer's Analysis Kit (HP/PAK) consists of the following products:

- *xps:* This tool displays per-process CPU utilization and some overall system statistics. Its functionality overlaps with other HP-UX commands such as top, GlancePlus, and sar.

- *dpat (Distributed Performance Analysis Tools):* This is a run-time profiling tool. dpat samples a running program's (process's) stack and gathers data on where (in which functions, subroutines, and such) the CPU is processing code. For a large number of samples, this data shows how much time is spent within each function or subroutine in the program.

- *hpc:* This tool provides run-time information also; however, it can display CPU time spent on each line of the program. The program must be compiled with the -g (debug) option, which provides the necessary source-level information in the final executable, which will be sampled when running.

19.20.1   xps

Figure 19.6 shows the output of

```
$ xps
```

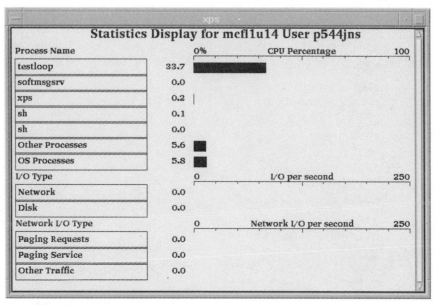

Figure 19.6 Process monitoring with *xps*.

xps works on X-windows/Motif displays; it does not support character terminals. The information displayed is

- CPU use by each of your processes.
- Total CPU use by OS processes. These are processes owned by root. The -ll option will display CPU use by each OS process.
- Total CPU use by all other processes. The -p option will display CPU by each of the other processes.
- Network I/O.
- Disk I/O.

The display is updated every 4 seconds; the -r n option specifies that the display is to be updated every *n* seconds.

19.20.2   dpat

dpat has both a text and an X-windows interface; we will look at the text interface in this section. There are two phases to dpat profiling: program monitoring and analysis. During monitoring, an existing process or a dpat-invoked program is sampled. The data is written to a file, datafile. During analysis, the contents of the datafile are used to display program profile information. Another dpat option, view, displays stack information every sampling interval while the program is running. Here is a C program we will profile. The program has three loops doing nothing much, simply consuming CPU time.

```
/* program has three loops consuming different amount of CPU time.
   The program is compiled with
$ cc -o loop loop.c

*/
#include <stdio.h>

loop1()
{
int i,j;
for (i=0; i<= 20000000; i++)
 {
   j=j + 1 ;
 };
printf("End of loop 1 \n");
}

loop2()
{
int i,j;
for (i=0; i<= 30000000; i++)
 {
   j=j + 1 ;
 };
printf("End of loop 2 \n");
}

loop3()
{
int i,j;
for (i=0; i<= 10000000; i++)
 {
   j=j + 1 ;
 };
printf("End of loop 3 \n");
}

main()
{
loop1();
loop2();
loop3();
};
```

Here is a sample dpat session that is profiling the executable loop. The HP/PAK tools are in the directory /opt/langtools/bin.

```
$ dpat -notext
dpat> monitor -invoke ./loop
Initializing image '/home/testjns/cloop/loop'...done.
Initializing image '/usr/lib/libc.1'...done.
End of loop 1
End of loop 2
End of loop 3
Monitoring lasted 14 seconds.
Target ran 10 seconds and used 9 CPU seconds.
Monitoring stopped after 101 samples.
dpat>
dpat> analyze
Samples    Samples      Cpu microseconds
In Only    In or Under  In or Under
```

%Total	%Total	Raw Count	Level	Routine
0	100	9420000	1	$START$
0	100	9420000	2	_start
0	100	9420000	3	main
31	31	2870000	4	loop1
52	52	4970000	4	loop2
17	17	1580000	4	loop3

```
Analysis has completed successfully.
dpat>
dpat> view -invoke loop
```

(Edited output; traceback info is displayed after each sample interval)

```
Initializing image '/home/testjns/cloop/loop'...done.
Initializing image '/usr/lib/libc.1'...done.
----TRACEBACK----
$START$
_start
main
loop1
----TRACEBACK----
$START$
_start
main
loop1
----TRACEBACK----
$START$
_start
main
loop2
----TRACEBACK----
$START$
_start
main
loop2
----TRACEBACK----
$START$
_start
main
loop2
End of loop 2
----TRACEBACK----
$START$
_start
main
loop3
End of loop 3
Monitoring lasted 14 seconds.
Target ran 9 seconds and used 8 CPU seconds.
Monitoring stopped after 6 samples.
dpat>
dpat> quit
$
```

In the preceding session,

- The analysis option displays per-function CPU use. Because dpat looks at stack contents and not at actual program counter position, reporting granularity is not at statement level. dpat can report profiling information on any process on the system. The hpc program described below reports CPU use for each statement; however, the program has to be compiled with the -g option.

- dpat has four options: monitor, analyze, view, and playback. Playback displays information similar to view in "slow motion"; however, unlike the case for view, the information is from the monitor output file, datafile. Playback requires an X-windows interface.

- Monitor can sample any running process with a command such as

```
dpat> monitor -existing 21624
```

- Analyze has filtering options to display information for a time range or to display functions and procedures accounting for at least a certain amount of CPU time.

19.20.3   hpc

Histogram Program Counter (hpc) displays what percentage of CPU time was spent on each of the program's statements. The program must be compiled with the -g option:

```
$ cc -g -o loop loop.c
```

Here is a sample hpc session. The program is the same as the one in the dpat example above.

```
$ hpc loop
Initializing image '/home/testjns/cloop/loop'...done.
End of loop 1
End of loop 2
End of loop 3
Monitoring stopped after 1925 samples.
Samples with line number information: 1925.
\\loop\loop2
      22       37.8 *************************************
      24       14.5 *************
\\loop\loop1
      12       22.5 *********************
      14        9.5 *********
\\loop\loop3
      32       10.8 *********
      34        4.9 ****
```

In this session,

- The numbers to the left of the histogram are line numbers.
- Only statements using more than 1 percent of CPU time are displayed. To change this limit, a command like this can be used:

```
$ hpc -limit 0 loop
```

- The -brief option displays one line for all the statements in each procedure or function. This can be useful when analyzing large programs.
- A running process can be analyzed with a command such as

```
$ hpc -existing 12363
```

- A histogram is displayed when the process terminates.

20

NFS Clusters

20.1 Introduction

In HP-UX parlance, clusters are systems consisting of one server and multiple clients. The clients load their operating system from the server. After loading the system software, the clients use the server as a file system; however, they operate as independent HP-UX systems. At most sites, the clients do not have any disks; hence, the term *clusters of diskless clients*. These clusters basically share files; they cannot be compared with Digital's OpenVMS Clusters, which support high availability, common system management, and scalable performance with many software products.

Before HP-UX V10.0, clusters were called DUX Clusters or Diskless HP-UX Clusters. DUX used proprietary software. Clusters are now called NFS Clusters and are based on the Network File System available on all Unix systems. Diskless systems used to be popular at sites having multiple systems because these systems were cheap and, to an extent, required less system administration. Today, however, disks have become cheap, and network traffic is increasing; hence, diskless systems are not as attractive as before. Nevertheless, clusters of diskless clients may be a suitable configuration

- When there are many users not familiar with Unix. These users should not be allowed to tamper with system files.

- The user, for security reasons, should not be given root access to the systems. A standalone system can be more easily modified by a user.

- Where system administrators find the setup more convenient than many standalone systems.

Diskless clusters may not be suitable when

- Each system is used for a separate application.

- Users have differing needs for system layered products.

- For security reasons, the users want to keep data on local disks.

- Booting off another system is not acceptable because of network configuration or low bandwidth.

- A powerful server is not available.

- A site considers Network File System (NFS) too insecure for its organization. NFS is required for diskless booting.

HP 9000 Model 700 (S700) systems can be clients; HP 9000 Model 800 (S800) systems cannot. Either S700 or S800 systems can be servers; if the server is an S700 system, the cluster is homogeneous; if the server is an S800, the cluster is heterogeneous. A typical cluster configuration would be a powerful S800 system (for example, model K400) serving a dozen S700 systems.

20.2 NFS Clustering Concepts

There are two major issues to be considered for a diskless client:

- How does a diskless client load the operating system?

- How should the directories on the server be configured? System files that do not change over the life of the operating system should be shared by all clients; client-specific configurations and other files cannot be shared.

The answer to the first question is that the firmware in the S700 systems supports bootp and tftp protocols to find booting server information and load files. Specifically, the client sends out a bootp broadcast using the UDP protocol of the IP stack. A server that has the client defined in the file /etc/bootptab responds with the client's IP address, boot file, and similar information. The client then uses tftp to load the boot file from the server. The boot file contains some esoteric code, which ultimately loads the kernel.

The answer to the second question is that HP-UX, starting with V10.0, uses the System V.4 directory layout, which specifies separate directories for dynamic and static files. See Chapter 2, which has a section on file system directory layout. Files and directories in /usr, /opt, and similar directories can be shared among clients. However, the server could be S800 while the clients are always S700. The executable formats are different for S800 and S700 (although they use the same PA-RISC CPU architecture). To address this issue, all servers contain an alternate root, normally, /exports/shared_roots/OS_700. This is the root shared by all the clients. If the server is an S700, the subdirectories are symbolic links to the server's root; for example, /exports/shared_roots/OS_700/usr will be a symbolic link to /usr. If the server is an S800, actual S700 files will be present in /exports/shared_roots/OS_700.

For each client, the root file system, /, corresponds to a directory such as /export/private_roots/clientname on the server. Most directories are pointed to via symbolic links from this directory. Consider the /usr directory. /usr, on any HP2DUX system, contains O/S-related commands like /usr/bin/patch and

/usr/bin/telnet; effectively, /usr contains static files. The client's /usr corresponds to /export/private_roots/clientname/usr on the server. Hence, /export/private_roots/clientname/usr is a symbolic link to /exports/shared_roots/OS_700/usr. What is the nature of a private directory like /home on a client? On the server, the directory corresponds to /export/private_roots/clientname/home. No symbolic links are involved. For a good understanding of file layouts, draw a diagram showing some private and some shared directories and corresponding symbolic links for two clients served by an S700 server and two clients served by an S800 server.

Additional software products normally installed under /opt have to be installed once on an S700 server, but twice on an S800 server: once for the server's use, and once into the alternate root for the client's use.

20.3 Shared and Private Roots

As mentioned before, each client's root, /, corresponds to /export/private_roots/clientname on the server. /export/private_roots/clientname is called a *private root*. There is one to /export/private_roots/clientname for each client. Directories that are not shared—i.e., are dynamic and client-specific—are allocated directly under the client's root. Directories that are static and shared with other clients are symbolic links from directories under /export/private_roots/clientname to directories in /exports/shared_roots/OS_700, which is called a shared root. On an S700, this directory contains symbolic links to directories under /. On an S800, this directory is set up, using SAM, to contain S700-specific root files. A server can contain multiple shared roots; for example, /export/common_applications can contain programs that can be used by all clients.

Directories under the shared root are /usr, /sbin, and such. Directories under the private roots are /etc, /tmp, /var, /home, /stand, /dev, and such.

20.4 Server Configuration

The /exports/shared_roots/OS_700 directory must be created and exported on the server.

- The directory contains symbolic links to / on an S700. This is done during the installation of two software products: Diskless and SystemAdmin. Hence, on an S700, install these two products.

- On an S800, /exports/shared_roots/OS_700 and subdirectories contain the root file system for an S700 architecture system. The files are in a bundle such as HPUXEngRT700. An example of an install command is

```
swinstall -r -s nodepqr:/swdepot HPUXEngRT700 @ /export/shared_roots/OS_700
```

- The SAM cluster area contains the menu item "Install OS for clients," which may be more convenient for the installation.

20.5 Diskless Client Configuration on the Server

A client is added with the *sam→clusters→NFS* cluster configuration, Actions menu item Define Clients. Once a client is created, the Install Defined Clients menu item must be navigated. SAM will perform the following tasks:

- Add client name, IP address, hardware address, network mask, and default route to /etc/bootptab.
- Create /export/private_roots/clientname. Create directories under it with symbolic links to directories under /exports/shared_roots/OS_700. Create default configuration files. Create client /etc/fstab.
- Create /export/tftpboot/clientname/stand and populate it with boot files for the client.
- Create entries in /etc/exports to export directories relevant to the client.
- Configure NFS, BOOTP, and TFTP if not already running.

Clients can now be booted.

20.6 The Client Booting Process

A new client must first be booted to the console firmware prompt. The primary boot path should be set with a command like

```
path primary lan.nnn.nnn.nnn.nnn.255.255
```

where nnn.nnn.nnn.nnn is the server's lan card IP address. After this, when booting, the client will use the bootp protocol to get information on client IP address, tftp boot file name, and such from the server. The boot file name is normally /exports/tftpboot/clientname/stand/uxbootlf. The boot file is loaded from the server by the client using the tftp protocol. Following that, /exports/tftpboot/clientname/stand/vmunix.fs and the kernel, /exports/ tftpboot/clientname/stand/vmunix, are loaded. vmunix.fs is a RAM file system which, through a sequence of events, sets the host name, configures the lan0 network interface, mounts the client private root as /, mounts files mentioned in /etc/fstab, and enables primary file system swap. Once all these initializations are done, the system continues a "normal" startup by executing /sbin/pre_init_rc and /sbin/init. For a first-time boot, the software will be configured (for example, device drivers for the system will be configured) and the client will reboot. The client is then ready for use.

20.7 Single-Point Administration

An NFS cluster essentially consists of independent systems sharing files. Some features are added to SAM to perform clusterwide tasks; however, these are minor enhancements:

- A printer can be added to any node on a cluster by defining it as a local printer on the system where it exists and as a remote printer on all other nodes. This can be done a system at a time; SAM allows you to perform this task for all systems automatically.
- /etc/passwd and /etc/group can be shared. This is achieved by using symbolic links on clients. The sharing is automated by the *sam ->clusters->NFS* Cluster Configuration, Action menu item "Set Cluster Policies." Home directories and mail can also be configured for shared use from this menu.

20.8   The swcluster Command

Software product installation or removal for a cluster is done with the *swcluster* command rather than the *swinstall* and *swremove* commands. The installation is into /export/shared_roots/OS_700. Configuration files are placed in each of the diskless client private roots. The software is configured for a client when the client boots.

20.9   The dcnodes Command

The *dcnodes* command displays nodes in the cluster. The command can be issued from any cluster node. Various qualifiers will display OS shared roots, active/inactive status, and such. The *dcnodesd* daemon must be running on all cluster nodes. The daemon is configured to start when diskless clients are configured by SAM.

A

dtksh: Desktop KornShell

A.1 Introduction

dtksh is a component of the Common Desktop Environment (CDE). It essentially consists of ksh-93 with GUI building extensions. The graphics commands of dtksh support many of the functions in libDT (which is a part of CDE), Motif widgets, Xt intrinsics, and Xlib. dtksh has some support for the ToolTalk service, which allows independent X applications to communicate with each other. If you know KornShell, then you mainly need to know the graphics features of dtksh. This chapter does not cover ksh, except for the newer features. Also, Motif and X programming issues are not covered in detail; there are many graphic programming books available.

dtksh is run by

```
# /usr/dt/bin/dtksh
```

A.2 Quick Start: dtksh Windows

There is a lot of terminology surrounding X programming; the best way to learn graphic programming is to look at and write programs. A dtksh program (script) using X-windows performs the following steps, like any other X program:

- Initialize the X Toolkit.
- Create widgets (and gadgets). Write functions which will process events via callback routines.
- Realize widgets.

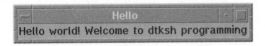

Figure A.1 Window created by a dtksh scribble script.

- Wait by calling a special X routine: Xtmainloop. Events are processed while waiting.

X calls can be made to Xlib, Xt intrinsics, or the Motif widget layers. Motif widgets are derived from Xt intrinsics, which are derived from Xlib, the lowest X layer that can be called. All X function names start with X or Dtksh.

Widgets are the entities you see on an X display. Example widgets are pushbuttons, scroll bars, list boxes, and dialog boxes and windows. Gadgets are efficient implementations of widgets. Widgets, like windows, can contain other widgets. Widgets have resources that have values. Examples of resources are widget color, position, title, and callbacks. Callbacks are functions called when specified actions take place. For example, a button widget can have an ActivateCallback resource that specifies a function. The function will be executed when the button is pressed by the user. Resources and callbacks are discussed later.

Here is a dtksh script that pops up the window shown in Fig. A.1.

```
#! /usr/dt/bin/dtksh
# File: hello.sh
XtInitialize TOPLEVEL helloAppName Hello Hello "$@"
XtCreateManagedWidget LABEL label XmLabel $TOPLEVEL \
       labelString:"Hello world! Welcome to dtksh programming"
XtRealizeWidget $TOPLEVEL
XtMainLoop
```

The program steps are:

- *XtInitialize:* This initializes the X toolkit and sets up the Xt intrinsic layer. The parameters are:

Top-level widget handle for your application. The specified variable contains the handle. The variable is *TOPLEVEL* in this example.

Application name used internally within widgets, *helloAppName* in this example.

Application class, used to specify a resource file, describe later; *Hello* in this example.

Application program name, displayed on the title bar; *Hello* in this example. Also used to define resource values for the widget (and child widgets).

Other parameters that are interpreted by the X toolkit. In this example the command line parameters are specified. Hence, if the program is run as

```
# hello.sh -iconic
```

the initial display will be an icon that has to be double-clicked to pop up the main window.

- *XtCreateManagedWidget:*   This is one of the many widget manipulation commands. The parameters are:

  Widget handle variable, *LABEL* in this example.

  Widget internal name, *label* in this example.

  Widget class, *Xmlabel* in this example.

  Widget's parent's handle. This determines where this widget is placed. *$TOPLEVEL* is the parent handle.

  Typically, simple widgets are created as managed widgets; the widgets are managed by the parent specified.

- *XtRealize:*   Widgets are assembled in memory but not displayed until this command is run. Child widgets are also displayed when the command is run.

- *Xtmainloop:*   Effectively, the program passes control to X. At this stage, X is waiting for an event to occur. Typical events are a key pressed, mouse moving over the window, mouse clicked. In the example, no event processing routines (callbacks) are declared to X; hence, X ignores most of the events. The window can be closed by selecting *close* from the menu, which pops up on clicking the button at the top left of the window.

  Syntax for the X commands is:

```
XtInitialize variable applicationName applicationClass prog-name [args ...]
XtCreateManagedWidget variable name class parent [arg:val ...]
XtRealizeWidget widget
XtMainLoop
```

The three commands XtInitialize, XtRealizeWidget, and Xtmainloop will be seen in most X programs. The key to dtksh graphic programming is mastering widget creation and writing callback routines.

A.3   Widgets

Widgets are the entities seen on the X screen and the corresponding data structures within the X-server. Widgets are classified in various ways.

A.3.1   Primitive and composite widgets

Primitive widgets are those that cannot serve as parents; composite widgets can have child widgets. Examples of primitive widgets are PushButton and Label; examples of composite widgets are MainWindow and FileSelectionBox.

A.3.2 Shell widgets

Many simple applications pop up a single window with widgets like menus, scroll bars, and text fields. Complex applications may pop more than one window. Windows other than the primary window are called *shell widgets,* and these are children of the primary window. The windows can be manipulated independently. Closing the primary window causes the child windows to be closed; however, closing a child window will not cause any other window to close. The primary window of an application is also called the ApplicationShell shell. The shells are:

- *ApplicationShell:*   Created by XTinitialize as a primary, top-level application window.

- *DialogShell:*   Used within Motif as parent of dialog widgets.

- *MenuShell:*   Used for creating different types of menus.

- *TopLevelShell:*   Behavior similar to ApplicationShell. This shell should be used by programmers to create additional top-level windows.

- *TransientShell:*   Similar to TopLevelShell, but cannot be independently iconified.

Here is the hello.sh program modified to create a second top-level window, which is shown in Fig. A.2.

```
#! /usr/dt/bin/dtksh
# File: Two-topwindows.sh
XtInitialize TOPLEVEL HelloAppName Hello Hello "$@"
XtCreateManagedWidget LABEL label XmLabel $TOPLEVEL \
      labelString:"Hello world! Welcome to dtksh programming"
#
XtCreatePopupShell NEWSHELL Newshell TopLevelShell $TOPLEVEL title:"NewShell"
XtCreateManagedWidget LABEL label XmLabel $NEWSHELL \
      labelString:"This is actually a child window"
XtPopup $NEWSHELL GrabNone
#
XtRealizeWidget $TOPLEVEL
XtMainLoop
```

The primary and the popup window are referred to by their widget handles and are manipulated very similarly in the program. Syntax for the new X commands is:

```
XtCreatePopupShell variable name class parent [arg:val ...]
XtPopup widget GrabNone|GrabNonExclusive|GrabExclusive
```

Figure A.2 A second top-level window in an application.

The grab options apply to the mouse focus. Shell widgets and KornShell are independent of each other.

A.3.3 Manager widgets

Manager widgets are widgets that manage the layout and geometry of child widgets. Examples of manager widgets are FileSelectionBox, Frame, MainWindow, Scale, and ScrolledWindow.

A.3.4 MainWindow widget

The preceding examples contained simple label widgets in the primary window. Many applications have a primary window having one or more of menu bars, work areas, scroll bars, and messages. To create a standard "look and feel" for such applications, Motif has a MainWindow widget which simplifies creation of windows for these applications.

A.3.5 Dialogs

Dialog windows are basically popup windows that display and optionally accept a small amount of data and then are closed. Example uses are prompting the user for confirmation of an action and displaying informational messages. There are two types of dialogs: message dialogs and selection dialogs. The message dialogs are Error, Information, Question, Warning, and Working. Selection dialogs are Selection, Command, FileSelection, and Prompt. Here is hello.sh modified to display a warning dialog box. The popup dialog window is shown in Fig. A.3. The response can be processed using callback functions.

```
#! /usr/dt/bin/dtksh
# File: Dialog.sh
XtInitialize TOPLEVEL HelloAppName Hello Hello "$@"
XtCreateManagedWidget LABEL label XmLabel $TOPLEVEL \
      labelString:"Hello world! Welcome to dtksh programming"
#
XmCreateWarningDialog WARNDLG $TOPLEVEL WARNING \
      dialogTitle:"Warning!" messageString:"System going down in 1 minute!"
XtManageChild $WARNDLG
#
XtRealizeWidget $TOPLEVEL
XtMainLoop
```

Figure A.3 A dialog box displayed from a dtksh script.

Syntax for the dialog commands is:

```
XtCreate{$1}dialog variable name class parent [arg:val ...]
```

where the appropriate word is substituted for {$1}.

Dialogs can be displayed as modal dialogs, in which case the user must respond to the dialog and dismiss it before he or she can continue other operations in the application.

A.3.6 Decoration widgets

The following widgets decorate an application:

- *Separator widget:*   Used to draw horizontal or vertical lines
- *Label widget:*   Used to display strings
- *Frame Widget:*   Used to draw a border around a child widget

Here is an example program using these appearance widgets; Fig. A.4 shows the program output. Note that the label widget was used before. The RowColumn widget arranges its child widgets in one or more columns (specified as a resource). If the labels had TOPLEVEL as a parent, only one of them would have been displayed because the TOPLEVEL application widget assumes that all child widgets are to be placed at the same starting point in the window unless specified otherwise.

```
#! /usr/dt/bin/dtksh
# File: Decorator.sh
XtInitialize TOPLEVEL TestAppName test Test "$@"
XtCreateManagedWidget COL1 col1 XmRowColumn $TOPLEVEL
#
XtCreateManagedWidget LABEL1 label1 XmLabel $COL1 labelString:"This is line 1"
XtCreateManagedWidget LABEL2 label2 XmLabel $COL1 labelString:"This is line 2"
XtCreateManagedWidget SEP1 sep1 XmSeparator $COL1
XtCreateManagedWidget FRAME1 frame1 XmFrame $COL1
XtCreateManagedWidget LABEL3 label3 XmLabel $FRAME1 labelString:"This is line 3"
#
XtRealizeWidget $TOPLEVEL
XtMainLoop
```

By now you should know how XtCreateManagedWidget is used to create most of the widgets.

Figure A.4 Decoration widgets.

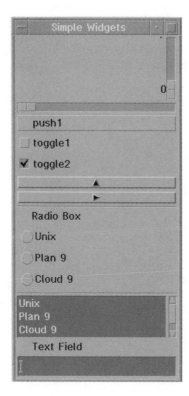

Figure A.5 Widgets created
from a dtksh script.

A.3.7   Other widget examples

Here is a script that displays assorted widgets. Figure A.5 is the output window. Note that normally action has to be taken when events occur. For example, actions like button pushes and text entry in text field have to be processed. This is achieved by callbacks, which are described later. Widget creation seems to be fairly simple; learning how to use each widget's resources is discussed in Section A.4.

```
#! /usr/dt/bin/dtksh
# File: widgets.sh
XtInitialize TOPLEVEL TestAppName test  Test "Simple Widgets" "$@"
XtCreateManagedWidget COL1 col XmRowColumn $TOPLEVEL
#
XtCreateManagedWidget SCALE1 scale1 XmScale $COL1 \
      maximum:150 orientation:vertical showValue:true
XtCreateManagedWidget SCALE2 scale2 XmScale $COL1 \
      maximum:200 orientation:horizontal  showValue:false
#
XtCreateManagedWidget PUSH1 push1 XmPushButton $COL1
XtCreateManagedWidget TOGGLE1 toggle1 XmToggleButton $COL1
XtCreateManagedWidget TOGGLE2 toggle2 XmToggleButton $COL1
#
```

```
# Changing toggle button state.
# Syntax: XmToggleButtonSetState $TOGGLE2 true|false  true|false
# The first true/false is state setting, the second is whether to display state.
#
XmToggleButtonSetState $TOGGLE2 true true
#
XtCreateManagedWidget ARROW1 arrow1 XmArrowButton $COL1
XtCreateManagedWidget ARROW2 arrow2 XmArrowButton $COL1 \
      arrowDirection:ARROW_RIGHT
#
# Radio boxes allow selection of one toggle button from a set.
XtCreateManagedWidget SEP1 sep XmSeparator $COL1
XtCreateManagedWidget LABEL1 label1 XmLabel $COL1 labelString:"Radio Box"
XmCreateRadioBox RADIO $COL1 radio
XtCreateManagedWidget TOGGLE3 Unix XmToggleButton $RADIO
XtCreateManagedWidget TOGGLE4 "Plan 9" XmToggleButton $RADIO
XtCreateManagedWidget TOGGLE5 "Cloud 9" XmToggleButton $RADIO
XtManageChild $RADIO
XtCreateManagedWidget SEP1 sep XmSeparator $COL1
#
# Scrolled Lists. Allow user to select one or more items.
XmCreateScrolledList OSLIST $COL1 oslist \
      visibleItemCount:3 selectionPolicy:MULTIPLE_SELECT
# Add items at position 1, beginning of list.
XmListAddItems $OSLIST 1 "Unix" "Plan 9" "Cloud 9" "OpenVMS"
XtManageChild $OSLIST
#
#Text widgets: scrolled text - user edits text in a scroll window
#             text - user edits text in a rectangular pane
#             text field - a one line text window.
XtCreateManagedWidget LABEL2 label2 XmLabel $COL1 labelString:"Text Field"
XtCreateManagedWidget TEXT2 text2 XmTextField $COL1 columns:8
#
XtRealizeWidget $TOPLEVEL
XtMainLoop
```

Other widgets not discussed in this brief section are:

- *Helpdialog:* This widget displays help. CDE has a comprehensive Help subsystem supporting SGML tags.

- *BulletinBoard:* This widget is a blank window. Children can be placed under it; however, the child's placement location must be specified relative to the top left of the window.

- *Form:* This is somewhat like a bulletin board widget; however, child widget positions can be specified relative to edges of the Form widget or other child widgets. This layout feature helps in maintaining a neat look when the form is resized.

- *PanedWindow:* Allows one or more window panes to be stacked, one on top of another. Vertical sizes of panes can be changed by a small square between panes called a sash.

- *MenuBar:* This widget is used to create a menu system. Supported options are pulldown and popup menus, cascaded menus, tearoff menus, and keyboard accelerators.

A.4 Resources

Resources define attributes and parameters associated with widgets. Example resource and their corresponding value

```
labelString:"This is line 1"
visibleItemCount:3
```

Resources have been used in examples before. For beginners, the term *resource* may be misleading. A resource is normally thought of as something that is consumed and deplenished. When used in X-windows parlance, a resource should be thought of as a parameter that has an associated value. Widget resources can be specified when the widget is created, as in

```
XtCreateManagedWidget LABEL1 label1 XmLabel $COL1 labelString:"This is line 1"
XmCreateScrolledList OSLIST $COL1 oslist visibleItemCount:3
```

Resources can be specified in a file that is read when the script is run. In this case, the name of the widget to which the resource applies must be specified. A resource in a file is specified as follows:

```
widget-path-name.resource.value
```

Recall that an application contains widgets which in turn contain child widgets, and so on. The widget-path-name identifies the widgets in the complete application to which the resource will apply. The application class is used as the top level of the widget name hierarchy. Hence, in the script

```
# File: hellonew.sh
XtInitialize TOPLEVEL helloAppName Hello "HelloNew" "$@"
XtCreateManagedWidget LABEL label XmLabel $TOPLEVEL \
        labelString:"Hello world! Welcome to dtksh programming"
XtRealizeWidget $TOPLEVEL
XtMainLoop
```

the application class is *Hello* and the widget name is *label*. Resources can be put in a file in the HOME directory with the file name the same as the application class name. In the example, the resource file will be $HOME/Hello. Contents of this file can be

```
Hello.label.foreground: gray
Hello.label.background: white
```

The foreground and background colors will be gray and white in the application window. In fact, the labelString specification shown above can also be put in the resource file as

```
Hello.label.labelString:Hello Folks! Let's learn how to use resources
```

Figure A.6 The *hello* script output with new resources.

Figure A.6 shows the window displayed when the script, without the labelString resource, is run and the three resources are specified in $HOME/Hello. Wildcards are allowed when specifying parent widgets. The following two resource specs are equivalent:

```
Hello.label.foreground: gray
*.label.foreground: gray
```

In fact, in a login resource spec, intermediate widgets can be wildcarded. The following resources are equivalent unless the specifications match other widgets, in which case the resource also applies to them:

```
Hello.scrollwin.winpane.rowcol.label.foreground: gray
*.label.foreground: gray
Hello*label.foreground:gray
Hello.scrollwin*label.foreground:gray
```

Note that the following is invalid because a widget is not specified just before the resource name:

```
Hello*foreground: gray      (Not valid)
```

Resources can be made available to all users on the system by putting them in a file under /usr/dt/app-defaults/C. (C is the world language locale, not to be confused with the C language.) The resources in the $HOME resource file will override the systemwide resource file.

The XtInitialize accepts resource specs for the application and for widgets with the -xrm parameter. Here is an example command which specifies black background for application widgets:

```
XtInitialize TOPLEVEL helloAppName Hello "HelloNew" -background black
```

Here is an example which specifies a red background for the *label* widget.

```
XtInitialize TOPLEVEL helloAppName Hello "HelloNew" \
                -xrm "Hello.label.background: white"
```

The $@ in the XtInitialize commands we have used allows us to specify additional parameters on the command line of the script. Hence, the scripts can be run with resource specifications as in

```
# hello.sh -xrm "*label.background: black"
```

Within the script, resource values can be specified and retrieved with the XtSetValues and XtGetValues commands, which have the syntax

```
XtSetValues widget arg:val ...
XtGetValues widget resource:variable ...
```

Here are example uses of these commands:

```
XtSetValues $LABEL foreground:green
XtGetValues $LABEL foreground:VAR1 background:VAR2
print $VAR1 $VAR2
0x33 0x1
```

A.5 Callbacks and Events

For many widgets, functions can be called when a button is clicked, an item is selected, the mouse moves over the widget, a key is pressed in a text field, and, in general, when an event occurs. The function called when an event is triggered is called a *callback*. A widget has a set of CallbackList resources. For example, the PushButton widget has a CallbackList resource called ActivateCallback. This callback is triggered when the button is pushed by the user. The XtAddCallback function declares a dtksh function that is to be called when the ActivateCallback is triggered. Effectively, you can execute a function in your script when the user clicks the button. Here is an example script:

```
#! /usr/dt/bin/dtksh
# File: callback.sh
XtInitialize TOPLEVEL TestAppName test  "Callback Test" "$@"

function Push1_clicked {  # called by pushbutton
        exit
}

XtCreateManagedWidget PUSH1 push1 XmPushButton $TOPLEVEL \
        labelString:"Click to exit"
XtAddCallback $PUSH1 activateCallback 'Push1_clicked'
XtRealizeWidget $TOPLEVEL
XtMainLoop
```

The window shown in Fig. A.7 is displayed. When the button is clicked, a message is displayed on the terminal window and the application exits. At times, additional information may be required in the callback routine. For example, the scale widget has a callback, valueChangedCallback, which can be used to call a function. The function may need to know what the current value is on the scale. The callback function is passed two variables, CB_WIDGET, which is the widget handle, and CB_CALL_DATA, which is a hierarchy of variables.

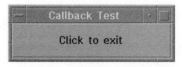

Figure A.7 A callback test application.

A.6 What's New in ksh-93?

ksh-93 supersedes ksh-88. The numbers represent the release year of the version of KornShell. ksh-88 is fairly popular, and there are a number of books available on how to use it. Features added to ksh-93 make it more of a programming language like C; a variable can point to another variable (like C pointers), hierarchical variable names (like C structures) are supported, and floating-point variables are supported. Without these extensions it would be nearly impossible to support the X-interface commands of dtksh. Major features not present in ksh-88 that have been added in ksh-93 are

- *Compound variables:* These are variables with one or more dots within them. The base variable has to be initialized. The variable can be indexed.

  ```
  cvar=                   Initialize base of compound variable.
  cvar.xval=5
  cvar.yval=12
  cvar.yval.imag=6
  cvar.zval[3]=23         Single dimensional array.
  ```

- *Typed variables:* By default, all variables are internally stored as strings. By specifying the type of a variable by typeset, the internal representation can be more compact and efficient.

  ```
  typeset -i ivar    Integer variable.
  integer ivar       Same as the above. Integer is an alias.
  ```

- *Floating-point variables:*

  ```
  typeset -E f1
  float f1           Equivalent to the line above.
  ```

- *Named reference variables:* These are variables pointing to other variables. The pointer variable is declared with a *typeset -n* or the equivalent *nameref* alias.

  ```
  var1=15
  typeset -n var2=var1    Variable var2 now references var1.
  nameref var2=var1       Equivalent to the line above.
  print var1 var2
  15 15
  var2=4
  print var1 var2
  4 4
  ```

- *Associative arrays:* ksh-88 supports single-dimensional arrays that have numeric subscripts:

  ```
  myarray[3]="test1"
  ```

ksh-93 now supports nonnumeric subscripts. Associative arrays must be declared with *typeset -A:*

```
typedef -A backupmode
backupmode["monday"]="fullbackup"
```

Such arrays are called associative arrays, because they allow keyed lookups.

- *Range of positional parameters:* $@ expands to all parameters specified on the command line. Additionally, in ksh-93, ${@:n:m} expands to *m* positional parameters starting at parameter *n:*

```
set "p1" "p2" "p3" "p4" "p5"       Override command line parameters.
print $@
p1 p2 p3 p4 p5
print ${@:2:3}
p2 p3 p4
```

- *C-style* for *loops:*   The ksh-88 *for* loop appears as

```
for j in s1 s2 s3
do
print $j
done
```

This loop will print the strings s1, s2, and s3, one per line. ksh-93 supports loops such as:

```
for (( j=0; j<5; j++ ))
do
print $j
done
```

This loop prints the numbers 1 to 5, one per line. Note that the C-style *for* statement has double parentheses.

B

Licensing
with
iFOR/LS

B.1 Introduction

ifor Licensing Suite (iFOR/LS) is a license management software used on HP-UX. iFOR/LS supports conventional node-specific or number-of-users–based licensing. In addition, it supports common license management for multiple systems on a network. Some of the products using iFOR/LS-based licensing are OmniBack, OperationsCenter, and SoftBench.

Product developers can make use of iFOR/LS features to control and monitor access to the product itself or any of its subcomponents. In that sense, licensing is a cooperative task between the product and iFOR/LS. Typically, the product issues calls to iFOR/LS to allocate a license or some units of a license; iFOR/LS checks which system on the network serves the license and refers to that system's license database to perform license checks. It is possible to set up a user file that controls access to licenses for individual users or controls the priority of individual users waiting to access a product. This last feature is not discussed here.

iFOR/LS is essentially developed by Gradient Technologies, Inc., and is available for IBM AIX and other platforms. DCE RPC is used by iFOR/LS to communicate between systems on the network; hence, centralized license management is supported across Unix platforms. iFOR/LS was previously known as NetLS.

Note that *codewords* are not a licensing mechanism. Codewords allow you to retrieve software for installation from CD and other media. A given codeword may allow you to retrieve only certain software, though there could be multiple software products on the media.

B.2   License Software Components and License Types

iFOR/LS consists of two major components: the Application Developer's Kit (ADK) and the Administrator's Runtime Kit (ARK). The ARK is required to run licensed products; the ADK is used by software developers who wish to include iFOR/LS with their products. The ARK is present on all HP-UX systems; the ADK is available as a separate product. In this chapter we will discuss only the ARK.

iFOR/LS supports the following types of licenses:

- *Nodelock:*   The software can be used only on a specified node.

- *Site license:*   The software can be used on any node in the network.

- *Concurrent access:*   The software can be used by a specified maximum number of users simultaneously.

- *Use-once:*   The software can be run only once. This type of license can be used for demonstration software.

A nodelock license is entered in the file /var/opt/ifor/nodelock. The complete license line has to be entered using an editor. Typically, nodelock licenses are used at sites that have few nodes or are evaluating a product. An example nodelock license entry is

```
#Comment line. K++ compiler.
670985ac8b34.02.0f.02.71.2b.00.00.00 32efzt9hspu47m82nn3qs62t8wk32 "K++ EVAL
15 MAR 1996
250 B 2500 C" "A.01"
```

No license daemons or processes have to be running for products to use nodelock licenses. All licenses that are not nodelocked are managed by the i4admin utility described later.

B.3   Target ID

Each node managed by iFOR/LS must be identified uniquely for licensing purposes. A node can be identified by a token such as a software-readable serial number. However, because iFOR/LS is supported on multiple platforms, it uses a unique ID called target ID for each node. A target ID has eight hex digits. A node's target ID can be displayed as:

```
$ /opt/ifor/bin/i4target
Permanent Target ID: de43dfe3c
```

B.4   License Management

Except for nodelock licenses, described in Section B.2, a license consists of

- *License details:*   A password and annotation. The password determines access type (for example, concurrent access), valid dates, and such.

- *Product:* What product the license applies to.

- *Vendor:* Product supplier.

For example, here is license information supplied by a hypothetical company, HAL, for its K++ language compiler on HP-UX.

Vendor information:

```
Vendor Password jdkgj36h443j8
Vendor Name : HAL SOFTWARE SOLUTIONS TORONTO
Vendor Id   : 5ca54ad53c2d.02.09.15.31.05.00.00.00
```

Product information:

```
Product name: HAL K++ for HP-UX
Product version: 3
Product password for targetid de43dfe3c: pci6xpi29zvwk9q49sc9tk25h6csa
```

When the license is installed on a system using i4admin, which is described later, the following encoded information is effective, as encoded in the product password pci6xpi29zvwk9q49sc9tk25h6csa:

```
license type      : Concurrent Access
start date        : 3/16/96
duration          : 19801
expiration        : 12/31/49
number            : 1
multi usage rules : Same user node.
target type       : HP-UX
target            : de43dfe3c
```

i4admin has a command line and an X-windows interface. Help on the command line can be displayed with

```
$ /opt/ifor/bin/i4admin -h
```

We will mainly discuss the X-windows interface. The program is started by

```
$ /opt/ifor/bin/i4admin
```

A window like the one in Fig. B.1 will pop up. Here is a list of entities that can be operated on and the operations that can be performed.

- *A license server:* This can be a node on the network serving one or more licenses to other nodes on the network. The list of known license servers is displayed. A vendor can be added to a license server node; information required is vendor name, vendor ID, and vendor password.

- *A vendor:* The list of vendors in the license database of the selected license server is displayed. New vendors are added as described in the pre-

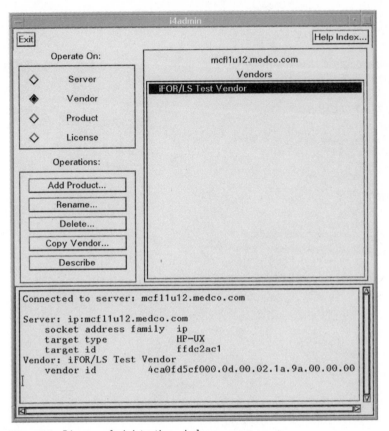

Figure B.1 License administration window.

vious item. A vendor's product can be added by specifying product name, product version, and license password.

- *A product:* The list of products is displayed. Typically, one license is installed when the product entry is created as explained in the previous item. Additional licenses can be entered by specifying license passwords.

- *A license:* The list of licenses for a selected product is displayed. Licenses can be deleted.

B.5   Setting Up iFOR/LS

As mentioned before, no setup is required to use nodelock licenses. For other licenses, no specific process needs to be running if the license is in the local license database, /var/opt/ifor/lic_db. If the product license is on another system, then the license management daemon, i4lmd, must be running on both nodes. Normally, the daemon starts on system boot if the following line is present in /etc/rc.config.d/i4lmd:

```
START_I4LMD=1
```

The i4lmd daemons communicate via the DCE RPC mechanism. Hence, the RPC daemon, rpcd, must be running on both systems. Also, the Global Location Broker (GLB) daemon, glbd, must be running. To start these daemon processes at system startup, /etc/rc.config.d/dce must contain

```
RPCD=1
```

and /etc/rc.config.d/ncs must contain

```
START_GLBD=1
```

The processes can be started without rebooting by executing the following commands:

```
$ /sbin/init.d/i4lmd start
$ /sbin/init.d/dce start
$ /sbin/init.d/ncs start
```

B.5.1 Reporting on license use: i4stat and i4report

The i4stat program displays information on licenses, licenses currently in use, how many users are waiting for licenses, and so on. The program is run by the command

```
$ /opt/ifor/bin/i4stat
```

Figure B.2 shows the displayed window. i4stat features are:

- Clicking *All Servers* causes all license daemons to be polled.
- Clicking *All Products* displays all products that are served by the license daemons.
- Clicking *Installed* displays all licenses.
- Clicking *Usage* displays all licenses and users of the licenses.
- Clicking *All Users* displays all users and the licenses they are using.
- Clicking *User* causes a popup window to prompt for a user name. Licenses in use by that user are displayed.
- The status message area at the bottom is where the information mentioned in the preceding items is displayed.

The i4report command does not have an X-windows interface. The command displays a report on actions performed on the license database. Here is a sample session:

```
$ /opt/ifor/bin/i4stat

i4report Version 3.0.0 HP-UX
```

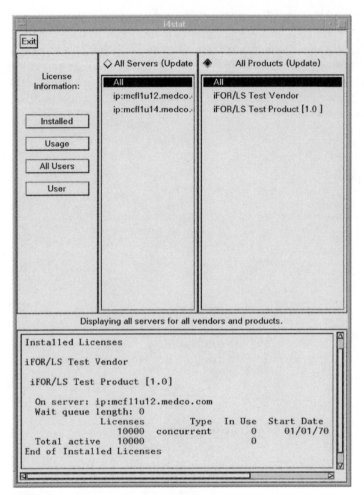

Figure B.2 License status reporting program.

```
N e t w o r k L i c e n s e S e r v e r L o g R e p o r t (3.0.0 HP-UX)
For: mcfl1u12.medco.com

Index       Vendor  Product            Vrsn    User Node     Group Amt Time
Event
-----       ------  -------            ----    ---- ----     ----- --- ----
-----
1           iFOR/LS Test Vendor (4) iFOR/LS Test 1.0    root
mcfl1u12.medco.com sys
1    4/15/96 10:37:41  G R A N T E D on mach type HP
2    ->1    iFOR/LS Test Vendor (4) iFOR/LS Test 1.0    root
mcfl1u12.medco.com sys
1    4/15/96 10:37:41  R E L E A S E D. time of use = 00:00
```

```
3            iFOR/LS Test Vendor (4) iFOR/LS Test 1.0    root
mcfl1u12.medco.com sys
1    4/18/96 10:38:29  G R A N T E D on mach type HP
4    ->3       iFOR/LS Test Vendor (4) iFOR/LS Test 1.0    root
mcfl1u12.medco.com sys
1    4/18/96 10:38:29 R E L E A S E D. time of use = 00:00
5            iFOR/LS Test Vendor (4) iFOR/LS Test 1.0 root mcfl1u12.medco.com
sys
finished.
```

C

SoftBench

C.1 Introduction

SoftBench is an integrated development framework that combines various program and project development components into a single interface. Major products integrated are

- Compilers
- *make* and similar products
- The dde debugger
- A Static Program Analyzer, which displays call graphs, function references, and similar information
- A run-time profiler, which is really a front end to dpat, described in Chapter 19, on programming
- Blinklink, a faster linker

User products can be integrated into the SoftBench environment. SoftBench runs under X-windows; a character mode interface is not supported. Some pluses and minuses of SoftBench are:

+ The programmer's interface to the system is more convenient, which may lead to better productivity.

+ The tools are well integrated; hence, for example, it is easy to jump from a compiler error line to the corresponding source program in another window.

+ The built-in editor and mail facility are easier to use than standard Unix products.

+ *make* files are automatically generated, once a few parameters are given via GUI windows.

− SoftBench is a separately licensed product.

− There is an above-average learning curve to become proficient with the SoftBench paradigm.

- Experienced programmers may have custom scripts that are faster than equivalent point-and-click operations within SoftBench. In some cases, scripts are required; for example, SoftBench cannot be used to submit a job to compile a complete project at night—at least not without additional setups within SoftBench.

- SoftBench is not seamlessly integrated with other HP-UX products; for example, the help system is unlike the standard helpview-based help facility used in many HP-UX software products.

C.2   SoftBench Components and Basics

Products integrated by SoftBench are called *tools*. Tools are managed by the *Tool Manager*. Tools communicate with each other and SoftBench via a process called the Broadcast Message Server (BMS). Tools also communicate with each other via a *message connector* protocol. Additional tools can be integrated into SoftBench using this protocol and the SoftBench Encapsulator software.

Here are the major tools supported within SoftBench. Typically, when a tool is invoked, a new window is displayed. Most tool windows have menu items that invoke other tools.

- *Tool Manager:*   The TM is the first window to show up when SoftBench is started. It displays what tools are running currently. The menu can be used to start new tools.

- *Development Manager:*   The DM coordinates file access. The DM window displays files in the current directory (context). Files can be checked in or checked out from the source control system, RCS, SCCS, or some custom system. The menus have file and directory manipulation commands like print, copy, and create directory.

- *Program Builder:*   *make* files are created and edited from here. *make* targets are also built from here. The menu has options to profile, run, and debug the target. Blinklink, the fast linker, is enabled by a menu selection.

- *Configuration Manager:*   This is a process that handles SoftBench requests to the source code configuration system, RCS or SCCS. No window is associated with this tool.

- *CBT (computer-based training):*   Some training on SoftBench features is available via this tool.

- *DEBUG:*   This tool runs the debugger on the current target. The debugger used is dde, which is described in Chapter 19.

- *Editor:*   A GUI-based program file editor.

- *Softmail:*   This is a GUI encapsulation of the Unix *mailx* program.

- *Monitor:*   Displays messages exchanged between tools.

- *Profiler:*   Used to analyze program run-time behavior.

- *File Compare:*   Used to visually study differences between two files.

- *Message Connector:*   Used to add tools and to customize SoftBench.

- *Static Analyzer:*   This tool is used to analyze a program's design as opposed to its run time behavior. Example uses are searching for all places where a variable is used, searching for statements that call a particular function, displaying all C++ classes, and displaying all derived classes of a specified class.

C.3 Quick Start

To use Softbench, change the current directory to one that contains a small program. In our example, the program is case.c in the directory /home/tmpdir. Here is the program listing:

```
/* program prints uppercase, lowercase and other counts in a line */
#include <stdio.h>

/* function counts uppercase, lowercase and other characters. */
strcase(char s[], int *ucase, int *lcase, int *ocase)
{
 int pos=0;
 char c;
 while ((c=s[pos++]) != '\0')
 {
  if (c >= 'A' && c <= 'Z') (*ucase)++;
  else if (c >= 'a' && c <= 'z') (*lcase)++;
  else (*ocase)++;
 }
} /* end of strcase */

main()
{
 char line[80];
 int uppercase,lowercase, othercase;
 printf ("Enter a string: ");
 gets(line);
 strcase(line, &uppercase, &lowercase, &othercase);

 printf("Input line: %s.\n",line);
 printf("Uppercase: %d, Lowercase: %d, Others: %d\n", \
             uppercase, lowercase, othercase);
} /* end of main */
```

SoftBench is started by:

$ /opt/SoftBench/bin/SoftBench

For a new setup, two windows, the Tool Manager (TM) and the Development Manager (DM) windows, show up. The Tool Manager is where tools are run from, though tools can also be run from other tools' menus. Figure C.1 shows an example Tool Manager window. The tools, ANNOTATOR, FILEMGR, SESSIONMGR, WORKSPACEMGR, and LICENSEMGR, do not have associated windows; they are processes supporting SoftBench and other tools. The TM menu options support the following functionality:

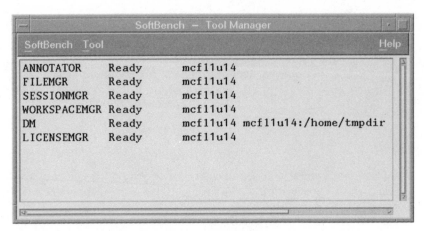

Figure C.1   Tool Manager: the starting window for SoftBench.

- *Save and restore toolsets:*   Other tools can be started and then saved so that they are started automatically the next time SoftBench is run. The default file is $HOME/.toolset.

- *Stop and start tools.*

- *Set context:*   The context determines where the project files are. Typically, the context is a directory.

The DM window displays the contents of the current context. Figure C.2 shows an example DM window. In this case, the current context is directory /home/tmpdir, which contains one program file, case.c. The TM menu options support the following functionality:

- Edit, rename, delete copy files selected from the main display area.

- RCS functionality: checkin , check out, show change log, create version, set version, and such. If SCCS is used for source code control, this menu will be changed accordingly.

- Directory create, delete, rename.

- Build targets, compile program, and perform static analysis.

- Browse files on whole file system.

To compile the program, the BUILD tool should be started from the Tool Manager, Tool menu. Figure C.3 shows the Program Builder window, which will pop up (actually, a build output is displayed because a build was done before screen dump). The Program Builder menu options support the following functionality:

- Create and edit Makefiles.

- Build, run, profile, or debug target.

- Enable Blinklink, the fast linker.

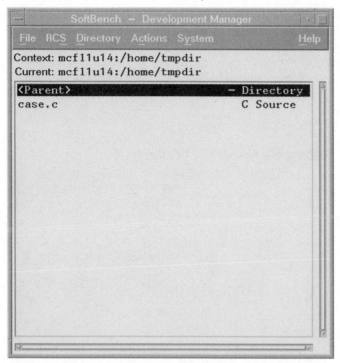

Figure C.2 Development Manager: performs file manipulations.

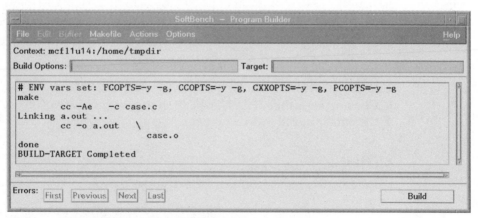

Figure C.3 Program Builder: compiles, links, and runs programs.

- If program errors are displayed, an error line can be clicked; a program editor window will pop up with the cursor at the file location where the error was encountered.

First, a make file will have to be made. The Makefile menu option *create/modify makefile* has to be selected. Various options can be specified; we need only specify *-Ae* in the *flags* field. This will allow compilation of case.c in ANSI mode, which supports function prototypes used in the program. The DM window will now display a new file, Makefile. The next step is to build the target, a.out. The Build Target option from the Action menu of the Program Builder window has to be selected. The target should build without errors. If there are errors, the source file can be edited by selecting the Edit option from the File menu.

The DM window will display more files:

- Static.sadb, used by the static analyzer
- case.o, the intermediate object file
- a.out, the executable for case.c

The Run Target option from the Actions menu of the Program Builder will cause a terminal window to pop up and the program will run there. Once execution is over, the terminal window closes and control returns to the Program Builder.

These are the basic steps to compile and run programs via SoftBench.

C.4 The Static Analyzer

The Static Analyzer can be run from the Tool Manager or the Development Manager. Figure C.4 shows the Static Analyzer window after the Show→ Functions→All Definitions option was selected from the menu. The Static Analyzer menu options support the following functionality:

- Show variable references, declarations, and definitions. Show functions, structures, typedefs, and global variables.
- Graph (diagram) of function calls and file references.
- Clicking on a function displayed causes the program editor to be run with the cursor at the point where the function declaration starts.

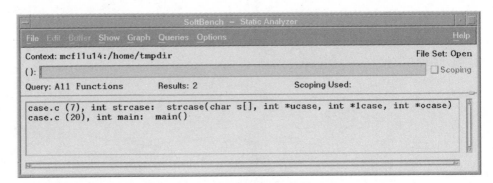

Figure C.4 Static Analyzer: displays source code information.

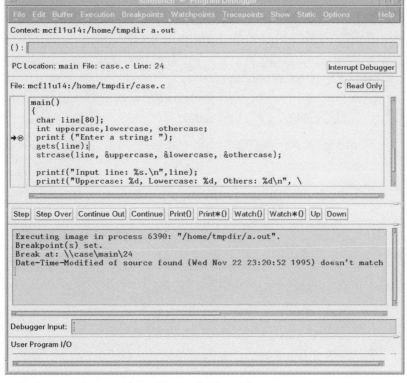

Figure C.5 Debugger: supports dde and SoftBench features.

C.5   The Debugger

The SoftBench debugger is a GUI front end to basic dde, Distributed Debugging Environment. The debugger can be started from the Tool Manager or the Program Builder menu: Actions→Debug target. Figure C.5 shows the initial screen. Chapter 19, on programming, describes dde; the SoftBench debugger has some menu items relevant to the SoftBench environment.

C.6   Other SoftBench Functionality

Blinklink is an incremental linker supported within the SoftBench Program Builder. Multiple modules can be compiled and linked together. When a single source module is modified, the module has to be compiled, and when the standard linker is being used, all modules have to be relinked. With Blinklink, only the modified module is relinked with the target. Blinklink can be used in the development phase; the standard linker can be used when the programs are put into production use.

The set_sbcompinfo system administration utility can be used to specify an alternate compiler for the same language. Be aware that Static Analyzer and some other SoftBench functionality may not work with non-HP compilers.

SoftBench supports embedded SQL statements; programs can be debugged at the source level even though the SQL preprocessor converts the SQL statements to equivalent language code.

D

PA-RISC:
Precision Architecture
and HP-UX
Assembly Language

D.1 Introduction

The design of HP's RISC chips is based on the HP Precision Architecture (HP-PA). All HP-UX systems, the HP 9000 series 8000 and series 700, are designed with PA-RISC CPU chips. Current architecture revision level is PA-RISC 1.1. There are about 140 machine instructions. Each instruction is a fixed 32 bits in length. There are no special I/O instructions; I/O is memory-mapped. The current implementations of HP-PA are the PA-7200 (32-bit) and PA8000 (64-bit) chips. HP-PA is typical of the RISC chips like IBM RISC/6000 and SUN's SPARC.

HP-UX assembler *as* fully supports PA-RISC 1.1. The assembly language syntax is typical of many other RISC processor assembly languages; macros and PIC are supported, and there are about three dozen assembler directives and pseudo-operations. General assembly language knowledge is assumed in this discussion. Assembly language programs are debugged using *adb,* which is not discussed here.

D.2 The PA-7200 CPU Chip

PA-7200, a 1.3 million transistor CMOS chip, has on-board integer and floating-point units. The chip is incorporated into HP-UX systems with varying operating frequencies and cache sizes, which determine the relative CPU performance. Some of the features of PA-7200 are:

- Up to 2 Mbytes data cache
- Up to 1 Mbyte instruction cache

- 64-line fully associative prefetch/miss cache
- Up to four-processor SMP support; MP cache coherency support
- Up to 120-MHz clock speed; SpecInt 92 performance in mid 100s
- Two-way superscalar execution
- Integrated memory management unit; 120-entry TLB, 16-entry block TLB
- Big and Little Endian support
- 64-bit multiplexed address/data bus
- Bus bandwidth > 700 Mbytes/s

D.3 Registers

These are the sets of registers:

- *General:* 32 registers, 32 bits wide each.
- *Space:* 8 registers, 32 bits wide each. These refer to virtual address spaces.
- *Control:* 25 registers, 32 bits wide each.
- *Floating-point registers:* 32 registers, 64 bits wide each. IEEE Standard implementation.

Each floating-point register can be referenced as a double-precision number, for example, %fr5; or as two single-precision numbers, for example, %fr5L and %fr5R. Effectively, there are 64 single-precision floating-point numbers. Figure D.1 shows the registers pictorially. Some registers have additional predefined mnemonics, some of which are:

```
%cr11 == %sar      Shift Amount Register
%r2   == %rp       Return Link
%r23  == %arg3     Argument word 3
%r24  == %arg2     Argument word 2
%r25  == %arg1     Argument word 1
%r26  == %arg0     Argument word 0
%r27  == %dp       Data pointer
%r28  == %ret0     Return value
%r30  == %sp       Stack pointer
%fr4  == %fret     Floating-point return value
%fr4  == %farg0    Floating-point argument
```

General register %r0 is always 0.

D.4 Spaces and Subspaces

A space is a range of addresses. The address is determined by one of the space registers and a 32-bit offset within the space. Hence, each space has 4 giga-

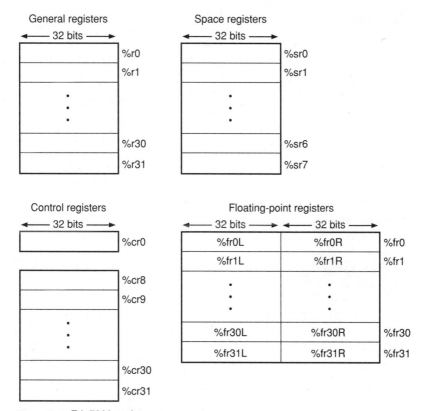

Figure D.1   PA-7200 registers.

bytes. Every HP-UX program has two spaces automatically assigned when loaded for execution; the spaces are *code* and *data,* which are identified by registers %sr4 and %sr5. The spaces are referred to as $TEXT$ and $PRIVATE$ in assembly language programs. The code space is read-only. Normally, all code for a single program is contained in one space; however, other space registers can be used to refer to other spaces. A space is declared with the .SPACE assembler directive.

Subspaces are a logical subdivision of a space. Different subspaces of a space are grouped together in the space by the linker. A subspace can be assigned attributes. For example, the access rights attribute determines whether pages in the subspace are executable only (right 0x2C) or readable-writable (0x1F). A subspace is declared with the .SUBSPA assembler directive. Example uses are:

```
.SPACE $TEXT$
.SUBSPA $CODE$, ACCESS=0x2c
(instructions)
.SPACE $PRIVATE$
.SUBSPA $DATA$, ACCESS=0x1f
(data)
```

D.5   Calling Convention

The calling convention standardizes the method for calling procedures. This is particularly useful when multiple languages are used. The beginning and end of each procedure are specified by the .PROC and .PROCEND directives. The .CALLINFO directive specifies information like the stack size. This information is used by the linker, among other things, to produce stack unwinding information.

Arguments to procedures should be given in %r26 to %r23, also known as %arg0 to %arg3. More than four arguments are stored on the caller's stack frame. Return value is stored in %r28 (%ret0). If the value is a double word, %r29 (ret1) is also used.

The .EXPORT and .IMPORT directives are used to export procedure names or data for use by other modules, and import names or data for use by the current module.

Data in $PRIVATE$ space should be accessed via %r27 (%dp). The standard run-time startup code, crt0.o, must be linked with every program. This code contains a symbol, $global$, whose address should be loaded in %dp at the start of program execution.

When calling a procedure, registers %r19 through %r22 must be saved by caller, if required, as the procedure can use them without saving them. The procedure is responsible for saving the values of %r3 through %r18.

D.6   Example Assembly Language Program

Assembly language program file names have an extension of .s. A program is assembled and linked as:

```
# as prog.s -o prog.o
# ld /opt/langtools/lib/crt0.o prog.o -o prog
```

In the example that will follow, the C run-time library function, printf(), is used; hence, the library, libc, has to be included as in:

```
# ld /opt/langtools/lib/crt0.o prog.o -o prog -lc
```

Here is an assembly language program which was created from a C language program.

```
; program prog.s.
; program prints "Integer int1 is 35".
; program is edited version of output of a C program.
;
        .SPACE   $TEXT$
        .SUBSPA $CODE$,ACCESS=0x2c
main
        .PROC
        .CALLINFO CALLER,FRAME=16,SAVE_RP
        .ENTRY
STW     %r2,-20(%r30)
        LDO      64(%r30),%r30
```

```
        LDI       35,%r1
        STW       %r1,-56(%r30)
        ADDIL     LR'M$2-$global$,%r27
        LDO       RR'M$2-$global$(%r1),%r26
        LDW       -56(%r30),%r25
        LDIL      L'printf,%r31
        .CALL     ARGW0=GR,ARGW1=GR,RTNVAL=GR    ;in=25,26 out=28
        BLE       R'printf(%sr4,%r31)
        COPY      %r31,%r2
        LDW       -84(%r30),%r2
        BV        %r0(%r2)
        .EXIT
        LDO       -64(%r30),%r30
        .PROCEND ;out=28;
        .SPACE $TEXT$
        .SUBSPA $CODE$
        .SPACE $PRIVATE$
        .SUBSPA $DATA$,ACCESS=0x1f
M$2
        .ALIGN 8
        .STRINGZ          "Integer int1 is      %d \n"
        .IMPORT $global$,DATA
        .SPACE   $TEXT$
        .SUBSPA $CODE$
        .EXPORT main,ENTRY,RTNVAL=GR
        .IMPORT printf,CODE
        .END
```

The C program that created the above code is:

```
# Compile this program like this to create assembly language output:
# cc -s prog.c
#include <stdio.h>
main()
{
int int1=35;
printf("Integer int1 is    %d \n", int1);
}
```

Here are comments on the assembly program:

- These statements declare the code area. Declaration for data comes later.

```
.SPACE $TEXT$
.SUBSPA $CODE$,ACCESS=0x2c
```

- Procedures must start and end with the .PROC and .PROCEND directives. The .CALLINFO directive specifies that this procedure calls other procedures (CALLER), a frame size of 16 bytes must be allocated on the stack (FRAME = 16), and the frame pointer of the previous procedure saves the value of Return Pointer (RP).

```
.PROC
.CALLINFO CALLER,FRAME=16,SAVE_RP
.ENTRY
```

- Store word from %r2 to -20(%r30) representing displacement(base). Note that r30 is stack pointer.

```
STW %r2,-20(%r30)
```

- Load offset into register.

```
LDO 64(%r30),%r30
```

- Load immediate value in register. LDI is pseudo-operation for LDO 35(0),%r1.

```
LDI 35,%r1
```

- Add immediate left part. L represents the high-order 21 bits, right justified. R represents the L result rounded to the nearest multiple of 8192. Effectively, LR' gets an 8192-byte page number.

```
ADDIL LR'M$2-$global$,%r27
```

- RR' represents the low-order 11 bits rounded to the nearest multiple of 8192 plus the difference of constant and rounded constant.

```
LDO RR'M$2-$global$(%r1),%r26
```

- Load word in register.

```
LDW -56(%r30),%r25
```

- Load immediate value in left part of register.

```
LDIL L'printf,%r31
```

- Specify where call values are stored for following BLE, on general registers or floating-point registers. General registers are used here.

```
.CALL ARGW0=GR,ARGW1=GR,RTNVAL=GR ;in=25,26 out=28
```

- Call the printf() routine in the C run-time library. BLE is Branch and Link External, used for procedure calls in another space.

```
BLE R'printf(%sr4,%r31)
```

- COPY is a pseudo-operation for OR %r31,0,%r2.

```
COPY %r31,%r2
```

- Vectored branch.

```
BV %r0(%r2)
```

- .ENTRY and .EXIT or .ENTER and .LEAVE must be used in every procedure.

```
.EXIT
.PROCEND ;out=28
```

- Data information follows.

```
.SPACE $TEXT$
.SUBSPA $CODE$
.SPACE $PRIVATE$
.SUBSPA $DATA$,ACCESS=0x1f
M$2
.ALIGN 8
.STRINGZ "Integer int1 is %d \n"
.IMPORT $global$,DATA
.SPACE $TEXT$
.SUBSPA $CODE$
```

- Procedures for global use.

```
.EXPORT main,ENTRY,RTNVAL=GR
.IMPORT printf,CODE
.END
.END
```

Figure D.2 shows an assembly listing file created with:

```
# as -l prog.s
```

The assembly listing syntax should be obvious to assembly language programmers.

```
HP92453-03 A.10.00 PA-RISC 1.1r3 Assembler Jan 14 1995 Copyright Hewlett Packard
1985,1993
    1                              .LEVEL 1.0
    2
    3                              .SPACE   $TEXT$,SORT=8
    4                              .SUBSPA
                                     $CODE$,QUAD=0,ALIGN=4,ACCESS=0x2c,CODE_ONLY,SORT=24
    5                 main
    6                              .PROC
    7                              .CALLINFO CALLER,FRAME=16,SAVE_RP
    8                              .ENTRY
    9 00000000 (6BC23FD9)          STW     %r2,-20(%r30)    ;offset 0x0
   10 00000004 (37DE0080)          LDO     64(%r30),%r30    ;offset 0x4
   11 00000008 (34010046)          LDI     35,%r1   ;offset 0x8
   12 0000000C (6BC13F91)          STW     %r1,-56(%r30)    ;offset 0xc
   13 00000010 (2B600000)*         ADDIL   LR'M$2-$global$,%r27     ;offset 0x10
   14 00000014 (343A0000)*         LDO     RR'M$2-$global$(%r1),%r26        ;offset 0x14
   15 00000018 (4BD93F91)          LDW     -56(%r30),%r25   ;offset 0x18
   16 0000001C (23E00000)*         LDIL    L'printf,%r31    ;offset 0x1c
   17                              .CALL   ARGW0=GR,ARGW1=GR,RTNVAL=GR ;in=25,26;out=28;
   18 00000020 (E7E02000)*         BLE     R'printf(%sr4,%r31)      ;offset 0x20
   19 00000024 (081F0242)          COPY    %r31,%r2         ;offset 0x24
   20 00000028 (4BC23F59)          LDW     -84(%r30),%r2    ;offset 0x28
   21 0000002C (E840C000)          BV      %r0(%r2)         ;offset 0x2c
   22                              .EXIT
   23 00000030 (37DE3F81)          LDO     -64(%r30),%r30   ;offset 0x30
   24                              .PROCEND         ;out=28;
   25
   26
   27
   28                              .SPACE   $TEXT$
   29                              .SUBSPA $CODE$
   30                              .SPACE   $PRIVATE$,SORT=16
   31                              .SUBSPA $DATA$,QUAD=1,ALIGN=8,ACCESS=0x1f,SORT=16
   32                 M$2
   33                              .ALIGN 8
   34 40000000 (496E7465)          .STRINGZ        "Integer int1 is   %d \n"
   35                              .IMPORT $global$,DATA
   36                              .SPACE   $TEXT$
   37                              .SUBSPA $CODE$
   38                              .EXPORT main,ENTRY,PRIV_LEV=3,RTNVAL=GR
   39                              .IMPORT printf,CODE
   40                              .END

   ->                               .SUBSPA $UNWIND$,QUAD=0,ALIGN=0x8,ACCESS=0x2c,SORT=64

   ->
                     **************SYMBOL TABLE**************

$DATA$      (00000000) SUBSPACE           $PRIVATE$   (00000000) SUBSPACE
$TEXT$      (00000000) SUBSPACE           $global$    (00000000) DATA UNSAT
M$2         (40000000) DATA LOCAL         main        (00000003) ENTRY UNIVERSAL
printf      (00000000) CODE UNSAT
```

Figure D.2   Assembler listing file.

E

OpenView

E.1 Introduction

OpenView was a network monitoring tool when released in 1989. The centralized monitoring and management paradigm was extended so that systems management, performance monitoring, software distribution, and similar functions can be performed with subproducts running under the OpenView framework. Typically, OpenView runs on an HP system with operators and other support staff using X-terminals to log into the system and run OpenView. Each support person probably uses one, or a few, of the subproducts integrated into OpenView. The network probably has more than a dozen systems and routers; centralized management is not likely to be cost-effective for environments with just a few nodes.

Some of the subproducts integrated in the OpenView umbrella are:

- *Network Node Manager (NNM):* This is actually part of core OpenView. NNM can display network topologies, monitor SNMP and OSI supporting nodes, and perform actions based on events on the network. SNMP-based management is extended to Unix and other systems that have an SNMP agent installed.

- *OperationsCenter:* This subproduct gets information from a monitored Unix or other system and performs specified actions. The information may be from system log files or sent by SNMP traps. The information, known as messages, is collated and filtered into categories. Actions can be specified for messages or groups of messages. Example actions are displaying an alarm and executing a script.

- *AdminCenter:* Centralizes some administrative tasks. Examples are user account and group maintenance, product installation, kernel modification, disk and file system maintenance, and spooler queue maintenance.

Some more OpenView products from HP are PerfView for performance monitoring, Software Distributor for centralized vendor software management, and OmniBack II for centralized backup management. Other vendors have also integrated their products in the OpenView framework; examples are Cisco, Inc., and Bay Networks, Inc., which have versions of CiscoWorks router management and Optivity hub management software added to OpenView. Note that all the products mentioned are licensed separately; OpenView is shipped only with NNM.

We will get into OpenView by first discussing NNM, since it is the most used of all OpenView components. A good basic understanding of SNMP and MIBs is required, since OpenView NNM is based on them. SNMP and MIBs are introduced in this appendix. Most subcomponents of OpenView use the X-windows interface; plain ASCII terminals cannot be used, because rich graphics are extensively used by the software.

E.2   NNM: Network Node Manager

NNM is used for monitoring and managing a TCP/IP network. The node where OpenView resides is called the *management station*. NNM will display network information when OpenView is started. IP Map is an NNM application that determines the network topology. As an example, NNM can be configured to automatically find out nodes, including routers and other systems, on the network. In automatic discovery mode, NNM

- Looks up the router of the local node (management station) and determines the IP subnet by looking up the subnet mask.

- Uses ICMP (ping) packets to determine what nodes are in the same subnet.

- Uses SNMP to poll discovered nodes to determine if they support SNMP MIBs.

- Uses SNMP requests to get information on nodes supporting SNMP.

- Branches off to other discovered subnets to get information on other nodes. The process is repeated until the network is traversed. The complete process effectively determines the network topology.

- Displays the network topology as maps.

The process can be speeded up if "seed" nodes are specified in a seed file. NNM will use the seed nodes as starting points for network traversal rather than the local node's router.

After OpenView is properly configured, it has to be started with the command

```
$ /usr/OV/bin/ovstart
```

Once started, a number of processes will be running to support OpenView operations. A user can start OpenView Windows with a command like

```
$ /usr/OV/bin/ovw
```

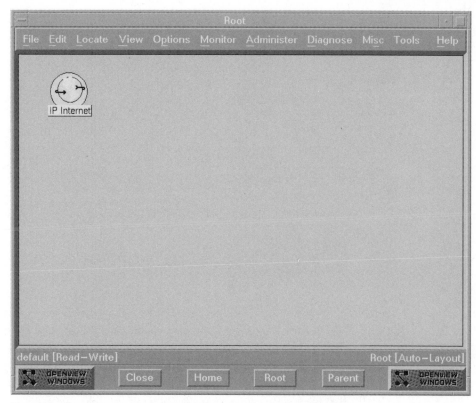

Figure E.1 OpenView main window displays a top-level network submap.

Two windows, shown in Figs. E.1 and E.2, will pop up. Figure E.1 is the main OpenView window, which displays submaps. Figure E.2 shows SNMP and other event groups and displays buttons whose color is determined by the severity of the most severe event in the group. The event categories are configured from the event browser window described later.

If automatic discovery mode is not set, the network can be manually created. Typically, the network is created once using the NNM discovery mechanism and then edited manually when network topology changes. This method is useful when operators are shown maps which do not update every time there is a network change; however, the network administrator has his or her maps update automatically. The network administrator may decide to manually update the operator maps.

E.3 Maps and Submaps

A map is a logical view of the network. It consists of a hierarchy of submaps (and related objects and symbols). A map may not be a representation of the

Figure E.2 Event window displays event groups and severity.

complete network; rather, a map can represent a logical subset of the network. Different users can see different maps; hence, an individual operator can manage a specified subset of the network. OpenView NNM displays submaps, not maps. Maps consist of four types of submaps arranged in order of detail level: Internet, network, segment, and node.

The top map in a hierarchy of submap displays is called a *root submap.* The user's *home submap* is the one displayed when OpenView is started by a user. Icons on a map may be *explodable,* in which case double-clicking on the item causes a *child submap* to be displayed.

Here is an example of submap hierarchy traversal. Figure E.1 shows an Internet submap. Icons represent nodes, networks, other Internet submaps, segments, and routers. Double-clicking on the only icon displays a more detailed Internet submap, shown in Fig. E.3. Clicking on one of the icons here can display a more detailed Internet submap, shown in Fig. E.4. Clicking on a network icon can display a network map, shown in Fig. E.5. Clicking on the segment icon can display a segment map, shown in Fig. E.6. The segment map shows all the nodes on a physical segment. Clicking on a node shows its interfaces, as shown in Fig. E.7.

Maps can be copied and modified with submenus of the Map menu, though, at any particular time, submaps are displayed from a single map. Submaps may be set for automatic layout, in which case the objects on-screen are placed by OpenView and cannot be repositioned. In manual layout mode, the mouse can be used to move objects around the screen, and there is a holding area at the bottom of the screen from which objects can be moved into the main display area. OpenView places newly discovered objects in the holding

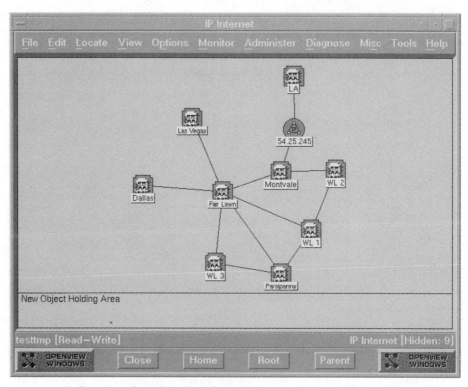

Figure E.3 An Internet submap based on physical locations.

area. There is an object database from which objects, like routers and workstations, can be added to a submap using the Edit menu.

E.4   Events

Events are generated by OpenView internally or by SNMP traps coming from other nodes on the network. Most events will be notification of abnormal events on other nodes on the network. All events are sent to the *trapd* process, which logs them in /usr/OV/log/trapd.log. trapd also sends a subset of the events to the event browser, which is the operator interface to monitoring and reacting to events. trapd also sends events to the *ovactiond* process, which can perform preprogrammed actions.

E.4.1   Event browser

The event browser is used to browse, acknowledge, delete, filter, and perform similar actions on events. The Fault menu on OpenView main window is used to bring up the browser window, shown in Fig. E.8. Actions that can be performed are:

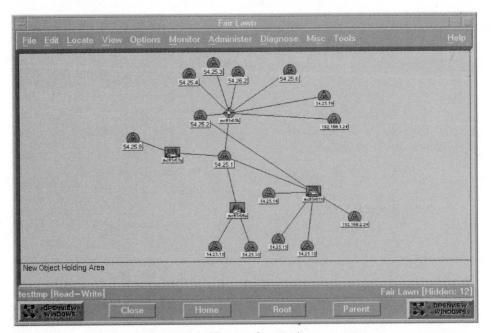

Figure E.4   An Internet submap based on IP networks at a site.

- Acknowledge events by clicking in the ack or severity field.
- Create and configure new event categories for display in the window shown in Fig. E.2. Configuration also allows additional actions when a specific event occurs—for example, pop up an alarm message or execute a specified script.
- Browse events with various filters like particular node, message strings, severity, and date.
- Delete events so that they are not seen or reflected in the button states in the event categories window.

E.5   SNMP: Simple Network Management Protocol

SNMP is a network management protocol used on TCP/IP networks. OpenView currently supports SNMPv1; the later SNMPv2 is not supported. Typically, SNMP is used by one system, called a manager, to get information from another, called an agent. A system can be both a manager and an agent. Either the manager gets the value of a variable (MIB value), or the agent sends an unsolicited message called a trap. For example, the manager can request an agent system to send the value of the variable

```
iso.org.dod.internet.mgmt.mib-2.system.sysObjectID
```

and the agent may send back a value

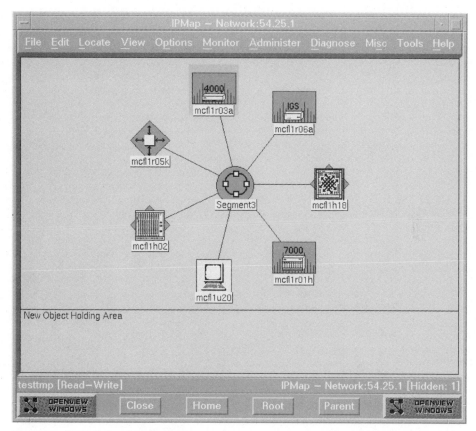

Figure E.5 A network submap.

```
iso.org.dod.internet.private.enterprises.hp.nm.system.hpux.hp9000s700
```

The basic commands that can be issued by the manager are

- *snmpget:* Get the value of a variable.
- *snmpnext:* Get the value of the next parameter in the variable tree hierarchy.
- *snmpset:* Set the value of a variable.
- *snmpwalk:* Traverse the variable tree hierarchy.

A manager system can register with an agent to accept traps. After that, the agent will send traps to the manager system. Traps can contain, for example, error messages on the agent's IP buffer overflows or faults on network interfaces. In OpenView, traps received can be seen in the event browser window.

A large network can be logically segmented into communities for SNMP purposes. Each node will have a *community name.* Managers and agents communicate via SNMP only if they are in the same community.

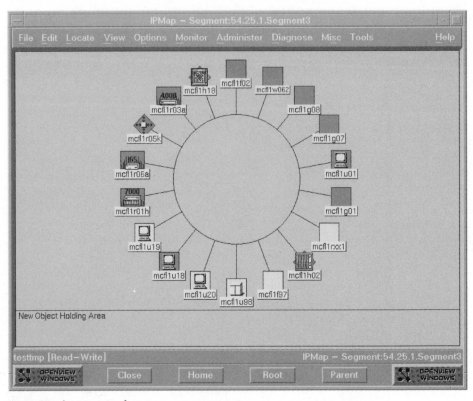

Figure E.6   A segment submap.

E.6   MIBs: Management Information Bases

A MIB is a fancy name for what is basically a hierarchical set of variables, or objects. The top level of the hierarchy is called *iso*. iso has only one leaf, *org,* which has only one leaf, *dod,* which in turn has only one leaf, *internet.* Starting from internet, the tree has multiple leaves. The exact structure is defined by some of the internet RFCs. Variables are the lowest level of the hierarchy. All variables are predefined in the RFCs except the ones under the subtree iso.org.dod.internet.private.enterprises. Vendors use this subtree to define variables pertaining to their products. For example,

```
iso.org.dod.internet.mgmt.mib-2.system.sysDescr
```

is a variable whose value is a description of the agent node. This variable is defined in the RFCs, while HP and Cisco define their private variables under the hierarchies

```
iso.org.dod.internet.private.enterprises.hp
iso.org.dod.internet.private.enterprises.cisco
```

Figure E.7 A node submap showing interfaces on a node.

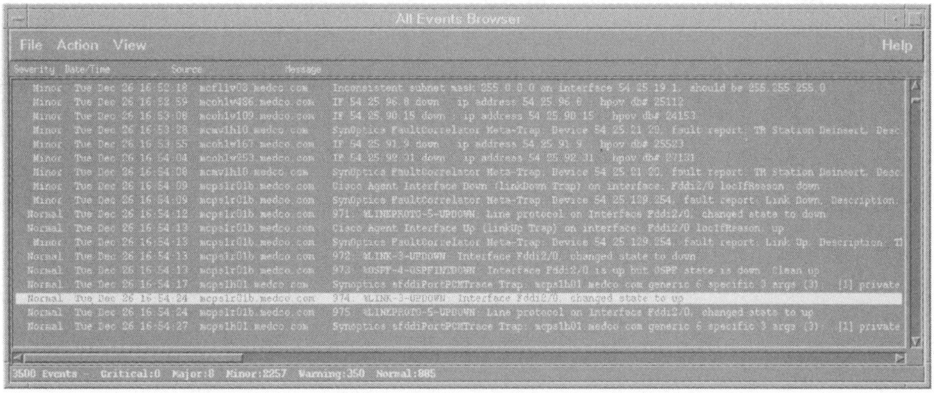

Figure E.8 Event management window.

The MIB hierarchy is quite large; hence, for convenience of manipulation, MIBs are organized in modules. A MIB module defines all the MIB objects under one subtree. Typically vendors ship MIB modules for their own extensions called *enterprise-specific MIBs*.

Note that although we have referred to MIB objects as variables, they may not have values stored in memory as is the case of conventional program variables. When a variable value is requested by the snmpget command, the agent may have to derive the value of the variable by running some code.

MIB-2 is merely an extension of the original MIB tree. RMON MIBs refers to remote monitoring MIBs. To understand the need for RMON MIBs, consider an example. Suppose you have a management station in New York and you wish to monitor a router in Ahmedabad, India. Assume the router is linked to New York with a 56-Kbit/s link. Using SNMP MIB–based monitoring, if you want to get the average CPU utilization for the last 30 minutes, you will have to poll the router at regular intervals to fetch the appropriate MIB object for CPU utilization and manipulate the data. However, this can generate a lot of network traffic, possibly flooding the slow link. RMON MIB support on the router will reduce such network loading by performing the calculations on its own and setting the value of a MIB object with the final result. What calculations are to be performed are parameter-driven; the manager node uses snmpset to set values of MIB objects, which are then read by the RMON MIB software. Effectively, RMON MIBs reduce network load and have a set of programs whose calculations are parameter-driven. Functions handled by an agent supporting RMON MIBs are:

- Gathering statistics
- Maintaining a history of statistics gathered
- Allowing thresholds and sampling intervals for alarms
- Maintaining statistics for the top n hosts
- Capturing packets based on filter patterns

E.7 Monitoring Systems and Applications: The Extensible SNMP Agent

Traditionally, SNMP was used to monitor routers, hubs, and similar devices, and recently SNMP has been used by many vendors to monitor power supplies, printers, and a host of other hardware products. The extensible SNMP agent allows Unix systems to be monitored. At the core, it consists of SNMP agent software running on the Unix agent system. The software is derived from the public-domain SNMP agent software developed by Carnegie-Mellon University. The software responds to manager SNMP requests and sends traps to the manager. MIB objects and their definitions are under the control of the person configuring the product. Hence, you can define MIB objects that will return CPU utilization, memory errors in the last hour, or even a list of printers on the system. OpenView treats the Unix system like other agents. The MIB modules in OpenView will have to be synchronized with the Unix agent MIB definitions.

The agent is started from /sbin/rc1.d/s560SnmpMaster, which effectively runs

```
/usr/sbin/snmpdm
```

which reads the configuration file /etc/SnmpAgent.d/snmpd.conf. The main
information in this file is trap destinations and community name. Log file is
/var/adm/snmpd.log. HP-UX–specific MIB is in /opt/OV/snmp-mibs/hp-unix. A
trap can be generated with the snmptrap command–for example,

```
$ snmptrap OVNODE "" "" 5 1 30 system.sysDescr.0 \
octetstringascii "HP-UX main prod. system "
```

Here the trap is sent to OVNODE, the generic trap number is 5, the specific
trap number is 1, and the time stamp is 30. A custom MIB can be written in
the file /etc/SnmpAgent.d/snmpd.extend. An example file is in
/use/OV/prg_samples/eagent/snmp.extend. Here is an extract from this file:

```
FLINTSTONES-MIB DEFINITIONS ::= BEGIN
—
— Test MIB - used for testing snmpd.ea (extensible agent)
—
—      @(#) HP OpenView Extensible SNMP Agent Release 3.0
—      snmpd.extend $Date: 94/01/19 15:35:35 $ $Revision: 3.7 $
—
internet       OBJECT IDENTIFIER ::= { iso(1) org(3) dod(6) internet(1) }
enterprises    OBJECT IDENTIFIER ::= { internet private(4) 1 }
flintstones    OBJECT IDENTIFIER ::= { enterprises 4242 }
fsys           OBJECT IDENTIFIER ::= { flintstones 1 }
fmail          OBJECT IDENTIFIER ::= { flintstones 2 }
fwidgets       OBJECT IDENTIFIER ::= { flintstones 3 }
fprinters      OBJECT IDENTIFIER ::= { flintstones 4 }
fdisk          OBJECT IDENTIFIER ::= { flintstones 5 }
fprocess       OBJECT IDENTIFIER ::= { flintstones 6 }
fconfig        OBJECT IDENTIFIER ::= { flintstones 7 }

fsysUsers  OBJECT-TYPE
        SYNTAX DisplayString
        ACCESS read-only
        STATUS mandatory
        DESCRIPTION
                "List of users on the flintstone machine
                READ-COMMAND: /usr/bin/users; exit 0
                READ-COMMAND-TIMEOUT: 5"
        ::= { fsys 1 }
fmemory OBJECT-TYPE
        SYNTAX INTEGER
        ACCESS read-only
        STATUS mandatory
        DESCRIPTION
                "Amount of memory (in megabytes) on system
                APPEND-COMMUNITY-NAME: true
                FILE-NAME: /usr/OV/prg_samples/eagent/memory"
        ::= { fsys 2 }
fUserRootProcessTable OBJECT-TYPE
        SYNTAX SEQUENCE OF FUserRootProcessEntry
        ACCESS not-accessible
        STATUS mandatory
        DESCRIPTION
                "List of root processes. Do not execute command more
                than every 60 seconds.
                FILE-COMMAND: /usr/OV/prg_samples/eagent/get_processes
                FILE-COMMAND-FREQUENCY: 60
                FILE-NAME: /usr/OV/prg_samples/eagent/root_processes"
        ::= { fprocess 1 }
```

```
fUserRootProcessEntry OBJECT-TYPE
        SYNTAX FUserRootProcessEntry
        ACCESS not-accessible
        STATUS mandatory
        DESCRIPTION
                "This macro documents the column that uniquely
                describes each row."
        INDEX { fProcessID }
        ::= { fUserRootProcessTable 1 }

FUserRootProcessEntry ::=
        SEQUENCE {
        fProcessID INTEGER
        fProcessName DisplayString
    }

fProcessID OBJECT-TYPE
        SYNTAX INTEGER
        ACCESS read-only
        STATUS mandatory
        DESCRIPTION
                "Process ID"
        ::= { fUserRootProcessEntry 1 }
        ::= { fconfig 1 }
...
END
```

Note how values of the MIB objects are file contents (FILE-NAME parameter) or Unix command output (READ-COMMAND parameter). The following command reads in the MIB information in snmp.extend:

```
$ snmp.ea -c
```

E.8   OperationsCenter

OperationsCenter (OpC) is a centralized operations management tool. It can run as an OpenView or as a standalone application. The central OpC station monitors clients, which can be multivendor Unix systems or HP MPE/iX systems. OpC client software, available for HP-UX, AIX, Solaris, and other Unixes, must be installed on all the managed systems. Monitored data comes from system log files and SNMP traps. Filters and thresholds are applied to the data and displayed on X-terminals, from which human operators are logged into the management station. When specific messages are received, automatic actions can be initiated, color of icons can be changed, or operators can start predefined actions. OpC is used by two types of users: an administrator and operators. The administrator, who has the OpC user name opc_adm, configures a management environment for each operator user. Each operator is assigned a subset of all possible tasks and managed nodes. OpC is run with a command like

```
$ /usr/OV/bin/OpC/opc
```

An OpC user name and password have to be entered. When an operator logs into the management station, four kinds of windows are displayed:

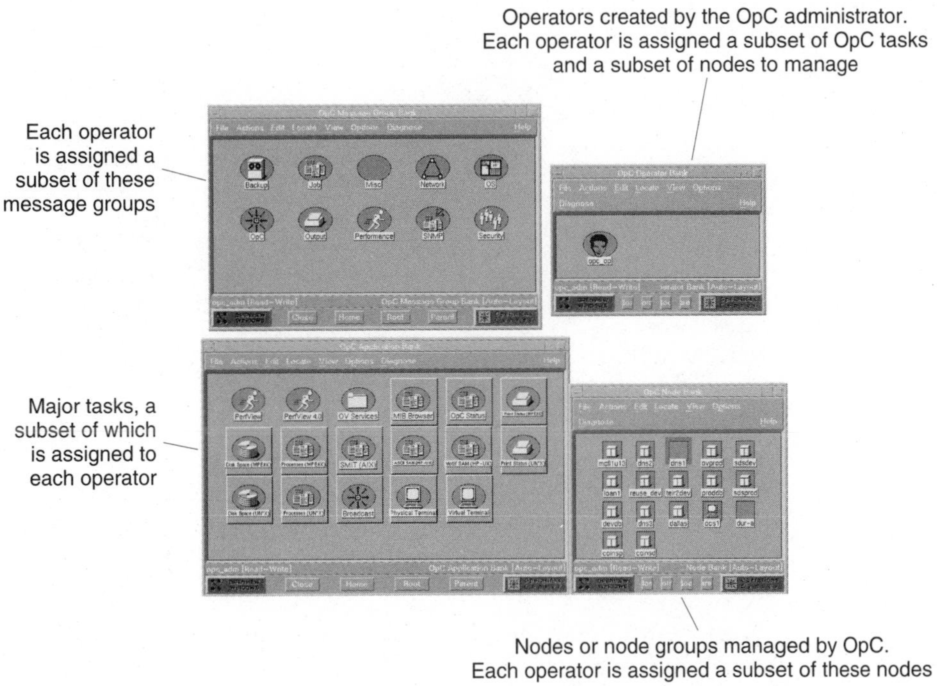

Figure E.9   The major OperationsCenter (OpC) administrator windows.

- *Managed nodes window:* Displays icons for nodes or groups of nodes. Color of icons can be changed by OpC depending on messages received from node.

- *Message groups window:* Displays message groups. Messages are grouped by location, application, or other classification.

- *Message browser window:* Displays all incoming messages, status of automatic actions, and such.

- *Application desktop window:* Displays a set of icons representing applications that can be started by the operator.

Figure E.9 shows the major windows seen by the overall administrator of OpC. Each operator can also pop up similar windows; however, the number of icons will be smaller, depending on what tasks and nodes the administrator has configured for the operator. Figure E.10 shows the message browser window, which is the focus of routine operations. Operators can check status of systems, filter messages, check status of automatic actions, and generate reports.

On each client managed, OpC's main function is to collect data from log files, filter it, and send it to the management station. This is done by OpC's Logfile Encapsulator. It can be configured to read a log file, process it, and keep monitoring the file for new entries. Filtering is achieved by a pattern-matching lan-

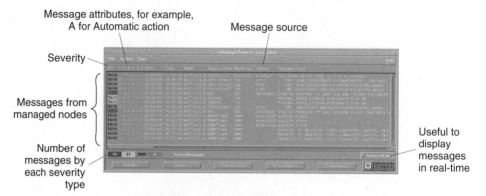

Message attributes, for example,
A for Automatic action

Message source

Severity

Messages from
managed nodes

Number of
messages by
each severity
type

Useful to
display
messages
in real-time

Figure E.10   OperationsCenter message browser window.

guage, somewhat like that used by *grep, sed,* and similar utilities. Messages
can be sent by scripts to the management station using the OpC API.

When properly implemented, OpC can simplify the task of operators in a
heterogeneous Unix environment. OpC presents a common view for all the
systems.

E.9   AdminCenter

AdminCenter (AdC) centralizes the management of objects on systems in a
heterogeneous Unix environment. Managed objects are users, groups, kernel,
swap space, file systems, network interfaces, interface cards, and spooler. A
large environment can be partitioned into domains each of which can be handled by a different set of system administrators. Policies like maximum and
minimum values for a specific field can be enforced. I find the product of limited use, since it cannot handle all types of fields for managed objects.

Terms may be listed here by either their full form or their acronyms. If you know only one form of a term and do not find it here, look in the index for help in determining the other form. Note that many terms that are sufficiently described in the book are omitted here, to avoid repeating material; use the index so that you can refer to the main text for terms not found here. Common Unix terminology is not included in this glossary, most terms are specific to HP-UX. Refer to the numerous available Unix books for standard Unix terms applicable to HP-UX.

100VG-AnyLAN One of the two 100-Mbit/s Fast Ethernet standards. HP supports the 100VG-AnyLAN standard with a number of hardware products.

Access Control List (ACL) List associated with a file (or another object) that defines who can access the file and the type of access (read, write, delete, and so on). ACLs provide an enhanced file access security mechanism when compared with the standard Unix protection based on user name and groups. The *chacl* command manipulates ACL entries.

AdminCenter Software package for centralized administration of databases, such as user accounts and printers, on multiple Unix systems. AdminCenter usually runs as a subcomponent of OpenView.

Adviser The component of GlancePlus performance monitoring software that can trigger alarms and perform actions when certain events occur. Adviser has a scripting capability that can be used to generate alarms based on performance events on a specific system.

Allbase HP proprietary relational database. Compare with Oracle, Sybase, and Informix.

alternate root Root directory for another system booting off the current system. Operating system and products are typically installed on an alternate root for use by NFS cluster systems.

Auto-discovery The mechanism through which OpenView Network Node Manager uses SNMP and ARP to automatically locate nodes to determine a network's topology.

biod   Daemon that performs I/O for the Network File System (NFS). On most systems, four or more biod processes will be running for good performance.

Blinklink   A fast linker. Normally, when a module is modified in a large project, the module is compiled and all modules are linked. Blinklink links only the modified module, not all the modules. The module is linked with a special-format executable. This reduces development time. Production code should use the normal Unix linker, ld.

bookshelf   A LaserROM term meaning a collection of related books.

cell (OmniBack)   A group of systems (somewhat like a domain) managed by an OmniBack configuration.

codeword   In installing software using the Software Distributor, a string of characters that has to be entered to extract protected software. HP ships a common set of CD-ROMs containing multiple software packages; codewords help reduce unauthorized use of products.

Common Desktop Environment (CDE)   X-window–based user interface to the system. CDE replaces VUE, Visual User Environment.

DDFA: Device File Access Utilities   Software to access DTC terminal servers.

DDS: Digital Data Storage   A tape-based data format commonly used on 4-mm tapes.

depot   Software Distributor term meaning a storage place for installation software.

Desktop KornShell (dtksh)   A scripting language that is part of the Common Desktop Environment (CDE). dtksh is standard KornShell with extensions for creating GUI applications.

Distributed Debugging Environment (DDE)   The standard source-level debugger for all languages on HP-UX. It replaces xdb.

DLPI: Data Link Provider Interface   Message communications interface to STREAMS-based network interface drivers. It provides program access to OSI Data Layer 2.

dpat: Distributed Performance Analysis Tool   Tool to profile a process's run-time behavior. dpat shows percent of CPU time spent in each procedure or function of a process.

DTC: Data Communications and Terminal Controller   Ethernet terminal server supporting inbound and outbound telnet connections.

dtlogin   Login process that controls login via CDE.

DUX: Diskless HP-UX   Software used to cluster HP-UX systems. DUX clusters are obsolete; they are replaced by NFS clusters.

ELM   Screen-oriented Unix mail package common on HP-UX.

Encapsulator   Subcomponent of the SoftBench set of products that allows you to extend the functionality of SoftBench.

Entria   A line of X-terminals.

Envizex   A line of X-terminals.

Enware   X software for HP X-terminals.

fbackup   A commonly used backup utility.

fence priority   Parameter set for print queues that determines which jobs are printed. Print jobs are submitted with a request priority using a command like

```
$ lp -p 3 file1
```

The job will be printed only if the request priority is greater than or equal to the queue's fence priority. Fence priorities have a value between 0 and 7 and can be changed using SAM or the *lpfence* command.

frecover   Utility to restore and list data backed up with fbackup.

Frontpanel   Window found on VUE and CDE that serves as "dashboard." Most VUE and CDE features are accessed via the Frontpanel.

GlancePlus   Real-time performance monitoring tool. More useful than common Unix commands like vmstat and iostat.

GSC+   An internal I/O bus.

HFS: High Performance Filesystem   Basically the same as the common Berkeley File System. HS and VxFS are the file systems found on HP-UX systems.

High Speed Interconnect (HP-HSC)   An internal I/O bus.

Human Interface Link (HP-HIL)   An interface standard for connecting keyboard, mouse, bar-code readers, touchscreens, and similar devices to HP terminals and workstations.

HP-FL   A fiber optics–based interface, particularly used for disk arrays.

HP-IB   Interface bus. An internal I/O bus.

HP-PB   Precision bus. An internal I/O bus.

HP/PAK: Programmer's Analysis Kit   Set of three tools, dpat, hpc, and xps, used to study run-time behavior of programs.

hpc   Histogram Program Counter. A program profiler.

hterm   Generic name for HP terminals. Main advantage over VT terms: supports use of eight programmable keys on top of HP keyboards and supports display of a menu for these keys on the bottom of the screen.

i4admin   Command to manage licenses based on iFOR/LS.

iFOR/LS   License Server. HP is using this license control mechanism for many new products.

inetd   A daemon (process) that handles incoming IP connections.

init   Process with PID 1. init is the parent of all processes on the system, except swapper.

Install root   Directory where a software is installed. / or alternate root. Alternate roots are used as roots by other systems booting off current system.

ioscan   Command that displays I/O devices connected to the system.

ITE: Internal Terminal Emulator   A kernel driver that supports graphics terminals as hpterm terminals.

JFS   Journaled File System. Same as Veritas File System, VxFS.

lanscan   Command that displays network connections.

LaserROM   The standard on-line documentation software.

LaserRX   PC software for analysis of performance data collected from HP-UX systems.

LLA   Link Level Access routines. Obsolete; replaced by DLPI.

LIF: Logical Interchange Format   HP proprietary data layout format typically used for booting purposes. LIF allows multiple operating systems to be booted off the same HP 9000 system.

logical volume   A volume managed by LVM.

Logical Volume Manager   Product that pools a collection of physical disks and partitions the space into logical volumes that are used as normal disks by HP-UX software.

/etc/lvmtab   An internal format file used by LVM; contains list of mounted logical volumes.

map   OpenView term representing a group of network components.

MC/ServiceGuard   Software product to create high-availability HP-UX systems. High availability is achieved with multiple HP-UX computers with some acting as standbys, lan cards, and disk mirroring, SCSI, or Fiberlink connections to multiple nodes. Of inferior design (but quick to market) when compared with Digital's OpenVMS Clusters, which allows parallel software execution on all nodes.

MDP   Modem Distribution Panel: hardware used to connect up to eight terminals, optionally connected via a modem, to the MUX port of the CPU cabinet.

Measurement Interface   Software to collect performance data from the HP-UX kernel.

Media Pool   OmniBack term meaning a group of tapes from which an arbitrary one can be picked for backup and similar purposes.

midaemon   Measurement Interface daemon. A process that collects performance data from the kernel.

netfmt   A program to format and print network-related data collected by NetTL.

NetMetrix Internetwork Response software   Software for monitoring network traffic and integrating data with PerfView.

NetTL   Network Tracing and Logging Facility. A network troubleshooting tool.

Network Node Manager   An OpenView component that monitors and manages devices on the network.

Network Time Protocol (NTP)   Protocol used to synchronize clocks on multiple systems, typically systems in an NFS cluster.

NFS clusters   Collection of HP-UX systems that share resources like boot directories and print devices. A common configuration of an NFS cluster is one powerful server HP-UX system and a number of diskless HP 9000 systems that boot off the server.

nfsd   Network File System daemon, process that handles client requests. Multiple nfsd processes will be running on most servers for good performance. See also **biod.**

OmniBack II   A powerful backup and restore utility. Supports network backups, jukebox devices, and tape management features such as retention period.

OnlineJFS   Software to fully support the Journaled File System.

OpC API   Program interface to OperationsCenter.

OpenSpool   Printer management utility providing functionality beyond the standard Unix lp commands.

OpenView   Framework for centralized management of systems and the network. Examples of products that run under OpenView are NNM for network management, OperationsCenter for systems management, and PerfView for multisystem performance management.

OperationsCenter   Package that centralizes system management on multiple systems.

OVc API   OpenView programmer's interface.

PA-7200   Precision Architecture 7200, the RISC CPU architecture for 32-bit HP 9000 systems.

PA-8000   Precision Architecture 8000, 64-bit RISC architecture.

PA-RISC   Precision Architecture–Reduced Instruction Set Computer; used in HP 9000 systems.

PerfRX   A graphical performance reporting package. Accepts data gathered from other HP-UX systems.

PerfView   A graphical performance reporting package for centralized performance gathering and integrating with OpenView.

Process Resource Manager   Software that interfaces with the HP-UX kernel to control CPU time allocation to processes.

Processor Dependent Code   Firmware on each HP 9000 model.

Pseudo-swap   Memory used as swap space.

SharedPrint   An extension of the lp subsystem using a client-server implementation.

smpsched   Process for multiprocessor scheduling found on systems with more than one CPU.

SoftBench   A programming environment supporting editing, compiling, debugging, and the like from a single interface.

softkeys   The eight programmable keys on an HP terminal keyboard.

Software Distributor   The standard product for software installation.

stand   The directory where the HP-UX kernel is stored; /stand/vmunix. Kernel rebuilds are performed under the /stand directory.

Starbase   Three-dimensional graphics library. Obsolete; use PEX and PHIGS instead.

statdaemon   An NFS process.

strmem   A STREAMS communications process.

strweld   A STREAMS communications process.

supsched   A STREAMS scheduler process.

swapper   The process with PID 0 on all systems. Handles swapping.

Switchover/UX   Software used to switch over to another HP-UX system when one system fails. Obsolete; use MC/ServiceGuard instead.

System Administration Manager (SAM)   A GUI tool for most system management activities on HP-UX.

Terminal Session Manager (TSM)   A utility to simulate multiple terminals with one physical terminal.

ToolTalk   A component of CDE for messaging among applications.

top   A command to display processes using the most CPU time.

Tornado   HP's highly integrated network and system monitoring framework.

Trusted Computing Base   The database used to manage security when the system is converted to a trusted system. The files are stored under /tcb.

trusted system   A system with a high level of security. HP-UX can be converted to a trusted system using SAM. Standard Unix security is enhanced with enforced password string requirements, shadow password file, password expiration, and the like.

unhashdaemon   A memory management and paging/swapping support process.

Veritas File System (VxFS)   An alternative to the standard file system, HFS. VxFS supports fast file recovery and on-line backups; however, it cannot be used for the root file system, and it requires more memory than HFS.

vhand   Process that handles paging to disk.

Viewport   Portion of a figure viewed with LaserROM that can be magnified and displayed in a separate window.

Visual User Environment (VUE)   User interface based on X-windows. Obsolete; replaced by CDE.

Volume Group   Group of physical disks under LVM treated as a single logical disk.

VT3K   A utility to connect HP-UX systems to HP's other operating system, MPE.

vx_*_thread   VxFS journaled file system processes.

workspace   Term used in VUE and CDE to represent a screen view containing a set of possibly related windows. Up to four workspaces are accessible from the Frontpanel.

xdb   A source-level debugger. Obsolete; use dde instead.

xps: X-window–based Process Statistics Viewer   A component of HP/PAK. xps displays CPU use per process.

G

Up-to-Date Sources of HP-UX Information

The *HP Direct* catalog is a good source of basic information on latest HP hardware and software. Available free to those qualified; call (800) 637-7740.

Associations

Usenix Association is a highly technical Unix group. It has a newsgroup: comp.org.usenix. It publishes the newsletter *;login* and the quarterly journal *Computing Systems.* The association holds Unix technical conferences at least twice a year and publishes the proceedings. For membership information, write to Usenix Association, 2560 Ninth Street, Suite 215, Berkeley, CA 94710; telephone, (510) 528-8649; fax, (510) 548-5738; e-mail, office@usenix.org, web site: http://www.usenix.org.

Interex (including Interworks) is an HP computing professionals organization. It holds conferences and distributes *hp-ux/usr,* a magazine discussing HP 9000 issues. Interex also has a software library. Telephone, (800) 468-3739; fax, (408) 747.0947; e-mail, membership@interex.org, web site: http:/www.interex.org.

Uniforum holds trade shows and conferences related to Unix systems. For membership information, write to Uniforum at 2901 Tasman Avenue, Suite 205, Santa Clara, CA 95054-1100; telephone, (408) 986-8840; fax, (408) 986-1645; e-mail: stephen_liebes@uniforum.org, web site: http://www.uniforum.org.

Usenet Newsgroups

The most important newsgroup is comp.sys.hp.hpux.

Get the newsgroup FAQ; it contains a lot of interesting material. Its World Wide Web URL is:

ftp://ftp.seas.gwu.edu/pub/rtfm/comp/sys/hp/hpux/comp.sys.hp.hpux_FAQ

An html version is at

http://www.cis.ohio-state.edu/hypertext/faq/usenet/hp/hpux-faq/faq.html

WWW Software Sites

Here are the URLs of some sites that have HP 9000 related software:

http://hpux.csc.liv.ac.uk

ftp://nic.funet.fi/pub/unix/hpux

http://www.cup.hp.com/netperf/NetperfPage.html   (Contains a network perfor-
                                                   mance monitoring tool)

http://col.hp.com

http://www.hp.com   (Mostly HP marketing hype)

ftp://iworks.ecn.uiowa.edu/pub/comp.hp

HP 9000–Related Magazines

HP Professional is an HP-related trade publication containing interesting tidbits. Published by Cardinal Business Media, Inc., 101 Witmer Road, Horsham, PA 19044; telephone, (215) 957-1500; fax, (215) 957-1050; e-mail, simpson@cardinal.com.

hp-ux/usr, published by Interex, was already mentioned under Associations.

The HP Chronicle, a tabloid magazine, is published by Publications and Communications, Inc., P.O. Box 399, Cedar Park, TX 78630-0399; telephone, (512) 250-9023; fax, (512) 231-3900; e-mail, {cs.utexas.edu, execu, texbell}!pcinews!wks.

Sys Admin, one of the better Unix technical magazines, is published by Miller Freeman, Inc., Sys Admin, P.O. Box 59170, Boulder, CO 80322-9170; telephone, (303) 678-0439; fax, (303) 661-1885; e-mail, sasub@rdpub.com.

Unix Review is a Unix-related trade magazine I like; published by Miller Freeman, Inc., 411 Borel Ave., Suite 100, San Mateo, CA 94402; telephone, (415) 358-9500; fax, (415) 358-9739; e-mail, abinstock@mfi.com.

HP Supportline

The Supportline web URL is:

http://us.external.hp.com

The line provides problem databases, patches, printer drivers, and such. Patches by e-mail and other services are available via Supportline. To get help on using the e-mail facility, send mail to:

support@us.external.hp.com

with the text portion containing a single line:

send guide

Bibliography

General Unix books are not listed here. A major bookstore should have books on Unix basics, awk, sed, ksh, vi, system administration, Unix networking, X and Motif programming, and myriad other topics.

Hewlett-Packard, *Using HP-UX,* Hewlett-Packard Company, Palo Alto, Calif., 1995. A useful introductory book for users who have not used Unix before.

Hewlett-Packard, *HP-UX System Administration Tasks,* Hewlett-Packard Company, Palo Alto, Calif., 1995. This manual is a must read for HP-UX system administrators.

Hewlett-Packard, *Programming on HP-UX,* Hewlett-Packard Company, Palo Alto, Calif., 1995. A starting point for HP-UX programmers.

Pendergrast, Stephen J., Jr., *Desktop KornShell Graphical Programming,* Addison-Wesley, Reading, Mass., 1995. An excellent guide and reference for writing GUI scripts.

Poniatowski, Marty, *The HP-UX System Administrator's "How To" Book,* Prentice Hall, Englewood Cliffs, N.J., 1994. One of the first HP-UX books. The second edition discusses HP-UX Version 10.0

Here is a partial list of HP manuals you can order by calling (800) 227-8164:

Analyzing Program Performance with HP/PAK
Assembly Language Reference Manual
Berkeley IPC Programmer's Guide
Configuring HP-UX for Peripherals
DCE Application Environment Specification
Developing and Localizing International Software
DLPI Programmer's Guide
DTC Device File Access Utilities and Telnet Port Identification
EISA 100VG AnyLAN Quick Installation Guide
FDDI/9000 Installation and Administration Guide
Getting Started with GlancePlus
Getting Started with HP PerfView
Guide to Writing DCE Applications
HP C Programmer's Guide
HP C++ Programmer's Guide
HP C/HP-UX Reference Manual
HP FORTRAN/9000 Programmer's Guide
HP FORTRAN/9000 Programmer's Reference
HP Help System Developer's Guide

HP Micro Focus COBOL for UNIX: Getting Started
HP Micro Focus COBOL for UNIX: System Reference
HP Micro Focus COBOL: Language Reference
HP Micro Focus COBOL User's Guide
HP Micro Focus COBOL/UX Programmer's Guide
HP OpenView AdminCenter Concepts Guide
HP OpenView OmniBack II Administrator's Guide
HP OpenView OperationsCenter Concepts Guide
HP OpenView SNMP Agent Administrator's Guide
HP OSF/Motif 1.2 Programming Manual
HP OSF/Motif 1.2 Reference Manual
HP OSF/Motif 1.2 Style Guide
HP Pascal/HP-UX Programmer Guide
HP Pascal/HP-UX Reference Manual
HP Process Resource Manager User's Guide
HP Visual User Environment 3.0 User's Guide
HP Xlib Extensions
HP-PHIGS C and FORTRAN Binding Reference
HP-PHIGS Development Product Read Me First
HP-PHIGS Graphics Techniques
HP-PHIGS Workstation Characteristics and Implementation
HP-UX Documentation: What's Available and How to Order It
HP-UX Floating-Point Guide
HP-UX Reference
HP-UX System Administration Tasks
HP/DDE Debugger User's Guide
Installing & Administering Internet Services
Installing & Administering LAN/9000
Installing & Administering NFS
Installing and Administering EISA/100VG AnyLAN
Installing and Administering FDDI
Installing and Administering Token Ring
Installing and Administering X.25/9000
Introduction to OSF DCE
Kermit Mailer
Mail Systems: User's Guide
Managing HP-UX Software with SD-UX
Managing MC/ServiceGuard (Series 800 only)
Managing Software Products with iFOR/LS
Networking Overview
Number Processing: User's Guide
OSF DCE Administration Reference
OSF DCE Application Development Guide
OSF DCE Application Development Reference
OSF DCE System Administration: Core Components
OSF DCE System Administration: Extended Services
OSF DCE User's Guide and Reference
Owner's Guide HP 9000 S800 Model E Computers
Owner's Guide HP 9000 S800 Model K Computers
PEXlib Development Read Me First
PEXlib Implementation and Programming Supplement
PEXlib Programming Manual
PEXlib Reference Manual
PEXlib Runtime Read Me First
Planning & Configuring HP DCE
POSIX Conformance Document
Programming on HP-UX
Programming with Threads on HP-UX
Read Before Installing PowerShade
Release Notes: SNAplus 10.0

SharedPrint/UX User and Administrator's Guide for HP-UX 10
Shells: User's Guide
SNAplus 3270/3179G Administration Guide
SNAplus 3270/3179G User's Guide
SNAplus 3270/TN3270 HLLAPI Programmer's Guide
SNAplus API Administration Guide
SNAplus API APPC Programmer's Guide
SNAplus API CPI-C Programmer's Guide
SNAplus Diagnostic Guide
SNAplus Link Administration Guide
SNAplus Link NetWork Management Administration
SNAplus Remote Configuration Guide
SNAplus RJE Administration Guide
SNAplus RJE User's Guide
SNAplus Text Configuration Guide
Software Portability with Imake
STREAMS/UX for HP 9000 Reference Manual
Terminal Control: User's Guide
Terminal Session Manager: User's Guide
Text Formatting: User's Guide
Text Processing: User's Guide
TN3270 User's Guide
Token Ring S700 10.0 Quick Installation
Token Ring S800 10.0 Quick Installation
Troubleshooting X.25/9000
Understanding DCE
Using HP-UX (Series 800 only)
Using Internet Services
Using Network Node Manager (OpenView)
Using Network Services
Using Serial Line Protocols
Using the Audio Developer's Kit
Using the HP DTC Manager/UX
Using the Image Developer's Kit
Using the X Window System
Using Your HP Workstation (Series 700 only)
X.25/9000 Programmer's Guide
X Toolkit Intrinsics Programming Manual
Xlib Programming Manual

Index

.dt, CDE, 179
.kshrc file, 16
.profile file, 16
.rhosts, 148
/.secure directory, 183
/dev, 35, 108
/etc/copyright, 85
/etc/inittab, 83
/etc/passwd, 156–157
/etc/profile file, 16
/etc/services, 148
/etc/syslog.conf, 32
/home, 35
/mnt, 35
/opt, 35
/opt/perf directory, 220
/sbin, 35
/sbin/init.d directory, 96–98
/sbin/rc, 85
/stand, 35
/stand/build directory, 252–253
/stand/system directory, 253
/stand/vmunix, the kernel, 83, 91, 251
/tcb directory, 182
/tmp, 35
/usr, 35
/var, 35
/var/adm/sw/products directory, 249
/var/adm/syslog/syslog.log, 32
/var/opt/perf directory, 220
/var/sam/log/samlog, 55
100VG-AnyLAN Fast Ethernet, 128
700 series workstations, 3
700/60 CRT terminals, 5
700/70 CRT terminals, 5
< (see I/O redirection)
> (see I/O redirection)
>> (see I/O redirection)

A3232A disk arrays, 5
Access Control Lists, 181, 186, 197
accounting, 189–195
acctcon command, accounting, 193
acctdisk command, accounting, 193
acctdusg command, accounting, 193

acctmerg command, accounting, 194
AdminCenter, 325, 338
Advisor, Glance, 224–226
alias, NIS, 15
alias, nodename in DNS, 149
Allbase relational DBMS, 339
alternate root, NFS clusters, 33
annotation, file, 172
ANSI C compiler, 266–267
Apollo computers, 1
areas, SAM, 51
arp command, 142
assembly language, 317–324
associative arrays, ksh-93, 298
audevent command, security, 184
auditing, security, 183
audsys command, security, 183
auto-configure, devices, 76
auto-discovery, OpenView NNM, 339–340
automounter, NFS, 31, 165–167
awk language, 28

Backdrop, VUE, 174
backplane, 101–110
backup levels, fbackup, 199
backup over network, 201, 206
backups, 197–218
bcheckrc, 85
bdf command, 117, 119
BDRA (see Boot Data Reserve Area)
BIND (see Domain Name Service)
biod, 340
biod process, 31
Blinklink, Softbench, 340
bookmark, LaserROM, 46
bookshelf, LaserROM, 39
Boot Data Reserve Area, disk, 121
boot devices, 87
boot information, 89
booting, 72–74, 83
bootp command, 145
bootpquery command, 145
Bourne shell, 14–15
Breakpoint, debugger, 272

ABOUT THE AUTHOR

Jay Shah is a Senior UNIX Systems Engineer at Merck-Medco Managed Care, Inc. in Fairlawn, New Jersey. He has more than 14 years of experience as a developer and systems administrator, and has worked on UNIX systems since 1981. Mr. Shah is the author of three other McGraw-Hill titles, including *VAX C Programming Guide*.